Legalines

Editorial Advisors:

David H. Barber
Professor of Law

Jonathan Neville
Attorney at Law

Robert A. Wyler
Attorney at Law

Authors:

David H. Barber
Professor of Law

Daniel O. Bernstine
Professor of Law

D. Steven Brewster
C.P.A.

Roy L. Brooks
Professor of Law

Charles N. Carnes
Professor of Law

Paul S. Dempsey
Professor of Law

Ronald W. Eades
Professor of Law

Jerome A. Hoffman
Professor of Law

Jonathan Neville
Attorney at Law

Norman R. Prance
Professor of Law

Arpiar Saunders
Professor of Law

Lynn D. Wardle
Professor of Law

Robert A. Wyler
Attorney at Law

Securities Regulation

Adaptable to Seventh Edition of Jennings Casebook

By David H. Barber
Attorney at Law

HARCOURT BRACE LEGAL AND PROFESSIONAL PUBLICATIONS, INC.

EDITORIAL OFFICES: 176 W. Adams, Suite 2100, Chicago, IL 60603

Legalines

REGIONAL OFFICES: New York, Chicago, Los Angeles, Washington, D.C.

Distributed by: **Harcourt Brace & Company** 6277 Sea Harbor Drive, Orlando, FL 32887 (800)787-8717

EDITOR
Roger W. Meslar, B.A., J.D.
Attorney At Law

PRODUCTION COORDINATOR
Sanetta Hister

Eighth Edition—1994

Legalines™

Features Detailed Case Briefs of Every Major Case, Plus Summaries of the Black Letter Law.

Titles Available

Administrative Law . . . . .Keyed to Breyer
Administrative Law . . . . .Keyed to Gellhorn
Administrative Law . . . . .Keyed to Schwartz
Antitrust . . . . .Keyed to Handler
Antitrust . . . . .Keyed to Areeda
Civil Procedure . . . . .Keyed to Cound
Civil Procedure . . . . .Keyed to Field
Civil Procedure . . . . .Keyed to Louisell
Civil Procedure . . . . .Keyed to Rosenberg
Civil Procedure . . . . .Keyed to Yeazell
Commercial Law . . . . .Keyed to Farnsworth
Commercial Law . . . . .Keyed to Speidel
Conflict of Laws . . . . .Keyed to Cramton
Conflict of Laws . . . . .Keyed to Reese
Constitutional Law . . . . .Keyed to Brest
Constitutional Law . . . . .Keyed to Cohen
Constitutional Law . . . . .Keyed to Gunther
Constitutional Law . . . . .Keyed to Lockhart
Constitutional Law . . . . .Keyed to Rotunda
Constitutional Law . . . . .Keyed to Stone
Contracts . . . . .Keyed to Calamari
Contracts . . . . .Keyed to Dawson
Contracts . . . . .Keyed to Farnsworth
Contracts . . . . .Keyed to Fuller
Contracts . . . . .Keyed to Kessler
Contracts . . . . .Keyed to Knapp/Crystal
Contracts . . . . .Keyed to Murphy
Corporations . . . . .Keyed to Cary
Corporations . . . . .Keyed to Choper
Corporations . . . . .Keyed to Hamilton
Corporations . . . . .Keyed to Vagts
Criminal Law . . . . .Keyed to Boyce
Criminal Law . . . . .Keyed to Dix
Criminal Law . . . . .Keyed to Johnson
Criminal Law . . . . .Keyed to Kadish
Criminal Law . . . . .Keyed to La Fave
Criminal Procedure . . . . .Keyed to Kamisar
Decedents Estates . . . . .Keyed to Ritchie

Domestic Relations . . . . .Keyed to Clark
Domestic Relations . . . . .Keyed to Wadlington
Enterprise Organizations . . . . .Keyed to Conard
Estate & Gift Tax . . . . .Keyed to Surrey
Evidence . . . . .Keyed to Kaplan
Evidence . . . . .Keyed to McCormick
Evidence . . . . .Keyed to Weinstein
Family Law . . . . .Keyed to Areen
Federal Courts . . . . .Keyed to McCormick
Income Taxation . . . . .Keyed to Andrews
Income Taxation . . . . .Keyed to Freeland
Income Taxation . . . . .Keyed to Klein
Labor Law . . . . .Keyed to Cox
Labor Law . . . . .Keyed to Merrifield
Partnership & Corporate Tax . . . . .Keyed to Surrey
Property . . . . .Keyed to Browder
Property . . . . .Keyed to Casner
Property . . . . .Keyed to Cribbet
Property . . . . .Keyed to Dukeminier
Real Property . . . . .Keyed to Rabin
Remedies . . . . .Keyed to Re
Remedies . . . . .Keyed to York
Securities Regulation . . . . .Keyed to Jennings
Torts . . . . .Keyed to Dobbs
Torts . . . . .Keyed to Epstein
Torts . . . . .Keyed to Franklin
Torts . . . . .Keyed to Henderson
Torts . . . . .Keyed to Keeton
Torts . . . . .Keyed to Prosser
Wills, Trusts & Estates . . . . .Keyed to Dukeminier

Other Titles Available:
Accounting For Lawyers
Criminal Law Questions & Answers
Excelling on Exams/How to Study
Torts Questions & Answers

All Titles Available at Your Law School Bookstore, or Call to Order: 1-800-787-8717

Harcourt Brace Legal and Professional Publications, Inc.
176 West Adams, Suite 2100
Chicago, IL 60603

SHORT SUMMARY OF CONTENTS

TABLE OF CONTENTS AND SHORT REVIEW OUTLINE

I. INTRODUCTION TO SECURITIES REGULATION

A. THE SECURITIES INDUSTRY GENERALLY

1. **The Capital Markets.** The securities markets are part of the broader financial markets that operate both within the United States and internationally. Many of these markets are in direct competition to finance industry and business. In the past several years, the line between the "securities markets" and other capital markets has become somewhat uncertain. For example, is the market that trades stock market indexes a "security market" and thus subject to regulation by the federal securities laws? Why are the so-called capital markets largely unregulated by federal securities laws? (For example, the huge market in government securities is largely beyond the jurisdiction of the S.E.C.) Possibly the answer so far is that the securities markets (i.e., stock exchanges, etc.) are ones where many individual investors participate, and they lack the bargaining power and financial sophistication to get the information they need without assistance. And second, these markets are important to regulate since they are perceived as central to the healthy functioning of the economy. Finally, business is now world wide, so domestic markets now compete with international capital markets. If the domestic market for capital is more highly regulated than international markets, our economy may lose out. Thus, constraints now exist to regulation that may not have existed in past years.

   a. **Conflict between regulatory agencies.** The jurisdiction of the S.E.C. over securities related matters is not always clear. For example, the Commodity Futures Trading Commission is authorized by federal law to regulate the trading of futures contracts, including futures on securities. New types of financial instruments are evolving all of the time, and it is often not clear what type of instrument is involved and who should be responsible for its regulation.

   b. **Application--Chicago Mercantile Exchange v. S.E.C.,** 883 F.2d 537 (7th Cir. 1989).

      1) **Facts.** The Commodity Futures Trading Commission has authority to regulate trading of futures contracts (including futures on securities) and options on futures contracts. The S.E.C. has authority to regulate trading of securities and options on securities. If an instrument is both a security and a futures contract, the CFTC has the sole right to regulate. [*See* 7 U.S.C. §2a(ii)] But if the instrument is both a futures contract and an option on a security, then the S.E.C. is the sole regulator. [*See* 7 U.S.C. §2a(i)] The statute, however, does not define "contracts for future delivery" or "option." Here a new financial instrument falls between the two.

      Index participations (IPs) are contracts of indefinite duration based on the value of a basket (index) of securities (the S & P 500, or some other index can be used). The seller of an IP (the "short" because the writer need not own the securities) promises to pay the buyer the value of the index as measured on a "cash-out day." The buyer pays cash on the date of sale and may borrow part of the price. Until cash-out, the IP may trade on the exchange; at the end of each quarter the short must pay the buyer a sum approximating the value of the dividends the stocks in the index have paid that quarter.

From the buyer's perspective, the IP is like a closed-end mutual fund. From the seller's perspective, he owns them only to reduce risk. He receives the long's cash, but must post margin equal to 150% of the value of the IP. This is held by the Options Clearing Corporation to ensure that there is value to cover cash-out. For the seller, then, this is like a futures contract that terminates on the cash-out date, plus an option by the buyer to roll over the contract to the next cash-out date.

Longs and shorts do not deal directly with each other. After the parties agree on price, the Options Clearing Corporation issues the IP to the long, receiving the cash; at the same time, the OCC pays the short and "acquires" the short's obligations to the long, to secure which it holds the short's 150% margin. As the quarter progresses, the short pays dividends. When a long cashes out, the OCC chooses a short at random to make the payment. Once the instrument has been formed, the long and the short do not relate to each other; each person's rights and obligations run to the OCC. This allows either party to close its position by making an offsetting transaction. If the seller, for example, buys an identical contract in the market, the OCC cancels the two on its books.

The Philadelphia Stock Exchange asked the S.E.C. in 1988 for permission to trade IPs. The American Stock Exchange then asked for permission to trade its version of the IP; and also the Chicago Board Options Exchange. All contended that the S.E.C. had exclusive jurisdiction because IPs are securities and not futures contracts. The Chicago Board of Trade and the Chicago Mercantile Exchange, supported by the CFTC, asked the S.E.C. to deny the requests, arguing that IPs are futures and not securities. The Investment Company Institute argued that if IPs are securities and not futures, then the OCC is an "investment company," offering a product combining features of closed-end and open-end mutual funds and must register under the Investment Company Act of 1940.

The S.E.C. granted the exchanges' requests and allowed the OCC to change its rules so that it could issue, settle, and clear IPs. The S.E.C. did this on the basis that IPs are "stock" within the meaning of section 3(a)(10) of the Securities Exchange Act of 1934 (the only attribute of stock missing from IPs is voting rights). The S.E.C. also found that IPs are not futures because they lack two features thought essential: futurity and bilateral obligation (futurity means that value is set in the future; bilateral obligation means that the contract is executory on both sides until expiration or settlement, while the long on an IP performs at the time of purchase, leaving only the short with executory obligations). Finally, the S.E.C. held that the OCC need not register under the 1940 Act since there was no "issuer" of a security as called for by that Act.

The futures exchanges and the CFTC appeal to the Circuit Court.

2) **Issue.** Who has jurisdiction to regulate IPs?

3) **Held.** The decision of the S.E.C. is set aside.

a) A futures contract is a fungible promise to buy or sell a particular commodity at a fixed date in the future. They are fungible since contracts have standard terms and each side's obligations are guaranteed by a clearing house. They are entered into without prepayment, although the markets and clearing house will set margins to protect their interests. Trading occurs in the contract, not the commodity. These contracts are used by investors to hedge risk. The regulatory jurisdiction of the CFTC is over regulating hedging instruments.

b) The jurisdiction of the S.E.C. is over the sale of "investments" for the purpose of raising capital.

c) Unfortunately, the distinction between capital formation and hedging falls apart when it comes time to allocate the regulation of options. The agencies reached an agreement on this issue, agreeing that jurisdiction over options follows jurisdiction over the things on which the options are written—the S.E.C. getting options on securities; the CFTC getting options on futures. The understanding was enacted into law by Congress. [*See* 7 U.S.C. §2]

d) As new instruments come to market, there is inevitable conflict, which will not be resolved unless the agencies are merged, or unless Congress changes the regulatory jurisdiction between the two agencies. Here we must decide who regulates IPs.

e) From the standpoint of the long, an IP is not stock. There is no issuer; there is no interest in an underlying asset. There is only a short on the other side. Further, the long does not fit into any of the other pigeonholes of section 3(a)(10).

f) From the standpoint of the CTFC, it found IPs to be futures contracts by looking at the short side. Shorts on IPs make the same pledge as shorts on stock-index futures contracts—to pay the value of an index on a prescribed day.

g) The S.E.C. argued there was no futurity and no bilateralism in the IP contracts, so they could not be futures contracts. There is, however, futurity (the IP contract tracks current value, but the short may only be forced to pay a future value, at maturity). There is no bilateralism; the long performs at the beginning, and executory performance is only due from one side, the short, thereafter.

h) The problem is that, depending on the perspective taken, the IP appears to be either a security or a futures contract. It has characteristics of both. It is no less one than the other. This will be true of many new instruments coming to the market. It is clear, though, that it is not an option on a security. Options are written out of the money, are limited in time, and establish a careful balance among premium, strike price, and duration; the writer retains the dividends. The IP does not have any of these characteristics.

i) In this situation, we have to hold that each agency has some leeway in applying its own statute to IPs. If each is entitled to some deference, then the IP is both a security (according to the S.E.C.) and a futures contract (according to the CFTC). It has some attributes of both, and all attributes of neither.

j) Since we broadly construe the securities acts to cover investments of all types, we must take the same approach with the CFTC—an instrument need not have all the characteristics of a futures contract to be governed by the CFTC.

k) Thus, here, since the IP is both a futures contract and a security, then the CFTC has exclusive jurisdiction. The S.E.C.'s orders approving the applications of the stock exchanges and the OCC are set aside.

2. The Securities Markets.

a. **Types of securities markets.** There are two basic types of securities markets.

1) **Markets for original distribution.** If Corporation XYZ is formed and issues some of its common stock to the public, this is an "original distribution" of securities.

2) **Continuous trading markets.** The second type of market is composed of the markets that exist for the continuous trading of securities after their original distribution. For example, after Corporation XYZ has issued its shares to the public, these shares may then be bought and sold (i) over a stock exchange, (ii) through the help of securities firms in the "over-the-counter" market (*see* the definition below), or (iii) directly between purchasers and sellers without the assistance of a market intermediary.

b. **Where securities are traded.** Once securities have been issued for the first time, they are then normally traded in one of two ways:

1) **On stock exchanges.** The securities of most of the large and important corporations are traded over stock exchanges (the most important of which is the New York Stock Exchange).

2) **Over-the-counter trading.** Securities traded outside of the stock exchanges are said to be traded "over the counter," which means that they are traded back and forth by securities firms (called "broker-dealers").

3) **Other markets.** There are also other markets for the trading of securities. One is the so-called third market (securities listed on stock exchanges and traded by broker-dealers in the over-the-counter market). Another is the "fourth market" (individual persons or firms owning securities that trade them without the assistance of a market intermediary). Note also that section 11A(a)(2) of the Securities Exchange Act of 1934 directs the S.E.C. to facilitate the establishment of a "national market system," which is slowly occurring through the development of computerized systems to provide information from many sources on the trading of securities.

3. The Securities Firms—Brokers and Dealers.

The federal securities laws also regulate the conduct of the securities firms that are involved in trading securities. These firms are called "broker-dealers."

a. **Broker.** A "broker" is an agent in buying and selling securities for his customer on a commission basis.

b. **Dealer.** A "dealer" acts as a principal in buying the security for his own account, then marks up the price of the security and sells it to his customer.

B. THE UNDERWRITING PROCESS

The process of distributing securities from the original issuer (e.g., XYZ Corporation) to the ultimate retail purchasers is called an "underwriting."

1. **The Underwriting Distribution System.** The following outline shows the original distribution of securities from the issuer of the securities to the retail purchasers.

   a. **The issuer.** The issuer decides to sell some of its common stock to the public in order to raise capital.

   b. **The underwriter.** The issuer goes to a securities firm (the underwriter) and makes an agreement with this firm to "underwrite" the securities issue (i.e., to buy the securities from the issuer, or to take responsibility for the sale of the issuer's securities on some other basis; *see* below).

   c. **Dealers.** The underwriter then reaches agreement with a number of other securities firms (the "dealers") to have them buy the securities for later resale to their retail customers.

   d. **Retail customers.** The dealers then sell the securities to their retail customers.

2. **Types of Underwriting Agreements.**

   a. **Stand-by underwriting.**

      1) **Issuer sells its own securities.** In this form of underwriting agreement, the issuer does not sell its securities to the underwriter. Rather, the issuer advertises the securities on its own and receives purchase orders directly from the public.

      2) **Insurance by the underwriter.** In the event that the issuer does not sell all of the securities, then the underwriter agrees, for a fee, to buy the portion of the securities issue that remains unsold. In effect, the underwriter acts as an insurer for the issuer.

   b. **Firm-commitment underwriting.** In a firm-commitment underwriting, the issuer sells its securities to the underwriter. The underwriter then resells the issue to the dealers and/or to the public.

   c. **Best-efforts underwriting.** In this form of underwriting, the underwriter simply sells the issuer's securities as an agent for the issuer (i.e., on a commission basis). The underwriter agrees only to use its best efforts to market the securities to the public. There is no guarantee that the issue will be sold.

    d.   **The issuer sells its own securities.** In situations where the company can market its own securities, it might not use an underwriter at all.

C.   THE SECURITIES AND EXCHANGE COMMISSION

The Securities and Exchange Commission (the "S.E.C.") is the federal administrative agency responsible for administering the federal securities laws.

1.   **The Functions of the S.E.C.**

    a.   **Rulemaking.**

    b.   **Interpretation** (interpreting the securities laws and the rules thereunder).

    c.   **Conducting investigations.**

    d.   **Formal proceedings** (seeking application of statutory remedies and sanctions for violation of the securities laws through appropriate proceedings).

        1)   **Civil injunctions** may be sought through the United States district courts.

        2)   **Criminal prosecutions** are brought by the United States Department of Justice.

        3)   **Administrative remedies** (such as suspension of trading by a securities firm) are initiated by the S.E.C. in administrative proceedings.

2.   **The Securities Acts Administered by the S.E.C.**

    a.   **The Securities Act of 1933.** This Act primarily regulates the original issuance of securities (e.g., XYZ Corporation issues 100,000 shares of its common stock to the public for $10 per share). The main thrust of the Act is to compel full disclosure to the public of all information material to an investor's determination of the real value of the securities being issued. A second purpose of the Act is to prevent fraud and misrepresentation in the interstate sale of such securities.

    b.   **The Securities Exchange Act of 1934.** This Act regulates a wide variety of transactions involving the securities markets.

        1)   **The registration and reporting requirements.** The Act requires that, under certain conditions, a company must register its securities with the S.E.C. and thereafter file periodic reports on the company's financial condition. [*See* SEA §§12 and 13]

2) **Proxy solicitation.** The Act also regulates the solicitation of voting proxies from shareholders of registered companies. [*See* SEA §14]

3) **Insider trading.** The Act contains provisions restricting and penalizing trading in a registered company's shares by company "insiders" (i.e., by company officers, directors, or owners of 10% of the outstanding shares of a registered class of equity securities). [*See* SEA §16]

4) **Margin trading.** The Act permits the regulation of margin trading (i.e., buying securities on credit). [*See* SEA §§7 and 8]

5) **Market surveillance.** The S.E.C. is also authorized to regulate certain security market trading practices which are based on fraud or market manipulation. [*See* SEA §9]

6) **Registration of securities exchanges, broker-dealers, and securities associations.** National securities exchanges (such as the New York Stock Exchange) and broker-dealers which conduct an interstate over-the-counter securities business must register with and make periodic reports to the S.E.C. [*See* SEA §§6 and 15]

   a) **Rules and regulations.** The S.E.C. is authorized by the Act to make rules and regulations to regulate the activities of broker-dealers and the national exchanges.

   b) **Self-regulation.** The Act also permits the exchanges to make their own self-policing rules. And organizations of broker-dealers that are self-policing may also organize and register with the S.E.C.

7) **Tender offer solicitations.** The Act regulates situations where one company seeks to acquire control of another by direct offer to purchase stock from the target company's shareholders. [*See* SEA §§13 and 14]

c. **The Public Utility Holding Company Act of 1935.** This Act was enacted to correct abuses in the financing and operation of electric and gas public utility holding companies.

d. **The Trust Indenture Act of 1939.** This Act relates generally to large issues of debt securities in excess of $1 million in total value. The Act contains provisions to protect the security holders, such as a requirement that the trust indenture covering the securities meet certain standards insuring the independence and responsibility of the indenture trustee.

e. **The Investment Company Act of 1940.** This Act regulates the activities of publicly owned companies engaged primarily in the business of investing in and trading securities. The Act regulates the composition of management, the capital structure of the company, its investment policies, etc.

f. **The Investment Advisers Act of 1940.** This Act provides for the registration and regulation of those in the business of giving advice to others concerning securities investments.

II. REGULATION OF THE ORIGINAL
DISTRIBUTION OF SECURITIES

The Securities Act of 1933 regulates the original distribution of securities from the issuer (e.g., XYZ Corporation) to the public.

A. OBJECTIVES OF THE 1933 ACT

1. **To Provide Full Disclosure to Potential Investors.** The first objective of the 1933 Act is to provide investors with full disclosure of all material information in connection with the original issuance of securities from the issuer (e.g., XYZ Corporation) to the public. To accomplish this, the issuer must file a "registration statement" with the S.E.C. prior to issuing its securities. This registration statement must contain all material investment information about the issuer and the issuer's securities. Also, the issuer must prepare a "prospectus" (a digest of the most important information contained in the registration statement) and give this prospectus to investors prior to the sale or delivery of the issuer's securities.

2. **To Prevent Fraud and Misrepresentation in the Interstate Sale of Securities Generally.** The second objective is to prevent fraud and misrepresentation in the interstate sale of securities. To accomplish this, the 1933 Act includes several liability provisions providing remedies to defrauded purchasers on a more lenient basis than formerly available under the common law. These liability provisions are discussed in detail, *infra*.

3. **Jurisdiction and Interstate Commerce.** The provisions of the 1933 Act apply only where interstate commerce is involved.

   a. **Statutory definition.** "Interstate commerce" is defined as "trade or commerce in securities, or transportation, or communication relating thereto, among the several states." [*See* SA §2(7)]

   b. **Expansive interpretation.** As one would expect, the S.E.C. and the courts have adopted a broad interpretation of what constitutes "interstate commerce."

      1) Under modern authority, interstate commerce is involved whenever the "means" of doing interstate commerce are used—such as the telephone, the mails, etc.—in any part of the securities transactions.

      2) The effect is that it will be a very rare case in which a securities transaction will be held exempt from the 1933 Act on the grounds that the transaction did not involve "interstate commerce."

B. THE REGULATION OF OFFERS AND SALES OF SECURITIES

Section 5 of the Act (which sets forth the registration requirement for newly issued securities) divides the underwriting process into three time periods and states the rules concerning making offers and sales of securities in these periods.

1. **The Pre-Filing Period.** This is the first period when an issuer is contemplating a public offering of its securities but *before* the registration statement has been filed with the S.E.C.

   a. **Basic prohibition.** During this period, it is unlawful (when means of interstate commerce are used) to offer to buy or sell, or to buy or sell, securities before filing a registration statement with the S.E.C. [*See* SA §§5(a)(1) and 5(c)]

   b. **Purpose.** The purpose of these sections is to ensure that investors are not presold on the issuer's securities by information other than that which will be contained in the registration statement.

   c. **Persons subject to the prohibitions.** These sections apply only to three classes of persons: issuers, underwriters, and dealers. [*See* SA §§5(a) and 5(c)]

   d. **Exemption for preliminary negotiations between the issuer and the underwriter.** "Preliminary negotiations or actual agreements" between an issuer and an underwriter are exempted by the Act from the prohibition against offers during the pre-filing period. [*See* SA §2(3)]

      1) This allows the issuer to make a firm deal to sell its securities prior to spending the large sum necessary to prepare the registration statement.

      2) Note that negotiations between the underwriters and the dealers are not permitted in this period.

   e. **Conditioning the market.** The prohibition against making "offers or sales" in the pre-filing period is much broader than a mere prohibition against common law offers or sales.

      1) **Rationale.** The objective in the pre-filing period is to see that potential purchasers of the securities that will later be registered with the S.E.C. do not have their minds made up by any information other than that contained in the registration statement.

      2) **Coverage.** Any material that might have the effect of "preconditioning the market" prior to the actual offer of the securities for public sale is prohibited. Thus, speeches by company officials, press releases, advertising, etc., could all violate section 5(c) if they had the unwanted effect. On the other hand, the S.E.C. does not intend to unreasonably interfere with an issuer conducting its business in a normal manner (i.e., advertising its products, etc.).

      3) **Applications.** Obviously, the issue that frequently arises in the pre-filing period in whether something communicated to the public by the issuer is an illegal "offer." The following examples illustrate what an issuer may and may not do during this period.

         a) **Soliciting advance orders.** An underwriter cannot give out a news release about the formation of a new company that names those who will underwrite the company's securities and gives misleading information about the assets and liabilities of the company. The court in this instance held that such a news release was designed to procure or solicit advance orders for the purchase of the security to be underwritten. [In the Matter of Loeb, Rhoades & Co. and Dominick and Dominick, 38 S.E.C. 843 (1959)]

b) **The checklist approach.** To give objective guidelines on news releases, the S.E.C. adopted a "checklist" in Rule 135. If a notice satisfies the items of this checklist, then it is deemed not to violate section 5(c).

   (1) **Items that must be mentioned.** Certain items must be mentioned in the press release, such as the fact that the offering will be made only by means of a prospectus.

   (2) **Permissible items.** An issuer may communicate about certain items (such as the title of the security, the basic terms, the time of the offering, the name of the issuer, etc.).

   (3) **Prohibited items.** Certain other items are prohibited from being mentioned (such as giving the name of the underwriter).

   (4) **An exclusive list.** The courts have held that Rule 135 is an exclusive list of what an issuer can say in a press release. Thus, an issuer cannot mention the "offering price" or the "value of the securities" being issued since these items are not included in Rule 135. [Chris-Craft Industries v. Bangor Punta Corp., 426 F.2d 569 (2d Cir. 1970)]

4) **Conflict with other policies of the securities acts.** The requirements of section 5(c) prohibiting premature disclosures in the pre-filing period may conflict with other policies of the securities acts that require a company to disclose material information to the public.

a) For example, in the *Chris-Craft* case, Bangor Punta Corporation planned a registered offering of its securities in order to buy Piper Aircraft. One of the issues concerned whether the "value" of the securities offered had to be disclosed as "material information" which might affect the decision of shareholders of Piper, the shareholders of Bangor Punta, and the investing public generally. The policy of the Securities Exchange Act of 1934 is to require such disclosures if the information is material. But Rule 135 prohibited such a disclosure in the pre-filing period. The court held that in this instance Rule 135 dominated and the price was not to be disclosed.

b) But recognizing that this conflict may often arise, the S.E.C. has indicated that a company does have a duty to disclose material developments (even when it is contemplating a registered offering of its securities). In these circumstances, in order not to violate Rule 135, the disclosures should be limited to factual reports—forecasts, projections, predictions, and/or opinions as to value should be avoided. The issuer should also avoid soliciting disclosure opportunities with securities and financial firms. [*See* SA Release No. 5180 (1971)]

f. Permissible dissemination of information by underwriters and dealers. In addition to the instructions given issuers in Rule 135, the S.E.C. has set forth guidelines for dealers concerning the information that they may disseminate about the issuer and its securities prior to the offering. The purpose of these guidelines is to allow dealers to conduct their normal business (such as the publication of market reports and security analysis) without undue interference with the objectives of the 1933 Act. [*See* SA Rules 137-139]

2. **The Waiting Period.** The "waiting period" is the period of time after the registration statement has been prepared and filed with the S.E.C. but before it has been declared to be effective by the S.E.C.

   a. **The objective in the waiting period.** The objective in this period of time changes—now it is to permit the underwriters and dealers to condition the market (i.e., to locate potential buyers so that when the registration statement does become effective the issue of securities may be sold very rapidly), but only certain types of information may be used in this pre-selling process.

   b. **Procedure for making offers.** Since in the waiting period certain types of offers may be made (but sales may not be concluded), the underwriter and dealers normally solicit offers to purchase which they may accept after the registration is effective.

   c. **Offers that may be made in the waiting period.**

      1) **Oral offers.** Oral offers may be made in the waiting period. [*See* SA §5(b)(1)]

      2) **Written offers.** Certain types of written offers are also permitted in the waiting period. [*See* SA §2(10)—which treats a written communication offering a security as a "prospectus"; §5(b)—which indicates that a "prospectus" must conform to the requirements of §10; and §10(b)—which specifies the permitted written offers]

         a) **The tombstone ad or identifying statement.** A "tombstone ad" or "identifying statement" is a short advertisement or announcement about a proposed offering of registered securities. Such ads typically appear in places such as the *Wall Street Journal*. [*See* §2(10)(b)]

            (1) **Purpose.** The tombstone ad may be used to announce a coming public offering, but the ad may only state certain things: the kind of security, the price at which it will be offered, by whom purchase orders will be executed, and the location where a prospectus may be obtained. [*See* SA Rule 134]

            (2) **Solicitations of interest.** The ad may not (by itself) be used to solicit indications of interest to purchase the registered securities. However, if the ad is sent to a prospective purchaser preceded or accompanied by a regular section 10 prospectus (and note that a preliminary or

summary prospectus, both of which are described below, would qualify), then the ad may be used in connection with the solicitation of an offer to buy or the solicitation of an indication of interest to buy. The ad must also state that no offer can actually be accepted in the waiting period and that an indication of interest is not biding on the prospective purchaser who gave it.

b) **The preliminary prospectus.** A second way in which written offers may be made is through the use of a "preliminary" or "red herring" prospectus. [*See* SA §10(b) and Rule 430]

    (1) **Defined.** The preliminary prospectus is exactly like the final prospectus that will be used to make sales once the registration statement is declared effective and sales begin, except that certain information to be included in the final prospectus is not yet available and so is omitted (such as the offering price of the securities, which is not decided until immediately before the registration statement is declared effective).

    (2) **Period of use.** Once the registration statement becomes effective, and a complete prospectus is available, then use of the preliminary prospectus must be discontinued.

    (3) **The S.E.C.'s policy of acceleration.** The registration statement is to become effective 20 days after filed, unless amended. Normally the S.E.C. suggests amendments, and the last amendment is generally the price at which the securities are sold. Once this is given, the underwriter wants to immediately begin selling. Hence, S.E.C. cooperation in the form of an acceleration order making the registration statement effective immediately is required. The S.E.C. has indicated that it will not give such an acceleration order unless the preliminary prospectus has been distributed to all underwriters and dealers who can reasonably be anticipated to participate in the distribution. [*See* SA Rule 460] Also, where the securities being offered are of a company that has never before offered its securities to the public and hence is not a "reporting company" under the 1934 Act, the S.E.C. will not accelerate the offering date unless the underwriters and dealers have sent copies of the preliminary prospectus to those persons who may reasonably be expected to be purchasers of the securities. [*See* SA Release No. 4468 (1969)]

c) **Summary prospectus prepared by the issuer.** The third form of written offer that is permitted in the waiting period is the offer by a "summary prospectus prepared by the issuer." [*See* SA §10(b) and Rule 431]

    (1) **Financial requirements the issuer must comply with.** The issuer must meet certain requirements of financial strength and stability in order to use this type of shortened prospectus.

    (2) **Period of use.** This prospectus can be used both during the waiting period and in the post-effective period.

d. **Organizing the selling group of dealers.** During the waiting period, the underwriters make arrangements for the assistance of dealers in selling the issue to retail customers as soon as the registration statement becomes effective. Of course, in making these arrangements, only approved information may be used.

e. **Illegal offers in the waiting period.** Everything said about illegal offers in the pre-filing period is also applicable to the waiting period.

3. **The Post-Effective Period.** After the registration statement is declared effective by the S.E.C., actual sales of the registered securities may be made. Thus, the offers solicited in the waiting period are normally accepted at this time. [*See* SA §5(a)]

a. **The objective.** The objective of this period of time is to see that all purchasers receive a copy of the final prospectus (called the "statutory prospectus"), which contains a summary of the most important investment information contained in the registration statement.

b. **Use of the statutory prospectus.**

1) **In connection with the delivery of securities.** A statutory prospectus meeting the requirements of section 10(a) must precede or accompany the delivery of securities where the mails or other interstate facilities are used in the delivery process. [*See* SA §§5(a)(2) and 5(b)(2)]

a) **The Rule 174 exemptions.**

(1) Normally in the 40-day period after the registration statement is declared effective and selling begins, all dealers (those who are not part of the offering but who are trading the securities in the secondary over-the-counter market, *and* those who have an allotment of securities in the offering) must deliver a statutory prospectus to the purchasers of the securities of the issuer. [*See* SA §4(3)]

(2) However, dealers who are not part of the dealer selling group and those dealers who are part of it but who have sold all of their original allotment of securities may be excused from this prospectus delivery requirement under the following conditions.

(a) Where the issuer has securities registered under the Securities Exchange Act of 1934 and is filing periodic reports with the S.E.C. under sections 13 or 15(d) of that Act.

(b) Where purchasers can already get information about the issuer equivalent to that which would be contained in the prospectus, and where the sales involve securities that have already entered the market for secondary trading (that is, the original issue or distribution is completed). [*See* SA Rule 174]

b) **Exemptions for certain sales.** The S.E.C. has made certain exemptions to the delivery requirements for sales made on exchanges and through brokerage firms not participating as dealers in the original distribution.

  (1) **Sales made over exchanges.** When a buying broker is a member of a stock exchange, the prospectus delivery requirements are fulfilled if the stock exchange has been supplied with enough prospectuses to fulfill requests made by its members. [*See* SA Rule 153]

  (2) **Delivery to brokers off the exchange.** If the broker is off of a securities exchange and is acting as an agent for the buyer of some of the issuer's securities, delivery of the prospectus to the broker is sufficient to meet the prospectus delivery requirements of the Act. [Loss, *Securities Regulation* 252 (1969)] However, if the broker is acting as a principal (buying the security for his own account and then reselling it), then the broker himself is responsible for meeting the delivery requirements of the Act (and the issuer, underwriter, or participating dealer need only see that the principal gets the prospectus).

2) **Written offers and confirmations.** After the effective date, any written offers that are made, or confirmations of sale sent by interstate means, must be accompanied by or preceded by a statutory prospectus. [*See* SA §§2(1)(a) and 5(b)(1)]

Diskin v. 3) **Effect of failure to supply prospectus--Diskin v. Lomasney & Co.,** 452 F.2d
Lomasney &   871 (2d Cir. 1971)
Co.

  a) **Facts.** Lomasney (D) offered to sell to Diskin (P) stock in Continental Travel "when, as and if issued." A registration statement had been filed but was not effective. Then a confirmation of sale was sent, and finally (when the registration statement had been declared effective) a prospectus. P then paid for the shares, but later brought an action to rescind the transaction under section 5(b)(1).

  b) **Issue.** Did D make an illegal offer in the waiting period and violate section 5(b)(1) in the post-effective period by sending a confirmation of sale that was not preceded or accompanied by a statutory prospectus?

  c) **Held.** Yes.

  (1) The conditional offer ("when, as and if issued") constituted an "offer" as defined by section 2(3) of the Act; it was not revocable by D. And the offer did not conform to the limited ways an offer can be made in the "waiting period." Also, the confirmation was sent before receipt of a statutory prospectus. Hence, section 5(b)(1) has been violated, even though P had a chance to read the prospectus before he actually paid for the shares.

4) **Innocent purchaser has right to rescind--Byrnes v. Faulkner, Dawkins &
Sullivan,** 550 F.2d 1303 (2d Cir. 1977).

    a) **Facts.** Byrnes (P) owned 148,000 shares of White Shield stock, which
was included in a registration statement filed by White Shield that became
effective on June 7, 1971. This was a "shelf registration," which permitted the selling shareholders to sell their shares periodically through registered securities dealers. P arranged for Tobey & Kirk, a registered S.E.C.
dealer, to sell its stock when the issue became effective. On June 7,
Tobey agreed to sell to Faulkner (D) at $14 per share; D was at the time a
market-maker of the White Shield stock. On the day of the sale Tobey
sent a written confirmation of the sale, but did not enclose a copy of the
final prospectus. When the stock was delivered on June 15, the final
prospectus was sent to D. The prospectus indicated that the selling
shareholders and the dealers who sold stock for them may be "underwriters." Later D rejected the stock certificates when tendered by Tobey,
claiming that the sale had violated section 5(b)(1) of the 1933 Act in that
the earlier written confirmation of sale had not been accompanied by a
section 10 prospectus. Tobey sold the stock at below $14 per share and
sued D in state court for breach of contract. After a series of complex
procedural moves, the case ended up in federal district court, and the court
granted D's motion for summary judgment. P appeals.

    b) **Issue.** In an over-the-counter transaction between broker-dealers, must the
selling dealer in a public offering, during the distribution period, give the
buying broker-dealer a section 10 prospectus when sending written confirmation of the sale?

    c) **Held.** Yes. Judgments affirmed.

        (1) The wording of section 2(10) of the 1933 Act indicates that, "unless
the context otherwise requires," a prospectus includes a written
confirmation of sale. Section 5(b)(1) requires that any prospectus
used in connection with a security for which a registration statement
has been filed must be a section 10 prospectus. This section, on its
face, has been violated. Also, the context does not require a different
result.

        (2) There are no exemptions available to P. P was an underwriter;
Tobey was a dealer. Section 4(3) does not apply since the transaction
occurred within the 40-day period of the offering of the stock to the
public. And the broker's exemption of section 4(4) does not apply
since the offering was being made for the issuer in a public offering.

        (3) There is no presumption that a market-maker in an over-the-counter
stock transaction who is publishing offers on the stock that is being
publicly offered already has a prospectus. Pursuant to Rule 153 a
different presumption might apply to a security traded over a national
exchange.

        (4) Section 12(1) of the 1933 Act gives an absolute rescission right to an
innocent purchaser of securities that are sold in violation of the
prospectus requirements. So the contract between P and D is not
enforceable because of the violation of the Act.

(5)   D's counterclaims are dismissed. They were based on Rules 10b-5 and 10b-6 of the 1934 Act, which do not allow punitive damages. Also, the stock went down after D canceled the sale, so D cannot claim that he could have sold the stock for a profit if the sale to D had not been a violation of the 1933 Act.

c.   **The use of supplementary sales literature.** After the effective date, supplementary sales literature may be used in addition to the statutory prospectus, as long as the statutory prospectus is also sent to the prospective purchaser with or previous to the selling literature. [*See* SA §2(10(a)]

d.   **Loophole in the Act.** Sales may be consummated in person or by telephone without the seller being required to furnish the buyer with a statutory prospectus in advance, as long as the prospectus accompanies or precedes any *later* written confirmation or delivery of the security using interstate means. Thus, it is clear that one of the major purposes of the Act can be circumvented, since registered securities may be sold where the investor is committed to the purchase prior to ever seeing the prospectus.

e.   **Length of time a prospectus may be used.** As long as the original distribution is taking place (i.e., during the time period in which any of the securities in the original issue have not been sold for the first time) and for a minimum of 40 days after the selling of the issue first begins (whether or not the original distribution has ended, except in limited circumstances—*see* Rule 174, discussed *supra*), the statutory prospectus must be used.

1)   **Mandatory updating.** If the period of use extends beyond nine months, there is a mandatory requirement that it be updated. [*See* SA §10(a)(3)]

2)   **Updating to avoid liability.** Furthermore, if the prospectus is misleading as to a material fact (whenever it is used), liability can result under sections 17(a) and 12 of the 1933 Act and section 10 and Rule 10b-5 of the 1934 Act.

a)   **Prospectus must be true and correct.** Implicit in the statutory requirements that a prospectus contain certain information is the requirement that the information be true and correct. Thus, a misleading prospectus, by implication, violates section 5(b)(2) of the Act (and section 12(1) liability may result since this section bases liability on any violation of section 5).

b)   **Effect of supplying inaccurate prospectus--S.E.C. v. Manor Nursing Centers,** 458 F.2d 1082 (2d Cir. 1972).

(1)   **Facts.** Manor (D) sold an "all or nothing" offering of securities, which indicated that if all of the shares of the offering were not sold in 60 days then all funds collected would be returned. The shares had not been sold in 60 days, but D kept the money for the shares that had been sold and continued to try to sell the remainder. Thus, since these facts were not disclosed in the prospectus, material misstatements occurred in connection with the continued offering. The S.E.C. brought an action pursuant to section 22(a) of the 1933 Act and section 27 of the 1934 Act,

S.E.C. v. Manor Nursing Centers

alleging violations of section 17(a) and section 5(b)(2) of the 1933 Act and section 10(b) and Rule 10b-5 of the 1934 Act.

(2) Issue. Did D violate section 5(b)(2) of the 1933 Act by delivering through the mails securities for sale which were accompanied by a prospectus that had not been amended to state all of the materials facts related to the securities being sold?

(3) Held. Yes. Judgment affirmed.

    (a)   Ds are guilty of a violation of section 17 of the 1933 Act and Rule 10b-5 of the 1934 Act (since they made misrepresentations in connection with the continued sale of the securities).

    (b)   Ds have also violated section 5(b)(2) of the Act (which prohibits the delivery of a security for the purpose of sale *unless* that security is accompanied by a prospectus that meets the requirements of section 10(a) of the 1933 Act), since the implication is that such a prospectus must contain true and accurate information as of the time it is used, and Ds did not amend the prospectus to make it accurate concerning the way the offering was being conducted subsequent to the time when the initial offering period had expired (i.e., there was no escrow, the time limit had passed, it was not being conducted as an "all or nothing" offering, etc.).

C. THE REGISTRATION STATEMENT

1. **Introduction.** Prior to the original issuance of securities by the issuer to the public, a registration statement must be filed with the S.E.C. The purpose of the registration statement is to provide the potential investor with all of the information needed to determine whether the securities offered are a good investment. The most important information in the registration statement is digested into a shorter document—the prospectus—which is the document given to a purchaser prior to purchase or at the same time as the purchased securities are delivered.

2. **Integrated Disclosure.** As the above material on the various securities acts makes clear, there are many disclosure requirements under the securities laws. With respect to the two main securities acts (the Securities Act of 1933 and the Securities Exchange Act of 1934), originally there were two separate and distinct disclosure systems established. Supposedly this approach was necessary since each act served a different purpose. However, this dual system spawned separate sets of registration statements, periodic reports, etc., each with its own set of instructions. Companies found themselves repeating information for several different reports, although often the format and the standards for reporting the information differed. For example, the financial statements included in an annual

report to shareholders required by the proxy rules of the 1934 Act had to conform to generally accepted accounting standards, but financials included in a 1933 Act registration statement had to conform to the more stringent standards of the S.E.C.'s Regulation S-X.

Recently the S.E.C. has made an effort to integrate the reporting requirements of the two Acts. Regulation S-K now prescribes a single standard set of instructions for filing forms under the two Acts, so that when the same type of information is required by the various forms under these acts a single set of instructions applies. Also, revisions to Form 10-K (the annual report of registered companies under the 1934 Act), Rule 14a-3 of the 1934 Act (the rule requiring an annual report to shareholders), Regulation S-K, and Regulation S-X resulted in a uniform set of financial disclosure requirements for all documents required to be filed under the 1933 or 1934 Acts. Undoubtedly the S.E.C. will continue to push for further integration of the reporting requirements in the future. [*See* "Proposed Rulemaking to Implement the Integrated Disclosure System," S.E.C. Executive Summary of Securities Act Release Nos. 6331-6338 (1981)]

3. **Preparing the Registration Statement.**

   a. **The objective of disclosure.** The objective of the registration statement is to provide potential investors with all of the information necessary in order to make an intelligent investment decision. This means that all information necessary in order to project what the issuer's future net earnings might be must be disclosed.

   b. **Statutory guidelines.** The starting point is the statutory guidelines.

      1) **Applicable sections and rules.**

         a) The registration process is governed principally by sections 6 and 7 of the Act and Schedule A.

         b) Regulation C sets forth the rules which apply to the registration statement itself.

         c) Regulation S-X gives accounting rules for disclosure of financial information.

         d) Regulation S-K gives rules for disclosing much of the information required by Schedule A.

      2) **Proper forms.** The S.E.C. has prescribed a number of different registration forms for use in particular situations. For example, Form S-1 is the general form to be used unless some other form fits the particular situation.

   c. **Indemnification and insurance.**

      1) **Indemnification.**

         a) **State law.** Officers, directors, and controlling persons may be exposed to substantial liabilities under federal securities laws.

The laws of the various states vary tremendously as to whether and to what extent these persons may be indemnified by the issuer. Some states do allow such indemnification (whether by specific contract or in the corporate bylaws).

b) **The policy of the S.E.C.** Whenever officers, directors, or controlling persons are indemnified, it is currently the policy of the S.E.C. that in order to approve a registration statement, such indemnification must either be waived by such persons or a statement must be made in the prospectus to the effect that the S.E.C. considers indemnification against the policy of the 1933 Act and unenforceable and that such persons promise to submit the question where it arises to a court of competent jurisdiction for a decision.

   (1)   The S.E.C. will deny acceleration of the effective date of the registration statement unless this statement is made in the prospectus.

   (2)   Note, however, that there is no direct judicial authority interpreting the 1933 Act as to whether indemnification is unlawful (but see the *Globus* decision *infra*). When it comes, such a decision will be based on policy considerations behind the 1933 Act.

c) **Underwriter indemnification.** Note that indemnification by the issuer of the underwriters is common and the S.E.C. has said nothing to discourage this.

   (1)   **Actual knowledge of violations.** The courts, however, have held that where the underwriter has **actual** knowledge of materially misleading statements or omissions contained in the registration statement, the underwriter cannot rely on an indemnification agreement to escape liability but is equally liable with the issuer.

   (2)   **Contribution among liable parties--Globus v. Law Research Service,** 318 F. Supp. 955 (S.D.N.Y. 1970).

Globus v. Law Research Service

   (a)   **Facts.** Globus, who bought Law Research (LRS) stock in a public offering, brought an action under sections 12(2) and 17 of the 1933 Act and Rule 10b-5 and section 15(c) of the 1934 Act against the company, its president, and the underwriter (Ds) for failure to disclose a material fact in the Regulation A offering circular. The underwriter, Blair, cross-claimed against defendant company on the basis of an indemnity clause in the underwriting agreement. In an earlier decision at 418 F.2d 1276 (2d Cir. 1969), the court of appeals affirmed the lower court judgment holding Ds jointly and severally liable to Globus, and denying Blair a recovery on its indemnity agreement with LRS. In this action, Blair is seeking judgment against the other Ds *for contribution* of one-third each of the sum Blair paid to Globus.

   (b)   **Issue.** Is contribution among joint tortfeasors available in a securities case under section 10(b) where the underwriting agreement provides expressly for such contribution?

   (c)   **Held.** Yes. Motion for judgment of contribution granted.

      1]   Since those sections of the securities acts which expressly provide for civil liability provide for contribution, contribution should be permitted even under sections which do not contain express provisions on liability.

   2] The main reason for denying the award of indemnity in the prior action was that it would dilute the deterrent impact of the securities laws. For the same reason, the other Ds should not be able to nullify their liability for damages by leaving the entire burden on Blair.

   (d) Comment. The courts have divided over the issue of whether there is an implied right of contribution among jointly and severally liable defendants *if* there is no express contribution agreement among the defendants.

2) **Liability insurance.** There is also an issue of whether the issuer can purchase liability insurance covering potential securities act liabilities.

   a) **Availability of insurance.** State law differs as to the extent that insurance may be acquired by an issuer to cover its officers and directors or the underwriters. But many states do allow it. Premiums are high for commercial policies and there are normally high deductible provisions. Also, the policies vary with respect to what standard of conduct they will insure against (but most do not insure against willful misconduct).

   b) **The S.E.C. policy.** The policy of the S.E.C. would seem logically to be against insurance (since it is against indemnification). But thus far a distinction has been made and insurance is not discouraged. The basis for this distinction is that otherwise the cost to the shareholders of the issuer from liability could be extensive—underwriters might refrain from marketing securities, and directors and others might be unwilling to serve where companies are involved in the registration process.

4. Standards of Disclosure.

   a. **The material required in the registration statement—discretion of the S.E.C.** The S.E.C. does not approve or disapprove of the investment merits of the securities being registered (it is only supposed to see that all material information is disclosed to the investor), but in performing its proper function the S.E.C. exercises broad discretion over what is put in the registration statement.

   1) The registration statement must contain the information specified in Schedule A of the Act, except that the S.E.C. by rules and regulations may provide that such information need not be put into the registration statement if it finds that disclosure is otherwise fully adequate for the protection of investors.

   2) Also, the S.E.C. can request additional information that it deems in the best interest of the investors. This same power exists with respect to the prospectus. [*See* SA §7]

b. **Financial information.** Financial information is a very important part of the information that must be disclosed.

1) **The balance sheet.** The balance sheet of the issuer normally must be of a date not more than 90 days before filing. [*See* Schedule A]

2) **Profit and loss statements.** The S.E.C. normally requires statements of the issuer's net income for at least the five past years (plus the issuer's statement for the year-to-date).

3) **Independent accountants.** The issuer's accountants who certify the issuer's financial statements as being according to generally accepted accounting principles must be "independent" of the issuer.

c. **Examples of material facts that require disclosure.**

1) **Integrity and conflicts of interest of key executives--In the Matter of Franchard Corp.,** 42 S.E.C. 163 (1964).

In the Matter of Franchard Corp.

   a) **Facts.** Glickman formed real estate limited partnerships as the general partner, selling limited partnership interests to the public. Franchard Corporation (D) was formed to hold all of Glickman's general partnership interests; Glickman was president and the controlling shareholder. D registered offerings with the S.E.C. to raise more capital. In the course of these offerings, Glickman borrowed funds from D without authorization or disclosure; he also pledged his controlling stock in D for additional personal loans. It also became apparent that Glickman was in personal financial trouble. The directors did not know of these transactions; when they discovered them, they forced the repayment of all the Glickman loans from D and charged an increased rate of interest (which had not yet been collected). Finally, Glickman was forced to resign when he continued making unauthorized loans to himself. The S.E.C. brings an action for a stop order to suspend the effectiveness of three of D's registration statements under which securities of D were still being offered.

   b) **Issues.**

   (1) Was the fact that a key executive was in serious financial trouble a material fact that must be disclosed?

   (2) Is the directors' standard of care in managing the corporation a material fact which must be disclosed?

   c) **Held.** (1) Yes. (2) No.

   (1) The fact that D's key executive (Glickman) had pledged all of his stock (a controlling interest in D) for large personal loans, was in personal financial difficulty, and had made unauthorized loans from the corporation were all material facts which should have been disclosed. These things reflect on the business ability, integrity, and likely motivation of the management of D. Also, they affect where control of the corporation might end up.

Furthermore, they are particularly relevant where the securities are being sold to the public largely on the reputation of the president (Glickman).

(2) The registration statement need not contain information as to whether the directors are properly performing their duties in overseeing the corporation since the 1933 Act does not define federal standards of directors' responsibility for management of the corporation. State law governs this issue and the responsibility differs with respect to different matters. If the 1933 Act required disclosures about how the directors were discharging their management responsibilities under state law, the disclosure requirements would be administratively impractical.

2) Other important disclosures:

a) All of the factors which make the securities of high risk, such as: (i) absence of an operating history for the issuer; (ii) lack of an earnings history, or an erratic pattern of earnings; (iii) competitive conditions in the industry; and (iv) the issuer's reliance on one product or on a limited product line.

b) Use to be made of the proceeds of the offering by the issuer.

c) Restrictions on the use of the issuer's earned surplus because of loan agreements, thus limiting the possibility of future dividends.

d) Recent drops of a substantial nature in the sales of the issuer.

e) Adoption of government regulations that could affect the business.

f) Pending or threatened litigation against the issuer of a substantial nature.

g) Proposals to or the intention of the issuer to enter new businesses or lines of business. [*See* SA Release No. 5395 (1973)]

h) The factors used to determine the offering price of the securities where the issuer is a new company. [*See* SA Release No. 5396 (1973)]

d. Required organization of the material. In addition to requiring that certain substantive material be disclosed, the S.E.C. has closely regulated the form in which the material is to be disclosed, the organization of the prospectus, the required use of certain types of graphs, charts, etc.—all in order to see that the material is communicated clearly.

e. Criticisms of the disclosure requirements. Many commentators have criticized the manner in which the S.E.C. has administered the disclosure requirements of the 1933 Act.

1) Disclosure of "soft information." According to business theory, the value of a security is the present value of the future cash flows to be received from owning the security (i.e., cash dividends received, capital gains from the sale of the stock, etc.). However, to make this kind of present value calculation, the issuer would have to disclose to investors its projected earnings per share for future periods of time, and the S.E.C. long resisted the inclusion of any such projections, estimates, or opinions (so-called soft information). Rather, the S.E.C. insisted that the registration statement contain only verifiable facts (so-called hard information).

a) **Shift in the S.E.C.'s position.** However, the S.E.C. has gradually modified its stance. It first indicated that management of the issuer may (but is not required to) include earnings projections in 1933 and 1934 Act filings—provided that such projections were: (i) made in good faith and had a reasonable basis; (ii) presented in an appropriate format; and (iii) accompanied by information adequate to allow the investor to make a judgment as to the probable accuracy of the projections. [*See* SA Release No. 5699 (1976)]

b) **Replacement costs.** Then the S.E.C. required that certain large companies (those with inventories and gross property, plant, and equipment which aggregate more than $100 million and which comprise more than 10% of the company's total assets) registering securities under the 1933 Act disclose in their financial statement the replacement cost of fixed assets and inventories (to reflect their current as opposed to historical values) and to show in the income statement what the cost of goods sold and depreciation expense would have been if replacement cost had been used rather than historical cost figures. (Such information is to be disclosed in a footnote to the financial statements.) [*See* S.E.C. Accounting Series Release No. 190 (1976)]

c) **Present S.E.C. position.** The S.E.C. has now taken the position that, in light of their importance to investor decisionmaking, projections of revenues, earnings and earnings per share (and, where relevant, of other financial information) are to be encouraged. [*See* SA Release No. 5992 (1978) and SEA Release No. 15305 (1975)]

  (1) Thus, issuers have the option of disclosing projections of future economic performance in 1933 Act registration statements or in filings under the 1934 Act.

  (2) Such projections must be made in good faith, have a reasonable basis, be presented in an appropriate format, and be made in such a way as to aid investor understanding (i.e., assumptions given, where relevant; warnings given against certainty of projections, where appropriate; etc.).

d) **"Safe harbor" rule.** The S.E.C. has gone even further and adopted a "safe harbor" rule to aid in its encouragement of the publication of future economic projections. [*See* SA Release No. 6084 (1979)] Forward-looking statements will not be found to be fraudulent if the requirements of the safe harbor rule are met.

  (1) The projection must be made in "good faith" and with a "reasonable basis." Experience or past accuracy in making projections may indicate that projections were made in good faith and with a reasonable basis.

  (2) In order to prove a cause of action where actual results do not match earlier made projections, a plaintiff has the burden of proof to establish the absence of a reasonable basis and good faith in making the projection.

(3) The safe harbor rule covers projections of revenues, earnings, and earnings per share and, in addition, other projections of financial items such as capital expenditures and financing, dividends, capital structure, statements of management plans, and objectives for the future, etc.

(4) Disclosure of assumptions behind projections are not mandatory, but in many cases may be necessary in order for the projections to meet the good faith and reasonable basis part of the test.

(5) Statements made by or on behalf of the issuer or by an outside (expert) reviewer retained by the issuer are also covered.

(6) Companies that file reports under the Securities Exchange Act of 1934 or that are filing registration statements under the 1933 Act are covered. (Note that projections of these companies made prior to or subsequent to these filings are also covered—not just their filings with the S.E.C.—if similar projections are also filed with the S.E.C., the companies are registered under the 1934 Act, or the projections are made in an annual report under the proxy rules of the 1934 Act.)

(7) There is a duty to update projections and restate assumptions when favorable or unfavorable information would indicate that the earlier statements no longer have a reasonable basis.

(8) Companies that are required to file 10-K (annual) reports under the 1934 Act with the S.E.C. must have filed the most recent report due in order to use the rule.

(9) The safe harbor rule does not apply to investment companies.

2) **Emphasis on negative information.** There has also been criticism of the fact that the S.E.C. requires the registration statement to focus on the negative aspects of the issuer in order to avoid potential liability under the 1933 Act for misrepresentations, rather than allowing it to present a balanced picture of the company (relating the positive as well as the negative aspects of the company).

   a) Critics argue that since registration statements thus lack much information that is relevant to making an intelligent investment decision, and since all registration statements are uniformly negative, they may no longer be taken seriously by investors.

3) **Presentation of complex information.** The argument has also been made that the complex information the S.E.C. requires to be disclosed (e.g., information on sophisticated products, financial information, accounting data, etc.) is impossible to present in a way that is understandable to the "average" investor. The solution offered by the commentators would be to draft the registration statement for the sophisticated or expert securities analyst, to whom the average investor looks for advice, and to dispense with the charade of trying to inform the investor himself.

4) **Management disclosure and analysis.** It is relatively easy to mask what is really going on with a business financially by manipulating numbers in the accounting process. For example, in recession years, companies typically have

huge write-offs, because they are less noticeable and less unexpected, hence they do not disturb investors. This is usually a way of cleaning up the accounting for charges that should have been written off in prior years; in this way also, earnings in the coming years will really be overstated. Now the S.E.C. requires that all publicly traded companies include, as part of the annual report, a Management Discussion and Analysis, in which management must discuss the company's prospects and the major factors that may affect future performance. Companies can be held liable for false or misleading statements or material omissions that are reasonably likely to have a material effect on the issuer's financial condition.

5. Processing the Registration Statement.

a. **Effective date of statement.** The registration statement becomes effective on the 20th day after its filing with the S.E.C., unless it is the subject of a refusal or stop order issued by the S.E.C. or becomes effective sooner by an S.E.C. acceleration order.

b. **Amendments to the statement.** Usually, several amendments will be required by the S.E.C. before it declares the registration statement effective. An amendment starts the 20-day waiting period running anew. However, the S.E.C. normally accelerates the effective date as soon as all of the problems with the registration statement have been worked out so that the issuance is not adversely affected by a delay.

c. **Review of the registration statement.** Once the registration statement is filed, the S.E.C. begins an examination of the statement to ensure that the issuer has complied with all disclosure requirements. [SA §8(e)] The Act provides that it is unlawful to offer or sell securities that are the subject of any proceeding under section 8(e) that was filed by the S.E.C. prior to the effective date of the registration statement. [SA §5(c)]

d. **S.E.C. authority.** The S.E.C. cannot legally compel the issuer to amend a defective registration statement; but by entering a "stop order" (*see* below), the S.E.C. can prevent the registration statement from becoming effective and thus effectively force the issuer to make the suggested amendments. Also, although there is no time limit on the duration of a section 8(e) examination, a court *can* compel the S.E.C. to make a determination whether to terminate the examination or institute an 8(d) proceeding (*see* below), at least where the S.E.C.'s inaction has the effect of prohibiting the sale of securities due to an unreasonably delayed completion of the 8(e) examination. [*See* Las Vegas Hawaiian Development Co. v. S.E.C., 466 F. Supp. 928 (D. Hawaii 1979)]

e. **Formal proceedings by the S.E.C.**

1) **Refusal and stop orders.** If, following an examination of the registration statement, the S.E.C. finds that the issuer has failed to comply with the Act's disclosure requirements, the S.E.C. may issue an order delaying or suspending the effectiveness of the registration statement.

a) **Refusal order.** A "refusal order" may be issued within 10 days after the filing of a statement that is clearly inadequate on its face. Such an order delays the effective date in order to allow the S.E.C. to take appropriate action; therefore it must always be issued prior to the effective date of the registration statement. [SA §8(b)]

b) **Stop order.** A "stop order" either delays the effective date or stops the selling of securities (if it has begun), so as to permit an investigation of the issuer and the securities offered. The S.E.C. may issue a stop order at any time—whether before or after the effective date. [SA §8(d)]

   (1) **Grounds for issuance.** A stop order may be issued only for "material" deficiencies in the registration statement.

   (2) **Note.** Correction of deficiencies by amendments filed by the issuer after institution of a stop order proceeding will not necessarily prevent issuance of the order. The S.E.C. has the power to communicate to the public, via the order, that the registrant disregarded the registration requirements. [*In re* Hazel Bishop, Inc., 40 S.E.C. 718 (1961)]

   (3) **Procedure for issuance.** Stop orders may be issued only after a hearing with notice. Such hearing may be initiated by the S.E.C. when, in the opinion of its staff, the issuer has filed a defective registration statement. The S.E.C. need not first give the issuer a letter of comment nor accept amendments offered by the issuer. However, S.E.C. orders are appealable to the courts.

2) **Effect of formal proceedings on underwriter.** The institution of S.E.C. administrative proceedings against an underwriter can have a tremendous effect on the underwriter's business. For example, in one case where the S.E.C. was investigating an underwriter's involvement in a Regulation A offering, it sent letters to all issuers that were using the underwriter, indicating that they would have to disclose in their registration statements that the S.E.C. was investigating their underwriter. [Koss v. S.E.C., 364 F. Supp. 1321 (S.D.N.Y. 1973)]

3) **S.E.C.'s use of acceleration power.** As a practical matter, the S.E.C. and issuers do not resort to formal grounds to delay the effective date. Issuers simply state on the registration statement that it will not be effective until S.E.C. approval. As a quid pro quo, the S.E.C. then grants acceleration immediately after the price amendment is filed. Note that depending on the S.E.C. to grant acceleration gives the S.E.C. a lot of informal power over what goes into a registration statement.

f. **Withdrawal of registration statement.** If, after filing, there are problems with the issuing company or its registration statement, the issuer may simply seek to withdraw the statement—in order to avoid adverse publicity and/or potential liability under the Act.

1) **S.E.C. approval required.** Withdrawal is permitted upon proper application by the issuer if the S.E.C., "finding such withdrawal consistent with

the public interest and protection of investors, consents thereto." [SA Rule 477]

2) Timing of request. A withdrawal request filed prior to the institution of stop order proceedings is always honored. However, if a stop order has been instituted in the post-effective period, the S.E.C. obviously will not permit withdrawal—since the stock (or part of it) has already been sold.

g. Shelf registrations. Many issuers are almost constantly involved in issuing new securities. It would obviously be easiest for such issuers if they could simply prepare one registration statement, thereby registering all securities that they may offer at any time in the future (a so-called shelf registration).

1) Problem—inadequate disclosure. The difficulty with this approach to registration is that the single registration statement may not provide adequate disclosure to investors; i.e., material events may occur subsequent to the filing of the registration statement that would make some of the information in the registration statement incorrect.

2) General prohibition on shelf registrations. As a result, the Act provides that the registration statement is deemed effective only as to the securities specified therein. [*See* SA §6(a)]

a) Note. The S.E.C. has indicated that it is materially misleading for an issuer to include in a registration statement more securities than are going to be offered presently; i.e., it is misleading to include securities that are to be offered at some remote future date. [*See In re* Shawnee Chiles Syndicate, 10 S.E.C. 109 (1941)]

3) Exceptions to prohibition. There have always been, however, a number of situations where "shelf registrations" were permitted; for example, where Company A is merged into Company B, and the controlling shareholders of A may wish to later offer their shares to the public but cannot without registration. Another exception is where the underwriters of an offering receive some of the securities of the issuer immediately before the registered offering, or are given warrants to buy shares after the offering at a price less than the offering price. [*See* SA Rule 415—general rules that apply to permitting shelf registration]

a) Registration requirement. Since underwriters normally sell this stock within a short time, the S.E.C. has held that this stock (called "cheap stock") must be registered at the time of the issuer's registered offering, even though it may be sold after the issuer's offering is completed. [*See* SA Release No. 4936 (1968)]

b) Updating necessary. However, since certain information that must be included when the underwriter's stock is actually sold is not then available (such as the offering price), the registration statement must be updated when the underwriters actually sell the stock.

4) Form S-3 registrants. There are advantages to shelf registrations for the issuer (flexibility in responding to changing markets, cost savings, etc.). The main concerns are the ability of underwriters to conduct their due diligence investigations and the adequacy of disclosure by the issuer.

Despite these concerns, the S.E.C. has moved recently to expand the situations where shelf registrations are available. [*See* SA Rule 415]

    a)   **Application—Form S-3 companies.** Rule 415 permits companies that may use registration Form S-3 to shelf register their securities. S-3 companies are those that are widely followed in the marketplace and that file reports pursuant to the 1934 Act. These reports may be incorporated by reference and the information in them need not be repeated again in the prospectus delivered to investors.

    b)   **Rationale.** The S.E.C. has suggested that continuous due diligence programs are developing that can take care of the problems of not permitting the underwriter of such shelf registrations to conduct a sufficient due diligence investigation before such securities are offered to the public. Such programs include making sure that a single law firm acts as the underwriter's counsel for all parts of the shelf registration offerings, and holding periodic due diligence meetings with management; also, due diligence requirements in this situation may be different than in regular underwriting situations. [*See* SA Rule 176]

h.   **Refusal of underwriter to proceed—material misstatements.** The underwriter normally conducts an independent investigation of the issuer during the waiting period to determine whether all material facts have been disclosed in the registration statement. (This relates to the underwriter's defense of "due diligence" in case there are material misstatements or omissions in the registration statement.) If there are material misstatements, the underwriter may refuse to proceed with the underwriting despite his contractual obligation to purchase and sell the issue.

    1)   **Rationale.** An underwriting contract that violates the 1933 Act because of material misstatements in the registration statement is void and therefore unenforceable. [Kaiser-Frazer Corp. v. Otis & Co., 195 F.2d 838 (2d Cir. 1952)]

    2)   **Opinion from counsel for issuer.** The underwriter also usually requires that the issuer's counsel (if the drafter of the registration statement) render the underwriter a legal opinion that he has no reason to believe that the registration statement contains any omissions or material misstatements.

i.   **Blue sky qualification.** The securities of a company going public must also be qualified under the "blue sky" or securities laws of each state in which they are intended to be offered, unless there is an exemption from qualification available under applicable state law.

j.   **NASD clearance.** The issuer must also receive clearance from the National Association of Securities Dealers that the underwriting commissions being paid are "fair" according to NASD rules.

k.   **Post-effective amendments and updates to registration statement.** There are two possible sources of error in the registration statement: (i) an intentional or unintentional material misstatement or omission may exist at the time the registration statement becomes effective; or (ii) everything may be correct at the time the registration statement becomes effective, but subsequent events may outdate the registration statement so that it contains material misstatements or omissions at the date of use. The Securities Act provides for a way to update the registration statement and the prospectus in each of these two situations.

1) **Errors existing at time of effectiveness.** Where the registration statement contains an error at the time it is declared effective, but the error is discovered only after the effective date, the appropriate way to update the prospectus is to file a "post-effective" amendment with the S.E.C. [SA Rule 423] Such filing is necessary in that section 11 of the 1933 Act provides a remedy against the issuer, the underwriters, and the others associated with the registration statement if the statement contains misstatements and omissions "when . . . it becomes effective." Since the amended statement is processed by the S.E.C., it has a new effective date and becomes a new registration statement. Section 11 liability is thus imposed on the new registration statement updated in this manner.

2) **Errors caused by subsequent developments.** However, where developments after the effective date of the registration statement make the information in the registration statement or prospectus misleading or false (although it was accurate at the effective date), a correction may be made simply by placing a sticker on the cover of the prospectus and supplying the correct information in the body of the prospectus. No filing or advance processing by the S.E.C. is required, as it is where errors existed at the effective date (above). [SA Rule 424] In this situation, section 11 liability does not apply. However, section 12(2) (prohibiting misrepresentation in the interstate sale of securities generally) does cover this situation. Consequently, correct information must be included in the prospectus whenever it is used if those connected with the offering are to avoid liability under the Act.

3) **Updating requirement.** Whether or not any errors are discovered, the Act requires that a prospectus still in use nine months after the effective date be updated to ensure that it contains information as of a date not more than 16 months prior to its use. This provision puts an outside limit on what can be considered "currently" accurate.

4) **Undertaking of underwriters.** As indicated earlier, if underwriters receive "cheap stock" and/or warrants in connection with registered offerings, the S.E.C. has required that the underwriters make a commitment in the issuer's initial registration statement to update the registration statement when the stock is sold. The S.E.C.'s position is that this updating must take the form of a post-effective amendment filed with the S.E.C. if the stock is sold by the underwriters after 90 days from the effective date of the issuer's offering. [*See* SA Release No. 4936 (1968)]

    a) **Effect.** This allows the S.E.C. to review the revised prospectus before it is used, and ensures that potential investors will be given current information (whereas a supplemental prospectus would not have to be processed by the S.E.C.).

    b) **And note.** In addition, it makes the amendment a new registration statement so that section 11 liability will apply to it.

    c) **Rationale.** In the initial registration, there is an undertaking to amend if and when the underwriters sell their stock. Thus, the registration statement is known to be incomplete when it is declared effective, and the S.E.C.

analogizes it to one requiring post-effective amendments under Rule 423 (above).

l. **Penny stocks and blank check offerings.** Many states pass on the merits of a security to be offered and if the offering does not meet certain criteria, then the security cannot be sold. The federal securities laws, for the most part, are based on disclosure of the facts so that investors can make their own decisions. However, the Securities Enforcement Remedies and Penny Stock Reform Act of 1990 was passed to target "blank offerings" (newly formed companies with no preexisting history or assets, no business plan (the proceeds can be used for anything), hence little disclosure). Often the securities of these offerings are then manipulated by the promoter, and proceeds are often siphoned off. Section 7(b) of the 1933 Act allows the S.E.C. to require issuers of such securities to provide additional disclosure, to place limitations on the use of the proceeds, and to provide that investors may rescind the purchase at any time.

D. WHAT IS A SECURITY?

1. **Application of the 1933 Act to "Securities."** In order to come within the registration requirement of section 5 of the 1933 Act, the offer or sale of a property interest must constitute the offer or sale of a "security."

2. **Categories of Securities.** Basically, the Act defines three categories of securities: [*See* SA §2(1)]

   a. **Any interest or instrument commonly known as a security.** These would include bonds, stocks, debentures, warrants, etc.

   b. **Types of securities specifically mentioned in the Act.** The Act specifically mentions the following as being "securities":

      1) Pre-organization subscriptions.

      2) Fractional, undivided interests in oil, gas or other mineral rights.

   c. **Investment contracts and certificates of participation.** The two most important clauses of section 2(1) are its broad, catch-all phases—"investment contracts" and "certificates of interest or participation in any profit-sharing agreement." [*See* SA §2(1)] The S.E.C. and the courts have applied these phrases to include many financial schemes not specifically mentioned by the Act as "securities."

S.E.C. v.
W. J. Howey
Co.

    1) **The traditional test for a security—leading case--S.E.C. v. W. J. Howey Co.,** 328 U.S. 293 (1946).

        a) **Facts.** Two Florida corporations (Ds) (owned by the same persons), one involved in planting citrus groves and selling interests in them to investors and the other involved in managing the groves, offered and sold small portions of land planted with citrus trees (as little as .65 of an acre) on warranty deed; in connection therewith a 10-year service contract was offered (and 85% of the land purchasers bought the service contract) whereby Ds took a leaseback of the land for a fee plus its expenses, managed the land, and harvested and marketed the citrus crop. Ds owned all of the machinery to do this and intermingled all of the harvest of all the plots together for sale. The S.E.C. brings an action for an injunction, alleging that a sale of a security is involved.

b) **Issue.** Were Ds involved in the sale of a "security" under the terms of the 1933 Act?

c) **Held.** Yes. Injunction issued.

(1) The offer of the land plus the service contracts is the offer of an "investment contract."

(2) The test for an investment contract is whether a person (i) invests money (ii) in a common enterprise and (iii) is led to expect profits (iv) solely from the efforts of the promoter *or* a third party. It is immaterial that the investor's interest is not evidenced by formal certificates.

(3) This is a flexible test capable of covering the countless schemes devised by those who seek the use of the money of others on the promise of profits.

(4) Something more is involved here than the sale of a piece of land plus a service contract. The investors here normally did not have the expertise to farm the land; the plots by themselves were not large enough to farm; it was a common enterprise, with management totally in the hands of Ds.

(5) It makes no difference that the investment is not speculative, nor that the land has value independent of the success of the enterprise as a whole.

(6) Since the Act covers offers as well as sales, it makes no difference that some of the purchasers chose not to buy the service contract.

2) **The trend of decisions.** The trend of decisions is toward expanding the scope of what is regulated as a "security." Whereas originally the scheme had to have a profit objective and the investor had to be totally passive in management, the S.E.C. and the courts have recently expanded the test to cover situations where investors do participate in management, and the form of benefit derived by the investor may be something other than cash profits.

3) **The modern tests.** Modern courts are applying the following criteria to determine whether an interest is a "security" under the 1933 Act.

a) Is the property interest one that is specifically mentioned in the Act?

b) Is it the type of interest that is commonly thought to be a security?

c) Is it an investment contract or a participation in a profit-making venture?

(1)   Does the investor invest money or something else of value?

(2)   Is there a "common enterprise" (several investors pooling resources together)?

(3)   Does the investor derive something of substantial benefit?

(4)   Is the management principally provided by a third party other than the investors? In particular, even if the investors are active in management, does control of the capital rest with a third party (the so-called risk capital test)?

d)   Is there a need for the protection of the Act?

4)   **The economic realities test.** Despite the traditional approach of classifying interests based on the three categories of section 2(1) of the 1933 Act, more recently the Supreme Court seemed to take the approach that there is really only one test for a security.

a)   **The preamble to section 2.** The preamble to section 2 of the 1933 Act states that the definition of a security in section 2(1) applies unless "the context otherwise requires." Thus, even if something is called a security, it may not be one if the context dictates that it not be. [*See, e.g.*, Exchange National Bank of Chicago v. Touche Ross & Co., 544 F.2d 1126 (2d Cir. 1976)]

b)   **Application.** In *United Housing Foundation, Inc. v. Forman, infra*, the Supreme Court adopted an economic realities test, refusing to find that the sale of "stock" in a nonprofit housing cooperative involved a security when (i) the stock did not have the normal indicia of stock, and (ii) the economic realities of the transaction dictated otherwise.

c)   **Not the exclusive test.** In *Landreth Timber Co. v. Landreth, infra*, the Supreme Court recently held that if something is called "stock" and has all the normal indicia of stock, it will be a security no matter what the economic realities of the situation. Thus, the latter test is just one of several tests for identifying a security.

5)   **Property interests that have been found to be "securities."**

a)   **Partnership and joint venture interests.** The sale of a general partnership does not normally constitute the sale of a security, since usually the partners take an active part in the management of the business. But there can be organizations which are structured to look like partnerships but which in reality are not (i.e., where a partner is really only a passive investor).

b)   **Limited partnership interests.** In contrast to general partnership interests, limited partnership interests are often held to be securities since the limited partners have little or no interest in the management of the business.

c) **Pyramid sales plans--S.E.C. v. Koscot Interplanetary, Inc.,** 497 F.2d 473 (5th Cir. 1974).

(1) **Facts.** Koscot (D) conducted a pyramid selling program: the lowest level was a "beauty advisor" who got the cosmetic product at a 45% discount from the retail price; the "supervisor" paid $1,000 and got the product at a 55% discount (so that he could sell to beauty advisors or to the public directly) plus $600 for each supervisor he recruited; and the "distributor" got the product at a 65% discount (so he could sell to supervisors and beauty advisors) and paid $5,000 (getting $3,000 for recruiting another distributor). "Investors" (supervisors and distributors) solicited prospects to attend "Opportunity Meetings," where Koscot put on a promotional program designed to recruit supervisors and distributors. The S.E.C. brings an action on the theory that the distributor solicitation program is a security.

(2) **Issue.** Is D's program for the solicitation of distributors a "security"?

(3) **Held.** Yes. The program for solicitation of distributors is an investment contract.

(a) The sale of cosmetics is separable from the solicitation of distributors. The program for the latter is the offer and sale of an investment contract.

(b) There is an investment of money.

(c) There is a common enterprise (i.e., the return of the investor is dependent on the success of the efforts of a third party—D; it makes no difference that the return of the investors is different among themselves).

(d) The success of the scheme is dependent on the third party's control of the essential managerial efforts, and the investor's realization of profits is inextricably tied to the success of the *promotional scheme*. It makes no difference that the investor also contributes some effort. If this were not the case the purpose of the Act could easily be evaded.

d) **Condominiums.** There are situations where condominiums can be securities. This occurs where, in addition to buying the condominium, the buyer gets some investment-type interest. For example, condominium units with a rental arrangement where the project manager rents the units when the owners are not using them and all units share expenses and revenues from rentals on a project basis were held to be securities. [*See* SA Release No. 5347 (1973)]

e) **Housing cooperatives--United Housing Foundation v. Forman,** 421 U.S. 837 (1975).

(1) **Facts.** Co-op City was a huge low-income rental housing project developed by a private, nonprofit corporation under state law. The corporation was formed for the purpose of building the project. It was financed by low-interest mortgage loans from the state plus "deposits" from prospective tenants; each step of the development process was supervised by the state

Housing Finance Agency; each prospective purchaser of an apartment purchased "stock" based on the number of rooms in the apartment ($1,800 for a four-room apartment) in the cooperative; the shares were tied to the apartment (they could not be transferred to a nontenant, nor pledged); they descended only to a surviving spouse; no voting rights attached to the shares since each apartment got one vote; and on termination of tenancy the stock had to be sold back to the cooperative at cost or to a qualifying tenant essentially at cost. The solicitation of tenants stated the estimated construction cost of the project and the projected monthly rent of the units. Approximately 10% of the cost of the project was to come from tenant stock purchases; the rest from the low-interest mortgage loan from the state. Actual costs of the project's construction were much higher and rent was, therefore, higher. Fifty-seven residents of Co-op City (Ps) bring a class action on behalf of all purchasers of the "stock." The state of New York, its housing finance agency, the construction company, the nonprofit development company and others (Ds) were all sued in this action. Ps claimed that the 1965 Information Bulletin soliciting deposits falsely represented that the construction company would bear all cost increases in building the project, and that there were several nondisclosures of material facts. Action is pursuant to section 17(a) of the 1933 Act and Rule 10b-5 of the 1934 Act. The district court dismissed on the basis that no "security" was involved. The federal circuit court reversed. The Supreme Court granted certiorari.

(2) **Issue.** Is the "stock" in the nonprofit housing cooperative a "security" for the purposes of the 1933 Act?

(3) **Held.** No. Judgment for Ds.

(a) Although the word "stock" is used in the definition of a security under section 2(1) of the Act, this is not determinative. The underlying test for a security is "the economic reality of the transaction."

(b) The 1933 Act was intended to regulate the capital markets for raising money in order to protect investors. So the question is whether this transaction meets that basic purpose of the Act.

(c) We do not say that the name is irrelevant. Sometimes the use of common names such as "stock" may lead the investor to assume that the federal securities laws apply. This did not happen here. They were purchasing an apartment for their own use, not making a securities investment in the common sense.

(d) This "stock" has none of the common characteristics of investment stock such as negotiability, voting rights, dividend rights, etc.

(e) The test for an investment contract or for "an instrument commonly known as a security" is the same—the economic reality of the transaction.

(f) There is no investment contract here, according to the *Howey* test.

   1] There must be a motivation for profits, either in the form of capital appreciation or a sharing in the earnings from the use of the investment capital. Here Ps were motivated by the opportunity to get an apartment and use it.

2] The attraction was not profit; the nonprofit nature of the project was emphasized. Also, there could be no resale of the units at a profit. Getting a tax deduction for the portion of the monthly rent that was represented by interest payments on the mortgage is not "profit," nor is getting rental space at lower rent than comparable space. Nor is having the rent reduced from commercial facilities (such as washing machines) on the project a profit, since such facilities were not mentioned in the sale of the stock and the purpose is only to provide a convenience to renters.

f) **Franchises.** The issue involving franchises is the same as that for partnerships—is the investor active in management or merely a passive investor? Where the franchisee is active, there is normally no security.

g) **Club memberships.**

(1) Memberships in purely social organizations or clubs are not normally construed to be "securities" (e.g., memberships in country clubs), but memberships in clubs that have some business aspect are generally held to involve the sale of securities. For example, where certificates are issued to members for loans there is an "investment contract." [United States v. Monjar, 147 F.2d 916 (3d Cir. 1944), *cert. denied*, 325 U.S. 859 (1945)]

(2) Also, the California Supreme Court held that where memberships are sold by promoters who will own the club in order to build the club and club members have an irrevocable right to use the club (for regular fees), a security is involved. [Silver Hills Country Club v. Sobieski, 55 Cal. 2d 811 (1961)]

(a) *Silver Hills* is interesting since the court indicated that profit-making is not the only test for a security.

(b) It indicated that the purpose of the securities laws was to protect against all schemes used to raise "risk capital."

(c) Note that although this is a state securities law case, it has frequently been cited by federal court decisions.

h) **Sale of a business is a security--Landreth Timber Co. v. Landreth,** 471 U.S. 681 (1985).

Landreth
Timber Co.
v. Landreth

(1) **Facts.** Landreth (D) owned 100% of stock in a sawmill, which was sold through a broker to Dennis. Shortly before the sale the mill was damaged by fire, but D made representations about rebuilding it and about other financial results. Dennis bought the stock and assigned it to Landreth Timber (P). D stayed on to manage the business. Rebuilding cost more than anticipated and the operation did not live up to expectations; it was sold at a loss. P sued under Rule 10b-5 and various sections of the 1933 Act. D moved for summary judgment based on the allegation that federal securities laws did not apply, since no "security" was involved. The district court granted the motion. P appealed.

(2) **Issue.** Is the sale of all of the stock of a company a securities transaction that is subject to the antifraud provisions of the federal securities laws?

(3) **Held.** Yes. Reversed.

(a) The specific language of section 2(1) of the 1933 Act mentions "stock."

(b) Just because something is called "stock" does not make it stock. The instrument must have the characteristics typically associated with stock. Here the stock had all the usual characteristics of stock (whereas the stock in the *United Housing Foundation* case, *supra*, did not).

(c) This is a context where an investor would expect that the securities laws would apply.

(d) Courts have also looked beyond form to analyze the economic substance of instruments.

    1] *United Housing* involved a situation where the instrument could not easily be classified as stock.

    2] Thus, the issue was whether the instrument fell under the broad category of an "investment contract."

    3] In making this determination, courts should look to economic realities.

    4] But where the instrument purports to be stock and has the characteristics of stock, it may be held to be a security without passing the economic realities test.

(e) The Acts were not just meant to cover passive investors. The Acts protect many classes of people, and there is no reason they should not protect entrepreneurs buying a business.

(f) Just because stock is covered literally by the Acts does not mean that there is no flexibility in defining other categories of instruments mentioned by the Acts (i.e., "notes," etc.). "Stock" represents the paradigm of a security: people dealing with stock have a high expectation that it is a security. The question of whether a note or a bond may be proven to be a security merely by showing that the instrument has this form and the usual characteristics will be left to other decisions.

(g) There are also strong policy reasons why the sale of business doctrine should not be applied in this case.

    1] Extensive fact-finding will often be necessary to determine whether plaintiffs are really controlling the corporation or are passive investors. Here, for example, D stayed on to help with the management of the mill.

    2] There is a difficult line-drawing problem in determining whether to apply the doctrine only to cases of 100% transfer of control or to situations of less control. Parties would never know until after litigation whether their situation was covered or not.

(4) Dissent.

    (a) Congress did not intend the antifraud provisions of the securities laws to apply to every transaction in a security described by section 2(1) of the 1933 Act. The sweeping definition given was to prevent evasion by people inventing new types of securities. But the courts should be able to interpret these terms in light of the purposes of the Acts.

    (b) Legislative history of the Acts indicates that Congress was primarily concerned with securities transactions in the public market where investors could not protect themselves by obtaining information and negotiating for contractual warranties.

    (c) All the economic realities of the situation should be taken into account for stock, notes, or other possible securities.

    (d) In summary, the antifraud provisions of the Acts are inapplicable unless the transaction involves (i) a publicly traded security, or (ii) an investor not able to negotiate protective warranties or get information before consummating the transaction.

i) Employee pension, profit sharing, and stock purchase plans. Qualified employee pension and profit sharing plans are tax-motivated arrangements permitting employers to make a deductible contribution to a fund that defers any tax to the benefited employees, with respect to both the employer's contribution and amounts of income generated by the plan until the employee actually receives the deferred distribution (typically upon retirement at age 65). All such plans are conceivably investment contracts involving the poolings of individual investments in an arrangement through which profits are expected as a result of the efforts of another. The S.E.C.'s historical approach to such arrangements, however, has been dictated in large part by the extent to which it perceives that an investor interest needs to be protected.

    (1) Pension and profit sharing plans. Where the offer or sale of an interest in these types of plans contemplates that the employee will make *voluntary* contributions to the plan, this has normally been held to be the offer and sale of a security. [*See* Opinion of Assistant General Counsel of the S.E.C. sent to Commerce Clearing House (1953)]

        (a) Exceptions. However, where the contributions are used merely for the purchase of annuity or insurance contracts (themselves exempt under section 3(a)(8) of the Act), it may be that the plan does not involve the offer of a "security." Also, where the plan has no contributions by employees, or where employee contribution is compulsory (i.e., involuntary), historically the S.E.C. regarded such plans as involving no "sale" of a security.

**(b) Noncontributory, compulsory pension plan not security--International
Brotherhood of Teamsters v. Daniel,** 439 U.S. 551 (1979).

1] **Facts.** In 1954, multiemployer collective bargaining between Local 705 of
the International Brotherhood of Teamsters, Chauffeurs, Warehousemen,
and Helpers of America and Chicago trucking firms produced a pension
plan for employees represented by the Local. The plan was compulsory
(all employees were automatically covered) and noncontributory (employees did not put up any contributions from their wages). Employees had no
choice as to participation in the plan, and did not have the option of
demanding that the employer's contribution be paid directly to them as a
substitute for pension eligibility.

The collective bargaining agreement initially set employer contributions to
the Pension Trust Fund at $2 per week for each man-week of covered
employment. The Board of Trustees of the Fund, a body composed of an
equal number of employer and union representatives, was given sole
authority to set the level of benefits but had no control over the amount of
required employer contributions. Initially, eligible employees received $75
a month in benefits upon retirement. Subsequent collective bargaining
agreements called for greater employer contributions, which in turn led to
a higher benefit payment for retirees. In order to receive a pension, an
employee was required to have 20 years of continuous service.

Daniel (P) began working as a truck driver in 1950, and joined Local 705
the following year. When the plan first went into effect, P automatically
received five years' credit toward the 20-year service requirement because
of his earlier work experience. P retired in 1973 and applied to the plan's
administrator for a pension. The administrator determined that P was
ineligible because of a break in service between December 1960 and July
1961. P appealed the decision to the trustees, who affirmed. P then asked
the trustees to waive the continuous service rule as it applied to him. After
the trustees refused to waive the rule, P brought suit in federal court
against Teamsters International, Local 705, and Louis Pieck, a trustee of
the fund (Ds).

P's complaint alleged that Ds misrepresented and omitted to state material
facts with respect to the value of a covered employee's interest in the
pension plan. Count I of the complaint charged that these misstatements
and omissions constituted a fraud in connection with the sale of a security
in violation of section 10b of the Securities Exchange Act of 1934 and the
Securities and Exchange Commission's Rule 10b-5. Count II charged that
the same conduct amounted to a violation of section 17(a) of the Securities
Act of 1933. Other counts alleged violations of various labor law and
common law duties. P sought to proceed on behalf of all prospective
beneficiaries of Teamsters pension plans and against all Teamsters pension
funds.

Ds moved to dismiss the first two counts of the complaint on the ground
that P had no cause of action under the Securities or Securities Exchange
Acts. The district court denied the motion. It held that P's interest in the
Pension Fund constituted a security within the meaning of section 2(1) of
the Securities Act and section 3(a)(10) of the Securities Exchange Act. It
also determined that there had been a "sale" of this interest to P within the

meaning of section 2(3) of the Securities Act and section 3(a)(14) of the Securities Exchange Act. It held that P "voluntarily" gave value for his interest in the plan because he had voted on collective bargaining agreements that chose employer contributions to the Fund instead of other wages or benefits.

The district court's order denying the motion to dismiss was appealed to the circuit court, which affirmed. According to the court, a "sale" took place either when P ratified a collective bargaining agreement embodying the Fund or when he accepted or retained covered employment instead of seeking other work. The court did not believe the subsequent enactment of the Employee Retirement Income Security Act of 1974 (ERISA) affected the application of the Securities Act to pension plans, as the requirements and purposes of ERISA were perceived to be different from those of the Securities Acts. The Supreme Court granted certiorari.

2] **Issue.** Does a noncontributory compulsory pension plan constitute a "security" for the purposes of the Securities Act of 1933 and the Securities Exchange Act of 1934?

3] **Held.** No. Judgment reversed.

a] Neither section 2(1) of the 1933 Act nor section 3(a)(10) of the 1934 Act indicate explicitly whether employee pension plans are securities. The question is whether pension plans are "investment contracts" under these sections.

b] The test for a security is whether the scheme involves investment of money in a common enterprise with profits to come solely from the efforts of others.

c] Here P did not make an investment since he did not give up a specific consideration in return for a separable interest with the characteristics of a security. P became an employee and as a result received, commingled with many other rights, a compensation package. He was selling his labor to make a living, not primarily to make an investment. Also, the employer did not make a contribution specifically on behalf of the individual employee—the employer made contributions on the basis of man-weeks worked, and all qualifying employees (whether in service 20 or 40 years) got the same benefit.

d] Here the return from the pension fund comes to the employees mostly from employer contributions and only a minimal amount comes from investment earnings on the contributed funds. Also, qualification to receive funds is not primarily a result of the management efforts of others, but rather of whether the individual can meet the requirements of the pension fund (such as length of service).

e] There are no actions of Congress that clearly indicate that its intent was to treat all pension plans as securities.

f] And the S.E.C.'s past actions would seem to indicate that it has never treated noncontributory pension plans as securities. Its position historically was that such plans did not constitute a "sale" as required by the Securities Acts. The S.E.C. now says that noncontributory plans are securities even if a "sale" does not occur, and that the "sale" requirement was required for the purposes of the registration provisions only and not for the antifraud provisions of the Acts. The historical position of the S.E.C. refutes its current argument.

g] The enactment of ERISA in 1974 (which requires pension plans to disclose specified information to employees and governs the substantive terms of pension plans) severely undercuts all arguments for extending the Securities Acts to noncontributory, compulsory pension plans. The possible benefits employees might have derived from the Securities Acts are now provided in definite form by ERISA.

4] Comment. The Court here is pursuing a conservative course of limiting the reach of federal securities law, particularly where other legislation clearly occupies the field.

(2) Stock purchase plans. If the employer simply sells stock to its employees at market price or at a discount in order to encourage employee ownership, this may amount to a public offering and registration would be required. The typical stock purchase plan consists of an arrangement by the company of an account with a brokerage firm. The company then deducts specified amounts from employee wages and the brokerage firm uses these amounts to purchase the company's stock *on the public market* on behalf of the employees.

(a) Whether or not registration of such plans is required depends on the degree and type of participation by the company in the program. [SA Release No. 4790 (1965)]

(b) Where an independent broker or other agent of the employees is responsible for the solicitation of the employees, then no registration is required where the company performs no more than the following functions: (i) announces the existence of such a plan to its employees; (ii) makes payroll deductions at the request of the employee; (iii) makes the names and addresses of the employees available to the brokerage firm, and direct communications concerning the plan are then carried on by the brokerage firm; and (iv) pays no more than its expense of the payroll deductions and the charges of the brokerage firm (its commissions and other reasonable charges for bookkeeping, etc.). [SA Release No. 4790 (1965)]

(c) Of course, where the employer directly supplies securities for purchase by the employees (from authorized but as yet unissued shares), then such a plan would clearly require registration unless some exemption applies.

Reves v. Ernst & Young

j) Notes as securities under the 1934 Act--Reves v. Ernst & Young, 494 U.S. 56 (1990).

(1) Facts. The Farmer's Co-operative was an agricultural co-op with 23,000 members; it sold promissory demand notes at higher than bank rates of interest in order to capitalize its operations, to both members and nonmembers, through newsletter ads. Arthur Young audited the co-op. The notes were not insured or guaranteed, although they were advertised as "safe." The co-op declared bankruptcy, with noteholders holding $10 million in notes. A group of noteholders sued D for misrepresentation in the value of the co-op's investment in a gasahol plant, which had it been given at its real value would have led the group not to buy the co-op's notes. Ps sue under the anti-fraud laws of the 1934 Act. The trial court found for Ps; the Eighth Circuit reversed; the Supreme Court granted certiorari.

(2) Issue. Are the notes in this case "securities" under the 1934 Act?

(3) Held. Yes.

    (a)   Congress enacted a definition of "security" sufficiently broad to encompass virtually any instrument that might be sold as an investment; but it did not intend to provide a federal remedy for all fraud. The courts, in interpreting the law, are not bound by formalisms, but instead take into account the economics of the transaction under review. Congress's purpose in enacting the securities laws was to regulate investments, in whatever form they are made and by whatever name they are called.

    (b)   The *Landreth* case held that stock is a special case and that it is a security if it has the indicia of normal stock.

    (c)   Notes are not the same as stock; but the 1934 Act (section 3(a)(10)) names notes as securities, so we begin with a presumption that every note is a security. This presumption is rebuttable, based on an analysis of the following factors:

        1]   What is the motivation of a buyer and seller to enter into the transactions? If the motivation is to raise money to finance a business, it is a security. If it is a consumer finance transaction, such as a note with a mortgage back, then it is not a security.

        2]   What is the plan of distribution? Is it like a public distribution?

        3]   What expectations do the investing public have? Do they think it is a security?

        4]   Is there another regulatory scheme that reduces risk so that the securities laws are not necessary?

    (d)   Here, by these criteria, the notes are securities.

    (e)   There is an exception in section 3 of the 1934 Act for "any note . . . which has a maturity at the time of issuance of not exceeding nine months." We hold that a demand note may be due immediately, or it might not in practice be redeemed for years, so it does not qualify for the exception.

    (f)   Eighth Circuit reversed.

(4) Concurrence. All of the Circuit Courts have held that when Congress spoke of notes with a maturity of nine months, it meant commercial paper, not investment securities. This should be the basis of the decision.

(5) Dissent.

    (a) The terms "note" and "maturity" have had generally accepted meanings for centuries, so at the time Congress adopted section 3(a)(10), the meaning of a demand note's being immediately due was the accepted interpretation. The majority has misconstrued the law.

    (b) It is also inappropriate to argue that the legislative history for section 3(a)(3) of the 1933 Act relative to notes can be relied on to interpret section 3(a)(10) of the 1934 Act. The language limiting short-term notes to commercial paper was taken out of the 1933 Act in its final version.

    (c) Finally, the exemption in section 3(a)(3) of the 1933 Act applies only to registration requirements; the anti-fraud requirements of the 1933 Act still apply; while excluding coverage of the 1934 Act excludes coverage as well of all anti-fraud provisions of the 1934 Act.

3. Exempted Securities. Certain types of securities are exempt from the registration requirements of section 5. Such an exemption means that the security may be sold and resold and never be subject to the registration or prospectus requirements of the Act. For example:

a. Bank and government securities. Section 3(a)(2) of the Act exempts the following securities:

    1) Securities issued or guaranteed by the United States, its territories or by the states; and

    2) Securities issued by banks, or securities of a common trust fund maintained by a bank for collective investment funds which are managed by the bank as the trustee.

b. Notes and other debt instruments. Notes, drafts, etc., which arise out of current transactions which have a maturity date not exceeding nine months are exempted. [*See* SA §3(a)(3)]

c. Charitable organizations. Securities issued by religious, educational, or charitable organizations are also exempted. [*See* SA §3(a)(4)]

E. TRANSACTION EXEMPTIONS AVAILABLE TO THE ISSUER OF SECURITIES

The 1933 Act contains certain exemptions for security transactions. [*See* SA §§3 and 4]

1. **Distinction Between Exempted Securities and Exempted Transactions.** The distinction between security transactions and exempted securities is an important one. If the security itself is exempted, then it can be sold and resold and never be subject to the requirements of section 5. However, if only the transaction is exempt, then the initial sale may be exempt from section 5 but a later resale may not be.

2. **The Private Offering Exemptions.**

   a. **Persons covered by the Act—issuers.** The registration requirements of the 1933 Act apply to all "persons" selling securities through the use of the facilities of interstate commerce. [*See* SA §5] However, the Act also exempts from the registration requirement securities transactions by persons other than an "issuer, underwriter or dealer." [*See* SA §4(1)] Thus, the registration requirements apply only to "issuers," "underwriters," and "dealers."

   b. **The definition of an issuer.** An "issuer" includes every person who issues or proposes to issue any security. [*See* SA §2(4)] Where an issuer makes a public distribution of securities, the registration requirements of section 5 of the Act apply.

   c. **Sections 4(2) and 4(6).**

      1) **Private offerings under section 4(2) of the 1933 Act.** Transactions by an issuer not involving a public offering (i.e., a "private offering" of securities) are exempted from registration. [*See* SA §4(2)]

         a) **Fact question.** Whether or not an offering is a "private offering" or a "public offering" is a question of fact.

         b) **Burden of proof.** The burden of proof to show that the offering is private is on the party claiming the exemption.

         c) **Primary factors considered.** The following are the primary factors which are considered by the courts in making the determination of whether an offering is a public or private one.

            (1) **Need for the protection of the Act--S.E.C. v. Ralston Purina Co.,** 346 U.S. 119 (1953).

            S.E.C. v.
Ralston
Purina Co.

               (a) **Facts.** Between 1947 and 1951, Ralston Purina (D) sold nearly $2 million of its stock to employees from all levels of the company (educational backgrounds, salary levels, etc.) without registration and, in doing so, made use of the mails. In each of these years, a corporate resolution authorized the sale of common stock to employees who, without solicitation by the corporation, inquired as to the manner in which common stock could be purchased from D. Sales in each year were to approximately 400 employees. The corporation classified all offerees who bought the stock as "key employees" in the organization. D claimed the private offering exemption. The trial court dismissed an action by the Securities and Exchange Commission, which sought to enjoin D's activities. The court of appeals affirmed. The Supreme Court granted certiorari.

(b) Issue. Was D's offering of stock to "key employees" a public offering?

(c) Held. Yes. The trial court erred in dismissing the S.E.C.'s action.

1] To be public, an offer need not be open to the whole world.

2] The design of the 1933 Act was to protect investors by promoting full disclosure of information thought to be necessary to informed investment decisions. Thus, the private offering exemption is available only where the protection of the Act is not needed (i.e., an offering to those able to fend for themselves).

3] Absent a showing of special circumstances, a corporation's employees are as much in need of protection as any members of the investing "public."

4] The burden of proof is on the issuer, who would plead the exemption.

5] Since the employees here were not shown to have access to the kind of information that registration would disclose, D was not entitled to the exemption.

6] The exemption applies whether the offering is made to few or many investors. However, it may be that offerings to a substantial number of persons would rarely be exempt, and the S.E.C. may adopt a numerical test in deciding when to investigate private offering exemption claims.

(d) Comments. Presumably, if the offer of securities is made to those able to "fend for themselves," then the transaction does not involve a public offering. This means that the basic issue concerns the level of sophistication of the persons (offerees) to whom the securities are offered for sale. That is, are they knowledgeable enough to ask the right questions, to demand and get the information they need to make an intelligent investment decision, to appreciate the risk of making securities investments, etc.?

(2) Access to investment information. Allied with the idea in *Ralston* of the level of sophistication of the offerees is the idea that investor access to material information is critical to an investment decision. And related to this is the concept that the offerees must be in or have a close relationship to the issuer and its management in order to have good access. [*See* S.E.C. v. Continental Tobacco Co., 463 F.2d 137 (5th Cir. 1972)]

(3) Distribution of material information. Some courts have stated that the mere access to material information is not enough. The issuer may have to actually distribute to its offerees the same type of information as would be contained in a formal registration statement. Further, the issuer may have to give the offerees access to any additional information that they request. [*See* S.E.C. v. Continental Tobacco Co.]

(4) **The number of offerees.** A "private offering" also seems to imply that the number of offerees will be few in number.

   (a) On the basis of this rationale, there is no question but that when the number of *offerees* (not actual purchasers) gets very large, no matter how sophisticated the investors might be or how much information they might have, the offering would be a public one and registration would be required.

   (b) This means that many of the criteria used by the courts to define a private offering are based on this same idea—it makes no difference whether the offerees get the same protection they would receive by registration; if it is a "public offering," it is a public offering and registration with the S.E.C. is required.

(5) **Other important factors.** In addition to the primary factors considered, there are several other factors that courts have indicated are important in making the determination of whether the offering is public or private.

   (a) **The size (amount) of the offering.**

   (b) **The marketability of the securities.** If the issuer has created the type of security which tends to be readily marketable (such as many small denominations, e.g., $1 per share), there is more reason to believe that the issue is made with the intent to distribute the securities to the public rather than to a few private persons.

   (c) **The diverse group rule.** The more unrelated to each other (i.e., without knowledge of or relationship to each other) and diverse the various investors are, the more the offering appears to be a public offering. [*See* S.E.C. v. Continental Tobacco Co.]

   (d) **The manner of offering.** The manner in which the offering is made (e.g., whether public advertising was used) may also be important. [*See* Hill York Corp. v. American International Franchises, 448 F.2d 680 (5th Cir. 1971)]

   (e) **Comment.** With all of these requirements for a private offering, the only thing not required is processing the registration statement through the S.E.C. As a result, many believed that the private offering exemption had been destroyed. The S.E.C. initially responded by passing Rule 146 (since rescinded). The courts also began to consider whether the private offering should be made available without such stringent requirements.

2) **Rule 146 exemption for private offerings.** After spending an inordinate amount of time analyzing and resolving alleged private offering sales under section 4(2), and also due to the fact that the rulings of the courts covering what constituted a private offering had grown so restrictive, the S.E.C. adopted Rule 146. This rule provides specific objective criteria for determining whether an offering is "private" and thus outside the registration requirements of section 5.

A discussion of Rule 146 is included only for historical interest since the S.E.C. subsequently rescinded Rule 146 and replaced it with Rule 506, which is discussed *infra* in association with the "small issue" exemptions.

a) **Relationship of Rule 146 and section 4(2).** It is important to remember that even if the issuer could not meet all of the specific requirements of Rule 146 it could still claim the private offering exemption if it could show that the offering complied with the broader criteria of section 4(2). [SA Release No. 5487 (1974)]

b) **Impact of Rule 146.** Because Rule 146 provided objective criteria, and more clearly defined terms that were somewhat ambiguous under section 4(2), it influenced judicial decisions as to what constituted a private offering under section 4(2). As a result, most issuers contemplating a private offering attempted to comply with the Rule 146 requirements.

Doran v. Petroleum Management Corp.

c) **Rule 146 applied--Doran v. Petroleum Management Corp.,** 545 F.2d 893 (5th Cir. 1977).

(1) **Facts.** Petroleum Management Corp. (D) organized a limited partnership to drill and operate four oil wells in Wyoming. Seven persons were offered "participant" interests and four accepted. Doran (P), a sophisticated investor, was offered a "special participant" interest, which he accepted. As a result he paid $25,000 into the partnership and signed a note for $113,000 to a supplier, which note was to be paid by P's production royalties. These royalties were insufficient to pay the note and the note holder sued P. P sued for damages and to rescind his purchase of the interest, claiming that D failed to register the securities. D claimed a section 4(2) exemption. The district court found for D; P appealed.

(2) **Issues.**

(a) Can a sophisticated investor, having adequate information, rescind a securities transaction otherwise exempt from registration under 4(2) if any of his fellow offerees were unsophisticated and/or lacked adequate information?

(b) Is the 4(2) exemption available when offerees are not insiders with a close relationship to the issuer?

(3) **Held.** Yes to both questions. Judgment for D reversed and the case remanded.

(a) To be a private offering, the number of *offerees* must be limited.

(b) Sophistication of one of the offeree-plaintiffs will not save a 4(2) exemption if any one of his fellow offerees is not sophisticated. Here, all of the offerees were sophisticated. In addition, each offeree must have available the information that registration would disclose. Under Rule 146, availability of information means *either* disclosure of *or* effective access to the relevant information. If access is relied on, then the offerees' relationship to the issuer is important. D has the burden of proof of showing such access.

(c)   Although Rule 146 does not directly control this case, it is unwise to constrict the scope of the private offering exemption more narrowly than does Rule 146. Thus, the offerees need not be insiders if they have access to or were provided with relevant information.

(4)   Comment. The Fifth Circuit caused much of the uncertainty concerning the private offering exemption that resulted in adoption of Rule 146. Here it tries to bring its interpretation of 4(2) closer to the tests set forth in Rule 146. That is, the *Doran* case seemed to hold that the issuer did not have to actually give investors the same information as would be included in a registration statement if the investors were sophisticated and had access to this same information. The court in *Continental Tobacco* would have required both access and the distribution of the same information. So Rule 146 apparently influenced *Doran* to retreat from the more severe holding of *Continental Tobacco*.

d)   Requirements under Rule 146. To have qualified as a private offering under Rule 146, all of the following conditions had to be met:

(1)   Method of offering. Securities could not be sold through any form of general advertising or solicitation—including newspapers, magazines, television, public seminars or meetings, letters, or written notices. (If the offerees were first "qualified" (below), seminars, meetings, or written communications could then be used.) [SA Rule 146(c)]

(2)   Qualified offerees and purchasers. The issuer had to have, after a reasonable investigation, reasonable grounds to believe and actually believe that:

(a)   Prior to the making of any actual offers, the potential offerees either: (i) had the knowledge and experience sufficient to properly evaluate the security; or (ii) were persons able to bear the risk of the investment—i.e., could afford a complete loss, or could hold the securities for an indefinite period. [SA Rule 146(d)(1)]

(b)   Prior to actually selling the securities: (i) the offerees had sufficient knowledge to evaluate the investment; or (ii) the purchasers and their representatives (who must themselves be qualified to evaluate the securities and be independent of the issuer) together had the requisite knowledge, and the purchaser was able to bear the risk of the investment. [SA Rule 146(d)(2)]

(3)   Access to information. Each offeree had to have access to the same kind of information included in a registration statement (i.e., have an employment, family, or economic position with respect to the issuer sufficient to enable the offeree to obtain such information), or the issuer must actually have given the offeree the same information normally included in a registration statement. [SA Rule 146(e)] (*Note*: There were different requirements for reporting companies under the 1934 Exchange Act and for nonreporting companies, in terms of what information had to be given to the offerees. Also, to make it easier on small businesses, Rule 146 provided that, for offerings under $1.5 million, the disclosures could approximate those required for a Regulation A offering rather than the more complex disclosures required in an S-1 registration.) In addition to either of the above, it was also required that:

(a) Offerees be given the opportunity to question the issuer about the terms and conditions of the offering, and to obtain any additional facts necessary to verify the information actually given; and

(b) The issuer had to disclose to each offeree in writing and prior to sale: (i) the fact that the purchaser had to take the securities for investment and bear the risk for the investment period (plus any other relevant limitations on disposition of the securities); and (ii) the existence of any material relationship between the issuer and anyone advising the offeree. [SA Rules 146(e)(2) and (3)]

(4) **Number of purchasers.** The issuer had to have, after a reasonable investigation, reasonable grounds to believe and actually believe that there were no more than 35 purchasers involved in the offering. In computing this number, parties related to the purchasers were not counted as purchasers—e.g., a corporation owned by a purchaser was not counted as an additional purchaser even though both bought the securities. [SA Rule 146(g)]

(a) **Note.** Large investors (i.e., persons who purchased $150,000 of the issued securities) were not counted as part of the 35. [*See* SA Rule 146(g)(2)(d)]

(5) **Limitation on subsequent disposition of securities.** Finally, the issuer had to exercise reasonable care to make sure that its purchasers were not and did not become "underwriters." The issuer could accomplish this by:

(a) **Making reasonable inquiry** to determine that the purchasers were acquiring the securities for themselves and not for public distribution;

(b) **Putting a "restrictive legend"** on the securities, stating that the securities had not been registered under the Act and that there were certain limitations on their transfer or sale;

(c) **Issuing "stop transfer" instructions** to the issuer's transfer agent; and

(d) **Obtaining signed written agreements** ("investment letters") from the purchasers that they would not sell the securities without registering them or qualifying for an exemption from registration. [SA Rule 146(h)]

(6) **Notification to the S.E.C.** The issuer also had to notify the S.E.C. when it made use of the rule. [*See* SA Release No. 33-5912 (1978)] This report had to be filed by issuers at the time of the first sale of securities in the offering. No report was required for offerings in which the proceeds totaled less than $50,000 during any 12-month period. The information required in the report included:

(a) **Basic information** regarding the issuer and its chief executive officer or natural persons who were the issuer's general partner(s), promoter(s), or controlling person(s).

(b) **Names and addresses** of organizers, promoters, and sponsors of, and offeree representatives involved in, the offering.

(c) **The title and dollar amount** of existing and planned sales of the securities in the offering.

3) **Integration of private offerings into public offerings.** Where the issuer has on several occasions attempted private offerings under section 412) (or Rule 146), an issue may arise as to whether these constitute several original distributions or only one offering. Although the issuer may attempt to convey the appearance of having made two or more private offerings, the S.E.C. might decide that they should be "integrated"—i.e., all of the offerings counted as one offering—which could thereby turn the separate private offerings into one public offering which could require registration.

   a) **Factors considered.** Factors the S.E.C. has considered in concluding that several offerings will be integrated into one include evidence that:

   (1) The different offerings are part of a "single plan of financing" by the issuer;

   (2) The offerings involve issuance of the same class of security;

   (3) The offerings are made at or about the same time;

   (4) The same type of consideration is to be received; and

   (5) The offerings are made for the same general purpose. [SA Release No. 4552 (1972)]

   b) **Safe harbor rule.** Rule 146 contained a "safe harbor" rule. If the issuer complied with all of the tests set forth in this rule, he could be assured that the S.E.C. would not challenge separate offerings on the basis that they should be integrated.

4) **Exemption for offerings to "accredited investors."** A new section, 4(6), was added to the 1933 Act by the Small Business Investment Incentive Act of 1980. This section, related conceptually to section 4(2) (the "private offering" exemption), provides an exemption from the 1933 Act's registration requirements for transactions involving offers and sales of securities by an issuer solely to one or more "accredited investors" if the aggregate offering price does not exceed the amount allowed under section 3(b) (currently $5 million). No advertising or public solicitation is permitted in connection with such transactions.

   a) **Exemption limited to "accredited persons."** A 4(6) offering may only be made to "accredited investors." Section 2(15) of the 1933 Act defines "accredited investors" as certain institutional investors and also others who qualify under S.E.C. rules (although to date the S.E.C. has not adopted any such rules).

   b) **Notice to the S.E.C.** Section 4(6) does not specify what information the issuer must give to accredited investors, and the S.E.C. has not yet elaborated on this point. However, any issuer relying on the exemption must file a notice of sales pursuant to the section with the S.E.C.

3. **The Small Issue Exemptions.** In addition to the other security and security transaction exemptions set forth in the Act, section 3(b) of the 1933 Act permits the S.E.C. to exempt security offerings from registration where the protection of the Act is not required and less than $5 million in securities is involved in the offering. Pursuant to this section, the S.E.C. has formulated several additional exemptions. Although formulated under section 3 of the 1933 Act for *security* exemptions, these small business exemptions are really *transaction* exemptions.

   a. **Regulation D.**

      1) **Introduction.** In a major initiative aimed at facilitating the capital formation needs of small business, the S.E.C. adopted Regulation D, which contains Rules 501-506. Rules 501 through 503 set forth definitions, terms, and conditions that apply generally throughout the regulation. Rules 504 and 505, respectively, replace prior Rules 240 and 242 and provide exemptions from registration under section 3(b) of the 1933 Act. Rule 506 replaces prior Rule 146 and relates to transactions that are deemed to be exempt from registration under section 4(2) of the 1933 Act. [*See* S.E.C. Release No. 33-6389 (1982)] These provisions apply only to the issuer; control persons may not use them. Regulation D is designed to:

         a) Simplify and clarify existing exemptions;

         b) Expand the availability of existing exemptions; and

         c) Achieve uniformity between federal and state exemptions.

      2) **Definitions and terms used in Regulation D.** Rule 501 sets forth definitions that apply to the entire Regulation D. One of these key definitions is that of "accredited investor," which includes eight categories:

         a) Institutional investors [*see* SA §2(15)(i)];

         b) Private business development companies [*see* Rule 501(a)(2)];

         c) Tax-exempt organizations [*see* Rule 501(a)(3)];

         d) Directors, executive officers, and general partners of the issuer of the securities [*see* Rule 501(a)(4)];

         e) $150,000 purchasers [*see* Rule 501(a)(5)];

         f) Natural persons with $1 million net worth [*see* Rule 501(a)(6)];

         g) Natural persons with $200,000 income [*see* Rule 501(a)(7)]; and

         h) Entities made up of certain accredited investors, such as an entity owned entirely by such investors [*see* Rule 501(a)(8)].

      3) **General conditions to be met.** There are several general conditions that apply to all offers and sales effected pursuant to Rules 504 through 506 (under Rule 502):

a) **Integration.** All sales that are part of the same Regulation D offering must be integrated. [*See* Rule 502(a)] The rule provides a safe harbor for all offers and sales that take place at least six months before the start of, or six months after the termination of, the Regulation D offering, so long as there are no offers and sales (excluding those to employee benefit plans) of the same securities within either of these six-month periods.

b) **Information requirements.** The type of disclosure that must be furnished in Regulation D offerings is specified. [*See* Rule 502(b)] If an issuer sells securities under Rule 504 or only to accredited investors, then Regulation D does not mandate any specific type of disclosure. But if securities are sold under Rule 505 or 506 to any investors that are not accredited, then delivery of the information specified in Rule 502(b)(2) to *all* purchasers is required. The type of information to be furnished varies depending on the size of the offering and the nature of the issuer (i.e., whether the issuer is a reporting or nonreporting company under the 1934 Act). Reporting companies in essence can use the information they are already filing with the S.E.C. (i.e., annual report, proxy statement and Form 10-K). The issuer, in a Rule 505 or 506 offering, must also give investors the opportunity to ask questions and to obtain any additional information which the issuer can acquire without unreasonable effort.

c) **Manner of the offering.** The use of general solicitation or general advertising in connection with Regulation D offerings is prohibited, except in certain cases under Rule 504. [*See* Rule 502(c)]

d) **Limitations on resale.** Securities acquired in a Regulation D offering, with the exception of certain offerings under Rule 504, have the status of securities acquired in a transaction under section 4(2) of the 1933 Act. [*See* Rule 502(d)] Issuers are required to exercise reasonable care to assure that purchasers of these securities are not underwriters and to make reasonable inquiry as to an investor's investment purpose. Also, a legend restricting transfer must be placed on the share certificates.

4) **Filing notice of sales.** There is a uniform notice of sales form for use in offerings under both Regulation D and section 4(6) of the 1933 Act. It is called "Form D." Issuers furnish information on Form D mainly by checking appropriate boxes. [*See* Rule 503] The notice is due 15 days after the first sale of securities in an offering under Regulation D. Subsequent notices are due every six months after the first sale and 30 days after the last sale.

5) **Exemption for offers and sales not exceeding $1 million.** An exemption under section 3(b) of the 1933 Act is provided for certain offers and sales not exceeding an aggregate offering price of $1 million (as of April 1988) during any 12-month period. [*See* Rule 504] This exemption is not available to investment companies or to 1934 Act reporting companies. Commissions or similar remuneration *may* be paid to those selling the offering in a Rule 504 offering.

Rule 504 does not mandate specific disclosure requirements. However, an issuer proceeding pursuant to the rule is subject to the antifraud and civil liability provisions of the federal securities laws *and must comply with any applicable state requirements*.

If the entire offering is made exclusively in states that require the registration and the delivery of a disclosure document, and if the offering is in compliance with these requirements, then the general limitations of Rule 502(c) (on the manner of the offering) and (d) (restrictions on transfer) do not apply.

6) **Exemption for offers and sales not exceeding $5 million.** An exemption under section 3(b) of the 1933 Act is also provided for offers and sales to an unlimited number of accredited investors, and to no more than 35 nonaccredited investors, where the aggregate offering price in any 12-month period does not exceed $5 million. [*See* Rule 505] Rule 505 is available to any issuer that is not an investment company.

7) **Exemption for offers and sales without regard to dollar amount.** Rule 506, which modifies and replaces Rule 146, relates to transactions that are deemed to be exempt under section 4(2) of the 1933 Act. Like Rule 146, Rule 506 exempts offers and sales to no more than 35 purchasers (accredited investors are not included in counting the 35 investors). Rule 506 modifies the offeree qualification principles of Rule 146 in two ways:

   a) Rule 506 requires that *only purchasers* have to meet the sophistication standard; offerees are not required to. If the purchaser himself cannot meet the sophistication standard (knowledge and experience in financial and business matters), then, similarly to Rule 146, the investor can employ a sophisticated person to represent him. [*See* Rule 506(b)(ii)]

   b) Rule 506 eliminates the economic risk test for qualifying offerees under Rule 146.

8) **The difference between Rule 505 and 506.** Note that the difference between Rule 505 and 506 is that a Rule 505 offering must be limited in amount (to $5 million or less) and that all investors in a Rule 506 offering must be either sophisticated (or be represented by a sophisticated person) or accredited, while in a Rule 505 offering the 35 nonaccredited investors need not be sophisticated or represented by a sophisticated person.

b. **The Regulation A exemption.** Offerings made pursuant to the Regulation A exemption are known as "Regulation A offerings."

1) **Shortened registration.** Regulation A is not a complete exemption from registration. Instead, it provides a simplified form of registration which costs less to prepare and takes less time to complete. [*See* Rules 251-263; Forms 1-A, 6-A]

2) **Issuers covered by Regulation A.** In order to rely on Regulation A, an issuer need only be a resident of, and have or propose to have its principal operations in, the United States or Canada. [*See* Rules 252(a)(1), (2)]

3) **Limitations on availability of Regulation A.**

   a) **Improper conduct by parties connected with the offering.** Regulation A may not be used where persons involved in the offering (e.g., underwriters, officers, and directors of the issuer) have engaged in conduct indicating that potential investors may need the protection of a full registration under section 5. [*See* Rule 252(c) and Rule 261]

b) **Limitation on type of securities offered.** Regulation A is not available where the securities being offered are fractional undivided interests in oil and gas or mineral rights or the securities of investment companies. [*See* Rule 252(b)]

c) **Limitation on dollar amount of securities offered.** The Regulation A exemption is limited to the offering of a small amount of securities by the issuer (and related persons).

(1) **General rule.** As a general rule, securities offered pursuant to Regulation A by the issuer, its affiliates, its predecessors, and (if offered within two years of death) by the estate of a deceased person owning the issuer's securities, together may not amount to more than $1.5 milion worth of securities during any one-year period. [*See* SA Rule 254]

    (a) **Further limitation on affiliates.** In addition, any one affiliate may issue no more than $100,000 worth of securities in a one-year period. Moreover, the affiliate must also have the issuer's permission to make such issuance, based on a finding by the issuer that the affiliate's offering will not interfere with any financing efforts under Regulation A contemplated by the issuer during the subsequent one-year period.

    (b) **Issues by noncontrol persons.** Shareholders other than the issuer and its control persons (affiliates) may also use Regulation A to offer $100,000 of securities each during a one-year period; but the aggregate amount offered by all such persons in any one year may not exceed $300,000. Offerings by these persons are not included in the $1.5 million ceiling. Hence, this provision may be useful to persons who purchased restricted securities in a private offering and wish to sell them prior to the end of their investment period. [*See* SA Rule 254(a)(1)(B); SA Release No. 5225 (1972)]

(2) **Calculation of offering price.** Since a Regulation A offering does not "come to rest" until it is acquired by the ultimate purchasers (i.e., those investors intending to hold the securities for investment), the dollar ceiling of $1.5 million is based on the sales price to these ultimate investors—not the offering price stated in the Regulation A registration statement. Thus, if underwriters or dealers hold part of a Regulation A offering to resell later at a higher price, it is the price at which these securities are finally sold that counts in calculating the dollar amount of the offering.

(3) **Special limitation on "unseasoned" companies.** In addition to the securities normally counted in calculating the $1.5 million limitation, all securities of "unseasoned" or "promotional" companies (below) previously issued for property or services must be included in the $1.5 million limitation. Likewise, all securities held by (or proposed to be issued to) officers, directors, or promoters of such companies, or underwriters, dealers, or security salesmen involved in the Regulation A offering of such a company, must also be counted. [*See* SA Rule 253]

    (a) **Purpose.** This additional limitation is designed to prevent promoters of thinly capitalized companies from thereafter drawing additional cash into the company through a Regulation A offering and then, once there is a public trading market established in the stock, selling their promotional stock at a price much higher than they paid for it.

(b) **Companies affected by the limitation.** The following companies are considered "unseasoned" or "promotional": (i) an issuer incorporated or organized within one year prior to filing of the Regulation A offering, and without net income from its operations; or (ii) an issuer incorporated or organized more than one year prior to the Regulation A filing date, but with no net income from operations in at least one of its two previous fiscal years. [*See* SA Rule 253]

(c) **Securities included in the limitation.** All securities of unseasoned companies issued to covered persons (i.e., officers, directors, etc.), or issued in return for property or services, are included in the $1.5 million limitation, even though issued prior to the normal one-year period. The per share value of such securities is based on the contemplated price under the Regulation A offering—at least where the securities were previously issued for noncash or nominal cash consideration.

(d) **Effect on control persons.** Where the additional limitation on unseasoned companies applies, only the issuer may use Regulation A to sell stock; i.e., control persons of such issuers may not use Regulation A.

(e) **Avoiding the limitation.** However, the additional limitation may be avoided where some means (such as an escrow arrangement) is used to assure that: (i) none of the covered securities will be offered to the public within one year after commencement of the Regulation A offering, and (ii) any reoffering of such securities will be made in accordance with the 1933 Act.

(f) **Example.** A promoter of the issuer purchased all of the issuing company's outstanding shares from a lender, recapitalized the company (putting in property and services and receiving the issuer's stock in return), and then registered a Regulation A offering of additional shares of the issuer's securities for public sale. Since the issuer had had no profits in the past two years, and no provision had been made to escrow the promoter's previously issued shares, Rule 253 was held to apply. Thus, all shares owned by the promoter were added to the securities in the Regulation A offering in calculating the requisite $1.5 million limitation. [*In re* Mutual Employees Trademark, 40 S.E.C. 1092 (1962)]

(4) **Limitation due to integration of issues.** If securities sold under another exemption to the 1933 Act are "integrated" by the S.E.C. with a Regulation A offering, the securities coming under the other exemption are counted in the Regulation A dollar limitation. However, the Commission will not invoke the integration doctrine where the former offering was registered pursuant to section 5 of the Act. [*See* SA Release No. 2410 (1940)]

(5) **Inclusion of securities sold in violation of section 5.** All securities sold by the issuer in violation of section 5 (e.g., purported private offerings that were really public offerings) within the year prior to the Regulation A offering are likewise included in the $1.5 million limitation.

4) Filing and processing procedures.

a) **The offering statement.** Formerly, Regulation A called for the filing of a notification on Form 1-A and exhibits to the form which included, among other matters, an offering circular prepared in accordance with Schedule I of Form 1-A. Now, a single document, designated the "offering statement," replaces the notification and the offering circular. The offering statement consists of three parts and is the basic form to be used by every issuer for every Regulation A offering:

(1) **Part I.** This part of the offering statement is similar to the former notification. Every issuer will be required to disclose the information called for in "Part I—Notification," which will be filed with the Commission and be publicly available but will not be circulated by the issuer to investors.

(2) **Part II.** This part of the offering statement consists of the offering circular to be distributed to investors. The structure of "Part II—Offering Circular" establishes a "pool" of disclosure items. The disclosure required by this pool ranges from basic items such as description of the business and management remuneration to more specialized items such as the description of the investment policies of a real estate investment trust. The general instructions to Part I of the offering statement indicate the items to which a particular issuer would be required to respond.

(3) **Part III.** This part of the offering statement is concerned solely with exhibits, which are treated in the same manner as formerly required by Form 1-A. They would be filed with the Commission, be publicly available, but would not be circulated to investors. Most of the exhibits formerly required by Form 1-A are required by "Part III—Exhibits," with the notable exception of the offering circular, which now becomes Part II of the offering statement.

b) **S.E.C. processing procedures.** A waiting period of at least 10 days must pass after filing of the offering statement before it can be declared effective and the selling of securities can begin.

(1) **Initial response after filing.** When the offering statement is filed by the issuer, the S.E.C. immediately comments on any matters requiring an amendment.

(2) **Commencement date where offering statement amended.** Once a definitive offering statement is filed (i.e., one amended to conform to S.E.C. comments), selling of the securities may generally commence—since the S.E.C. usually waives the 10-day waiting period in such cases.

(3) **Continuing responsibility of issuer.** In any event, even after the issuer has responded to all S.E.C. comments, it remains responsible for any misstatements or omissions in the offering statement.

c) **S.E.C. enforcement procedures—suspension of offering.** At any time after filing of the offering statement, the Commission may order a "temporary suspension" of the Regulation A offering if it has "reasonable grounds" for believing that any possible basis for suspension exists. If the temporary suspension is not lifted, the exemption is lost; and the issuer, its affiliates, and any underwriters involved may not make a Regulation A offering for a period of five years.

(1) Grounds for suspension. The following grounds will cause the S.E.C. to suspend a Regulation A offering:

(a) Failure to meet the requirements for the exemption.

(b) Misleading statements or omission of material facts in the offering statement.

(c) Events after filing which would have made the exemption unavailable had they occurred prior to filing. (Here, a temporary suspension may be ordered by the S.E.C. until the problem is corrected; *see supra*.)

(d) Actions initiated against the issuer or its predecessors or affiliates for offenses involving securities transactions (*see supra*).

(e) Actions against the directors, officers, principal security holders, present promoters, or underwriters of the issuer for securities transaction offenses (*see supra*).

(2) Suspension procedures. If the issuer takes no action (i.e., fails to request a hearing) within 30 days after issuance of a temporary suspension order, the order becomes permanent. Where a hearing is requested, the S.E.C. may either allow the necessary corrections to be made or it may make the suspension permanent. Normally, temporary suspensions will be lifted where it is shown that noncompliance was in good faith and is correctable.

5) Offers and sales pursuant to Regulation A exemption.

a) No offers prior to commencement date. In a registered offering, section 5 permits certain solicitations of offers to be made during the period after filing of the registration statement and before the effective selling date (i.e., the "waiting period," *supra*). However, the rules are more stringent for Regulation A offerings.

(1) Offerings through an underwriter. The S.E.C. has amended Regulation A to permit the use of a preliminary offering circular for offerings sold by or through underwriters who are registered broker-dealers.

(2) Issuer underwriting own issue. If the issuer is underwriting its own issue, however, it may not use a preliminary offering circular to solicit interest in an offering. It must wait until after the offering statement is declared effective by the S.E.C.

(3) Rationale. The new rule permits underwriters of Regulation A offerings to disseminate information to potential investors and get a reading on marketability of an upcoming offering prior to the effective date.

b) Offering circular required after commencement date.

(1) As to offers. After the commencement date of a Regulation A offering, no written offer of any kind may be made unless the offeree is concurrently or previously given a copy of the offering circular.

    (a) Exception—tombstone ads. The only exception to this rule permits a "tombstone ad" to be used to advertise the issue without delivering a circular to all readers.

    (b) Additional sales material. An offeree may be given additional sales material contemporaneously with or after receiving the offering circular, provided such material was previously filed with the S.E.C. and meets all antifraud provisions of the 1933 Act.

(2) As to sale. In addition to offers, no actual sale may be concluded unless an offering circular is furnished to the purchaser in accordance with the following rules:

    (a) "Forty-eight hour" rule. As a general rule, a purchaser must be furnished an offering circular at least 48 hours before any mailing of confirmation of sale.

    (b) Reporting companies. However, where the issuer is subject to the reporting requirements of the 1934 Act, the offering circular may be furnished with the confirmation of sale, at the seller's option. [*See* SA Rule 256(a)(2); SA Release No. 33-5397 (1973)]

(3) "Ninety-day" rule. The Regulation A exemption recognizes that the offering may continue after all securities in the offering have been sold for the first time, until the issue really comes to rest in the hands of more or less permanent investors. Therefore, the S.E.C. rules arbitrarily designate the length of the secondary trading period as 90 days after commencement of the offering. [*See* SA Rule 256(f)]

    (a) Effect of "ninety-day" rule. Unless the issuer is subject to the reporting requirements of the 1934 Act, or an offering circular has previously been mailed or delivered to the purchaser of securities in a secondary trade, any dealer trading in this period must furnish an offering circular to the purchaser either prior to or at the time a confirmation of sale is received.

    (b) Commencement of ninety-day period. This dealer-delivery requirement continues for 90 days from the date on which the securities were first bona fide offered to the public under the Regulation A offering. [*See* SA Rule 256(g); SA Release No. 33-5397 (1973)]

    (c) To whom rule applies. These delivery requirements also apply to underwriters who have sold their allotments and are acting as dealers in the secondary trading markets. However, if a dealer fails to comply with Rule 256(g), this does not destroy the Regulation A exemption for other persons involved in the underwriting and distribution.

(4) **Period of circular's use.** Unless used in connection with certain specific types of offerings (such as employee stock purchase plans), the original circular may be used for a period of nine months. After this time, a revised circular must be filed with the S.E.C. [*See* SA Rule 256(e)]

(5) **Post-effective amendments.** The offering circular and sales material in a Regulation A offering must continue to correctly represent all material facts throughout the period they are used. Hence, material changes in the issuer during the course of the offering may require suspension of the offering and an amendment to the circular. [*See* SA Rule 256(e)]

In the Matter of Shearson, Hammill & Co.

6) **Effect of failure to follow proper procedure--In the Matter of Shearson, Hammill & Co.,** 42 S.E.C. 811 (1965).

a) **Facts.** USAMCO sold $300,000 of common stock to the public in a Regulation A offering. It was not disclosed that the underwriter of the issue was in fact the broker-dealer (D) and its branch office manager (who was a member of the board of directors of the issuing company). Also, a trading market to support the issue price was begun before the stock was actually fully distributed to the public.

(1) Personnel of D purchased a significant number of the issuer's shares and then gave out false information about the prospects of the company to firm customers. Also, the daily quotation price was continually raised arbitrarily. Furthermore, no sale orders were accepted from customers unless orders to buy an equal amount of shares were available at the time.

(2) After completion of the offering, D's personnel sold their shares in preference to sell orders of their customers. When they had all been taken out of the market, the market for the company's stock was allowed to collapse. And in fact, the company had never been profitable.

(3) The S.E.C. found numerous violations of the securities acts, including section 5 of the 1933 Act and Rule 15[c]1-2 of the 1934 Act.

(4) The action by the S.E.C. (for suspension of brokers associated with the broker-dealer) was brought under sections 15(b), 15A and 19(a)(3) of the 1934 Act against D and several of its representatives and officers.

b) **Issue.** Should the management of a broker-dealer be suspended pursuant to provisions of the 1934 Act for failure to adequately supervise its employees in the underwriting and subsequent trading of a company's securities?

c) **Held.** Yes. Members of the Executive Committee of D in New York (who were supposed to supervise the Los Angeles office of the firm) are suspended for a substantial period of time. This sanction is imposed rather than a general broker-dealer suspension or revocation of the firm's Los Angeles office.

    (1)   The offending sales personnel had already been terminated by the firm.

    (2)   The firm was involved in lawsuits with customers who had been hurt, or had settled the claims of these persons.

    (3)   The firm had also instituted closer supervision practices.

    (4)   Nevertheless, the public interest still demands the sanction as a penalty for the lax supervision methods employed by the firm.

c.   **Registrations on Form S-18.** The S.E.C. has adopted Form S-18 as an alternative to Regulation A for corporate issuers who are not required to file reports under the 1934 Act with the S.E.C. This form of registration has particular significance for small businesses. The issuers which qualify may offer up to $5 million of their securities with lesser disclosure requirements than under an S-1 registration and lesser reporting requirements than are ordinarily imposed on other issuers under the 1934 Act. This procedure allows an issuer, over a period of time, to raise a limited amount of capital and gradually come into compliance with the full disclosure and reporting requirements. Form S-18 may also be used for secondary sales by selling shareholders (such as control persons) for amounts up to $1.5 million.

4.   The Transaction Exemption for Intrastate Offerings.

a.   **Introduction.** Securities which are offered and sold only to persons residing within a single state, where the issuer of the securities is also a resident of and doing business in that same state, are exempt from registration under section 5 of the Act. This is known as the "intrastate offering" exemption. The purpose of the exemption is to facilitate the raising of local capital for local businesses. [*See* SA §3(a)(11)]

    1)   **Transaction exemption.** The intrastate offering exemption is a transaction exemption. Thus, securities sold under this exemption may have to be registered later when offered in a secondary distribution (as by a control person).

    2)   **Antifraud provisions of the Act apply.** Even though an issuer using this exemption does *not* have to register the securities being offered, still the general antifraud provision of the 1933 Act apply to the offering (*see* the discussion of sections 12(2) and 17 of the Act, *infra*).

    3)   **Rule 147.** Over the years, a great deal of uncertainty arose in the meaning of some of the terms of the exemption, leading to uncertainty in its application. For this reason, the S.E.C. adopted Rule 147, which sets forth a specific, objective set of criteria, which, if followed by an issuer, will ensure that the intrastate offering exemption

will apply. However, if the issuer cannot qualify an issue under Rule 147, the issuer may still qualify it under the general terms of section 3(a)(11).

b. The general requirements of the intrastate offering exemption—section 3(a)(11).

1) The issue concept. The entire issue must be offered and sold to residents of one state. [*See* SA Release No. 4434 (1961)] Thus, a single *offer* to a nonresident will destroy the exemption.

a) Integration with other offerings. The issuer must be very careful not to lose the exemption through the integration of an attempted intrastate offering (pursuant to the exemption) with another offering of the same type of securities.

b) Restricting transfers—the good faith test. It is the responsibility of the issuer, the underwriter, and any participating dealers to make sure that the offering is made only to residents and that no resales (which would destroy the exemption) are made to nonresidents.

(1) Those participating in the offering must act in good faith, according to a standard of due care, to see that only appropriate offers and sales are made.

(2) The standard of due care requires that: (i) a reasonable investigation be made to determine the residence of each offeree and purchaser (purchasers might also be required to give letters affirming their residence in the state); and (ii) reasonable precautions must be taken to prevent resales to nonresidents, such as placing a restrictive transfer legend on the stock certificates and instituting transfer restrictions with the registrar and transfer agent.

c) Resales—the coming to rest test. Resales to nonresidents are possible without destroying the exemption, but only *after* the original distribution to residents is complete (i.e., only after the offering has come to rest in the hands of residents).

(1) The intent of the purchasers. The question whether the issue has come to rest depends on the intent of the original purchasers. If they purchased the securities with the intention of keeping them for investment, then the issue is complete and resales to nonresidents may begin. However, if the purchasers took with the intent to make a further distribution or resale, then the issue has not "come to rest" and resales to nonresidents will destroy the exemption.

(2) Objective standard. Whether the issue has come to rest is a fact question, to be determined according to objective factors.

(a) For example, it has been held that resales to nonresidents prior to 90 days after the original purchase by residents will defeat the exemption.

(b) A holding period of one year or more may be adequate to prove the necessary investment intent.

2) Residence within the state. The exemption also requires that the entire issue be confined to a single state where the issuer, the offerees, and the purchasers are residents.

a) Offerees and purchasers. With respect to offerees and purchasers, the mere presence in the state is *not* sufficient to establish residence. The test for residence is something like "domicile" (i.e., the purchaser must reside in the state with the intent to remain in the state).

b) Underwriters and dealers. Underwriters and dealers participating in the offering need not be from the same state as the issuer and the offerees.

c) Control persons. Control persons may use the exemption, even though such control persons are not residents in the state where the offering is made.

d) The issuer. There are two requirements that the issuer must meet in order to establish "residence":

(1) Residence in the state. The issuer must be a resident in the state where the offering is made. For a corporation, the state of residence is the state of incorporation.

(2) Doing business test. Since the purpose of the rule is to finance local business, the tests used to establish "doing business" in the state are (i) whether the issuer is doing a majority of its business in the state, and (ii) whether the proceeds of the offering are used in the state.

(3) Application--S.E.C. v. McDonald Investment Co., 343 F. Supp. 343 (D. Minn. 1972).

S.E.C. v. McDonald Investment Co.

(a) Facts. A Minnesota corporation (D) is selling securities to Minnesota residents (installment promissory notes), and has its only office located in Minnesota. However, D is lending the money to non-Minnesota real estate developers. S.E.C. seeks an injunction against the sale without registration; D claims the 3(a)(11) exemption.

(b) Issue. Is D "doing business" in the state?

(c) Held. No. Judgment for S.E.C.

1] The issuer must conduct a predominant amount of its business within the state.

2] This means that the issuer must conduct within the state income producing activities of the business in which the issuer is selling the securities. Here the income producing operations are located outside the state (i.e., the loans to the developers).

3) **Use of the mails and the facilities of interstate commerce.** The exemption is not dependent on the nonuse of the mails or other instruments or means of interstate commerce. Thus, securities issued in connection with the use of the exemption may be offered by use of general newspaper advertising, as long as the advertisement indicates that offers are being made only to residents of the state.

c. **The requirements of Rule 147—an objective test for the intrastate offering exemption.** The S.E.C. has little control over intrastate offerings, since the initiation and the progress of such an offering is never reported to the commission. Hence, many violations of the exemption occurred, and much uncertainty arose over the meaning of some of the terms and conditions involved in the section 3(a)(11) exemption. This resulted in the adoption by the S.E.C. of Rule 147, which is a specific, objective set of criteria for qualifying an issue for the 3(a)(11) exemption.

1) **Integration of offerings.**

a) **The general rule.** All of the transactions involving securities that are part of an integrated offering must meet the requirements of Rule 147, or none of the parts of the offering will qualify under the Rule. For example, where there are two offerings that are separately made but the S.E.C. integrates them into one offering, then both offerings must meet the requirements of Rule 147 or no part of the offering will qualify.

b) **Exemption—the safe harbor rule.** Certain exceptions to the general rule are made. [*See* SA Rule 147(b)(2)] Transactions occurring pursuant to either section 3 or section 4(2), either six months before or six months after a section 3(a)(11) transaction, will not be integrated with the intrastate offering.

2) **Residence.** The issuer, offerees, and the purchasers must be residents of the same state. Rule 147 gives specific definitions to the term "residence."

a) **Issuer.**

(1) **Residence in state.** Residence is defined in Rule 147 as follows:

(a) **Corporation.** The state of incorporation.

(b) **Partnership.** The state where the principal place of business exists.

(c) **Individual.** The state of principal residence.

(2) **Doing business.** An issuer is deemed to be "doing business" in a state if: (i) 80% of consolidated gross revenues are derived there; (ii) 80% of consolidated assets are held there; (iii) 80% of the proceeds from covered transactions are to be used in the issuer's operations there; and (iv) the issuer's principal office is located there. [*See* SA Rule 147(c)(2)]

b) **Offerees and purchasers.** Definitions are also given for determination of the state of residence of the offerees and purchasers.

    (1) **Corporations and business organizations.** Business organizations are deemed residents of the state in which their principal business office is located. [*See* SA Rule 147(d)(1)]

    (2) **Individuals.** Individuals are deemed residents of the state where their principal residence is located. [*See* SA Rule 147(d)(2)]

3) **Resale of intrastate securities.** Rule 147 provides an objective standard for the "coming to rest" test. No sales can be made to persons not resident in the state of issue during the time the securities are being offered and sold by the issuer *and for an additional period* of nine months following the last sale by the issuer of the offering. [*See* SA Rule 147(e)]

4) **Transfer restrictions.**

    a) **Legend and stop transfer instructions.** To insure that securities issued under the Rule 147 exemption do not enter securities markets prior to the time allowed under Rule 147(e) (i.e., nine months), the S.E.C. requires the issuer to have a restrictive legend (conforming to Rule 147(e)) on each certificate and to lodge stop transfer instructions with the transfer agent for the issued securities. [*See* SA Rules 147(f)(1)(i) and (ii)]

    b) **Transfer letters.** Also, to insure that only resident offerees and purchasers are involved in covered transactions, Rule 147 requires the issuer to obtain a written representation from each purchaser regarding his place of residence. [*See* SA Rule 147(e)(1)(iii)]

5. **The Exemptions for Reorganization and Recapitalizations.** This section deals with a number of exemptions that relate to the reorganization or recapitalization of business enterprises.

a. **"Offers" or "sales" for value.**

    1) **Introduction.** The registration requirements of section 5 of the Act apply only where there is "security" which is "offered or sold" "for value." The "sale" and "for value" requirements are stated in section 2(3) of the Act.

        a) **Definition of a "sale."** The term "sale" includes "every contract of sale or disposition of a security or interest in a security, for value." [*See* SA §2(3)]

        b) **Definition of an "offer."** Section 2(3) also provides that an "offer" includes "every attempt to dispose of a security, for value."

2) **For value.** The words "for value" in section 2(3) are very important. For example, if securities are the subject of a gift, then there is no offer or sale "for value," and the registration requirement of section 5 is not applicable to the securities transaction.

3) **Transactions where there is no offer or sale for value.**

    a) **Rights offering to existing shareholders.** Where XYZ transfers rights to its shareholders to purchase additional stock (e.g., one "right" to purchase one new share of common stock is issued for each 10 shares of common stock already owned; thus, A, owning 100 shares, gets 10 "rights." If A exercises the rights, he buys 10 new shares of common stock at the offered price). If the rights are issued without consideration (e.g., XYZ issues the 10 rights to A for no consideration), the rights are "securities," but since there is no sale for value, there need be no registration of the rights. Of course, the underlying security which may be purchased for value on the exercise of the rights (i.e., the common stock) is being offered for value and, if the warrant or right is immediately exercisable, the underlying security must be registered under the Act.

    b) **Stock dividends and stock splits.** Suppose that XYZ issues a stock dividend of one new share of common stock for each 10 shares of common stock already outstanding. Here again, there is no transfer for value and the shares given in dividend (or in a stock split) need not be registered.

        (1) Even where the corporation gives the shareholder the choice of taking the stock dividend or taking the cash equivalent, there is no "sale" for "value" if the shareholder takes the stock.

        (2) But if the corporation declares a cash dividend and then the shareholder takes stock instead of the cash, there is a "sale" for "value." The theory is that the shareholder in this case got cash and then purchased the securities. [*See* SA Release No. 929 (1936)]

b. **Corporate reorganizations and recapitalizations through exchanges between issuer and issuer's security holders.** Any security voluntarily exchanged by the issuer with its existing security holders exclusively, where no commission or other remuneration is paid or given directly or indirectly for soliciting such an exchange, is exempt from registration under section 5 of the Act. [*See* SA §3(a)(9)]

1) **Example.** Thus, where XYZ Corporation exchanges a new debt issue of securities with a longer maturity date (e.g., 10 years) but a lower interest rate, for an outstanding issue of a shorter duration (e.g., five years) but higher interest rate, the exchange may qualify for exemption.

2) **Restrictions on the application of this exemption.**

    a) **Must be offered to the issuer's security holders exclusively.** The exchange may occur only between the issuer and its already existing security holders. For example, the exemption would be destroyed if the issuer sold part of an issue to its security holders and the remainder to the public. [*See* SA Release No. 2029 (1939)]

b) **Commission.** No commission or remuneration may be given for soliciting the exchange with the shareholders.

c) **Consideration paid by the security holders.**

(1) In situations where the security being surrendered by the issuer's security holders is more valuable than the security they are receiving from the issuer, *the issuer may also distribute cash* to the security holders to make up this difference.

(2) But the exemption will be destroyed if the issuer asks for the old security plus cash from the security holders. This provision is to avoid turning what is called a recapitalization exemption into an attempt to raise new capital (cash) for the issuer without a full registration of the new securities. [*See* SA Rule 150]

d) **Rationale of the restrictions.** The rationale for each of the restrictions is that the exemption is designed to apply to situations where the issuer is not really raising new capital (where the purchasers need the protection of a registration and prospectus) but is simply exchanging securities as part of a corporate recapitalization.

3) **The effect of Rule 145.** The S.E.C. has also adopted Rule 145 (below), which also deals with certain types of corporate reorganizations and recapitalization exchanges. In some situations both section 3(a)(9) and Rule 145 may apply to a given transaction. Thus, the issuer may qualify the transaction under either.

c. **Selling or merging businesses—Rule 145.** Rule 145, which provides for a limited type of registration, is applicable to certain situations where companies are bought by or merged into other companies.

1) **Example.** Suppose that Corporation A offers its common stock to purchase the assets of Corporation B. The S.E.C. formerly held that the term "sale" embodied the idea of a volitional act on the part of the buyer of a security, so that in certain types of corporate reorganization transactions where the required individual volition was absent (here only a majority of the shareholders of Corporation B had to approve for B to sell the assets of Corporation B for the common stock of A), no registration was required. [*See* former SA Rule 133]

a) **Sale of assets.** In the sale of assets transaction (discussed above), since no single shareholder could really determine (by himself) whether to make the investment in the offered securities (i.e., the securities of Corporation A), there was held to be no volitional act and thus no "sale." Thus, no registration was required.

b) **Stock-for-stock transaction.** If, however, Corporation A had offered its common stock directly to the shareholders of B for their common stock (a stock-for-stock exchange), then each shareholder of B would have had to make up his own mind whether to sell. Hence, here the S.E.C. held that there was a voluntary sale, and registration of A's securities was required (unless an exemption was available).

    c)   **Abuses.** Rule 133 led to a number of abuses of the rationale of the 1933 Act. For example, see the discussion concerning spin-off transactions (discussed *infra*).

2)   **Replacement by Rule 145.** Thus, the S.E.C. has repealed Rule 133 and replaced it with new Rule 145, which provides that securities issued in certain corporate reorganization transactions must be registered and that certain persons (such as control persons) of the acquired company (B) must have transfer limitations placed on the stock they receive in the transaction (from A).

3)   **Transactions covered by Rule 145.**

    a)   **In general.** Rule 145 establishes registration procedures for certain kinds of corporate reorganization transactions where the security holders of the selling corporation are required by state law to give their approval before consummation of the transaction. The rationale is that these "corporate acts" really do involve individual shareholder volition and thus a "sale" is involved within the contemplation of section 2(3) of the Act.

    b)   **Specific transactions covered.**

        (1)   **Reclassifications.** Any reclassification of securities (other than certain simple transactions such as a stock split; e.g., XYZ Corporation splits each of its $1 par value common shares into ten .10 par value shares) which involves the substitution or exchange of one security for another is covered. [*See* SA Rule 145(a)(1)]

        (2)   **Mergers or consolidations.** Also covered is a statutory merger or consolidation or similar plan of acquisition of one corporation or entity (for example, A) by another (B) in which securities of such corporation or person (A) held by its security holders (A's security holders) will become or be exchanged for securities of the other corporation or person (B), *except* where the sole purpose of the transaction is to change an issuer's domicile (e.g., where Corporation A is incorporated in California and forms a new Corporation B in Delaware in order to merge into B and become a Delaware corporation). [*See* SA Rule 145(a)(2)]

        (3)   **Transfer of assets.** A transfer of assets by one person or corporation (A) to another (B) in exchange for the issuance of securities by the latter corporation or person (B) is covered by Rule 145, but only if:

            (i)   The plan or agreement of transfer provides for the dissolution of the corporation or person whose security holders are voting (i.e., A's security holders); or

            (ii)   The plan or agreement of transfer provides for a pro rata distribution of the exchanged securities (B's) to the security holders (of A) that are voting; or

(iii) The board of directors of the corporation (A) adopts a resolution with respect to the provisions in (i) or (ii) above within one year after the vote or consent to the transaction has taken place; or

(iv) Notwithstanding (i), (ii), or (iii) above, a subsequent dissolution or distribution is part of a preexisting plan for distribution of the securities.

Note that in each of these four situations, registration is required since the securities of the purchasing entity are being distributed to the public within a short time of the purchase of assets transaction.

c) **Relationship of Rule 145 to other exemptions for corporate reorganizations and recapitalizations.** Note that some reorganizations and/or reclassification transactions covered by the terms of Rule 145 may still be exempt from registration by some other exemptions in the Act. For example, *see* the discussion of section 3(a)(9) (discussed *supra*) and section 3(a)(10) (discussed *infra*).

d) **Application.** Suppose that Company X wants to acquire 80% of the outstanding common stock of Company Y by offering its common stock to Company Y shareholders in a stock-for-stock exchange. Is Rule 145 applicable? Answer: NO. Rule 145 does *not* apply to stock-for-stock exchanges. [*See* SEA Release No. 10661 (1974)] However, this transaction would be covered by section 5 of the 1933 Act, and if no exemption were available, then the stock of X would have to be registered.

4) **Registration under Rule 145.** If no exemptions are available for the above described business transactions, Rule 145 provides for *a limited form of registration* as a substitute for full registration pursuant to section 5 of the Act.

a) **The prospectus requirement of Rule 145.**

(1) **Form and content of the prospectus.**

(a) **The general form.** Form S-4 is the registration form to be used in Rule 145 transactions. The information required by S-4 is not nearly as extensive as that required by Form S-1.

(b) **Alternative form.** Registration amounts to a great financial and time burden to companies engaged in these types of business transactions, so the S.E.C. has provided that the disclosure requirements under Rule 145 can be satisfied if the information required under the *proxy regulations* of the Securities Exchange Act of 1934 is disclosed to those receiving the issuer's securities (*see* Rules 14a-2, 14a-6, 14c-5 of the 1934 Act and the discussion of the 1934 Act, *infra*). Thus, the issuers who have to file proxy statements anyway (which will be the case in most situations of corporate acquisitions made by companies whose securities are publicly traded) are not caused any additional work by the requirements of Rule 145.

(2) **Delivery of the prospectus.**

(a) **Persons receiving a prospectus.** All security holders of record of the company to be acquired in the Rule 145 transactions who are entitled to vote on the proposed transaction must be given a prospectus. [*See* SA Rule 153A]

(b) **Time of delivery.** Delivery of the prospectus must be made prior to the time when the vote on the transaction is taken. [*See* SA Rule 153A]

(3) **Communications not subject to the prospectus requirements.** Certain written communications made to the shareholders of the selling company are deemed *not* to be a prospectus (under section 2(10) of the Act) or an "offer to sell" (under section 5 of the Act) and thus they may be distributed to the security holders without complying with the strict requirements of the Act. Allowing such communications facilitates the completion of Rule 145 transactions without the delay which normally surrounds the full registration process.

(a) **A preliminary proxy statement.** For example, a communication which meets the information standards of a "preliminary proxy statement" (*see* Rule 14a-12 of the 1934 Act and the discussion of proxy regulation, *infra*) may be sent to the shareholders (after previous filing with the S.E.C.). [*See* SA Rule 145(b)(2)]

(b) **"Bare bones" statement.** In addition, a statement that contains certain specific and limited information may be given to the security holders (containing items like the name of the issuer; the name of the other parties to the transaction; a brief description of the businesses of the parties; the date, time, and place of the meeting where a vote will be taken; a description of the transaction involved, etc.). This is called a "bare bones" statement. [*See* SA Rule 145(b)(1)]

b) **Persons and parties deemed to be underwriters in Rule 145 transactions.** Certain parties to the transactions covered by Rule 145 are deemed by the terms of Rule 145 to be "underwriters," and thus there are restrictions on their subsequent transfer of the securities they receive in a registered Rule 145 transaction. The rationale for this restriction is to prevent a control person (A) of Company X (who could not distribute his stock to the public without a registration) from having X merge into Company Y (A receiving Company Y stock) in order for A to sell his Y stock to the public without registration.

(1) **Underwriters defined.** Any party (except the issuer), or person who is an affiliate of a party (i.e., a control person) to a Rule 145 transaction, is deemed to be an underwriter if that party sells or offers to sell the securities acquired in connection with the Rule 145 transaction. [*See* SA Rule 145(c)]

(2) **The definition of a party.** A "party" means the corporations or persons (other than the issuer of the securities) whose assets or capital structure are affected by the transaction (for example, if Corporation A sells its assets to Corporation B for B's common stock, A would be a party to the transaction since its capital structure or assets would be affected).

(3) **Control persons of the acquired company.** Thus, the real effect of these provisions is to limit the subsequent transfer of securities received by control persons of acquired companies in Rule 145 transactions. For example, if Corporation A is purchased by Corporation B and X is a control person of A, then X is deemed to be an underwriter.

(4) **Limited resales permitted.** However, those covered as "underwriters" may make limited sales of their securities without re-registration. [*See* SA Rule 145(d)]

(a) **Sales pursuant to the terms of Rule 144.** Such resales by control persons may be made if the person or party follows subsections (c) (distribution of current public information), (e) (limitation on the amount of securities sold), (f) (manner of sale), and (g) (sold in a broker's transaction) of Rule 144; or, such person or party is not affiliated with the issuer and has held the securities for at least two years, and the issuer is subject to the periodic reporting requirements of sections 13 or 15(D) of the 1934 Act, has been subject to such sections for at least the preceding 12 months and has filed all required reports (*see* the discussion of Rule 144, *infra*). Note that the two-year holding period of Rule 144 does not apply to underwriter sales under Rule 145.

(b) **Registration alternative.** Alternatively, underwriters in Rule 145 transactions may register their securities for resale pursuant to Form S-4.

d. **Court or government agency approved reorganizations.**

1) **Introduction.** The Act also provides an exemption from registration for business reorganization or reclassification transactions where a new security is issued in exchange for already outstanding securities, claims, or property interests (or partly in exchange for cash), where the terms and conditions of the exchange are approved (after a hearing upon the fairness of such terms and conditions at which all persons to whom it is proposed to issue securities in such exchange have the right to appear), by: (i) any court, or any official or agency of the United States; or (ii) any state or territorial banking or insurance commission or other governmental authority expressly authorized by law to grant such approval. [*See* SA §3(a)(10)]

2) **Example.** XYZ Insurance Company wishes to form a financial services holding company. It organizes a new corporation (ABC), and after a hearing conducted by the state insurance department on the terms and conditions of the exchange, exchanges stock in the holding company for the stock of the insurance company. The transaction is exempt from registration.

3) **Specific authorization by law.** In order for this exemption to apply to state authorized transactions, the state government authority must have specific authorization in state law to approve such transactions. In the hypothetical above, the insurance commission can approve such transaction

(and the federal securities law exemption apply) only where there is a state statute which permits it to do so. Note that this requirement does not apply to transactions approved by federal authorities.

e. **The bankruptcy exemptions.** A new United States bankruptcy law was passed in 1978. The main provision is chapter 11, which provides for the reorganization of bankrupt companies.

1) **Appointment of examiners.** The basis for an acceptable reorganization plan (i.e., where existing debtors may be asked to exchange their debts for new debt or equity securities, etc.) is left to be determined by the bankruptcy court on a case-by-case basis. However, where the debts exceed assets by $5 million or more, the court is required to appoint an examiner to investigate the debtor for fraud by insiders, etc. This provision is meant to protect public shareholders of large public companies. In addition, the S.E.C. or any other party having an interest in the outcome of the reorganization plan may attend and be heard at all public hearings involving the plan.

2) **Disclosure requirements.** Restructuring of the debtor's capital and debt structure usually involves an exchange of new debt and/or equity securities for the outstanding securities. The Bankruptcy Act provides for disclosure obligations in issuing these securities, which is done under the supervision of the bankruptcy court. Thus, when the Bankruptcy Act applies, the issuer is exempt from the other federal and state securities laws. [*See* 11 U.S.C. §1145]

   a) The Bankruptcy Act provides that the issuer must provide information which is adequate in light of the nature and history of the debtor and the conditions of its accounting records so that the typical holder of claims or interests of the relevant class can make an informed judgment about the proposed exchange.

   b) This information must be given to creditors at or prior to the solicitation of acceptance of the reorganization plan.

   c) The S.E.C. and/or state securities commissioners may appear and contest whether the disclosure statement proposed by the bankruptcy court is adequate.

3) **Debt securities.** The Bankruptcy Act does not allow the sale by the debtor of equity securities to raise new capital (equity securities may only be issued in exchange for old debts). It does, however, permit the trustee to issue debt securities to raise additional funds to operate the business. [*See* 11 U.S.C. §364] This is a transaction exemption. In addition, section 3(a)(7) of the 1933 Act appears to provide a "security" exemption for debt securities issued under court approval in order to finance the receivership, bankruptcy or reorganization proceedings.

4) **Resales, sales by control persons and other provisions.** The Bankruptcy Act also sets forth standards under which a creditor or control person acquiring securities under the reorganization plan can resell the securities. [*See* 11 U.S.C. §1145(b)] A limited exemption for brokers selling such securities is also provided. [*See* 11 U.S.C. §1145(a)]

f. **Integration of exemptions.** The 1933 Act provides a series of distinct exemptions from the registration requirements of section 5. We have examined sections 4(2) and 4(6), Rules 505 and 506 (all private offering exemptions); Regulation A and Rule 504 (limited offering exemptions); section 3(a)(11) and Rule 147 (the intrastate offering exemption), and sections 3(a)(9) and 3(a)(10) (exchange exemptions). All of these provisions provide for the possibility of an integration of offerings that are made to appear as separate offerings but which, in fact, are part of one plan of financing. However, each of these integration provisions must be examined separately, as their terms differ somewhat. Also, these terms must be carefully studied to determine which offerings can be integrated with securities offerings under other exemption sections of the 1933 Act (e.g., Rule 147(b)(2) provides that a Rule 147 offering may be integrated during certain time periods with other Rule 147 offerings, or offerings pursuant to section 3 or 4(2) of the Act, or offerings done pursuant to a registration statement).

g. **The spin-off transaction.** There have been many attempts to rely on section 2(3) (the theory of no sale for value) in order to achieve a public distribution of securities without going through a registration. One of these attempts is known as the "spin-off transaction."

 1) **The reaction of the S.E.C.** The S.E.C. first warned that a public company participating in such spin-off distributions could be held to be an "underwriter" under the Act. [*See* SA Release Nos. 4982 and 8638 (1969)] Then the S.E.C. adopted a rule which requires that any broker-dealer quoting a security in a dealer quotation system has to have available certain comprehensive information concerning the issuer in order to trade in the issuer's securities (only a few companies are exempted). This rule works to thwart the trading of securities normally associated with spin-off transactions since little information concerning such companies is normally available. [SEA Rule 15[c]2-11]

 2) **Registration required for issuance of spin-off shares--S.E.C. v. Datronics Engineers, Inc.,** 490 F.2d 250 (4th Cir. 1973), *cert. denied,* 416 U.S. 937 (1974).

S.E.C. v. Datronics Engineers, Inc.

   a) **Facts.** Datronics (D) was a public company with 1,000 shareholders and an active trading market for its stock. Without any apparent business purpose of its own, D and its officers formed new companies or used D's existing subsidiaries to merge private companies. The promoters behind the private companies would retain a majority interest in the shares of their companies. D would either receive stock in the merger from the private companies or buy it at a nominal price. D's officers and directors also received part of the securities in the private companies for services rendered (such as for legal services in forming the subsidiaries, etc.). As part of the agreement, D would then distribute a portion of the stock it received from the merger to its 1,000 shareholders in a dividend distribution. D would keep part of the stock it received. Immediately after the dividend distribution, D's shareholders would begin trading the stock of the new company, the price would go up, and D and the promoters of the new company would begin selling their shares to the public at a profit. The S.E.C. sought an injunction on the basis that a public distribution of the private companies' stock, without registration, had taken place. The trial court granted D's summary judgment, and the S.E.C. appealed.

    b)   **Issue.** Has there been a public distribution of securities for value without registration or exemption from registration in violation of section 5 of the 1933 Act?

    c)   **Held.** Yes, judgment for the S.E.C.; summary judgment for D reversed and case remanded for trial.

        (1)   D is an "issuer," or a "co-issuer" with the new company.

        (2)   This is a different case than an ordinary dividend, since here there was a contractual obligation with the private companies for D to make the dividend distributions (i.e., on the front-end, as part of a distribution of unregistered shares).

        (3)   There is a "sale" of a security, since "sale" includes a "disposition" of a security.

        (4)   The "for value" requirement is fulfilled since D always kept part of the stock that was distributed as a dividend and when the subsequent trading began it profited from the scheme.

        (5)   D is also an "underwriter," since it took (purchased) the stock in the new company with the intent of making a distribution of it to the public.

        (6)   There is also a violation of Rule 10b-5 of the 1934 Act since, in connection with the distribution (sale of the securities), D made misstatements to its shareholders as to the purpose of the transactions (i.e., that it was impractical for it to run the companies so it was "spinning them off." As a matter of fact, it could not run the companies, owning only a minority interest. This was a subterfuge to cover D's stock manipulations).

    d)   **Concurrence.** The decision does not apply to situations involving companies having legitimate business purposes even though the transaction may also have the effects resulting in the public distribution of securities that would otherwise have to be registered under the Act.

F.   **THE OBLIGATION TO REGISTER ON RESALES OF SECURITIES BY PERSONS OTHER THAN THE ISSUER**

    1.   **Introduction.** The registration requirement of the Act applies to all "persons" selling securities through the use of the facilities of interstate commerce. [*See* SA §5] However, the Act also exempts from the registration requirement securities transactions by persons other than "issuers," "underwriters," or "dealers." [*See* SA §4(1)] Thus, the registration and prospectus requirements are really only applicable to "issuers," "underwriters," and "dealers."

2. **The Definition of an Issuer.** An "issuer" is defined to include every person who issues or proposes to issue any security. [*See* SA §2(4)] Where an issuer makes a public distribution of securities, the registration requirements of section 5 of the Act apply.

3. **Underwriters.** "Underwriters" also must comply with the registration requirements of section 5 of the Act. The Act defines three classes of persons to be "underwriters." [*See* SA §2(11)]

   a. **Persons who purchase securities from the issuer with a view to a public distribution.** The first definition of an "underwriter" is one who purchases from an issuer with a view to "distribution." [*See* SA §2(11)] "Distribution" means essentially a "public offering" (i.e., an offering to a substantial number of people who do not purchase the securities to hold them for a long time as an investment).

   b. **Persons who offer or sell for an issuer in connection with a distribution.** The second definition of an "underwriter" concerns those persons who actually offer or sell securities for an issuer in connection with the issuer's public distribution.

      1) **Persons who purchase from or sell for control persons.** Note that for the purpose of determining who are "underwriters," the term "issuer" includes any person directly or indirectly controlling or controlled by the issuer, or any person under direct or indirect common control with the issuer. [*See* SA §2(11)]

         (i) This section makes an "underwriter" out of a person who purchases securities from a "controlling person" for the purpose of a public distribution, or who offers or sells for such a controlling person in connection with a public distribution.

         (ii) The Act defines a "control person" as one having the "power to direct or cause the direction of the management and policies of a company." [*See* SA Rule 405] This may occur through stock ownership, a position in management, influence with the management, or any combination of these factors.

         a) **Classifying broker as underwriter--In the Matter of Ira Haupt & Co.,** 23 S.E.C. 589 (1946).

In the Matter of Ira Haupt & Co.

            (1) **Facts.** Schulte owned 22% of Park & Tilford stock; a trust run by his sons owned 67%; a corporation he controlled owned 2%; the public owned 9%. The stock was selling at about $57 per share. The Price Administration controlled the retail price of liquor, but the demand for it was so high (during the war) that it could be resold at a higher price. Schulte called in a broker-dealer (D) and

indicated that Park & Tilford was going to declare a dividend of its liquor inventory to its shareholders and that in connection therewith it wanted to sell some of its stock as the stock moved up in price. D was authorized to sell 73,000 shares for the trust at $80 or better and 200 shares on each quarter point the stock moved up for Schulte personally. The dividend was declared and the stock went up rapidly (eventually to $90 per share). D sold the stock over the New York Stock Exchange, eventually disposing of all but 1% of Schulte's personal interest, all of the corporation's interest controlled by Schulte, and about 50,000 shares of the trust's interest (24% of the corporation) in a five-month period before the Price Administration ruled that those purchasing the stock and receiving dividend rights could not resell the right to buy the liquor; the stock price then fell dramatically to about $30 per share. No registration statement was in effect for the sales. The S.E.C. brings an action under the 1934 Act to revoke D's registration as a broker-dealer and expel D from membership in the National Association of Securities Dealers.

(2) **Issue.** Is there an exemption from registration available for D?

(3) **Held.** No. D suspended from NASD for 20 days.

(a) D is an underwriter because Schulte was a control person and D effected a distribution in a control person's stock. A "distribution" is the entire process by which a block of securities is dispersed to the public. It *makes no difference* that when the distribution began D might not have known the exact number of shares that were to be distributed, nor that there were certain conditions (such as price) attached to the sale. On the facts, D *knew* that a large number of shares were to be sold. D knew of the dividend plan and that the stock would go up. D had specific authorization to sell a large number of shares. Thus, D had the necessary intent to make a distribution for a control person (for the purposes of the liability section being applied here—1934 Act).

(b) An offering done for a control person is a "new offering." Thus, the exemption of section 3(a)(1) (which applies to offerings completed before enactment of the 1933 Act) does not apply; neither does the dealer exemption of section 4(1) (which exempts offerings after one year from the date of the offering).

(c) The exemption for brokers in section 4(2) of the Act does not apply. The Act was meant to provide possible investors with reliable information on which they could reach informed decisions as to whether to buy securities offered publicly. This rationale applies whether the securities are newly issued or are being sold by control persons (a secondary distribution). Section 4(1) and the dealer exemption make a distinction between the "distribution period" and subsequent "trading." The distribution of securities is not exempt. But to allow trading during the distribution period, section 4(2) was enacted, which allows trading during this period when a "broker's transaction" is involved. However, here a full-scale distribution for a control person took place. This exemption does not overlap section 4(1) (the dealer exemption), since the broker exemption allows trading by an individual when distribution is halted, as for example, when a stop order by the S.E.C. is in effect.

(d)   Due to the fact that there has been administrative doubt concerning the availability of section 4(2) for distributions on behalf of control persons, it is not in the public interest to revoke D's registration. A 20-day suspension is appropriate.

b)   **Control person as issuer--United States v. Wolfson,** 405 F.2d 779 (2d Cir. 1968), *cert. denied*, 394 U.S. 946 (1969).

   (1)   **Facts.** Wolfson (D) controlled Continental Enterprises, Inc., and with his family and close associate (Ds) owned 40% of its stock. Over a period of 18 months, Ds sold 55% of their own holdings (25% of the corporation's outstanding shares) without registration. The United States brought criminal charges of conspiracy to sell unregistered stock and an action for selling unregistered stock. Ds were convicted and appeal their conviction.

   (2)   **Issue.** Are transactions between control persons and brokers exempt from registration when the brokers are considered underwriters under section 2(11) of the 1933 Act (which makes the control persons issuers)?

   (3)   **Held.** No. Ds' conviction is upheld.

      (a)   Ds argue that section 4(1) should apply since they are not issuers, underwriters, or dealers; but section 4(1) *applies only to transactions*, not classes of persons. Under section 2(11) the brokers who sold for Ds are considered underwriters, so the stock was sold in "transactions by underwriters," which are not exempt under section 4(1).

      (b)   The section 4(4) exemption is unavailable to Ds since it is designed only to exempt the brokers' part in securities transactions. The seller has to have its own exemption and cannot rely on the broker's exemption. Also, the volume of sales by Ds indicates a distribution rather than an ordinary brokerage transaction, so the broker here may *not* have an exemption.

      (c)   Ds' contention that they were unaware of the securities laws and that sections 4 and 5 of the Act are unconstitutionally vague do not mitigate their culpability.

   (4)   **Comment.** The brokers were able to claim the section 4(4) exemption because they were unaware that Ds' part in the transaction was not exempt. Ds later sued the brokers for misrepresentation of the legality of the sale but lost, the court finding that Ds' conviction estopped their claiming ignorance of the law at the time of sale.

2)   **Directors, officers, and employees of the issuer.** Directors, officers, and employees of the issuer who engage in selling activity on its behalf may be "underwriters." The issue is whether in selling the issuer's securities they are performing their usual corporate functions (in which case they are not underwriters) or whether they are engaged in a separate selling function for the issuer (in which case they are underwriters). The following tests are used to make this determination:

a) Do the officers, directors, or employees receive additional compensation for selling the issuer's securities? If so, they are underwriters.

b) Do they spend a major portion of their time in selling the issuer's securities? If so, they are underwriters.

c) Are they hired specially in connection with the selling activity? If so, they are underwriters.

3) **Any "selling for" relationship.** A person may be an underwriter under this part of the definition ("selling for the issuer") even though he has no contractual relationship with the issuer.

a) **"Selling for the issuer"--S.E.C. v. Chinese Consolidated Benevolent Association,** 120 F.2d 738 (2d Cir. 1941).

(1) **Facts.** The Chinese Government was selling bonds; a benevolent society of United States Chinese (D) held mass meetings and put out advertisements to solicit purchasers for the bonds, in some instances collecting the money and transmitting it to the agent United States Bank and delivering the bond certificates after issuance in China. D had no contractual relationship with the Chinese Government and received no remuneration. S.E.C. seeks an injunction against D as an "underwriter" of an unregistered offering.

(2) **Issue.** Is D an underwriter?

(3) **Held.** Yes. Judgment for the S.E.C.

(a) The purpose of the 1933 Act is upheld by finding that D is an underwriter, since the purpose is to limit distribution of securities to the public without an adequate disclosure of relevant information.

(b) D has solicited offers to buy, which constitutes an assistance in the selling process of an unregistered public offering.

(c) D is also an underwriter by virtue of having "participated" in the underwriting.

(4) **Dissent.** D did not sell for the issuer.

c. **A person who participates in a distribution.** The third definition of an "underwriter" is one who "participates" in a distribution. Obviously, this makes the definition of an "underwriter" under section 2(11) very broad.

1) **The "participation" test.** The test is purely one of "participation" in some fashion or other in the underwriting. It is not necessary that a person have a financial interest in the underwriting.

a) For example, a person who supplies financing to enable the distribution to take place is an underwriter (i.e., getting money for the expenses, assisting in getting names of dealers to sell the securities, assisting to convince persons to buy the securities, etc.). This is true whether or not the person receives any monetary compensation for these services.

b) Also, a person who arranges for quotes on the securities being issued in the newspapers may be an underwriter.

c) However, a person who receives a fee for bringing the issuer and the underwriter together (a "finder") and does not participate thereafter in the underwriting is not an underwriter.

(1) A "finder" may also help bring the underwriter and the subordinate underwriters together.

(2) But if the finder receives compensation based on part of the proceeds from the offering, or receives a part of the issue to be distributed, or goes in any way beyond the traditional role played by a finder, then he may become an underwriter.

2) Exemptions from the participation test.

a) **Agreements to purchase unsold securities.** A group of persons that would otherwise be underwriters under the participation test are excluded by Rule 142 of the Act. These are persons whose sole function in the distribution is confined to an undertaking entered into with one of the principal underwriters (but not the issuer) to purchase all or a portion of the securities remaining unsold after some specified period of time has elapsed, if the purchase is for investment purposes (i.e., holding for a significant period as an investment).

b) **Exclusion of dealers.**

(1) **Where dealers sell for a normal commission.** Dealers who are part of the selling group of dealers in an underwriting would normally be covered by the participation test and be "underwriters." However, these dealers, where they receive merely a commission from an underwriter or dealer "not in excess of the usual and customary distributors' or sellers' commission," are excluded from the definition of "underwriters" by section 2(11) of the Act. [*See also* SA Rule 141]

(2) **Definitions.**

(a) **Commissions.** "Commissions" include the remuneration, commonly known as a "spread," which is received by a dealer who buys and sells as a principal, as long as it is not more than is customary or normal in the circumstances of the particular issue concerned.

(b) **From the issuer.** The commission may not be received by the dealer directly from the issuer. [*See* SA §2(11)]

(c) **Underwriters.** A person is an "underwriter," regardless of the amount of his commission, if his function is the "management of the distribution of all or a substantial part of the particular issue," or if he "performs the functions normally performed by an underwriter or underwriting syndicate."

d. **Sales by pledgees of securities pledged by control persons.** A special instance of the problem of defining who is an underwriter for the purposes of the 1933 Act sometimes arises in connection with the pledge of securities to a lender (such as a bank).

1) **The issue.** Suppose X, a control person owning stock in Y Corporation, pledges this stock with a bank for a loan, then defaults on the loan, causing the bank to sell the shares publicly in order to repay the loan. This creates an issue as to whether the bank is an "underwriter."

2) **Applications.**

a) **A spurious pledge.** Where there is not a bona fide pledge involved (i.e., where the pledge of the securities is really a device to give the pledgor-control person cash) the pledgee-bank is held to be an underwriter. [*See* S.E.C. v. Guild Films Co., *infra*]

b) **Weak loan.** The same is true where the bank has not made a reasonable investigation into whether there is a good loan (i.e., where there is not a reasonable basis for a bank determination that the pledgor can repay the loan without the sale of the securities).

c) **Bona fide pledge and loan.** The difficult cases are those where the loan is bona fide. No case has specifically held that a good faith loan and pledge requires registration of the control person's shares before the bank or pledgee can make a distribution of the shares; nevertheless, dicta to this effect in *S.E.C. v. Guild Films Co.*, below, has widely been interpreted to the effect that all pledgees take the shares with a view to distribution and thus there must be a proper registration before a public distribution of the pledgee's securities can be made.

S.E.C. v. Guild Films Co.

d) **Sale of stock held as collateral--S.E.C. v. Guild Films Co.,** 279 F.2d 485 (2d Cir. 1960).

(1) **Facts.** Roach was an officer, director and controlling shareholder of Jacobs Co., which owned Scranton, which owned W-R Corp. and Rabco. Roach borrowed $60,000 from two banks (Ds), giving Jacobs stock as collateral, due in 90 days. Guild Films (D) made a deal with Rabco and W-R to issue shares of D's stock for certain film rights; D's stock had a restrictive legend indicating that the stock could not be transferred without registration under the 1933 Act. Roach was financially pressed; the Jacobs stock was suspended from trading on the exchange and dropped in price; the banks called the loans; Roach put them off and then finally gave them 50,000 shares of D's stock (one of the certificates issued to Rabco). Two days later the

banks learned that all trading in Jacobs stock had been suspended; they called the loans (which had been renewed), brought a state court action to have the D stock transfer agent transfer the 50,000 shares into their names, and sold part of the stock to the public to repay the Roach loan (even though the S.E.C. had issued an adverse opinion that the stock could not be sold without registration). The banks bring an appeal against a lower court judgment in favor of the S.E.C. preventing further sale.

(2) Issue. Are the banks underwriters?

(3) Held. Yes. Judgment for the S.E.C. affirmed.

(a) On the facts, the banks saw the restrictive legend on D's shares; they knew that Roach was in financial trouble.

(b) It makes no difference that the banks did not "purchase" the shares directly from D. The Act covers every disposition for value of a security. [*See* SA §2(3)]

(c) It makes no difference that the banks did not have contractual privity with the issuer (D).

(d) The policy of the Act is implemented by covering the banks.

(e) It makes no difference that the banks were in "good faith" in accepting the stock. This would not help purchasers of worthless stock.

(4) Comment. Note that the statement saying that it makes no difference that the banks were in "good faith" is dictum, since the banks obviously were not in good faith in accepting the stock.

4. **Dealers.** Dealers also appear to be covered by the Act (since section 4(1) seems to include them in the registration and prospectus requirements; however, a limited exemption is included in the Act for dealers by section 4(3), which was discussed in the *Ira Haupt* case, *supra*.

a. **Definition of a dealer.** A "dealer" (in this context) is any person who engages either for all or part of his time (directly or indirectly) as agent, broker, or principal, in the business of offering, buying, selling or otherwise dealing or trading in securities issued by another person. [*See* SA §2(12)]

1) Note that this definition includes those persons who might normally be called "brokers."

2) Also, here the definition of "dealer" depends on the person's usual activities and not merely on his activities with respect to a particular offering or transaction.

b. **The distinction between the "distribution period" and the "post distribution trading period."**

    1) **The concept of a distribution.** The concept of a "distribution" involves the idea of moving the issuer's securities through the underwriter, the dealers, the initial investors and into the hands of purchasers who intend to hold the securities for investment (i.e., for some substantial period of time). In a normal distribution, the dealers sell to some initial investors who intend to hold for only a very short time and then take their profits by an early sale (once the securities have moved up in price, which often happens in the first hours or days of a new offering). A "distribution" has occurred when the securities have come to rest in the hands of those that intend to hold for a substantial period of time.

    2) **Definition of the "distribution period."** Section 4(3) of the Act defines the "distribution period" in terms of a specific time period: Forty days following the effective date of the registration statement, or 40 days following the commencement of the offering, whichever date occurs later. The period after this time is defined as the "post-distribution trading period." The exemption for dealers operates in the "post distribution trading period."

c. **Where a registration statement has actually been filed.** Where a registration statement has been filed, every dealer is subjected to the prospectus delivery requirements of section 5 for 40 days following the effective date of the registration statement, or for 40 days following the commencement of the public offering, whichever date occurs later. In this "distribution period," the Act deems it essential that investors receive a prospectus. Thereafter, the Act deems the "distribution" to have come to an end. [*See* SA §4(3)(B)]

    1) **Dealers affected.** Note that the requirement that a prospectus be delivered in the distribution period applies to *all* dealers—those who are participating in the offering and those who are not but who happen to be trading in the securities. The rationale for including the dealers who are not actually participating in the offering is that in the 40-day period after the offering begins, resales that are part of the "distribution" will still be going on and these dealers will be involved in these resales.

    2) **The securities involved.** The securities that are subject to the prospectus requirements are those that are newly offered as part of the registered offering. This is important where the issuer already has shares of the same class of security outstanding (example: XYZ has already issued its common stock; now it has a new offering of some additional shares of common stock; it is only these new shares that are subject to the requirements of the Act); although the outstanding shares are not subject to the Act, a dealer may not be able to tell the difference and so may comply with the prospectus requirement in the "distribution period" with all transactions involving the class of stock that is the subject of the offering.

3) **New companies.** Where the securities being offered are by a company which is offering its securities to the public for the first time, then the distribution period lasts 90 days rather than 40. [*See* SA §4(3)(B)]

4) **Exemption does not apply as long as the original allotment is being sold.** The exemption from the prospectus delivery requirements in the post distribution trading period does not apply to dealers who are participating in the offering and who have not yet sold out their original allotment of securities. The rationale is that as long as the securities that are part of the offering are still being sold for the first time, the distribution is still going on and the investors need the protection of receiving a prospectus. [*See* SA §4(3)(C)]

d. **Unregistered offerings.** Where a registration statement should have been filed but was not (and the securities were offered to the public anyway), the Act provides that 40 days after such offering first began, dealers are exempt from the prospectus delivery requirements of the Act. The rationale is that even though the offering was illegal, after some period of time the harm has been done and unsuspecting dealers trading in the securities should not be held to be in violation of the Act.

e. **Issues of companies reporting under the 1934 Act.** The 40-day dealer prospectus delivery requirement of section 4(3) is eliminated for the issues of corporations already required to file regular and periodic reports with the S.E.C. (under either sections 13 or 15d of the 1934 Act; *see supra*).

1) The rationale is that the information normally included in these reports and investors interested in it may get the information from the S.E.C.

2) This exemption, however, does *not* apply where a dealer is part of the offering and still is selling the securities of its original allotment.

5. **The Broker's Transaction Exemption.** The Act also provides a transaction exemption for certain broker's transactions. [*See* SA §4(4)] This exemption was also discussed in the *Ira Haupt* case.

a. **Definition of a "broker."** The definition of a "dealer" given above includes in it all brokers. Thus, where a broker has the dealer exemption of section 4(3) available to him, the exemption of section 4(4) is of no assistance.

b. **Broker's transactions.** However, where the dealer exemption is not available (such as where the transaction occurs in the "distribution period"), then the broker's exemption may apply.

1) Broker's transactions, executed on the customer's order on any exchange or in the over-the-counter market, are exempt (but solicited buy orders are not exempt).

2) This exemption does not focus on whether the broker-dealer normally or usually acts as a broker or a dealer; it is an exemption for a specific transaction and the broker-dealer must be acting in this transaction as a broker (selling on a commission basis) to qualify.

c. **Purpose of the exemption.** The purpose of the exemption is to allow a broker to execute an unsolicited brokerage sell order at any time without complying with the prospectus delivery requirement. There is no limitation such as the 40-day distribution period of the dealer's exemption.

1) **An open market.** In this way, the ordinary investor may sell his securities (purchased as part of the new offering of securities) at any time (even when an S.E.C. stop order may be in effect, which halts the distribution process involving the issuer, underwriters, and all dealers). Thus, there would always remain an open trading market in the securities of the issuer where they may be traded at a price which reflects their current trading value.

2) **Applicable only to the broker.** The exemption applies only to the broker and does not extend to the selling customer. The customer must find his own exemption in order to sell the securities without violating the Act.

   a) The ordinary customer normally has no trouble in doing this since he is not an issuer, underwriter, or dealer (*see* section 4(1)).

   b) But the control person may not be able to rely on section 4(1) and thus might not be able to sell through the broker.

d. **Requirements for the broker's exemption.**

1) **The usual brokerage function.** The exemption applies only where the broker is performing no more than the usual broker's function.

   a) Delegation of unusual authority by the seller of the securities to the broker (as to the time and manner of the execution of the order) may go beyond the usual broker's function.

   b) So does the payment of more than the usual brokerage commission.

2) **The prohibition on the broker's solicitation of orders.** The exemption is lost if the broker solicits the orders to buy.

   a) **Rationale.** The rationale is that the Act was designed primarily for the protection of buyers rather than for the protection of sellers. Buyers should receive all of the information required by the Act.

   b) **Solicitation.**

      (1) Advertising for business generally does not amount to solicitation, and a broker may call another broker or dealer who has made a bid for the security (such as in the printed quotation sheets). Or the broker may simply execute the sell order over the exchange.

(2) But the broker may not call another broker or dealer on the telephone to see "if he is interested." Nor may the broker approach another member of the exchange to see if he is interested.

e. Sales by control persons through brokers. The situation frequently arises where a control person attempts to sell securities through a broker.

1) **Control person's exemption.** The control person must either register the securities or find an exemption from registration.

   a) The broker's exemption does not apply, since it only applies to the broker.

   b) Normally, the control person would rely on Rule 144 to establish an exemption (*see* the discussion of this rule, *infra*).

2) **Where the control person has no exemption.** If the control person has no exemption, and the broker knows this or has reasonable grounds to believe that the control person has no exemption, then the broker may be acting as an "underwriter" (since he is participating in an underwriting) for the control person, in which case the broker cannot rely on the broker's exemption (*see* the *Ira Haupt* case discussed *supra*). This means that in order for the broker to claim the exemption of section 4(4), the broker, before selling securities, must make a reasonable investigation to determine whether the sales are for a control person and if so whether the control person has the needed exemption.

f. Amendments and updates to the registration statement.

1) **Where there are errors at the time of effectiveness.** Section 11 of the Act, which provides a remedy against the issuer, the underwriters and others associated with the registration statement, applies only to misstatements and omissions contained in the registration statement "when . . . it becomes effective." Thus, in order to avoid liability under section 11, where an error is discovered in the registration statement after the effective date, the appropriate way to update the prospectus is to file a "post-effective" amendment with the S.E.C. [*See* SA Rule 423]

2) **Where subsequent developments occur.** However, where developments after the effective date make the information in the prospectus misleading or false (although it was accurate at the effective date), then the section 11 liability provision does *not* apply. But section 12(2) (which prohibits misrepresentation in the sale of interstate securities generally) covers this situation. So it is clear that correct information must be included in the prospectus whenever it is used. In this situation a correction may be made simply by placing a sticker on the cover and supplementing the material in the prospectus. [*See* SA Rule 424] No advance processing by the S.E.C. is required.

3) **Note time period.** Section 10(a)(3) of the Act requires that a prospectus used nine months after the effective date be updated to contain accurate information.

4) Undertaking of underwriters. With respect to "cheap stock" and warrants received by underwriters in connection with registered offerings, the S.E.C. has required that the underwriters make a commitment in the issuer's registration statement to file a *post-effective amendment* with the S.E.C. if the stock is sold by the underwriters after 90 days from the effective date of the issuer's offering. This allows the S.E.C. to review the revised prospectus before it is used and ensures that the potential investor will be given current information. Also, it makes the amendment a new registration statement and section 11 of the Act will apply to it.

6. Restrictions on Resale of Restricted Securities by Nonaffiliates Prior to Rule 144.

a. Introduction. Suppose the issuer (XYZ Corporation) intends a private offering and initially issues common stock to six sophisticated investors (a private offering under section 4(2)). At that point, however, the six original investors immediately sell their stock to 90 new investors. The XYZ offering has now arguably become "public," since (as noted previously) a "distribution" of securities encompasses the entire process by which a block of securities is dispersed until it ultimately comes to rest in the hands of a group of purchasers for investment (i.e., to hold for investment).

b. Buyer's intent crucial. In this situation, the intent of the *original purchasers* in buying the securities is very important.

1) Purchasers as underwriters—registration required. If the original purchasers buy the securities with a view toward distribution (i.e., resale to the public), they are "underwriters" (*see* the discussion, *supra*). And if a public distribution actually does take place without registration, there is a violation of section 5 of the Act.

2) Purchasers with investment intent—private offering. The opposite of taking for resale is purchasing for "investment"—i.e., to keep or hold securities for a significant period of time. If this is the intention of the original investors, and they otherwise satisfy the criteria for a private offering (e.g., limited number, sophisticated, etc.), no registration is required.

c. Factors showing investment intent. Whether the original purchaser bought for investment or for distribution is a *question of fact*—i.e., what was the purchaser's intent at the time of purchase? Objective facts must be examined to determine this subjective intent, and the following factors are especially relevant:

1) Investment letters. To establish investment intent, it is a common practice to require that the original purchasers give the issuer a letter indicating that they are buying for investment purposes rather than for resale.

2) Restrictive legends on stock certificates. To show that the issuer has made a reasonable investigation and also to establish reasonable precautions by making unlawful secondary transfer difficult, the issuer claiming a private offering exemption often places a legend on its stock certificates to the effect that the certificates cannot be transferred without the issuer's permission.

3) **Length of holding period.** The longer the securities are held by the original purchasers before resale, the more likely it is that the original purchase was for investment and that the private offering exemption still applies. (At one time, the S.E.C. gave opinion letters on the subject—i.e., that a one-year holding period was sufficient to show investment intent—but it no longer does so.) However, the length of time is not conclusive evidence of investment intent. The other factors referred to above must also be considered.

4) **Significance of holding period--United States v. Sherwood,** 175 F. Supp. 480 (S.D.N.Y. 1959).

   a) **Facts.** Sherwood (D) had purchased shares from the issuer and from another shareholder of the issuer. He owned 8% of the outstanding stock, but was not an officer or director; furthermore, he had had a falling out with the president. D had held the stock for more than two years. He had also consented to an S.E.C. decree that he would not sell the stock without registration, *if* a registration statement were needed. D sold 12,000 shares over various exchanges in daily transactions and the S.E.C. (P) brings a criminal contempt action, alleging that D is a control person who has made an unlawful public distribution and/or that he is an "underwriter" since he took from the issuer with a view to a public distribution.

   b) **Issue.** Does D have an exemption to sell the shares without registration?

   c) **Held.** Yes. Judgment for D.

      (1) D is *not* a control person, and the shares he bought from a control shareholder do not remain control shares in his hands. Thus, D need not register the shares he sold on this basis.

      (2) Furthermore, it has not been shown that D is an underwriter. He took the privately sold shares and held them for over two years, which rebuts any inference that he took them with a view to distribution.

5) **Compare—proof of "investment intent" under Rule 144.** Because of frequent confusion and ambiguity in determining whether an investor had the requisite "investment intent" to establish a private offering, the S.E.C. adopted Rule 144 to specify the circumstances under which purchasers in a private offering of securities may resell without violating the Act (*see* the discussion of Rule 144, *infra*).

d. **Knowledge of subsequent resales imputed to original purchasers.** In determining whether the original purchasers in a purported private offering have become "underwriters" in an unlawful public offering because of subsequent resales of stock, such initial buyers are charged with knowledge of both vertical distributions (i.e., what their purchasers do with their stock) and horizontal distributions (i.e., what other purchasers from the issuer do with their stock).

1) **Reasonable and actual belief that offering is private.** To avoid liability, purchasers must therefore show that they had a reasonable and bona fide belief that the offering was a private one. With respect to their own offerees, this means showing that they took reasonable precautions to prevent resales.

2) **Change of circumstances doctrine--Gilligan, Will & Co. v. S.E.C.,** 267 F.2d 461 (2d Cir. 1959).

    a) **Facts.** S.E.C. (P) brings an action under section 15 of the 1934 Act against Gilligan, Will (D) and its partners to have its broker-dealer registration under the 1934 Act suspended based on alleged violation by its partners of the registration provisions of the 1933 Act. Elliot was authorized to make a private placement of $3 million of Crowell Collier's convertible debentures; he was also given an option on $1 million more. Elliot informed D that he was going to sell $500,000 to his wife and the remainder of the $3 million issue to friends; also that the lawyers for Crowell Collier had said the sale was exempt from registration. Almost no information about Crowell Collier was given. On August 5, D took $100,000 of the debentures and signed an investment letter on the stock. It then sold $45,000 to Alter, offered $10,000 to a customer, sold $5,000 to another customer, and put $5,000 in its trading account. These purchasers signed investment letters. Nine months later, noticing that the advertising in Crowell Collier's publications was not increasing, the partners converted all of the debentures and sold them at a profit over the American Stock Exchange, where D was a specialist in the stock. Then in the same month D, on very little information, bought through Elliot $200,000 of a $1 million issue of debentures; sold $50,000 to Alter, put the remainder in a joint account with another person, and signed an investment letter. The debentures were immediately converted into common stock. In addition, D assisted Elliot to place another $200,000 with a mutual fund and received 50,000 warrants to purchase common stock, which it shared with several parties involved in the sale. Again, investment letters were signed. The S.E.C., after a hearing, suspended D for five days; D appealed to the circuit court.

    b) **Issue.** Was there an unregistered public offering of the debentures? If so, were the partners of D "underwriters"?

    c) **Held.** Yes. Judgment affirmed.

        (1) Looking only at D—there was a public distribution by D of the debentures it purchased, making D an underwriter.

            (a) D did not buy for investment; it bought for distribution.

            (b) There was not sufficient information on Crowell Collier available or distributed to investors.

            (c) The number of purchasers is not alone determinative of whether there is a public offering.

        (2) In addition, there was a public distribution of the first debenture issue and D "participated" in it.

(a) D knew of all of the Elliot sales, as well as its own sales.

(b) To avoid liability, D would have to establish a reasonable and bona fide belief that the number involved in the private placement was within the exemption.

(c) The sale of the common stock over the exchange further indicates the public distribution. D had not established its investment intent with respect to the debentures, and there was no valid change of circumstances to justify the termination of D's investment holding period. Thus, the section 4(1) exemption was not available to D. To purchase with intent to hold only as long as the issuer remains profitable is equivalent to purchasing with an intent to make a distribution.

(3) It is not necessary to consider the second issue of debentures.

(4) D's acts were "willful" within the meaning of section 15(b) of the 1934 Act.

d) **Comment.** The first issue of debentures were sold to over 27 persons and firms (including D), who then redistributed to many others (as an end result, there were at least 79 purchasers, representing 88 individuals and firms). Note also the "change of circumstances" doctrine. This doctrine allowed investors in private placement stock to resell before the bidding period was up (two years, according to *Sherwood*) *if* they suffered an unexpected financial "change in circumstances."

7. Applicability of Rule 144 to Resale of Privately Offered Securities and Sales of Securities by Control Persons.

a. **Scope of Rule 144.**

1) **Resale of privately offered securities ("restricted securities").** A person may properly resell securities he received in a private offering (referred to as "restricted securities" in Rule 144) if the requirements of Rule 144 are met. That is, Rule 144 provides *objective criteria* for determining whether the purchaser has met the "investment intent" which permits the purchaser to resell without becoming an "underwriter."

a) **"Restricted securities."** The term "restricted securities" in Rule 144 encompasses two types of securities:

(1) Privately offered securities acquired directly or indirectly from the issuer or a control person.

(2) Securities issued pursuant to Regulation D (Rules 504-506), *supra*, or a section 4(6) of the Act (*see supra*).

b) **Rule 144 is the preferred standard for private offerings.** While a seller of restricted securities can still rely on pre-Rule 144 criteria to establish investment intent (*see* the discussion *supra*), there is a heavy burden of proof on this issue where the facts deviate from what is required by Rule 144. In these situations the S.E.C. has indicated that it will pay particular attention to (i) the availability of information, (ii) the length of the holding period, and (iii) the impact on the trading markets (i.e., whether the volume sold could affect the market price of the stock). These are three of the requirements of Rule 144 (*see* the discussion, *infra*). This seems to indicate that lawyers will be very careful in giving opinions which suggest that investment intent has been satisfied if the requirements of Rule 144 are not satisfied. [*See* SA Release No. 5223 (1972)]

c) **Example.** A buys 100 shares from XYZ in a private offering by XYZ to sophisticated investors. After holding the shares for two years, A desires to sell but does not wish to violate any securities laws in doing so. If he complies with Rule 144, A can rest assured that his sales are not unlawful (i.e., will not turn the private offering into an unregistered public offering).

2) **Sales of securities by control persons.** Rule 144 also applies to the sale of securities owned by control persons. When the Rule is complied with, those selling for the control person will not be deemed "underwriters." A control person may wish to sell either of two types of securities: (i) restricted securities (i.e., those which the control person purchased in a private offering); or (ii) nonrestricted securities which the control person acquired as part of a registered public offering of the issuer's securities. The two-year holding period of Rule 144 (*see* below) does ***not*** apply to sales of nonrestricted securities by a control person, but all other provisions of the Rule do apply.

a) **Example.** When XYZ Corporation was formed, A received 25% of the stock; A now serves on the board of directors. Hence, A is a control person of XYZ. After holding his stock for several years, A wishes to sell. If he complies with Rule 144, there will be a private offering no matter how many people he sells to.

b. **Requirements of Rule 144.** The following criteria must be met to qualify a sale under Rule 144.

1) **Adequate public information about the issuer.** Whether sales by control persons (of restricted or unrestricted securities) or sales of restricted securities by any person are involved, adequate information about the issuer must be available to the public at the time of sale. *Rationale*: Information analogous to that contained in a registration statement must be publicly available to the purchaser to justify application of the Rule. [*See* SA Rule 144(c)]

a) **Public reporting companies.** Adequate information is ***presumed*** to be available where companies are required to report—and have actually reported for a certain period of time—under sections 13 or 15(d) of the 1934 Act (these reporting requirements are discussed *infra*).

b) **Other companies.** For issuers not reporting under the 1934 Act, all the information concerning the issuer set forth in Rule 15[c]2-11 of the 1934 Act must be publicly available, or the issuer must make such information available. This is approximately the same information required of public companies under section 13 or 15(d) of the 1934 Act—i.e., financial statements and other important information on the condition of the company is required.

   (1) The real issue concerns what is meant by "made publicly available." The S.E.C. has indicated that supplying the required information to the broker handling the sale for the seller is *not* sufficient.

   (2) But supplying such information to the issuer's shareholders and to brokers trading regularly in the issuer's securities, plus the publication of financial information about the issuer in a recognized financial service, are sufficient. [*See* SA Release No. 5306 (1972)]

2) **Holding period for restricted securities.** Second, Rule 144 requires that a person desiring to sell restricted securities (i) must be the beneficial owner of and have borne the economic risk of the investment in those securities for at least two years prior to the sale; and (ii) must have fully paid for the securities prior to the sale thereof. (Note that a control person selling nonrestricted securities need *not* comply with the two-year holding period.)

   a) **Rationale.** This requirement ensures that the investor purchased the securities as an investment, rather than for public distribution.

   b) **Purchase with promissory notes and collateral.** In order to show that the original purchaser has "borne the risk of the investment," he must have purchased the securities from the issuer for cash or, where a promissory note or installment contract was used, the note or contract must have been a full-recourse obligation secured by collateral (*other than* the securities themselves) having a fair market value at least equal to the amount of the note. And in any case, full payment for the securities must have been made prior to any sale under Rule 144. Note that where the purchaser has borrowed the money (as from a bank or other independent party) to pay the issuer (and the loan is not guaranteed by the issuer), then the holding period will be counted even if the purchaser only pledges the restricted stock as collateral for his full-recourse loan from the bank. [*See* Decorator Industries, Inc., Fed. Sec. L. Rep. CCH 78,847 (1972-73)]

   c) **Calculating the two-year holding period.** There are special rules for computing the two-year holding period in certain situations. For example:

   (1) **Options.** The time period during which the seller holds options on securities which are later purchased is *excluded* from the requisite two-year holding period under Rule 144. Thus, if A had an option on 100 shares of XYZ common stock for one year, at the end of which time he exercised the option, the one-year option period could not be counted as part of the two-year holding period. [*See* SA Rule 144(d)(3)]

   (2) **Stock dividends or stock splits.** The holding period for securities acquired through stock dividends or splits relates back to the acquisi-

tion date of the original securities. Thus, where A buys 100 shares of XYZ common stock in 1974 and XYZ in 1975 pays a dividend of one share for each 10 shares owned, the holding period for the 10 dividend shares would relate back to the 1974 date of purchase on the original securities.

(3) **Gifts.** A donee can relate back to the acquisition date of his donor. [*See* SA Rule 144(d)(4)(E)]

3) **Limitation on amount of securities sold.** The volume of restricted securities or securities owned by a control person that may be resold under Rule 144 is limited so that during any three-month period only the following amounts of securities may be sold:

a) **Sales by control persons.** Sales of restricted and other securities by control persons (or sales of restricted securities by noncontrol persons who cannot meet the qualifications to remove the volume limitations; *see infra*) during the three-month period may not exceed:

(1) One percent of the shares outstanding of the class of security; or

(2) If the security is traded on an exchange, the average weekly reported volume of trading in such securities on all exchanges and/or reported through the automated quotations systems of a registered securities association for the four weeks prior to a filing of the notice of sale; or

(3) The average weekly reported volume of trading in such securities reported through a consolidated transaction reporting system pursuant to Rule 11Aa3-1 of the 1934 Act during the four-week period preceding a filing of the notice of sale. [*See* SA Rule 144(e)]

b) **Sales by noncontrol persons of restricted securities.** The volume limitations do not apply if (i) the securities have been beneficially owned for at least three years, and (ii) the issuer satisfies the relevant current public information requirement of the Rule (*see* section 354, *supra*). [*See* SA Rule 144(k)]

c) **Securities otherwise acquired.** When restricted securities are pledged, given as a gift, placed in trust or acquired in a decedent's estate, the respective sales by the pledgor, donor, settlor or decedent (as the case may be) must be combined with the sales made by the pledgee, donee, trust, or estate within the relevant time period in calculating the total volume for the Rule 144 limitation. [*See* SA Rule 144(e)(3)]

4) **Limitation on manner of sale.** In order to preserve the "nonpublic" nature of Rule 144 sales, the rule requires that sales thereunder be made in transactions directly with a "market maker" (as defined in section 3(a)(38) of the 1934 Act) or in "broker's transactions" within the meaning of section 4(4) of the 1933 Act (*see supra*). Thus, the following limitations apply in a broker's transaction:

(i) The broker may only execute the order to sell and cannot receive more than the customary commission;

(ii) The broker may not solicit the order to buy, although he may contact other brokers who have expressed an interest within the previous 60 days, or customers expressing an interest within the previous 10 business days;

(iii) The broker may publish bid and ask quotations in an interdealer stock quotation system, as long as the broker has been "making a market" (i.e., trading regularly) in the security to be sold; and

(iv) The broker must make a reasonable inquiry to assure that the person claiming the right to sell without registration is entitled to do so.

    a)   **Exception.** Note that if the seller is selling restricted securities and qualifies to avoid the volume limitations (*see* section 368, above), then the manner of sale limitations does *not* apply.

5)   **Notice of intent to sell.** The final requirement of Rule 144 requires that the seller file with the S.E.C. a notice of his intention to sell the restricted securities. [*See* SA Rule 144(h)] This requirement does not apply where the seller of restricted securities qualifies to avoid the volume limitations.

6)   **Nonexclusive rule.** Rule 144 is not exclusive with respect to nonaffiliation sales of restricted stock, nor with respect to affiliates' sales thereof (whether of restricted or nonrestricted securities). The affiliate or nonaffiliate may also effect such sales pursuant to a registration statement, another exemption, or a Regulation A offering. [*See* SA Rule 144(g)]

c.   **Alternatives to Rule 144.** While Rule 144 did make the criteria for selling unrestricted securities more definite, in some respects it also made them more stringent. Therefore, at the time Rule 144 was adopted, the S.E.C. also provided certain alternative ways for holders of restricted securities to sell their shares without destroying their private offering exemption.

1)   **Exemption for ordinary investors—Rule 237.** Rule 237 provides that persons other than the issuer, control persons, or brokers and dealers—in other words, "ordinary investors" holding restricted securities—may sell their securities without registration if:

    a)   The issuer has been an active, going concern for at least five years;

    b)   The seller has been the beneficial owner of the securities and they have been fully paid for, for at least five years;

    c)   Sale of the securities of the issuer, its predecessors and all of its affiliates by the seller during a one-year period do not exceed the lesser of $50,000 or the proceeds from the sale of 1% of the issuer's shares outstanding in that class of securities; and

    d)   The sales transactions are negotiated other than through a broker or a dealer (i.e., privately). [*See* SA Release No. 5224 (1972)]

2)   **Regulation A exemption.** The S.E.C. has also amended Regulation A—a shortened form of registration available to certain issuers (discussed *supra*)—so that a noncontrol person, or group of noncontrol persons, can generally sell restricted securities pursuant to that exemption without affecting the availability of Regulation A to the issuer.

3) **Section 4(1)—sales by persons not an issuer, underwriter, or dealer.** Another alternative, of course, is for the person selling restricted securities to argue that the sale is exempt because the sale is not by a person covered by the 1933 Act (i.e., it is a sale by a person *other than* an issuer, underwriter, or dealer). [*See* SA §4(1)]

    a) **Sales of restricted securities by noncontrol persons.** Suppose, for example, that A, a noncontrol person of XYZ Corporation, has purchased some of XYZ's common stock in a private offering by XYZ under section 4(2) of the 1933 Act. A desires to resell some of these restricted securities. He cannot appeal to section 4(2) since this section applies only to "issuers," and A is not an issuer. If A is also not an "underwriter" or "dealer," then presumably he can resell under section 4(1).

        (1) A is not an underwriter if he does not purchase from, or sell for, or participate in a "distribution" for the issuer (XYZ) (*see* section 2(11) and the discussion *supra*). The S.E.C. and the courts have traditionally resorted to the concepts related to a "public offering" to determine the meaning of the word "distribution," although this area of the law is presently confused and there is substantial disagreement as to exactly what is required in the section 4(1) context (i.e., sophistication of investors, access to information on the issuer, manner of offering, etc.).

        (2) Thus, if the sale by A of some of his restricted stock does not destroy XYZ's initial private offering (that is, if the offering in which A got his stock has "come to rest"), then there is general agreement that A may resell his stock in any manner he chooses; the stock is freely trading stock.

        (3) If, on the other hand, the XYZ offering in which A bought his stock has not come to rest, then if A sells his stock pursuant to section 4(1), he could be an "underwriter" (*see* the *Gilligan, Will* case, *supra*) if the result of his sales is to create a distribution by XYZ. On the other hand, if A's sales can be made without creating such a distribution by XYZ (and thus A would not become an underwriter for the issuer), then section 4(1) provides an exemption for A's resales. The question becomes, in this situation, what are the requirements of section 4(1)? The better view is that this section only imposes the requirements that the offering be private in manner and that the purchasers be few in number. [*See* Report from Committee on Federal Regulation of Securities, "The Section 4 (1½) Phenomenon: Private Resales of Restricted Securities," 34 *Business Lawyer* 1961-1978 (1979)]

    b) **Sales by control persons.** Control persons may also rely on section 4(1) to resell their securities, whether restricted or not. If the securities being sold are restricted securities, then all of the problems just mentioned above with respect to ordinary investors (i.e., would the resales create a public distribution of the original offering by XYZ?) would apply. In addition, the control person must not himself make a public distribution of his securities (whether restricted securities or not), since those selling for him would become underwriters and he would be an issuer, and the section 4(1) exemption would be lost (*see* section 2(11) and the discussion *supra*). Rule 144 defines what is not a public distribution by a control person and may be definitive therefore of what sales could be made by a control person pursuant to section 4(1) of the 1933 Act. [*See* Fogelson, "Rule 144—A Summary Review," 37 *Business Lawyer* 1519 (1982)]

4) **Resale of restricted securities; changes to method of determining holding period of restricted securities under Rules 144 and 145.**

a) **New Rule 144A.** The S.E.C. has adopted a new Rule 144A, which sets forth a safe harbor rule from the registration requirements of section 5 for the resale of restricted securities *to specified institutions* by persons other than the issuer of such securities.

b) **Private persons.** Persons other than issuers, control persons, and dealers are deemed not to be engaged in a distribution of securities, and hence are not underwriters.

c) **Dealers.** If the rules are followed, dealers are also held *not* to be a participant in a distribution of securities pursuant to section 4(3)(C) of the Act and not to be underwriters.

d) **Eligible securities.** Rule 144A does not extend to the offer or sale of securities that, when issued, were of the same class as securities listed on a national securities exchange registered under section 6 of the Exchange Act or quoted in an automated inter-dealer quotation service.

e) **Institutions covered.** Except for registered broker-dealers ($10 million), to be a qualified institutional buyer, an institution must in the aggregate own and invest on a discretionary basis at least $100 million in securities.

f) **Information requirement.** Where the issuer does not file periodic reports under the 1934 Exchange Act, then the holder of the securities must have the right to receive certain basic information from the issuer, and the purchaser must receive that information at or prior to the purchase of the securities.

g) **Comment.** Note that the objective of this provision is to keep the United States capital markets internationally competitive. Rule 144A allows foreign companies to issue their securities on a private placement basis to United States investors because these institutional investors now have at least a limited resale market (without registration) for the securities they purchase.

5) **Regulation S—offers and sales of securities (outside the United States).** In a measure related to Rule 144A, the S.E.C. has adopted a new safe harbor rule to indicate clearly when an offer or sale of securities occurring outside the United States is *not* subject to the 1933 Act requiring registration.

a) **General conditions.** There are two conditions which apply to three different safe harbor situations.

(1) **Prohibition against "directed selling" efforts in the United States.** This prohibition is to prevent securities sold abroad without 1933 Act registration from ending up in the United States. Thus, the United States markets may not be preconditioned prior to or at the time of the foreign offering.

(2) **The transaction must be an "offshore" offering.** The offering must actually take place outside the United States. The buyers must be (or the seller reasonably believe they are) outside the United States at the time the buy orders are originated, and both the execution and the delivery of the transactions must occur outside the United States. This allows United States citizens abroad (or who go abroad) to buy these offerings.

b) **Categories of offerings.** There are three safe harbor categories.

(1) **Category one.** There is a category one safe harbor for foreign offerings where there is no "United States market interest" for the foreign issuer's securities that are being offered. Various criteria are set up to determine whether the foreign issuer has a United States market interest (i.e., whether a substantial amount of its securities trading occurs on United States markets). Assuming there is no such interest, then the foreign issuer only need comply with the two general conditions set forth above. Even if there is a United States market interest, if the foreign issuer is offering an issue that is an "overseas directed offering" (one that is directed into a single foreign country in compliance with its laws), then it is still a category one offering.

(2) **Category two.** If there is a substantial United States market interest, then debt and equity offerings by foreign issuers filing reports under the 1934 Act's reporting system (and debt offerings by non-reporting foreign issuers) become category two offerings. Here the requirements for avoiding 1933 Act registration are (i) legends on the offering documents, (ii) contractual undertakings by participants in the offering to comply with Regulation S, (iii) certain confirmation notices to securities professionals, and (iv) a restricted period of 40 days where offers or sales to United States persons (other than original participants) may not be made.

(3) **Category three.** This category applies to all other offerings where there is a United States market interest, including offerings by non-reporting foreign issuers and debt offerings by non-reporting United States issuers. In addition to the restrictions of category two, there are many additional restrictions.

c) **Liability rules** still apply (such as Rule 10b-5, 1933 Act provisions, etc.) to Rule 144A and Regulation S offerings.

d) **Relationship to Rule 144A.** Regulation S securities are "restricted securities." Thus, an underwriter could buy them abroad and resell them in the United States in private placement under Rule 144A.

III. REGULATION OF SECURITIES TRADING

The Securities Exchange Act of 1934 deals with many aspects of the trading of securities subsequent to their original distribution.

A. OVERVIEW OF THE 1934 ACT

1. **Purposes of the Exchange Act.** The purpose of the 1934 Act is to protect interstate commerce and the national credit, and to insure the maintenance of fair and honest securities trading markets. [*See* SEA §2]

2. **Registered Securities and Reporting Companies.** The 1934 Act requires that certain securities be registered with the S.E.C. Once a company has registered its securities, it is subject to continued reporting under the Act and to regulation of many of its other activities.

   a. **Corporations required to register their securities.** Companies whose securities are traded on a national securities exchange, *or* companies having assets of $5 million or more and a class of equity security held by 500 or more persons, *must* register such equity securities with the S.E.C. [*See* SEA §12] Companies that have registered a security are typically referred to as "registered" and/or "reporting companies."

   b. **Information required.** Section 12 requires that the registering company supply information similar to an S-1 registration statement under the 1933 Act.

   c. **Exemptions.** There are numerous exemptions from the registration requirement of the 1934 Act, for example, securities of investment companies (i.e., "mutual funds") registered under section 8 of the Investment Company Act of 1940.

   d. **S.E.C. exemptive power.** In addition, the S.E.C. has the power to exempt securities from registration if such an exemption is in the public interest and does not endanger investors. [*See* SEA §12(h)]

   e. **Reports required of companies which have offered their securities to the public.** Every issuer of a security which was registered in the past year under the 1933 Act must also file periodic reports with the S.E.C. (which are similar to those reports required of registered companies under section 12 of the 1934 Act). [*See* SEA §15(d)]

3. **Additional Registrations Required Under the 1934 Act.** The 1934 Act contains other registration requirements in addition to those under section 12.

   a. **Registration of national securities exchanges and associations of over-the-counter broker-dealers.** The 1934 Act defines a "national securities exchange" [*see* SEA § 3(a)(1)] and requires that they register with the S.E.C., unless exempt. [*See* SEA §§5 and 6] Note that the 1934 Act regulates the functions of stock exchange members. Under section 15A, associations of over-the-counter broker-dealers may register with the S.E.C. These associations may regulate and discipline their members. Under section 19, the S.E.C. has broad oversight authority over the rules of these associations and the national stock exchanges.

b. **Registration of broker-dealers.** The 1934 Act provides for the registration with the S.E.C. of all brokers and dealers who transact a securities business in interstate commerce. [*See* SEA §15(a)(1)]

1) **Standards of conduct.** The 1934 Act authorizes the S.E.C. to adopt and enforce rules for broker-dealers with respect to training, broker qualifications, financial responsibility, etc. [*See* SEA §15(b)(8)] Alternatively, broker-dealers may belong to a national securities association registered under section 15A of the Act (which provides for this same type of control).

2) **National association of securities dealers.** The NASD has registered under section 15A of the 1934 Act and is very influential in regulating broker-dealers who are not members of a national securities exchange.

3) **Regulation by the Securities and Exchange Commission.** Alternatively, broker-dealers may choose to be regulated by the S.E.C. and not belong to and be regulated by the NASD.

c. **Registration of information processors.** "Securities information processors" (i.e., persons distributing information about securities quotations or transactions) are required to register with the S.E.C. and make periodic reports. [*See* SEA §11A(b)]

d. **Registration of clearing agencies.** Also, transfer agents, clearing houses, and others involved in the mechanical completion of securities trades are required to register and make periodic reports. [*See* SEA §17A]

4. **Additional Reporting Requirements Under the Act.**

a. **Reports by 5% owners of registered securities.** The 1934 Act requires that the purchaser of 5% or more of a class of equity securities registered under the Act must file certain information with the S.E.C., the issuer of the securities, and the exchange (if the securities are traded on a national exchange) concerning itself, the source of the funds used to purchase the securities, any plans it may have to acquire more of the same securities, and plans it may have to attempt to change the issuer's business or corporate structure. This provision is aimed at regulating "tender offers" (i.e., situations where Company A makes an offer to buy the shares of Company B by approaching Company B's shareholders directly). [*See* SEA §13(d) and the discussion, *infra*]

b. **Reports by officers, directors, and 10% security holders.** Officers and directors of the issuer, and 10% owners of a class of security registered under section 12, must file a report with the S.E.C. of their holdings and a monthly update of any changes therein. [*See* SEA § 16(a) and the discussion, *infra*]

c. **Reports by national securities exchanges and securities associations.** National securities exchanges and securities associations are required to file reports concerning changes in their rules, etc. [*See* SEA §§6 and 15]

5. **Margin Requirements.** The Board of Governors of the Federal Reserve System is granted power over margin requirements (i.e., over loans to purchase securities and broker-dealer borrowings from regulated banks). [*See* SEA §§7 and 8 and the discussion *infra*]

6. **Market Manipulation.** The S.E.C. has the power to control certain practices designed to manipulate securities market prices and to regulate short sales and stop-loss orders. [*See* SEA §§9 and 10 and the discussion *infra*]

7. **Regulation of Practices Relating to Stock Ownership.** The 1934 Act also regulates the following matters relating to stock ownership:

    a. **Proxy solicitation.** The Act governs the manner in which voting proxies are solicited from the shareholders of companies having securities registered under section 12 of the Act. [*See* SEA §14 and the discussion *infra*]

    b. **Tender offers.** And sections 13 and 14 also govern the practices used in making a tender offer (offers directly to shareholders to buy their holdings in order to gain control of the issuing company). [*See* discussion *infra*]

8. **Creation of a National Market System.** In 1975 the 1934 Act was amended in several respects to move in the direction of a "national market system." Section 11A was added, which establishes this goal and creates a Market Advisory Board. Securities information processors and clearing agencies are required to register and are subject to regulation by the S.E.C. [*See* §17A] An exemption from registration for municipal broker-dealers was eliminated; new section 15B provides for their registration and regulation; a Municipal Securities Rulemaking Board was also created. The S.E.C. was given oversight powers over the exchanges and the over-the-counter broker-dealer associations (section 19) to initiate as well as review actions. Certain restrictive practices of the exchanges, such as rate fixing and prohibition of off-board transactions were prohibited, or the S.E.C. had power to prohibit them. Reporting requirements were imposed on certain "institutional investment managers." [*See* SEA §13(f)] Limitations were placed on broker-dealer transactions for their own account (and for certain accounts for which the broker-dealer exercised investment discretion, such as mutual funds) over the exchange. [*See* SEA §11]

9. **Regulation of Certain Bank Activity.** The Government Securities Act of 1986 eliminated the exemption for government securities broker-dealers (usually banks). Section 15C provides for their registration and regulation by the S.E.C.

10. **The Role of the S.E.C. in Administering the 1934 Act.**

    a. **Powers of the commission.** The Act grants specific powers to the S.E.C. for administration of the 1934 Act. The S.E.C. has investigatory and study powers [*see* SEA §§19, 21, and 22], rulemaking power [*see* SEA §23], enforcement powers [*see* SEA §§15, 19], and injunctive power [*see* SEA §21].

b.   **Liability provisions.** There are several important liability provisions of the 1934 Act.

    1)   Some of these liability provisions expressly provide for private damage actions. For example, section 18 of the 1934 Act provides liability for making any false or misleading statement in any document filed pursuant to the 1934 Act or any rule or regulation adopted thereunder.

    2)   Other liability provisions do not expressly provide for private damage actions, but in many instances a private right of action has been implied by the courts. [*See*, e.g., SEA §10(b) and Rule 10b-5, discussed *infra*]

11.   The Role of the Courts.

a.   **Jurisdiction.** The district courts of the United States have exclusive original judicial jurisdiction over actions for violations of the 1934 Act or its regulations and over actions brought to enforce liabilities or duties thereunder. [*See* SEA §27] Nationwide service of process is available.

b.   **Judicial review.** Appeal from district court decisions is first to the circuit court, then by certiorari to the United States Supreme Court. Appeal from decisions of the S.E.C. is also to the circuit courts. S.E.C. decisions must be based on a record, and its decision on factual issues is conclusive if based on "substantial evidence."

B.   REGULATION OF THE SECURITIES MARKETS

1.   National Securities Exchanges.

a.   **Definition.** An "exchange" is any organization, association or group of persons providing a market place or facilities to match purchases and sales of securities. [*See* SEA §3(a)] An example is the New York Stock Exchange.

b.   **Listing for trading.** In order to trade its securities on an exchange, an issuer must "list" the security with the exchange. The exchanges have set up rules by which an issuer can qualify its securities for trading (i.e., such as the size of the firm in sales and assets, the net worth, etc.).

c.   **Registration with the S.E.C.** Once the issuer has listed a security with a national securities exchange, then the security must be registered with the S.E.C. under section 12 of the 1934 Act (*see supra*).

d.   **Exchange membership.** In addition, each exchange sells memberships to securities firms or individuals in the securities business. Membership carries with it the privilege of executing transactions over the exchange.

e.   **Broker and dealer functions.** In order to make the exchange work effectively, various broker and dealer functions have been developed for those members and their agents participating in the trading that takes place on the exchange. For example, a "specialist" (discussed *infra*) is supposed to ensure that there is a continuous market (i.e., a purchase or a sale in a listed security can always be made, at some price) in the securities listed on the exchange for which he is responsible.

f. **Proprietary trading systems as exchanges.**

1) **Introduction.** The growth in computer technology and the growth in institutional trading of securities among themselves without the use of an exchange have created some trading systems that look a lot like exchanges. The issue is whether they must register with the S.E.C. under section 6 of the 1934 Act. The traditional exchanges want them to.

2) **Application--Board of Trade of the City of Chicago v. S.E.C.,** 923 F.2d 1270 (7th Cir. 1991).

> Board of Trade of the City of Chicago v. S.E.C.

a) **Facts.** RMJ, a broker, Delta, a clearing agency, and a bank created a trading system for options on federal government securities, and they registered as a clearinghouse with the S.E.C. The Board of Trade and the Chicago Mercantile Exchange argued that this was an "exchange" and must register and be regulated by the S.E.C. The Seventh Circuit remanded to the S.E.C. for determination whether the system was an exchange, which the S.E.C. said it was not. The case is now being reviewed again by the Seventh Circuit.

Some of the terms of the option to be traded are fixed; others are left open to the parties to negotiate. The traders are securities dealers, banks, pension funds, etc. They put their buy and sell orders into RMJ's computer. Delta notifies the traders when it sees a match and helps complete the transaction (without telling the parties who they are dealing with); Delta guarantees that buyer and seller will honor the terms of the contract.

b) **Issue.** Does this trading system meet the definition in 1934 Act, section 3(a)(1) of a national securities exchange so that it must register and be regulated as such by the S.E.C.?

c) **Held.** No, it is not an exchange.

(1) Section 3(a)(1) provides that an exchange is "any organization, association, or group of persons . . . which constitutes, maintains, or provides a market place or facilities for bringing together purchasers and sellers of securities or for otherwise performing with respect to securities the functions commonly performed by a stock exchange as that term is generally understood."

(2) This system is an electronic marketplace for securities traders. Appellants argue that it is an exchange if it brings together buyers and sellers. The S.E.C. looks at the broader language and says that it is not what is generally understood to be an exchange (it has no trading floor, no specialists, no broker-dealer members who trade for their own account and for clients;

this is not a membership organization as required by section 6).

    (3)   This is not an exchange:

        (a)   The language is broad; the S.E.C. has power to bring entities under regulation. Here the S.E.C. felt there was no need to. Administrative agencies have broad discretion to interpret relevant statutes, and they are in a better position to do so than the court.

        (b)   Further, it makes no sense to interpret the statute in a way that prevents competition for exchanges from an entity that poses no threat to the safety of investors from its not registering with the S.E.C. (each firm is comprehensively regulated).

    d)   **Dissent.** The statute is clear: if the trading system brings together buyers and sellers, it is an exchange; it may also be an exchange if it is what is commonly understood as an exchange.

g.   **Institutional trading on the exchanges.**

    1)   **Accumulation of money in financial intermediaries.** Over the years the savings of individuals have accumulated in financial institutions (such as insurance companies, banks, pension plans, etc.), which invest large pools of money in large blocks, rather than many individuals investing in small blocks. Many of the problems affecting the national exchanges in recent years have arisen as a result of the effects of institutional investing.

        a)   For example, it is much more difficult to maintain a continuous trading market at relatively even prices when huge blocks of stock are being traded (relatively infrequently) than when small amounts of stock are being traded continuously by many small investors.

        b)   In addition, the exchanges (particularly the New York Stock Exchange) have attempted to preserve the economic position of their members by rules which are anticompetitive (such as by prohibiting transactions by member firms in listed securities from occurring outside the exchange). The institutions that do a lot of business in these listed securities have increasingly sought ways to save the expenses involved (such as commissions) in their securities transactions. These opposing pressures (institutions pushing for a more competitive market and the exchanges seeking to preserve their economic position) have resulted in many of the recent changes in the law affecting the national exchanges.

2.   **Competing Markets and a National Securities Market.**

a. **A national market.** Congress has directed that the S.E.C. use its authority under the 1934 Act to facilitate the establishment of a national market system for securities. [*See* SEA §11A]

b. **The motivation to encourage competition.** Whereas previously the actions taken by the S.E.C. may have been influenced strongly by the exchanges (and thus served to preserve the anticompetitive posture of the exchanges), the direction of the actions taken by the S.E.C. is now clearly toward encouraging a breaking down of these competitive restraints between security markets in order to move in the direction of a national securities market.

c. **Elements of the national market.** The following items have been suggested by Congress as important aspects of a national market system:

   1) A nationwide system for disclosure of market information so that price and volume information is available in all markets.

   2) Elimination of artificial impediments to dealing in the best available markets created by exchange rules or otherwise.

   3) Establishment of terms and conditions under which qualified broker-dealers could negotiate access to all exchanges.

   4) An auction trading market which would provide price priority protection for all public orders.

   5) The type of securities to be included in the system would be dependent on their characteristics and not on where they were traded. [SEA Release No. 14416 (1978)]

3. **Self-Regulation of the Exchanges and S.E.C. Supervision.**

   a. **Registration of the exchange with the S.E.C.** A broker-dealer is prohibited from effecting transactions on a securities exchange unless such exchange has registered with the S.E.C. according to the provisions of section 6 of the 1934 Act, or is exempted by the Act from such registration. [*See* SEA §5]

   b. **Self-regulation of the exchanges.** Extensive self-regulation of member activities by a national securities exchange is provided for. [*See* SEA §6]

      1) For example, the exchange may propose rules and adopt policies and procedures for implementing its rules. Formerly, the S.E.C. had limited supervisory power over adoption of these rules.

      2) However, under recent amendments to the 1934 Act, proposed rule additions, deletions, or changes must now first be approved by the S.E.C. [*See* SEA §19(b)]

      3) In addition, the S.E.C. may exercise its power to abrogate, add to, delete, or amend the rules of the exchanges where necessary to insure the fair administration of the exchange or to conform its rules to the purpose and rules of the Act. [*See* SEA §19(c)]

4) And if the exchange imposes any disciplinary sanction on any exchange member, or denies membership to a firm, then the exchange must notify the S.E.C., and the S.E.C. may review (on its own motion or on the motion of the aggrieved party) the actions taken by the exchange. [*See* SEA §19(d)]

5) Finally, the Act provides the S.E.C. with the power to sanction the exchanges, exchange members, and persons associated with exchange members. [*See* SEA §19(h)]

4. Accommodation of Exchange Rules with the Antitrust Laws.

a. **Introduction.** The Securities Exchange Act of 1934 regulates the national exchanges; but extensive power of self-regulation (with S.E.C. overview) is given to the exchanges themselves. This power of exchange self-regulation and S.E.C. regulation involves the power to regulate member firms in their business practices. Through this power the exchange and/or member firms may possibly engage in conduct which violates the antitrust laws (since many things an exchange does or would like to do involve protecting the economic position of member firms from outside competition).

Historically, this anticompetitive impulse has expressed itself in three major ways:

(i) Restricting membership on the exchange and restricting the opportunity to deal on the exchange to members.

(ii) Prohibiting members from executing orders off the exchange in securities listed on the exchange.

(iii) Setting fixed commission rates.

One of the ways utilized by those who have wanted to change these anticompetitive rules has been the antitrust laws.

b. **A policy of accommodation.** The courts have indicated that the Securities Exchange Act does not exclusively occupy the field, but that the 1934 Act must be reconciled or accommodated with the antitrust laws.

Gordon v. New York Stock Exchange

1) **Application--Gordon v. New York Stock Exchange,** 422 U.S. 659 (1975).

a) **Facts.** Richard A. Gordon (P) brings a class action under the Sherman Antitrust Act on behalf of a group of small investors, challenging the rules of the New York and American Stock Exchanges (Ds) that fix minimum commission rates to be charged by member firms. Section 19(b) of the 1934 Act provided that the S.E.C. had supervisory power over exchange rules, including specifically the fixing of commission rates, "which must be reasonable." Historically the S.E.C. had repeatedly exercised this supervisory power. Finally, in 1975 Congress added new section 6(e), providing (with exceptions) that the national exchanges could provide for fixed fees to be charged by members. The district and circuit courts found that in these circumstances the antitrust laws did not apply. The Supreme Court granted certiorari.

b) **Issue.** In this factual context, is application of the federal antitrust laws excluded by the federal securities laws?

c) **Held.** Yes. Judgment for Ds.

(1) The principle decided on by *Silver v. New York Stock Exchange*, 373 U.S. 341 (1963), is affirmed. That is, the antitrust laws are repealed *only* where necessary to make other regulatory provisions work (such as those of the 1934 Act), and then only to the extent minimally required to coordinate the efforts of the two acts.

(2) The Court decided in *Silver* that there was no implied repeal of the antitrust laws in that factual context because nothing in the 1934 Act provided for the S.E.C. to review particular applications by the exchanges of rules enacted by the exchanges.

(3) But here the S.E.C. had direct regulatory power over commission rates and had consistently exercised it (and subsequent to the filing of this action adopted Rule 19b-3, which abolished all fixed commission rates), so this is an appropriate case to exclude the antitrust laws.

(4) *Thill Securities Corp. v. New York Stock Exchange*, 433 F.2d 264 (1970), *cert. denied*, 401 U.S. 994 (1971), is distinguished on its facts. There, no evidence existed of the S.E.C.'s review of the challenge of exchange rule, and the item involved in the exchange rule was not specifically itemized as a matter for S.E.C. regulation by section 19(b).

d) **Comment.** In light of the amendments that have given the S.E.C. total supervisory power over the national exchanges, it might seem that the rationale of *Gordon* would enable the S.E.C. to totally exclude the effect of the antitrust laws from the regulation of the securities exchanges. However, it is likely that the Supreme Court will preserve a place for application of the antitrust laws as a means of ensuring that progress toward a competitive securities market is made.

c. **Fixed commission rates.** For a long time, the New York Stock Exchange set minimum commission rates for member firms to charge their customers. With pressure from the third market (i.e., the trading of listed securities in the over-the-counter market), exchange members began to find ways to get around these minimum rates.

1) **Avoidance devices.** For example, in one practice, a customer would pay the exchange member the full commission on the trade, but would then direct the member firm to "give up" part of the commission to some other party (regardless of the involvement of this party in the transaction). In a direct or indirect way the customer would have an interest in the "give-up"

(i.e., the customer might receive other services from the party to whom the commission was given up).

2) **Negotiated commissions.** Finally, the exchange abolished "give-ups" and the 1934 Act was amended with the intention of abolishing fixed rates.

    a) The 1934 Act now provides that no national securities exchange may impose any schedule or fix rates of commissions charged by its members. [*See* SEA §6(e)]

    b) The S.E.C. may permit exceptions if it finds: (i) that such fixed rates are reasonable in relation to the costs of services, and (ii) that the rates do not impose any burden on competition not necessary or appropriate. [*See* SEA §6(e)]

    c) The S.E.C., by rule, has now acted pursuant to section 6(e) and has abolished fixed commission rates. *See* Rule 19b-3, which prohibits the exchanges from fixing the rates that member firms must charge. [*See* SEA Release No. 11203 (1975)]

3) **An approved form of "give up."** Give-ups went out with the abolition of fixed commission rates. However, money managers still engaged in the practice for other reasons: e.g., they might allow a higher than market commission to a broker for executing trades in return for various services (research, advisory services, computer facilities, etc.). These services might or might not benefit the client for whom the manager was having the trade executed. To protect themselves, institutional money managers got section 28(e) added to the 1934 Act. It creates a "safe harbor" that allows money managers to pay above-market commission rates in return for these special services.

d. **Institutional membership.** The institutions (such as banks, insurance companies, etc.) which are controlling the trading on national exchanges to an increasing extent for a long time desired to have membership on the New York Stock Exchange directly or to acquire subsidiaries (broker-dealers) who had such membership. In this way, the institution that was constantly trading in securities could save the commission expenses otherwise paid to exchange members.

1) With the abolishment of fixed minimum commission rates, the demand for institutional membership should subside somewhat.

2) Currently the 1934 Act prohibits any member of a national securities exchange from effecting a transaction on such an exchange for its own account, the account of an associated person (such as a parent or subsidiary company), or for an account with respect to which it or an associated person exercises investment discretion, subject to specific exemptions. [*See* SEA §11(a); *see also* SEA Release No. 12055 (1976)] This has effectively prohibited institutional membership on the exchanges since it would prohibit an institutional member from handling its own transactions (and thus saving commissions).

5. The Regulation of Trading—Specialists and Market Makers.

a. The specialist system.

1) The work of the specialist. A specialist is a member of a stock exchange who engages in the buying and selling of securities on the exchange of one or more specific listed securities. He may act as either a broker (buying and selling for other brokers on the exchange) or as a dealer (buying or selling for his own account).

    a) The concept of a specialist is that he is supposed to buy when stock is offered but other bids for the purchase of the security are not available.

    b) He is supposed to sell when there are offers to buy but other offers to sell are not available.

2) Function of the specialist. In other words, the specialist is supposed to see that there is a continuous market in the specific securities he is responsible for; i.e., that a security may always be bought or sold at some price.

    a) Specialist for each stock. Thus, each listed security has at least one specialist who is responsible for it.

    b) Key role. The specialists obviously occupy a key position in the functioning of the stock exchanges. They actually purchase and sell a substantial portion of all the securities sold on the exchanges.

    c) Types of orders executed. Typically, the specialist executes the following types of orders:

        (1) Limited price orders. This is an order to buy or sell a stated amount of a security at a specified price or at a better price if obtainable. For example, the specialist may receive an order to buy 100 shares of XYZ when the price drops to $10 per share or less.

        (2) Stop-loss orders. This is an order to buy or sell a stated amount of a security at the market price if and when a transaction occurs at a designated price. For example, the specialist may receive an order to sell 100 shares of XYZ if the price ever drops below $10 per share (and the specialist may then sell at the market price).

        (3) Market orders. Specialists execute very few market orders (i.e., orders to buy or sell at the current market price), since these orders are normally executed between brokers at the "post" (i.e., the location on the exchange where the stock is traded). But where the order is at a price different from the current market price, the order is typically given to the specialist (who remains permanently at one post) to execute.

d)   Recording orders. Thus, the specialist records each buy or sell order which is for execution at a price above or below the current market price. As the market moves, the specialist executes these orders.

3)   Objections to the specialist system. Most of the objections to the system of having specialists on the exchange arise in connection with specialists trading for their own accounts.

   a)   The specialist has the advantage of special knowledge and superior bargaining power in buying and selling for his own account.

   (1)   For example, knowing what the limited orders to sell are above the market price may assist the specialist to decide whether a stock can advance in price or not. If there are a lot of sell orders (say at $5 per share) just above the market price (of say $4 per share), the specialist would probably not buy for his own account, since as soon as a price advance begins, it will run into all of the sell orders and probably the stock will retreat (back to the $4 price).

   (2)   In addition, most specialists have augmented the information they get from actually trading in the stock by developing relationships with people inside the companies whose stock they trade.

   b)   The specialist by personal trading can stimulate public interest and encourage speculation. There is no question but that the specialists are in a position to manipulate the market. For example, specialists make income from commissions on buying and selling. The more trading activity in a stock, the more commissions. Specialists might attempt to create interest in a stock by stimulating trading volume. Knowing where all of the buy orders are below the market price, the specialist might begin to "churn" the stock (buy and then immediately resell) to create interest in a security.

   c)   Specialist trading may accentuate the price trend of the securities. Rather than stabilize the market, the specialist may actually accentuate the trend. Knowing or being able to forecast the trend of the market, the specialist in trading for his own account may accentuate this trend.

4)   Contentions in favor of the specialist system.

   a)   Specialist trading contributes to price continuity and increases liquidity.

   b)   Acting as a dealer and profiting thereby enables the specialist to assume substantial risks to ensure an orderly market.

5)   Regulating the activities of specialists.

   a)   Maintenance of orderly market. The S.E.C. originally adopted Rule 11b-1, which indicated that if a specialist could act as both a dealer and a broker by the rules of the exchange, then he had to restrict his activity as a dealer (so far as practicable) to those activities "reasonably necessary to permit him to maintain a fair and orderly market."

      (1)   Disclosure of the specialist's book. It was unlawful for a specialist to disclose "information in regard to orders placed" with him to anyone but an exchange official, an S.E.C. representative, or another specialist acting in his place, except that order disclosure could be made generally to all other exchange members in accordance with the S.E.C. rules.

(2) **Exchange rules.** The New York Stock Exchange adopted the following rules to regulate specialists (pursuant to Rule 11b-1):

(a) **Registration and cancellation.** Specialists had to be registered with the exchange. Further, if a specialist was found to engage in "continued dealings" for his own account and not for the objective of maintaining an orderly market, he could be suspended.

(b) **Orderly market.** A specialist could not exercise a trade in which he was personally interested unless the objective was to maintain an orderly market.

(c) **Trading regulations.** There were numerous rules which were adopted to implement the basic objective to be achieved (maintenance of an orderly market) by specialists. For example: (i) when adding to his own position in a security, the specialist could not purchase at a price above the price of the last sale in the same session; and (ii) when decreasing his position, the specialist could not liquidate substantially all of his position at a price below the last different price. Both of these rules were to prevent specialist trades from accentuating market trends.

(d) **Capital requirements.** The exchange rules require that specialists be able to assume positions of a certain amount in each stock that they are responsible for and that specialists have net liquid assets of a certain amount.

(e) **Relationship with issuing companies.** The relationship of specialists with issuing companies was also regulated (for example, the rules forbid the execution of purchase or sale orders received directly from the company or any of its officers, directors, or 10% shareholders).

b) **Current and possible future changes.**

(1) **Introduction.** It is clear from recent changes in the 1934 Act that there are going to be substantial changes in the manner in which the specialist system works. Not all of these changes can be set forth at this time, since much of what will happen will depend on specific action to be taken by the S.E.C. pursuant to these amendments in the Act. But the general future direction can be outlined.

(2) **Dealer transactions on the exchange—in general.** The 1934 Act has been amended to prohibit any member of a national securities exchange from effectuating transactions on the exchange for its own account, the account of an associated person, or an account with respect to which it or an associated person has investment discretion (so-called covered accounts), subject to certain specified exceptions. [*See* SEA §11(a)]

(a)   In addition to the specified exceptions, the S.E.C. was given the authority to exempt other transactions from the prohibitions of section 11(a). [*See* SEA §11(a)(1)(H)]

(b)   And the S.E.C. may also regulate or prohibit (i) exchange transactions by members for covered accounts (even though they are otherwise permitted by section 11(a)), (ii) over-the-counter transactions for covered accounts, and (iii) exchange transactions by nonmembers of the exchange for covered accounts. [*See* SEA §11(a)(2)]

(3)   **The dealer exemptions.** Section 11(a) of the Act provides for specific exemptions from the prohibition against dealer transactions by members of the exchange. For example:

(a)   **Market-maker transactions.** A specific exemption is given in the Act for transactions by a dealer acting in the capacity of a "market maker." A market maker is defined to be any specialist or any dealer holding himself out as being willing to buy and sell a particular security on a regular or continuous basis. [*See* SEA §11(a)(1)(A)] This exception generally permits the specialists to continue performance of their traditional functions.

(b)   **Where priority is given to outside orders.** In addition, the Act provides that transactions may be effected for the account of members of the exchange where they are executed in compliance with the rules of the S.E.C. that ensure the maintenance of a fair and orderly market and where priority and precedence are given in execution of these orders to orders for the account of persons who are not members of the exchange or associated with members. [*See* SEA §11(a) (1)(G)] The S.E.C. has adopted Rule 11a-1-1(T) to implement this exception where the following requirements are met:

(i)   The member of the exchange buying for its own account must disclose to any member with whom the offer to purchase is placed for execution (including the specialist), and to anyone else who participates in the execution of the order, that the order is for its own account.

(ii)   Also, if a member is representing a second member in executing an order for the second member's account, it must be clearly announced to the specialist and to other members of the exchange present when the trading takes place that the order is for the account of the second member. Specialists (who often are executing orders for other exchange members) need not comply with this rule when they are executing orders for other brokers.

(iii)   The exchange member executing an order for its own account or for the account of another member must yield to any bid or offer for the account of a person who is not a member of the exchange if such offer is at the same price (irrespective of the size of this other offer or the time when it was entered).

(iv)   Fifty percent or more of the revenues executed in the preceding year must have been derived from certain specified sources (traditional securities industry revenues, such as from underwriting, acting as a broker, etc.). Note that this exception is not available for transactions for the account of a person associated with the member or an account over which a member or an associated person exercises investment discretion.

Obviously, if the specialist is not performing his role as a market maker (which is the essence of his function), then he is subject in buying for his own investment account to section 11(a)(1), and must look to this exception when he acts as a dealer.

c)   **The national market system.**

(1)   **Introduction.** The establishment of a national securities market is clearly going to have an impact on the specialist system. The exact dimensions of these changes cannot be predicted at this time, however.

(2)   **A national book.** But the S.E.C. has already suggested that the information technology is present to create a "national book" of offers to purchase and sell securities that would include not only those made over the exchanges (the province of the specialists) but third market makers as well. This in itself, when it comes about, will have a profound effect on the function of the specialist. [*See* SEA Release No. 11942 (1975)]

b.   **Off-the-exchange transactions.**

1)   **Introduction.** In recent years, there has been tremendous pressure on *exchange member firms* to participate in off-the-exchange transactions. The pressure has come principally from institutions (banks, trusts, insurance companies, etc.) which buy and sell large amounts (and large blocks) of securities. They want to avoid the normal brokerage commissions set by the exchanges. Thus, they found that they could deal with each other and with nonmember brokers and dealers and avoid the minimum commission rates established by the New York Stock Exchange. This off-the-exchange market is called the "third market."

2)   **Block transactions.** In addition, many member firms found that they were unable to handle the purchase or sale of the large blocks of securities being traded by institutions in normal exchange transactions and that, in order to facilitate such transactions for their customers, they had to negotiate the transaction off the exchange (as by finding off-the-exchange brokers or dealers to participate, or finding other institutions in the third market that wished to participate, etc.).

3)   **Exchange rule.** Yielding to the pressure of exchange members, on the recommendation of the S.E.C., the New York Stock Exchange adopted Rule 394, which allowed off-the-exchange trading in order to facilitate block trading.

a) **The basic rule.** Member firms had to obtain the permission of the exchange before engaging in an off-the-exchange transaction involving a listed security.

b) **Solicitation of nonmember market makers to participate in transactions off the floor of the exchange.** Under certain conditions, an exchange member firm could approach a nonexchange broker-dealer making a market in the listed security (if such market maker was a broker-dealer registered with the S.E.C.) to participate in a nonexchange transaction. Efforts had to first be made to fill the order or make the sale over the exchange, and specialists had to first be allowed to participate in the transaction at the same prices as would occur in the off-the-exchange transaction.

4) **Permission to trade off the exchange.** Recognizing that the prohibition of off-the-exchange trading was anticompetitive (since it prevented over-the-counter brokers from trading on the exchange and exchange brokers from competing with over-the-counter brokers) and essentially contradicted the 1934 Act's express purpose of creating one central competitive market for securities transactions, the S.E.C. has required that the national exchanges abandon in most instances the prohibition against off-the-exchange trading by member firms. [*See* SEA Rule 19c-1 and SEA Release No. 11942 (1975)]

a) When acting as an *agent* (broker) in a securities transaction, a member firm may effect a securities transaction in securities listed on a national exchange, on exchanges other than the one on which the security is listed, or with a market maker in the third market.

   (1) The exchange rules may still require that members effecting such transactions first satisfy orders at the same or a better price than are listed with the exchange specialist.

   (2) The exchanges may also still adopt rules which would prohibit the member firms from effecting transactions "in house" (i.e., acting as agent for both the buyer and the seller).

b) Where, however, the member firm is acting as a *principal* in the transaction (for example, it might be selling securities which it owns in its investment account), then the member firm must still comply with exchange rules regulating off-the-exchange sales. (However, the S.E.C. indicated that it believed that the problems associated with removing this restriction were less than the adverse effects of the lessening of competition in the marketmaking function which such a prohibition created, and that after further study and recommendations from the National Market Advisory Board it would probably recommend that the restrictions on off-the-exchange principal transactions be removed.)

c) In 1979 the S.E.C. followed up Rule 19c-1 with a further step toward reducing off-board trading restrictions. It prohibits all off-board trading restrictions on stock listed on an exchange after April 26, 1979.

c. **Floor trading.**

1) **Introduction.** "Floor trading" is the purchasing or selling for a broker-dealer's own account while on the floor of the exchange engaged in trading for others. All of the objections raised to specialists are also applicable to floor trading (*see* above); in addition, floor trading was not limited to "maintaining an orderly market" as specialists trading was supposed to be, so floor trading may even be more detrimental to an orderly market.

2) **Current regulation of floor trading.**

    a) **Effective prohibition.** Floor trading is effectively prohibited unless specifically permitted by rule of the S.E.C. (*see* the discussion above of section 11(a)).

        (1) The exception for dealer purchases under section 11(a)(1)(G) would not normally apply since a floor trader would not normally derive 50% of his revenues from traditional security industry type business.

        (2) The exception of section 11(a)(1)(A) for market makers would not apply since floor traders are not normally making a market in the stocks they purchase.

    b) **Probable exceptions.** The S.E.C. is likely to permit some special exceptions to the prohibition, such as one to allow members to effectuate block transactions.

d. **Additional steps toward a national market system.** In addition to those mentioned above, since the adoption of section 11A, there have been several other substantial steps made in the direction of creating one national trading market for securities.

1) **The possible system.** It would be possible technically to create one large computer system for the execution of all orders for securities (whether market or limit orders), the orders being executed automatically, with all qualified market participants having access to the computer to carry out the trading. If this happened, then the existing exchanges would disappear. For this reason, although many steps can technically be taken toward such a securities market, there is great resistance to taking these steps, and the S.E.C.'s position seems to be not to go this far, but to link up the various markets in several other ways.

2) **Consolidated transaction reporting; composite quotation system.** There now exists a system which will report transactions in the same security in whatever market they may have taken place. There is also a quotation system that will transmit bids and offers for securities to all markets from whatever market they may originate. These systems cover securities listed on exchanges and over-the-counter securities that are part of the national market system.

3) **Market linkage systems.** There are several market linkage systems being experimented with. One is the Intermarket Trading System, which links the principal exchange markets, permitting orders for the purchase and sale

of multiple-traded securities to be sent directly by specialists from one market to the others for execution.

4) Limitations. In other respects, the attempt to create a national market system has proved elusive. For example, the S.E.C. has been very cautious about allowing exchange specialists to make markets in over-the-counter stocks. And even when multiple markets in the same security exist, the S.E.C. has not enacted a rule establishing and defining a duty to give the customer the "best execution price."

e. Regulation of the over-the-counter markets.

1) Introduction. Securities which are traded outside the exchanges are said to be traded "over-the-counter." Often securities firms act as the agents of the buyer and seller in such securities transactions. And, of course, sometimes the securities firms act as a principal (i.e., owning the security and acting as either a buyer or seller in the transaction).

2) Registration of broker-dealers. The 1934 Act provides for the registration with the S.E.C. of all brokers and dealers who transact in securities in interstate commerce. [*See* SEC §15(a)] Essentially, these are the broker-dealers involved in the over-the-counter securities markets. These broker-dealers may then choose to be regulated by either the S.E.C. or a registered national securities association.

3) Regulation by the S.E.C. The S.E.C. may adopt and enforce rules for registered broker-dealers with respect to training, broker qualifications, capital requirements, etc. [*See* SEA §15(b)]

4) The National Association of Securities Dealers. Alternatively, the broker-dealers may choose to belong to a registered national securities association.

a) Securities associations. The 1934 Act provides that securities associations of broker-dealers doing an interstate business in securities may register with the S.E.C. [*See* SEA §15A] The only such association to do so to this date has been the National Association of Securities Dealers (NASD).

b) Self-regulation. The securities associations are authorized by the Act to adopt and enforce rules for member broker-dealers with respect to training, broker qualifications, capital requirements, etc.

c) Supervision by the S.E.C. The S.E.C., however, exercises close supervision over the NASD.

(1) Proposed rule additions, deletions, or changes must first be approved by the S.E.C. [*See* SEA §19(b)]

(2) In addition, the S.E.C. may exercise its power to abrogate, add to, delete, or amend the rules of the association where necessary to ensure fair administration and to accomplish the purposes of the Act. [*See* SEA §19(c)]

(3) And if the association imposes any disciplinary sanction on any member, or denies membership, then the association must inform the S.E.C. and the S.E.C. may review (on its own motion or the motion of an aggrieved party) the actions taken by the association. [*See* SEA §19(d)]

(4) Finally, the S.E.C. has the power to sanction members and persons associated with members. [*See* SEA §19(h)]

5) Application—commission and mark-up policies.

a) **NASD policy.** The NASD has adopted a policy that its members may not effect securities transactions at any price "not reasonably related to the current market price of the security" or charge a commission "which is not reasonable." [*See* NASD Rules of Fair Practice, art. III, §§1, 4]

    (1) **Five percent mark-up policy.** The NASD has indicated that a mark-up of 5% *probably* will *not* violate sections 1 and 4. The following factors, however, are to be considered in determining whether a mark-up is "reasonable":

        (a) The type of security involved;

        (b) The availability of the security in the market generally;

        (c) The unit price of the security;

        (d) The total amount of dollars involved in the transaction;

        (e) Whether disclosure of the mark-up is made to the customer.

        (f) The pattern of the broker-dealer's mark-ups;

        (g) The types of services and facilities offered by the broker-dealer.

    (2) **The mark-up base.**

        (a) **Introduction.** The NASD rules indicate that the mark-up is to be based on the "market price" *or*, where evidence of market price is not available, on the broker-dealer's own contemporaneous cost.

        (b) **Determining market price--Merritt, Vickers, Inc. v. S.E.C.,** 353 F.2d 293 (2d Cir. 1965).

            1] **Facts.** The NASD brought an action to expel Merritt, Vickers (D) from membership in the NASD and to revoke Merritt's and Vickers's individual registrations as brokers. D firm is charged with selling securities it owned as a principal and charging customers unfair prices not reasonably related to current market prices of the securities (in violation of NASD Rules 1 and 4 of article III). In 47 transactions the mark-up was computed from the base price that D had purchased the securities for on the same day

Merritt, Vickers, Inc. v. S.E.C.

(and averaged 40.5% over cost). In 73 transactions the mark-up was based on ask quotations in the quotation sheets for over-the-counter stocks published by the National Daily Quotation Bureau (and averaged 30%). Several other violations were also found (such as failing to disclose that D was acting as agent for both buyer and seller in a securities transaction). D applied to the S.E.C. for review under section 15A(g) of the 1934 Act; the S.E.C. denied the review on the basis that D could have produced before the NASD the additional evidence now offered. D appeals to the circuit court based on section 25(a) of the 1934 Act.

2] **Issue.** Were the bases used by the NASD for calculating mark-ups fair to D?

3] **Held.** Yes. Judgment against D is affirmed.

a] The NASD may rely on same-day costs of the broker-dealer as the base for determining reasonable mark-ups. Or, alternatively, the quotations of the National Daily Quotation Bureau are proper (even though these quotes are not firm offers to buy or sell a fixed number of securities).

b] D has the burden to prove special circumstances which made the bases chosen unreasonable or make the excessive mark-ups reasonable.

c] The S.E.C. was proper in denying review; there was no reasonable ground for D's failure to present its additional evidence before the NASD.

d] The penalties imposed on Ds are proper. Ds had experience in the securities business, were the managers of the firm, and knew what was going on.

b) **The S.E.C. policy.** For broker-dealers who are not members of the NASD, there are no specific rules against excessive mark-ups. However, there is the general rule which requires that brokers must observe high standards of commercial honor and just and equitable principles of trade, and this has been construed to cover the problem of excessive mark-ups and commissions. [*See* SEA Rule 15b10-2]

c) **The problem of profits.** If the base used for mark-ups is the broker-dealer's cost, then the mark-up rule might limit the broker's ability to earn profits on his dealer transactions. This is the reason that in *Merritt*, the court only used cost for same-day transactions. In other transactions the S.E.C. referred to quotes on market prices.

d) **Underwriter's compensation.**

(1) **State law.** Many states have securities laws which limit the amount and type of compensation that an underwriter may receive in an original distribution offering.

(2) NASD regulation. The NASD has also undertaken to regulate underwriter compensation to determine if the compensation is fair and consistent with equitable principles of trade. [*See* NASD Rules Art. III, §1]

(a) The standard. Compensation received by the underwriter must be "fair and reasonable" under all of the circumstances.

(b) Advance review. Underwriting agreements for "unseasoned companies" (new companies or those without an established earnings record) must be reviewed in advance of the underwriting.

(c) Compensation factors and guidelines.

1] Compensation which exceeds 18% to 20% of the gross dollar amount received by the issuer in the offering will probably be held to be excessive.

2] All types of the issuer's securities received or purchased (prior to, at the time of, or subsequent to the underwriting) by the underwriter may be considered part of the underwriter's compensation. The rule of thumb is that securities amounting to no more than 10% of the total number of shares offered by the issuer may be received by the underwriter as compensation.

3] Other factors involved in underwriter compensation are expenses payable by the issuer, cash commissions received, consulting and advisory fees, options and warrants granted to the underwriter, etc.

C. REGULATION OF THE TRADING ACTIVITIES OF BROKER-DEALERS

1. Regulation of Manipulation of the Market.

a. Market manipulation—in general.

1) Introduction. Market manipulation is an attempt to set prices or other important criteria of stock market performance through transactions specifically having the purpose of such manipulation.

2) Applicable sections of the 1934 Act. The following sections of the 1934 Act are applicable to "market manipulation" activities:

a) Prohibition of manipulative activity with regard to listed securities. The Act prohibits "any person" or "any member of a national securities exchange" from using the instrumentalities of interstate commerce or the facilities of "any national securities exchange" to engage in certain specified manipulative activities with respect to securities listed on a national securities exchange. [*See* SEA §9(a)]

(1) Per se violations. A series of per se violations (such as attempting to create a misleading appearance of active trading) are listed by section 9. [*See* SEA §§9(a)(1)-(5)]

(2) Possible violations. Certain other types of market transactions are violations if done in contravention of rules adopted by the S.E.C. [*See* SEA §§9(a)(6), 9(b), and 9(c)]

(3) Limited use of section 9. Section 9 has received limited use by the S.E.C., due to several factors.

(a) Applicable only to listed securities. Section 9 applies only to securities listed on a national securities exchange. Rule 10b-5 applies to both listed and over-the-counter securities. So does Rule 15c1-2 (but it is limited to broker-dealer transactions).

(b) Burden of proof. Under section 9, the S.E.C. must show "intent" or "purpose" to engage in an unlawful act on the part of the defendant in order to get injunctive relief.

1] And a plaintiff in a private damage action must show "willfulness." [*See* SEA §9(e)]

2] In contrast, the less burdensome proof elements and broad coverage of Rule 10b-5 has resulted in its use in market manipulation cases (instead of using section 9).

b) Prohibition of manipulative activity with regard to over-the-counter securities.

(1) General liability provision. Rule 10b-5 applies to listed securities *and* over-the-counter securities. Thus, Rule 10b-5 has had broad application in market manipulation cases (and the prohibitions of section 9 of the Act with respect to listed securities have been held to be incorporated into Rule 10b-5). [*See* S.E.C. v. Resch-Cassin & Co., 364 F. Supp. 964 (S.D.N.Y. 1973)]

(2) Liability provisions specifically applicable to broker-dealers.

(a) General fraud provisions. Section 15(c) is a general fraud provision worded similarly to section 9 and Rule 10b-5, relating to transactions by *broker-dealers* in the over-the-counter markets.

(b) Rule making. Pursuant to section 15(c), the S.E.C. has adopted rules prohibiting certain manipulative and deceptive practices. [*See* SEA Rules 15cl-2 through cl-9] Note that the specific requirement of "willfulness" is not present in a section 15(c) action (as it is in a private damage action brought under section 9).

   (c)   **Enforcement.** The S.E.C. has specific enforcement powers against broker-dealers and it may review disciplinary proceedings brought by the NASD against any of its broker-dealer members.

c)   **Regulation of short-selling.** In a short sale, an investor sells (by borrowing it) a stock he does not own, and then buys it back later (replacing the borrowed stock), hopefully at a lower price. Short-selling is regulated pursuant to section 10(a) by the S.E.C. because it can lead to acceleration of market downturns.

   (1)   Rule 3b-3 defines a short sale.

   (2)   Then Rule 10a-1 prohibits a short sale in a falling market. Thus, since the S.E.C. can regulate short-selling of any listed security, no matter where it is traded, it has determined that no short sale can occur at a price lower than the last previous trade. So if the stock traded at $20.25, the short sale has to be at $20.25 or better.

   (3)   Other rules prescribe the methods to be used in covering short sales, short-selling in anticipation of a public offering of the same securities, etc.

d)   **Making a market--In the Matter of Shearson, Hammill & Co.,** 42 S.E.C. 811 (1965).

   (1)   Facts. This is an S.E.C. action pursuant to sections 15(b), 15A, and 19(a)(3) of the 1934 Act and section 203(d) of the Investment Advisers Act of 1940 to determine whether remedial actions should be taken with respect to Shearson, Hammill (a registered broker-dealer), some of its New York office partners, and personnel in the branch office in Los Angeles—one of whom is "Dunbar"—(Ds). USAMCO was organized in July 1960 to engage in the vending machine business by United States Chemical Milling Corporation. Seven hundred thousand dollars in convertible notes were sold, and a Regulation A offering of $300,000 was put together in November 1960. The company was never profitable; in fact, it lost money at everything it tried. Six days after the offering began, Shearson's Los Angeles office began trading the stock and making a market in it.

   (2)   Issue. Did Ds violate various provisions of the securities laws in assisting with the marketing of the USAMCO stock?

   (3)   Held. Yes.

      (a)   It was not disclosed in the offering circular that Shearson was an underwriter. In fact, Shearson was disqualified from acting as such an underwriter for a Regulation A offering. The circular indicated that the company would act as its own underwriter; but, in fact, at least 46% of the offering was sold to employees of Shearson or its customers. So, Shearson and those of its salespersons who participated in the offering are underwriters, and in violation of Rule 252(e)(1) of the 1933 Act. Also, the trading began before the distribution of the offering was complete; hence, the $300,000 Regulation A limitation was exceeded (since such trading counts in computing the limitation amount). Finally, no registration statement was in effect with respect to the offering. Hence, sections 5(a) and (c) were violated.

(b) Rule 10b-6 was violated in that Ds purchased or sold the stock while a distribution of the same stock was being conducted. Also, from November 1960 until the end of 1961, Shearson was the only market maker; it put continually increasing prices into the quotation sheets, but would not fill sell orders. Instead, the employees of D (and other insiders) were allowed to sell their stock. They did not disclose this practice to persons whom they were soliciting to buy the stock. In addition, the stock was never analyzed; untrue earnings reports and progress reports were fabricated by personnel of the Los Angeles office and used to solicit customers. False press releases were sent out; misleading oral predictions were also given to customers.

(c) Also, there was a failure on the part of the broker-dealer to adequately supervise its Los Angeles office.

(d) As a remedy, members of the Executive Committee in New York (who were supposed to supervise the Los Angeles office) are suspended for a substantial period of time. This sanction is imposed rather than a general broker-dealer suspension or termination of the firm's Los Angeles office.

The offending personnel have been terminated; the firm is involved in many lawsuits brought against it by customers, or has settled the claims of these persons; the firm has already instituted closer supervision methods; but still the public interest demands the sanctions given.

b. Market stabilization.

1) **Definition.** "Stabilization" is an attempt to set a price for a security in the market by offering to buy all the shares that are offered at a lower price than the desired price.

a) **In connection with public distributions.** Market stabilization usually occurs in connection with an original public distribution of shares, where the underwriters stabilize the price until the entire public issue is sold (particularly in the situation where securities of the same class are already outstanding; it is critical to maintain the market at the offering price long enough to get the new issue sold out).

b) **Arguments against stabilization.** The argument against stabilization is that manipulation of the market price almost always involves stabilizing.

(1) For example, the classic manipulation case is where the defendant artificially raises the price of a security, then gets people to purchase it at this price.

(2) In the public distribution context, it is argued that stabilizing results in losses to purchasers, since (i) often the price of a security is pegged artificially high from the true market demand, and when stabilizing stops the market price falls, and (ii) it allows the issuance of securities at artificially high prices. [*See* SEA Release No. 2446 (1940)]

2) Regulation of distribution situations.

a) **Overview.** The 1934 Act prohibits transactions for the purpose of pegging or stabilizing the price of a security only when such transactions are in contravention of rules and regulations adopted by the S.E.C. [*See* SEA §9(a)(6)] Pursuant to this section, the S.E.C. has adopted several rules that apply specifically to the distribution situation.

b) **The general prohibition.** Any issuer, underwriter, prospective underwriter, or dealer is prohibited from bidding for or purchasing any security that is the subject of a distribution (or any security of the issuer of the same class or series), if he is a participant in such distribution, except in conformity with the stabilization rules of 10b-7 or 10b-8 of the Act. [*See* SEA Rule 10b-6]

(1) **Relevant time periods.**

(a) **Beginning.**

1] **Purchases on an exchange.** The prohibition against unregulated stabilizing begins for purchases of the issuer's securities on an exchange: (i) as soon as a *dealer* agrees to participate in the original distribution; and (ii), for the *underwriter*, as soon as he becomes a "prospective" underwriter.

2] **Over-the-counter purchases.** For unregulated purchases over-the-counter, the prohibition begins 10 days before the offering for solicited purchases or bids. Five days before the actual offering begins, the underwriters and dealers must get totally out of the over-the-counter market (i.e., they cannot accept even unsolicited offers to sell the issuer's securities). [*See* SEA Rule 10b-6(a)(11)]

3] **Regulated purchases.** Note that "regulated purchases" (i.e., those accomplished pursuant to Rules 10b-7 or 10b-8) may be made prior to the commencement of the offering, although this seldom happens in practice.

(b) **Termination.** The rule against unregulated bids and purchases lasts as to each underwriter or dealer until he has completed his participation in the distribution. [*See* SEA Rule 10b-6(a)]

1] With respect to the underwriter, the restrictions apply until the underwriting syndicate manager gives the underwriter notice that the syndicate has been terminated (even though the particular underwriter may have previously sold all of his own allotment). [*See* SEA Rule 10b-6(c)(3)]

2] The restrictions on the issuer continue until the distribution is completed.

3] Also, although normally the prohibitions terminate with respect to participating dealers when they finish distributing their allotment, the dealer may still not make a market in the security being distributed if it is acting at the instigation of the underwriter, knowing that the underwriter is having trouble distributing the entire issue. [*See* S.E.C. v. Resch-Cassin & Co., 362 F. Supp. 964 (S.D.N.Y. 1973)]

c) **Legal stabilization in connection with a public distribution.** Stabilization in support of a public distribution may occur where "necessary to prevent a decline in the open market price of the security being distributed." [*See* SEA Rule 10b-7]

   (1) **Stabilizing levels.** Stabilization may not be commenced at a price higher than the highest current independent bid price, or above the price at which the security is being offered to the public. [*See* SEA Rule 10b-7]

      (a) Thus, the stabilizing price cannot be raised. The stabilizer can follow the market down (attempting to stabilize it), but he cannot follow the market up. [*See* SEA Rule 10b-7(j)]

      (b) So stabilizing at "the market price" is illegal. [*See* SEA Rule 10b-7(g)] This occurs when the stabilizing bid is represented to be "at the market." This is misleading since the market price itself is (in part) the result of the stabilized bid.

   (2) **Publicity.** The fact that the underwriters may be stabilizing the price of the issued securities must be disclosed at or before the completion of the transaction with a purchaser. Normally the fact that stabilizing may occur is stated in the prospectus. Also, the stabilizer must report on actual stabilizing transactions to the S.E.C. [*See* SEA Rules 10b-7(k) and 17a-2]

Jaffee & Co. v. S.E.C.

   (3) **Rule 10b-6 violation--Jaffee & Co. v. S.E.C.,** 446 F.2d 387 (2d Cir. 1971).

      (a) **Facts.** Jaffee & Co. is the successor broker-dealer to an earlier firm; it is 90% owned by Jaffee. While Jaffee was with the predecessor firm, a secondary offering of 28% of the outstanding stock of Solitron was registered with the S.E.C. under the 1933 Act to be offered in the "proximate future" through Lee & Co. (a broker-dealer). Jaffee owned the largest block of this stock. Sales began in May 1963. Just prior to that time and afterwards, Jaffee bought and sold Solitron stock. The S.E.C. charged a violation of Rule 10b-6 (which prohibits any person on whose behalf a distribution is being made, or any person who has agreed to participate in such a distribution to bid for or purchase any security which is the subject of such distribution until after he has completed his participation in the distribution) against Jaffee and seeks to suspend Jaffee and Jaffee & Co. (under section 15(b)(5) of the 1934 Act).

(b) **Issue.** Must the S.E.C. prove intentional fraud in order to prove a violation of Rule 10b-6?

(c) **Held.** No. Judgment of suspension against Jaffee is affirmed. Judgment against Jaffee & Co. is vacated.

1] Jaffee has clearly violated Rule 10b-6. This is not a case where the underwriter of Jaffee shelved or suspended an offering and then bought or sold shares. The transactions occurred while there was clear intent to make a distribution. No fraudulent intent need be shown to prove a violation. All that need be shown is a violation.

2] Section 15(b)(5) of the 1934 Act governing suspension for a willful violation of the securities acts only requires that the act which constitutes a violation be intended. Jaffee clearly intended the act which constituted the violation.

3] Interstate commerce is involved since Jaffee put his offer to buy in the "pink sheets" distributed in interstate commerce by the National Quotation Bureau.

4] Section 15(b)(5) allows suspension of the broker-dealer when a person associated with it (whether prior to or after the association of such person) willfully violates the securities laws. However, a condition of revocation is that the broker-dealer be given notice and an opportunity to be heard, which was not done in this case. Therefore, the order suspending Jaffee & Co. is vacated.

(4) **In nonpublic distribution situations.** Since section 9(a)(6) indicates that stabilization is prohibited only when the S.E.C. has adopted rules prohibiting it, and the S.E.C.'s rules relative to stabilization (Rules 10b-6 to 10b-8) all speak concerning stabilization in connection with a public distribution, it is arguable (but it has not been decided) that stabilizing for other purposes is unlawful.

(a) For example, a person who pledges stock for a loan might purchase additional shares on the market to maintain the price of the stock which has been pledged.

(b) Section 15(c) of the 1934 Act and Rule 10b-5 could possibly be applied to these nondistribution stabilization transactions.

c. **The "hot issue" problem.**

1) **"Hot issue" defined.** A "hot issue" is one where there is tremendous demand for the offered security that is the subject of the public distribution. Thus, the hot issue will typically be oversubscribed (more offers to purchase than available shares).

2) **The problem.** Normally a "hot issue" comes to the market and immediately rises to a premium price over the initial offering price. In this situation, underwriters and dealers may attempt to profit from the hot issue, to the detriment of the public, by:

   a) Holding back a portion of the initial issue to be sold later, at higher prices.

   b) Allocating part of the issue to employees, relatives, etc., for later sale.

   c) Allocating part of the issue to other broker-dealers, who will immediately put quotes in the quotation services raising the price of the issue, and then all will sell at a substantial premium over the offering price.

3) **Prohibition of certain practices.**

   a) **The S.E.C. position.** The S.E.C. has indicated that all of the above devices are violations of the securities acts. [*See* SEA Release No. 6097 (1959)] Possible violations include violation of section 5 of the 1933 Act (misrepresentation that the offering will be made to the public, at the offering price), section 2(11) of the 1933 Act (parties taking part of the offering for resale would be underwriters), and the antifraud provisions of the 1934 Act (including Rules 10b-6, 10b-5, and 15cl-8).

   b) **The NASD and "free riding."** The NASD has also adopted rules prohibiting "free riding" (i.e., sales by members of the distribution groups at prices above the offering price, or holding back part of the offering for later sale, etc.).

2. **Regulation of the Other Trading Activities of Broker-Dealers.**

   a. **Introduction.** The 1934 Act provides for the registration of all brokers and dealers with the S.E.C. if they undertake to effect security transactions in interstate commerce. [*See* SEA §15]

      1) **Self-regulation.** Section 15A provides for the self-regulation of these broker and dealers through a registered national securities association, subject to supervision and review by the S.E.C.

   b. **Areas of regulation.**

1) **The general antifraud provisions.** The 1934 Act contains several general fraud provisions which are applicable to the activities of broker-dealers. [*See* SEA Rule 10b-5 (discussed *infra*) and SEA Rule 15cl-2 (based on §15(c)(1))]

Rule	Applicable to Sales of Securities?	To Purchases?	Applicable to Brokers?	Dealers?	Any Person?
10b-5	Yes	Yes	Yes	Yes	Yes
15-cl-2	Yes	Yes	Yes	Yes	No (Only to broker-dealers)

2) **The shingle theory.**

   a) **Intentional fraud.** The language of sections 10(b) and 15(c)(1) (and the rules adopted thereunder) seem to require that actions brought thereunder require a showing of actual fraud by the defendant (i.e., intentional fraudulent conduct or misrepresentations) in order for there to be a recovery by the plaintiff.

   b) **Implied representations.** It has been held, however, that when a broker-dealer goes into business ("hangs out its shingle"), it impliedly *represents* that (i) it will deal fairly and competently with its customers and (ii) there will be an adequate basis for any statements (as of value, possible future earnings) or recommendations it makes to its customers. [*See* Charles Hughes & Co. v. S.E.C., 139 F.2d 434 (2d Cir. 1943), *cert. denied*, 321 U.S. 786 (1944)] This "shingle theory" allows a court to find statutory fraud under one of the statutes mentioned above in situations where an *intentional* misstatement or omission by the broker-dealer could not otherwise be proved.

   c) **Applications of the implied representation theory.** In the following situations, a broker-dealer has been held liable:

      (1) Broker-dealer made optimistic statements to his customers about a security without any actual basis for doing so. [*See In re* Alexander Reid & Co., SEA Release No. 6727 (1962)]

      (2) The broker-dealer sold securities to a customer at a price far in excess of market value, without a disclosure of the actual market value. [*See* Charles Hughes & Co. v. S.E.C., *supra*]

3) **Boiler room operations.**

   a) **Definition.** Boiler room operations are securities sales operations using high-pressure tactics (e.g., direct mail offers and telephone follow-up by the broker) where, typically, misrepresentations concerning the security being sold are made. Normally the securities of a single issuer are involved.

   b) **Indirect control.** Prior to 1964, in order to shut down a boiler room operation, the law required that the S.E.C. proceed directly against the broker-dealer in a proceeding to revoke the broker-dealer's registration where it was found that the broker-dealer had willfully violated the securities laws. [*See* SEA §15(b)] Statutory law then indicated that other broker-dealers registered with the NASD could not hire the sales representative who had been found to be the "cause" of the first broker-dealer's revocation (without prior approval of the S.E.C.). [*See* former SEA §15A(b)(4)] This was a form of "indirect control" against the individual salesperson responsible for violating the securities acts (since nothing in the law provided that the S.E.C. could proceed against the salesperson directly; of course, those customers damaged by the sale to them of misrepresented securities could bring a private damage or rescission action under Rules 10b-5, 15cl-2, etc.).

c)   **Direct control.**

(1)   **S.E.C. actions.** Amendments were made in 1964 to the 1934 Act. Now the S.E.C. can proceed directly against "any person" (including the broker-dealer's salesperson) and censure or bar him from associating with *any* broker-dealer, in the event that he has willfully violated the securities acts. [*See* SEA §§15(b) (7) and (b)(5)(D)] Also, the S.E.C. can proceed for revocation against the employer broker-dealer in a boiler room operation under section 15(b)(5)(E), on a charge that the employer has "willfully aided, abetted, counseled, commanded, induced or procured the violation" by the employee.

(2)   **NASD and S.E.C. rules.** In addition, the NASD passed a rule which required that no sale of speculative, low-priced securities could be made without an inquiry into the customer's holdings, financial situation, etc. [*See* NASD Manual (CCH) §2152] Also, the S.E.C. adopted its own "know thy customer" rule. [*See* SEA Rule 15b10-3] These rules make it difficult to conduct the classic "boiler room" operation.

4)   **The suitability issue.**

a)   **Introduction.** The "know thy customer" rules of both the NASD [*see* art. III, §2; NASD Manual (CCH) §2152] and the S.E.C. [SEA Rule 15b10-3] require that all ***broker-dealers*** must have reasonable grounds for believing that any purchase or sale recommendation made to a customer is "suitable" to the customer. Note that the New York Stock Exchange has a similar "know thy customer" rule. [*See* N.Y.S.E. Rule 405, N.Y.S.E. Manual (CCH) §2405] And the cases have made it clear that this rule applies independently to all ***salespeople*** as well. [*See* Hanly v. S.E.C., 405 F.2d 589 (2d Cir. 1969)]

b)   **The NASD and the S.E.C. approach.**

(1)   **The duty to investigate.** Both the NASD and the S.E.C. rules place a duty on the broker-dealer to investigate (i) the customer's other holdings, (ii) his financial condition, and (iii) his ability to make additional financial commitments.

(2)   **Duty to make suitable recommendations.** And the broker-dealer's recommendation must be based on the discovered facts and be "reasonably related to the customer's unique situation."

5) The duty to supervise. The 1934 Act provides for a censure, denial of, suspension, or revocation of a broker's or dealer's registration for failure to adequately supervise its associates (i.e., its salespersons and employees), where the result is a violation of the securities acts or registrations pertaining thereto. [*See* SEA §15(b)(5)(E)]

    a) NASD rules. The NASD rules also contain a supervision requirement. The registered principal (i.e., the person in charge of the broker-dealer organization) must supervise all transactions and correspondence of its employees. [*See* art. II, §27 of NASD Rules]

6) The prohibition against "churning."

    a) Definition. The 1934 Act prohibits "churning" [*see* Rule 15cl-7], which is excessive trading by a broker-dealer in a customer's account, with the primary purpose of generating commission income. Normally, "churning" occurs when the broker-dealer has discretionary accounts with which he may effect trades without prior approval of the customer.

    b) Two elements of damages--Nesbit v. McNeil, 806 F.2d 380 (9th Cir. 1990).

Nesbit v.
McNeil

        (1) Facts. Mr. Nesbit died, leaving his estate to his wife, with securities in a Nesbit Trust and the other securities in her name. Ms. Nesbit was unsophisticated; the value of the securities was going down. McNeil, working for Black & Co., was a friend of a friend. Nesbit told him her objectives were stability, income, and growth. Over 11 years the equity in Nesbit's personal account rose $180,000 and the trust rose $92,000; but there were over 1,000 trades in 150 securities, worth $4.4 million, and commissions were $250,000. Many of the stocks were speculative, with no income. In 1984 Nesbit questioned McNeil about the trades; they decreased in number. In 1985 he apologized for the losses in the portfolio. Nesbit terminated the brokerage agreement and a year later sued McNeil and Black & Co. under Rule 10b-5 for churning and under the State of Oregon securities laws. The federal district court dismissed the Oregon claim and submitted the federal churning claim to the jury. The jury found for P, awarding damages in the amount of the commissions earned by the excessive trades. Ds appeal.

        (2) Issue. Where a portfolio increases in value, may damages be given to a plaintiff that claims that there was still excessive trading so that the account was charged excessive commissions?

        (3) Held. Yes.

            (a) There is sufficient evidence for the jury to have found that churning of the account occurred. P must show (i) excessive trading in light of her stated objectives; (ii) that the broker exercised control over the account; and (iii) that the broker acted with the intent to defraud or with willful and reckless disregard for the interests of the client. Here P was unsophisticated, relied on the broker, who has de facto control. D knew that his trades did not meet the client's investment objectives.

As to excessive trading, no single factor identifies it (turnover ratio, commission ratio, etc. may help). Here an expert testified that 1,000 trades and the high commissions in relation to the value of the accounts, indicated churning.

(b) As to damages, if D is shown to have churned the account, then there are two possible measures of damages. First, if there are portfolio losses and the broker disregarded the client's investment objectives, then there may be damages for these trading losses. Second, even if there are portfolio gains, P may still recover if trading was excessive, by the commissions charged for those excessive trades. Ds cannot deduct the costs they incurred in making the trades that they must reimburse commissions for.

c) **Damages.** Normally, the plaintiff customer may recover the total amount of commissions paid on the securities transactions, although no recovery is allowed for losses in the market value of the securities purchased. [*See* Hecht v. Harris, Upham & Co. (above); *but see* Fey v. Walston & Co., 493 F.2d 1036 (7th Cir. 1974) (which takes the position that plaintiff can recover his out-of-pocket loss)]

7) **The Penny Stock Reform Act of 1990.** This Act is one of the most significant attacks on securities fraud and white collar crime in many years. The first four titles of the Act deal with civil enforcement remedies, allowing the S.E.C. to impose fines for violations involving manipulation of penny stocks. Title V is the Penny Stock Reform Act, which authorizes the S.E.C. to protect investors in low priced securities defined as "penny stocks." Penny stocks are defined in new paragraph 3(a) of the 1934 Exchange Act. Of the 55,000 publicly traded stocks in the United States, 3,500 are listed on the New York and American Exchanges; 4,970 are quoted on NASDAQ. So 47,000 stocks fall outside an exchange or NASDAQ. The issuance and trading of these securities has been an increasing means of defrauding investors. Formerly the fraud occurred in connection with hot "new issues" of low priced stocks. Now "blank check" offerings, where false rumors are started *after issuance* (driving up prices), or merger after the offering with a private company (which then has no regulation in its going-public process) occurs. Then once the stock price is driven up, the parties distributing the stock sell out, the price goes down, and the company fails.

Therefore, a number of new provisions have been added to attack these problems: for example, new subparagraph (6)(A) has been added to section 15(b)(6) of the 1934 Act which expands the S.E.C.'s authority to exclude sanctioned persons from participating in the distribution of penny stocks; new paragraph (g) has been added to section 15 to establish more comprehensive disclosure and regulatory oversight for the penny stock market (including requirements that brokers or dealers give customers a risk disclosure statement when dealing in penny stocks; that prior to entering transactions, customers be given accurate bid and ask prices, or other pricing information if such accurate bids and ask prices are not available; that customers having penny stocks in their accounts be given monthly statements indicating the market value of these stocks, or an indication that such a market value cannot be determined, etc.); section 29(b) of the 1934 Act has been amended to make voidable contracts in violation of the rule(s) which have been adopted; section 7(b) has been added to regulate blank check offerings; and section 15A has been amended to mandate the NASD to establish a toll-free telephone listing to answer customer inquiries concerning the disciplinary history of its members.

8) Regulation of market makers.

a)   **Definition of a market maker.** A "market maker" is a broker-dealer who publishes (in the NASDAQ system or some other quotation service) bona fide "two-way" quotations with respect to any over-the-counter security.

(1)   This means that the broker-dealer is quoting both a bid price (what he will buy the security at) and an ask price (what he is willing to sell the security for).

(2)   It implies that the broker-dealer stands ready to either buy or sell in reasonable quantities.

(3)   The "market maker" may also engage in simultaneous transactions where he buys from one customer and sells to another. Such transactions are, of course, subject to the NASD "mark-up" policy (discussed *supra*).

b)   **Rules controlling market-making activity.**

(1)   A broker-dealer may not represent to a customer that a transaction is occurring at the "market" price unless it has reasonable grounds to believe that a trading market in the security in fact exists (other than one made or created by the broker-dealer). [*See* SEA Rule 15cl-8]

(2)   Also, under the general fraud provisions (i.e., the "shingle theory"; *see* the discussion, *supra*), every sale by a broker-dealer carries with it the implied representation that the price is reasonably related to that prevailing in an open market.

c)   **Single market makers.** These rules create a problem for the firm which is the only one making a market in a security (i.e., only firm which regularly is quoted as willing to buy and sell the security), which often occurs in the over-the-counter market.

(1)   **Close scrutiny.** Thus, it is not per se illegal to be the only market maker in a security. But such a situation will be closely scrutinized for representations made to customers.

d)   **Several or many market makers.** It has been held that even when there are several firms making a market, it is still necessary in order to avoid liability under Rule 10b-5 for a broker-dealer to disclose its position as a market maker to its customers (i.e., this is a *material* fact).

e)   **Market maker position must be disclosed--Chasins v. Smith, Barney & Co.,** 438 F.2d 1167 (2d Cir. 1971).

Chasins v. Smith, Barney & Co.

(1)   **Facts.** Smith, Barney & Co. (D), a brokerage firm, underwrote several over-the-counter securities and made a "market" in these stocks (i.e., maintained a position in the stocks as a principal). D

was also Chasins's (P's) stockbroker and analyzed P's portfolio of securities, recommended sale of several of his securities, and then recommended and sold P several of the securities in which it made a market. The confirmation slips indicated that D was acting as principal, but did not disclose the price D had paid for the securities or that it was making a market in the stocks. P sues under Rule 10b-5 for damages (difference between what he paid and the amount he later sold the stock for). District court found for P. D appeals and P appeals a finding that there was no breach of a common law fiduciary duty by D.

    (2)   **Issue.** Is the fact that D is making a market in a stock a "material fact" that must be disclosed to a buying customer under Rule 10b-5?

    (3)   **Held.** Yes. Judgment for P affirmed.

        (a)   The issue is not whether P bought at a fair price.

        (b)   It is whether a reasonable person would attach importance to the fact that the brokerage firm was making a market in stocks it recommended for purchase.

        (c)   Disclosure of market-making activity would reveal D's possible adverse interests.

        (d)   Since a violation of Rule 10b-5 has been shown, the issue of a breach of fiduciary duty need not be considered.

    (4)   **Motion for rehearing.**

        (a)   **Majority.** Denied.

        (b)   **Dissent.** Rehearing should be granted. Since it is not, the case must be limited to its narrow facts.

           1]   P's complaint did not allege a violation of the securities laws due to nondisclosure of market-making activity by D. It alleged that P may not have gotten the best price because of D's position. But it is clear that the best price in a security is from a market maker (at least when, as here, the market maker is a reputable firm and there are several other firms also making a market in the same stocks).

           2]   Everything about D's position in the stocks was disclosed in documents given to P, except D's role as market maker. But in this factual situation, fears cited by the court that a market maker can set an arbitrary price (to the detriment of its customers) are unwarranted.

    (5)   **Comment.** The dissent has paid more careful attention to what really happens in the market and to the particular facts of this case.

  9)   **Margin requirements.**

a) **Introduction.** In order to generate greater sales volume, broker-dealers often encourage their customers to buy securities on credit (i.e., on "margin"). Section 7 of the 1934 Act regulates this area. The regulations developed in this area under section 7 are the province of the Federal Reserve Board. But the S.E.C. brings enforcement actions for violations by broker-dealers.

b) **The regulations.**

   (1) Federal Reserve Board *Regulation T* governs the extension of credit by market intermediaries in securities transactions (such as broker-dealers).

   (2) Federal Reserve Board *Regulation U* governs extension of credit by commercial banks for the purpose of buying securities.

   (3) *Regulation G* governs lending by persons other than broker-dealers and banks, where the credit extended is secured by the stock purchased.

   (4) *Regulation X* governs borrowing from domestic or foreign lenders.

   Note that these regulations only allow the extension of credit to buy specific exchange-listed and over-the-counter securities.

c) **Margin amount.** Under Regulation T, a "margin" amount may be set. Thus, if the margin amount is 50%, then the amount of the loan cannot be any more than 50% of the market value of the securities.

d) **Implied right of private action for margin rule violations.** Neither section 7 of the 1934 Act nor Regulation T provides for a private civil cause of action to enforce their provisions or to compensate for damage done pursuant to violation of the rules. However, a few courts have found an implied civil action against broker-dealers for such violations.

D. TENDER OFFERS AND REPURCHASES OF STOCK

A "tender offer" is the offer to purchase the securities of one corporation (A) made directly to the shareholders (of A) by another corporation (B). This offer may be made *in cash* or *in stock* (of B). The offer may be made with knowledge and cooperation of the management of the first corporation (A) or without this cooperation.

1. **Inadequacies of Earlier Regulation.** Prior to 1968, several provisions of the securities laws were applicable to tender offers, but there were inadequacies in the coverage of these provisions.

a.   **The Securities Act of 1933.** If the offer to purchase was a cash offer, then (since it was an offer to purchase securities rather than an offer to sell securities) the 1933 Act was *not* applicable and there were no affirmative disclosure requirements on the offeror (B corporation in the example above). Also, the antifraud sections of the 1933 Act (sections 11, 12, and 17) did *not* apply (since they apply only to defrauded *purchasers* of securities).

b.   **The Securities Exchange Act of 1934.**

    1)   **Rule 10b-5.** The antifraud provisions of Rule 10b-5 are available to plaintiff-sellers who sell their stock where there has been a material misrepresentation made or a failure to disclose material facts by the offeror (B corporation). However, since there was doubt whether the tendered corporation itself (A) and the shareholders who do not sell could bring an action (since 10b-5 requires that a plaintiff be an actual purchaser or seller of securities; *see infra*), this section was not thought to adequately cover the tender offer area either.

    2)   **The proxy rules.** The proxy rules (applicable where a vote of shareholders is required on a corporate transaction) of section 14 are of limited applicability since in many tender offers there is no solicitation of proxies that takes place (*see infra*).

    3)   **Market manipulation.** If market manipulation is involved on the part of either the offeror (B) or the management of the tendered company (A), then the other party might have recourse to section 9 or Rule 10b-5 of the 1934 Act. But the proof problems and the limited range of section 9 coverage (*see* the discussion, *supra*) made this section inadequate for all of the problems that arose in tender offers, and the problems involved in tender offers are broader than those of market manipulation.

2.   **Jurisdiction to Regulate.** Jurisdiction of the federal government to regulate tender offers is based on their effect on interstate commerce (and on the use of the mails or other means of interstate commerce in effectuating the transaction) and because these transactions are squarely within the purposes of the 1934 Act.

3.   **Overview of the Rules Relating to Tender Offers.** The following sections of the 1934 Act apply to tender offers.

a.   **The basic provision.** Section 14(d) is the basic section regulating the making of tender offers. Under this section the party making a tender offer must make an appropriate disclosure prior to commencing the offering.

b.   **Antifraud provision.** Section 14(e) is an antifraud provision making it unlawful for any party making a tender offer or defending against one to make untrue statements concerning material facts, or to omit to state material facts, or to engage in any fraudulent, deceptive, or manipulative acts or practices in connection with any tender offer.

c.   **Reporting requirement.** Section 13(d) is a reporting section. It requires that any party acquiring 5% or more of an equity security registered under section 12 of the 1934 Act must report such acquisition and its intentions with respect to the issuer of such security.

4. **The Preliminary Reporting Requirement of Section 13(d).** The preliminary reporting requirements of section 13(d) are framed so that anyone making significant acquisitions of registered equity securities must disclose his plans with respect to the issuer of those securities at a very early stage. Schedule 13D of the 1934 Act specifically indicates what must be filed in connection with the reporting requirement of section 13(d).

   a. **Ownership criteria.** Any person having acquired beneficial ownership of more than 2% of a class of equity security registered under section 12 of the 1934 Act within a 12-month period—*and* who thereby owns 5% of the outstanding shares—must, within 10 days after the acquisition, file an information statement with the S.E.C. (and send copies to the issuer and any exchanges on which the security acquired is traded).

      1) **Updating.** Section 13(d) requires the updating of this material if there are any material changes of fact that subsequently occur.

      2) **Equity securities.** Section 13(d) is applicable to the acquisition of any class of registered equity security (and the 5% requirement relates to each class separately). Thus, if A acquires 5% of the convertible debentures of XYZ Corporation, the reporting requirements apply even though, if the debentures were converted into common stock, A would not own 5% of the underlying common stock.

   b. **Required information.** The following information must be disclosed:

      1) **Information about the purchasers.** The purchaser must disclose the background and identity of the persons involved in the purchase.

      2) **Information about consideration.** The sources and amounts of consideration used in the purchases must be disclosed.

      3) **Information about the purpose of the purchases.** The acquiror must disclose whether the purpose of the purchases is to acquire control of the issuer, and if it is, any present *plans* the purchaser has to liquidate the issuer, to sell its assets, to merge it with any other entity, or to make any other major changes in its business or corporate structure.

      4) **Information about ownership.** The purchaser must disclose the number of shares owned beneficially, the existence of any rights to purchase additional shares, etc.

      5) **Information about contracts, arrangements, or understandings relating to the issuer.** The purchaser must disclose the existence of any such matters relating to the issuer and its securities.

   c. **Exemptions.** The following exemptions apply:

1) Offers for an acquisitions of shares made by means of a 1933 Act registration statement (but not acquisitions pursuant to any exemptions under the 1933 Act or a Regulation A offering under the 1933 Act).

2) Acquisitions where less than 2% of the tendered class of security are purchased within a 12-month period. Thus, if 2.1% is acquired within 12 months but only 4.9% is owned, the reporting requirements are not triggered. Also, if 1.9% is acquired in the period of 12 months and 5.1% is owned, the reporting requirements are *not* triggered.

3) Acquisitions made by the issuer of its own equity securities.

4) Acquisitions exempted by rule or regulation of the S.E.C.

5. **The Tender Offer Rules of Section 14(d).** A "tender offer" is *not* defined in the Act. Generally a "tender offer" is thought to be one that is made "publicly." Generally, the S.E.C. applies a broad definition so as to accomplish the basic remedial purposes of the 1934 Act.

   a. **Tender offers unlawful except under certain conditions.** It is unlawful for any person to make use of the means of interstate commerce to actually make a "tender offer" for any class of equity security registered under section 12 of the Act *unless* certain conditions are met. [*See* SEA §14(d)(1)]

      1) **Disclosure of information.** The offeror must make the following disclosures in connection with the tender offer:

         a) **To the S.E.C.** Prior to the offering, the offeror must give the S.E.C. the information requested in section 13(d) (which is discussed *infra*) and any other additional information which the S.E.C. may by rule or regulation require. In addition, copies of the offer, any advertisements used, and any soliciting materials used must be filed with the S.E.C.

         b) **To the issuer.** Copies of the information filed with the S.E.C. must also be sent to the issuer at a date not later than when such material is first published.

         c) **To the exchange.** The information must also be sent to any exchange where the security being tendered is traded.

      2) **Special requirements.**

         a) **Withdrawal period.** There is a period during which the offeree may change his mind and withdraw the securities which he tendered and deposited with the offeror. [*See* SEA §14(d)(5)]

         b) **Pro rata purchases.** Where the offeror tenders for less than all of the issuer's outstanding stock and a greater number of shares are offered than the offeror intends to purchase, then the offeror must purchase pro rata from each person tendering shares. [*See* SEA §14(d)(6)

c) **Change in offer terms.** If the offeror changes the terms of the offer, then the same terms (if better than offered to prior offeree-sellers) must be offered to those previously selling their stock. [*See* SEA §14(d)(7)]

d) **No purchases outside the offer.** The S.E.C. has adopted Rule 10b-13, which prohibits the tender offeror from purchasing securities of the class tendered outside the tender offer at prices higher than those offered in the tender offer. [*See* SEA Release No. 8712 (1969)]

3) **Offers requiring registration under the 1933 Act.** Where a tender offer involves the public offer of the offeror's securities to the tendered shareholders, the offeror-tenderer must register the offered shares under the 1933 Act (unless some exemption is available).

b. **Exemptions.** The tender offer rules do not apply to the following situations:

1) **Five percent limitation.** Section 14(d)(1) is *not* applicable if, after consummation of the offer, the person making the offer is not the owner of at least 5% or more of the class of equity security tendered. Beneficial ownership is what counts. Beneficial ownership is determined by whether the person controls the voting of the shares. But section 14(d)(3) provides that a group of persons can form a group to make a tender offer and together own the requisite 5%.

a) **Aggregations of voting power subject to tender offer rules--GAF Corp. v. Milstein,** 453 F.2d 709 (2d Cir. 1971).

GAF Corp. v. Milstein

(1) **Facts.** GAF (P) filed a complaint alleging that the four Milsteins (Ds) had failed to file section 13(d) reports and had filed false reports. Together Ds owned 10.25% of the convertible preferred stock of P. P alleges that sometime after July 19, 1968, Ds formed an intent as a group to take over P but then failed to file a 13(d) report. P cites in support the attempt of Ds to put a representative on the board of directors, attempts to disparage management, and a lawsuit charging mismanagement. Later, two of the Ds bought additional shares of common stock, filed 13(d) reports denying any intent to take over the company or buy more shares (which on several occasions were followed by more purchases within a short time). Finally, Ds waged a proxy contest (to elect directors) for control of P (and lost). P seeks an injunction prohibiting Ds from acquiring more stock, soliciting proxies from P shareholders, or voting any shares acquired during the alleged conspiracy. Ds moved for summary judgment, which was granted. P appeals.

(2) **Issue.** Is organizing a group that owns more than 10% of a class of equity security with a view to seeking control of a company a reportable event under section 13(d)?

(3) **Held.** Yes. Reversed and remanded for a full trial.

(a) Section 13(d)(3) provides that any persons acting as a group for the purpose of acquiring, holding, or disposing securities as a group will be deemed a "person" for the purpose of section 13(d).

(b) The complaint alleges that Ds agreed to hold their shares as a group for the purpose of acquiring control of P.

(c) If the complaint is true, then the group "acquired" a voting interest in each other's share for their common purpose. The legislative history of section 13(d) indicates that Congress was interested in reaching any new conglomeration of voting power which might result in a shift in corporate control.

(d) An agreement among a group of shareholders to act together has the same effect as though a single person buys the required amount.

(e) It may be difficult to show when a group is formed; that is the plaintiff's problem and it has the burden of proof on the issue.

(f) There is a private right of action implied under section 13(d). Also, the obligation to file reports under 13(d) implies that the reports be truthful and the issuer of the securities has standing to sue for an injunction requiring that the reports be truthful.

(4) **Comment.** Although section 13(d) requires a "person" to file only if *acquiring* more than 2% of a class of registered stock within a 12-month period, the group was held to have "acquired" a beneficial interest in the prior, individual holdings of its members. The burden of proof is on the plaintiff to show that the defendant "group" has been formed for a "common objective" covered by section 13(d) (e.g., gaining control or ousting current management). Moreover, plaintiff is normally required to show such purpose by objective acts. [*See* Bath Industries v. Blot, 427 F.2d 97 (7th Cir. 1970)] Note that this court, contra to *Milstein*, required additional purchases of shares after formation of the group, and pursuant to group agreement, in order to trigger the reporting requirements of section 13(d).

2) **Equity securities.** Only equity securities registered under section 12 of the 1934 Act are covered by section 14(d)(1) (i.e., registered common stock as opposed to debt securities such as bonds).

3) **Offers made by the issuer for own securities.** Offers made by the issuer for its *own* securities are not covered.

4) **Limited purchases.** Acquisitions made by offerors, where the purchases made in the preceding 12 months do not exceed 2% of the class outstanding, are excluded.

5) **Transactions exempted by rules or regulations of the S.E.C.**

S.E.C. v.
First City
Financial
Corp., Ltd.

6) **Remedies for violation of the tender offer rules--S.E.C. v. First City Financial Corp., Ltd.,** 890 F.2d 1215 (D.C. Cir. 1989).

a) **Facts.** On March 4, 1986, Marc Belzberg (Belzberg), V.P. of First City (D), called the C.E.O. of Bear, Sterns, a Wall Street brokerage firm, and asked Greenberg to buy a large block of shares of Ashland Oil. Belzberg indicates that he only suggested that it would be a "good buy"; Greenberg testifies that Belzberg told him to buy the stock for First City. If purchased for First City, the shares would have pushed First City's Ashland holdings above 5%, triggering the 10-day reporting period of section 13(d) of the 1934 Act, which disclosure statement would have had to be filed on March 14. Between March 4 and 14, Greenberg bought another 330,700 shares. On March 17, Belzberg arranged for a written purchase of all these shares, dressed up to look like the stock had really not been purchased until March 17 (i.e., the price from Bear, Sterns was only slightly above its cost, although the price rose between Greenberg's purchase dates and March 17). Between March 17 and 25, Ds bought another 890,100 shares. Then Ds sent a letter to Ashland proposing a takeover; Ashland rejected the offer and issued a press release disclosing that Ds held between 8 and 9% of its stock. The stock rose 10%, to $52 per share. The next day, First City filed a Schedule 13D disclosure statement, indicating it held 9% and intended to launch a tender offer at $60 per share. The stock rose to $55.75. The District Court discounted Belzberg's testimony and found the stock had been purchased on March 4. The court permanently enjoined Ds from future violations and ordered them to disgorge $2.7 million (the profits on 890,000 shares of Ashland acquired between March 14 and 25, (which were eventually sold back to Ashland), based on the fact that had Ds made the 13(d) disclosure on March 14, they would not have been able to buy the 890,000 shares as cheaply as they did. Ds appeal.

b) **Issue.** Did the District Court abuse its discretion in ordering the injunction and disgorgement of·profits?

c) **Held.** No.

   (1) Any formal or informal means by which a person owns investment or voting power in stock is beneficial ownership. There is sufficient testimony here that Ds owned more than 5% on March 4.

   (2) Ds claim that the Court abused its discretion in ordering disgorgement of profits, and that the measure of disgorgement was excessive.

      (a) Disgorgement, an equitable remedy to prevent unjust enrichment, is given the court by the very fact that it has jurisdiction vested in it.

      (b) Disgorgement is used in insider trading cases; here Ds say the violation is of a technical statute (giving notice). But the 13(d) requirement is at the heart of the tender offer rule, and Ds benefited by not giving the notice (in that they could buy the stock at a lower price than had they given notice on March 14).

   (3) Disgorgement must be related to the wrong; only profits causally related to the wrong done may be ordered returned. Ds argue that there were other variables besides the 13(d) disclosure that caused the

stock to rise after March 25 (which did not exist in the March 14-25 period). For example, Ds say that they held 9% after March 25, while they owned less on March 14. However, it is hard to say exactly how the market would have reacted to different situations, so the rule for calculating disgorgement may not be able to separate legal from illegal profits in an exact manner. The disgorgement holding only need be a reasonable approximation of the profits causally connected to the violation. The S.E.C. met this standard of proof. The burden then shifts to Ds to clearly demonstrate that the disgorgement figure was not such a reasonable approximation. Ds point to four facts; for example, by the 25th they had 9% rather than 5% on the 14th. But, had Ds known they had to disclose on the 14th, they might have purchased the 9% by that date. So Ds failed to meet the burden of proof.

    (4)   This holding may result in actual profits becoming the typical disgorgement measure of damages when section 13(d) is violated.

c.   **Definition of "tender offer."** A "tender offer" is *not* defined in the Act. Generally a "tender offer" is thought to be one that is made "publicly." Generally, the S.E.C. applies a broad definition so as to accomplish the basic remedial purposes of the 1934 Act.

    1)   **Application.** A tender offer has also been found where an offer was made by letter to purchase the stock owned in the Hoover Company by all members of the Hoover family (41%), where the remainder was publicly owned and traded. [*See* Hoover Co. v. Fuqua Industries, Inc., Fed. Sec. L. Rep. (CCH) 97,107 (N.D. Ohio 1979)] The court in *Hoover* cited the seven factors used by the S.E.C. to determine whether a tender offer exists:

        a)   Is there active and widespread solicitation of shareholders?

        b)   Is the solicitation for a substantial percentage of the issuer's stock?

        c)   Is a premium price offered?

        d)   Are the terms of the offer firm?

        e)   Is the offer contingent on the tender of a fixed minimum number of shares?

        f)   Is the offer open only for a limited period?

        g)   Is there pressure on the owners to sell?

    2)   **Compare.** On the other hand, purchase of a 10% interest in Kennecott Copper, where the purchases were made from 50 shareholders over the exchange and from a dozen institutional investors off the exchange, was held not to be a tender offer. The court found no pressure on shareholders to make ill-considered decisions. [*See* Kennecott Copper Corp. v. Curtis-Wright Corp., 584 F.2d 1195 (2d Cir. 1980)]

3) **Corporate acquisition of own stock not tender offer--S.E.C. v. Carter Hawley Hale Stores, Inc.,** 760 F.2d 945 (9th Cir. 1985).

a) **Facts.** Limited made a cash tender offer to purchase 55% of Carter Hawley Hale (D) at $30 per share (D's stock was trading at $24). After some delay D gave a press release opposing the tender and announced that it was selling 1 million shares to General Cinema along with an option to purchase D's subsidiary, Walden Books. The agreement allowed D to direct General Cinema as to how to vote its shares. D also announced that it was going to buy up to 15 million shares of its stock in order to defeat Limited's attempt to take control. Appropriate documents were sent to the S.E.C. and a letter from D's chairman was sent to D's shareholders. From April 16 to April 22, D bought 15 million shares at a price of between $25 and $26 per share; it then increased its authorized amount and bought another 2.5 million shares; it then controlled over 50% of its own stock. After the price reached a high of $32 per share, Limited dropped its competing tender offer, and D's stock fell to $21 per share.

The S.E.C. then brought an injunctive action, arguing that D's purchases were a tender offer in violation of section 13(e) and Rule 13e-4 of the 1934 Act. The district court denied the request for an injunction. The S.E.C. appealed.

b) **Issue.** Was D's market purchase program a "tender offer"?

c) **Held.** No. Affirmed.

(1) The Williams Act was designed to see that investors responding to tender offers get full disclosure of relevant information and that neither management nor the tendering party gets unfair advantage.

(2) Issuer repurchases are governed in part by section 3(e) and Rules 13e-1 and 13e-4.

(3) Rule 13e-1 prohibits an issuer from repurchasing its stock during a third-party tender offer unless it discloses certain information. By inference, however, this section recognizes that not all issuer purchases during a third-party tender offer are themselves tender offers.

(4) Rule 13e-4 indicates that issuers repurchasing their shares may be engaging in tender offers and should be regulated accordingly.

(5) The regulations do not, however, say when a repurchase is a tender offer and when it is not. This decision should be made according to the eight-factor test set forth in *Wellman v. Dickinson*, 475 F. Supp. 783 (S.D.N.Y. 1979), *aff'd on other grounds*, 682 F.2d 355 (2d Cir. 1982), *cert. denied*, 460 U.S. 1069 (1983):

(a) Was there active and widespread solicitation by D? No. The only public announcements were those required by the S.E.C.

(b) Was the solicitation of a substantial percentage of the outstanding stock? The "solicitation" issue is covered in factor one and the "substantial percentage" by factor eight.

(c) Was a premium paid over the market price? No. The relevant price is the existing market price at the time of the offer, not the pre-third-party tender offer market price. A premium will always exist after a third-party tender offer.

(d) Are the terms of the tender offer firm and fixed? No. D engaged in a number of different transactions at different prices.

(e) Was the offer contingent on the tender by shareholders of a fixed minimum number of shares? No. D went into the market and simply bought the number of shares it wanted.

(f) Was the offer open only a limited time? No. It was kept open long enough for D to purchase the shares it wanted. But no specific deadline was set.

(g) Were there shareholder pressure and public announcements accompanying a large accumulation of stock? There was no undue pressure put on shareholders. But D did accumulate a large percentage of the stock.

(6) The district court was within its discretion to have held that not enough of the *Wellman* factors were present to have found a tender offer.

(7) The tender offer test set forth in *S-G Securities* should not be applied.

(a) The test in that case is whether there is publicly announced intention by the purchaser to acquire a block of stock to control the target company and the subsequent rapid acquisition by the purchaser of large blocks and stock through open market purchases and privately negotiated transactions.

(b) This test is too vague and does not give guidance to an issuer as to when its conduct will come under Rule 13e-4 as opposed to Rule 13e-1.

Hanson Trust PLC v. SCM Corp.

4) **Private purchase of shares after termination of tender offer not tender offer--Hanson Trust PLC v. SCM Corp.,** 774 F.2d 47 (1985).

a) **Facts.** Hanson (D) publicly announced its intention to make a cash tender offer of $60 per share for all outstanding shares of SCM (P). D filed the tender offer documents required under the Williams Act. P then announced the formation of a new entity with Merrill Lynch to acquire all shares of P at $70 per share in a leveraged buyout. D increased its tender offer from $60 to $72 per share. D reserved the right to terminate its offer if P granted anyone any option to purchase assets owned by P on terms D believed to be a "lock-up" device.

P entered into a new leveraged buyout agreement with Merrill at $74 per share. The agreement provided that if any group or investor other than Merrill acquired more than one third of P's outstanding shares, Merrill would have the option to buy P's two most profitable businesses. In light of this "poison pill" provision, D terminated its offer. On the same day that D terminated its offer, D made five privately negotiated cash purchases and one open-market purchase of P's stock, acquiring 25% of P's outstanding shares.

P brought suit in the district court for a restraining order to prevent D from acquiring more of P's stock for 24 hours. The TRO was extended by consent pending the court's decision. D claimed that the idea of making market purchases of P's stock was considered only after its tender offer was terminated. P argued that D's cash purchases immediately following the termination of D's tender offer amounted to a *de facto* continuation of D's tender offer and was an attempt to avoid the requirements of the Williams Act. P argued that, unless a preliminary injunction issued, P and its shareholders would be irreparably injured because D would acquire enough shares to defeat the P-Merrill offer. The district court found that D's actions were an attempt to avoid the Williams Act and granted a preliminary injunction.

b) **Issue.** Does the negotiation of private purchases and open market purchases of a target corporation's shares immediately after the purchaser's termination of a tender offer for such shares constitute a tender offer within the meaning of the Williams Act?

c) **Held.** No. Preliminary injunction vacated.

(1) The typical tender offer consists of a general, publicized bid to buy shares of a publicly owned company, the shares of which are traded on a national securities exchange, at a price substantially above the current market price. The offer is usually accompanied by newspaper and other publicity, a time limit on the offer, and a provision fixing a quantity limit on the number of shares to be acquired.

(2) The Williams Act was intended to protect shareholders from being forced to rapidly respond to tender offers without adequate knowledge upon which to base their decisions. Section 14(d) of the Act requires pre-acquisition disclosure of information by solicitors seeking beneficial ownership of more than 5% of the outstanding shares of any class of any equity security registered on a national exchange.

(3) Many of the conditions leading to the enactment of section 14(d) are absent in the case of privately negotiated transactions. Whether a solicitation constitutes a "tender offer" within the meaning of section 14(d) turns on whether, based on the totality of the circumstances, it appears likely that there will be substantial risk that solicitees will lack necessary information to carefully consider the proposal unless the pre-acquisition filing provisions are followed.

(4) D's privately negotiated purchases do not qualify as a tender offer. While the Williams Act was intended to apply in public solicitation involving large numbers of sellers, only six sellers are involved here. At least five of the sellers were highly sophisticated sellers well aware of the essential facts of the transaction. The sellers were not pressured to sell. There was no widespread publicity or public solicitation. The sellers did not receive a premium price. The purchases were not contingent upon the buyer's acquisition of a fixed number or percentage of outstanding shares, and there was no time limit involved.

(5)   D's private purchases did not constitute de facto continuation of the tender offer. D terminated the offer because of the "poison pill" provision. Because D's termination was valid and final, there was no tender offer to continue. There is no indication that D considered the private purchases prior to the termination of the tender offer.

(6)   Section 14(d) was never intended to apply to all acquisitions of more than 5%. If that were the case, there would be no need for section 13(d)(1), which requires disclosure after the acquisition of more than 5%. As D is complying with section 13(d)(1), that is all that is required by the Act.

5)   S.E.C.'s proposed definition. The S.E.C. has proposed, but not yet adopted, a definition of a tender offer. There is a tender offer when:

(i)   During any 45-day period offers are made to more than 10 persons for the acquisition of more than 5% of a class of a registered equity security, *except* that offers made over an exchange or the over-the-counter market at current market prices by brokers or dealers (on behalf of the offeror) in *unsolicited* transactions are exempted.

(ii)   In addition, although not ordinarily covered by paragraph (i) above, if the offer is widely disseminated, and is at a price which is the greater of 5% or $2 above market value, and there is no meaningful opportunity for the shareholders to negotiate the price of the offer, then there is a tender offer.

[SEA Release No. 16385 (1979)]

MAI Basic Four, Inc. v. Prime Computer, Inc.

d.   Who is the "bidder"?--MAI Basic Four, Inc. v. Prime Computer, Inc., 871 F.2d 212 (1st Cir. 1989).

(1)   Facts. MAI and Brooke Partners are trying to take over Prime Computer, Inc. with a cash tender offer. Basic filed a complaint attacking a Massachusetts's takeover statute; Prime counterclaimed that Basic had violated the takeover provisions of the 1934 Act by failing to provide sufficient information concerning the involvement, interests, and financial condition of its investment advisor Drexel Burnham, on the basis that Drexel was a "bidder" as defined by the Act and relevant S.E.C. rules. Prime sought a preliminary injunction, which was granted, pending further disclosures. Basic appeals.

(2)   Issue. Is Drexel a "bidder" so that it must meet the disclosure requirements of section 14(d) of the 1934 Act and S.E.C. rules?

(3)   Held. Yes. Drexel must make further disclosures.

(a)   Drexel is the investment adviser on all phases of the takeover deal; it is to arrange placement of $875 million in notes to finance the deal (and it may agree to buy the notes if it cannot place them); it has an equity interest of 5% in Basic, with a right to buy another 9%; it owns one-third of Brooke's corporate general partner, and 17% in Brooke itself (Brooke is putting up $20 million, the only equity money being put up); in addition, Drexel had the right to appoint one of the three directors of Brooke's corporate general partner (which it had recently relinquished). Prime wants Drexel to disclose its financial statements and the other information required by Schedule 14D-1.

(b) Is a "bidder" the entity formally making the tender offer (and those that control it)? Or does it include others who are central to the offer, motivating forces behind it, and principal players?

(c) In the event of doubt on disclosure questions, courts should err on the side of forcing disclosure rather than limiting it. The statute (section 14(d)(2) defines "person" as an entity or group for the purpose of acquiring securities of the issuer; S.E.C. Rule 14d-1(b)(1) uses the word "bidder" as any person who makes a tender offer or on whose behalf a tender offer is made) includes the "group concept." Other than that, no clear test is given.

(d) So, even though Drexel does not control a majority of the stock of Basic, it is so central to the success of the venture that the district court did not err in finding that it is a "bidder."

(e) Next, the question arises whether the information sought by Prime is material (a substantial likelihood that a reasonable shareholder would consider it important in tendering his shares). It is material since shareholders would want to know the ability of the bidder to pay for the securities sought in the offer and to repay any loans taken out to make the payment. If the bidder is strong, a shareholder might want to wait for a higher price; if weak, then the shareholder might want to sell immediately and take the money. Here Prime valued its stock at $23 to $28 per share; Basic is offering $20. So Drexel's financial condition and a disclosure about a recent plea bargain it made (and other legal difficulties) is material information.

(f) It does not appear, however, that it is material to have Drexel disclose all of the items in Schedule 14D-1.

(g) On making a full disclosure, the injunction should be vacated.

6. **Defensive Tactics.** Most managements of companies which are tendered for, under the threat of losing their jobs, attempt to fight the takeover attempt. They do this in a number of ways.

a. **Litigation.** Management may bring an immediate action against the offeror, alleging that there have been misrepresentations or omissions of material facts in the tender offer. If management is successful in getting even a preliminary injunction, then this will probably kill the tender offer (since the offeror will not want to spend large sums of money to fight a court battle with no certainty that when it is over conditions will be suitable to continue with the offer).

b. **Persuasion of the shareholders.** Management may attempt to persuade the shareholders not to tender their shares. Any such solicitation or recommendation to the holders of a tendered security to accept or reject a tender offer must be made in accordance with rules and regulations set up by the S.E.C. These rules and regulations are contained in section 14(d)(4) and Rule 14d-4 of the 1934 Act.

c. **Issuance of additional shares.** Another strategy is to issue additional shares so that the tender offeror has to buy more to gain control.

d. **Pac-man defense.** The target company may turn on its pursuer and itself make a tender offer for the shares of the initial offeror.

e. **Poison pills.** The essence of this defense is that "rights" are issued to all of the the shareholders of the corporation that is the target, entitling them (i) to purchase additional shares of common stock at a price that is a fraction of the market price upon the happening of certain "triggering events," and (ii) to purchase stock of the tender offeror at the same discounted price after a merger of the target company into the tender offeror.

f. **Stock exchange rules for listing securities and the voting rights of the securities.**

1) **Introduction.** These issues concerning special securities that may be issued as part of a takeover plot, connect with another issue: the power of the S.E.C. to regulate the voting rights relating to securities by regulating the right of stock exchanges to list those securities on the exchanges.

2) **The relevant law.** Section 19 of the 1934 Act gives the S.E.C. authority over the rules of self-regulatory organizations (stock exchanges and associations of brokers and dealers). Section 19(b) requires these organizations to file with the S.E.C. any proposed change in their rules. The S.E.C. is to approve them if it finds they are consistent with the requirements of the Act and the rules and regulations thereunder applicable to the self-regulatory organizations. Then section 19(c) allows the Commission on its own initiative to amend the rules of a self-regulatory organization as it deems necessary or appropriate (i) to ensure the fair administration of the self-regulatory organization, (ii) to conform its rules to requirements of the 1934 Act and the rules and regulations thereunder applicable to such organizations, or (iii) otherwise in furtherance of the purposes of the Act.

3) **Adoption of Rule 19b-4.** General Motors wished to issue a second class of common stock, with one-half vote per share (when compared with regular common stock), as part of its acquisition of Electronic Data Systems, Inc. The New York Stock Exchange filed an amendment to its listing rules with the S.E.C. to permit a change in its one share, one vote rule.

The basis of the NYSE's proposal was that there was competition for listings with other exchanges, and that it had to adopt such changes if other exchanges were going to. Second, public companies, subject to hostile takeover attempts, were increasingly looking to disparate voting rights plans as a defensive tactic. Third, the NYSE wanted to give corporate issuers flexibility in raising capital, structuring acquisitions, and devising their own capital structures. And finally, other protections (such as the requirement of independent boards) provided shareholders adequate protection.

Other exchanges began to follow with similar proposals.

However, the S.E.C. adopted Rule 19b-4, which provided that the rules of exchanges and associations would be amended to prohibit them from listing or continuing to list or from authorizing for or continuing quotations and/or transaction reporting through any inter-dealer quotation system, any of the common stock and equity securities of an issuer that on or after May 15, 1987, issued any securities, or took other corporate action, that had the effect of nullifying, restricting, or disparately reducing the voting rights of shareholders of an outstanding class or classes of common stock registered pursuant to section 12 of the 1934 Act. Rule 19b-4 provided a certain amount of flexibility by permitting an exchange to issue rules, subject to Commission review, that would specify the types of securities issuances or corporate actions covered by, or excluded from, the prohibitions contained in Rule 19c-4. For example, it was clear that the rule would permit initial public offerings or subsequent offerings of stock with equal, lesser, or restricted voting rights (than other outstanding types of stock) because in this situation shareholders willingly and knowingly would purchase such shares with an understanding of the stock's limitations (as opposed to the situation where existing shareholders give up some of their voting rights in complicated transactions involving the ongoing corporation, and it is not very clear what the implications of such a transaction are). [*See* SEA Release No. 24263 (1987)]

4) **Court challenge.** In *The Business Roundtable v. S.E.C.*, 905 F.2d 406 (D.C. Cir. 1990), the court held that the S.E.C. did not have the authority to adopt rule 19c-4; the matter was not a disclosure issue; instead it intruded on an area traditionally left to the states.

g. **Purchase of its own shares.** The management of the tendered company may attempt to have the corporation (or its pension fund, etc.) buy enough shares on the open market to prevent control from going to the offeror.

1) **No outright prohibitions.** There are no outright prohibitions against this. There are, however, some provisions which provide disclosure requirements.

   a) Rule 13e-2 does not relate specifically to tender offers, although its limitations on purchases by issuers of their own securities would apply (*see* discussion of this rule, *infra*, in connection with the subject of a corporation buying its own shares).

   b) Rule 13e-1 of the 1934 Act does preclude an "issuer" from purchasing its own shares during a tender offer being made by another party after that party has filed its Schedule 13D statement and given the issuer notice, but the prohibition *only lasts until* the issuer has filed certain information with the S.E.C. and distributed this information to its equity security holders (such as the amount of securities to be purchased, the purpose of the purchases, etc.).

2) **Purchases by a defensive merger partner—applicable liability provisions.** Section 9(a)(2) (applicable to purchases and sales of securities listed on a national exchange; *see supra*) and Rule 10b-5 (applicable to all securities transactions; *see infra*) have been applied in situations where one company purchased shares on the market in order to defeat the tender offer attempt of another company. In, e.g., *Crane Co. v. Westinghouse Air Brake Co.*, 419 F.2d 787 (2d Cir. 1969), the court held that purchases on the exchange of the tendered company's shares by a rival merger candidate, when accompanied by off-the-exchange sales at less than the prices being paid on the exchange, constituted illegal manipulation in violation of section 9(a)(2) of the 1934 Act.

h. **Merge with another company.** When a tender offer is attempted, the tendered company often looks for another company (a "white knight") to merge with that will promise to employ the management of the tendered company. The rationale given by management for such a merger is that the merger is a "better deal" for shareholders than the tender offer.

i. **Control provisions.** Corporations often take measures in advance of any tender offer in order to prepare for one. These measures are aimed at making it more difficult for a successful tender offer to gain control of the company. For example, the company might stagger the election of its board of directors (elect them serially over a three-year period) so that it is more difficult for the offeror to control the tendered company's board of directors.

j. **Greenmail.** Here the target company buys off a possible bidder by repurchasing its shares from the bidder, either at a premium over the market or at the market price in a market that is inflated by takeover rumors, and then requiring that the bidder sign a "standstill agreement" whereby the bidder agrees not to acquire additional shares of the target company for some period of years.

k. **Lockups.** Sometimes when faced with a tender offer, or as a preventive measure in the event one occurs, management may give an option to buy a key division or key corporate assets (the "crown jewel") to management or some third party.

l. **Standards of state law for reviewing defensive actions.** This area of state corporate law is evolving rapidly, and the tests are not totally clear. On the one hand, officers and directors cannot get by with exercising mere "business judgment"; shareholders are owed more of a duty than this to have their financial interests in maximizing their return from owning stock looked after. On the other hand, courts hesitate to impose a strict duty of loyalty on directors and officers only to look at maximizing present value to the shareholders. In Delaware, the courts have held that defensive actions taken must be "reasonable" in relation to the threat posed. [*See* Unocal Corp. v. Mesa Petroleum Co., 493 A.2d 946 (Del. 1985)] Further, where a company does put itself up for sale, *then* management must act "fairly" in giving consideration to all competing offers; management must also act carefully in fulfilling its fiduciary duties to shareholders (i.e., get accurate facts, expert opinions on value, etc.). [*See* Revlon, Inc. v. MacAndews & Forbes Holdings, Inc., 506 A.2d 173 (Del. 1986)]

The following case is an update on all these possible duties:

1) **A merger plan prior to a hostile cash offer--Paramount Communications, Inc. v. Time, Inc.,** 571 A.2d 1140 (Del. 1989).

   a) **Facts.** Time had 16 directors, 12 of them outside directors. In 1983 several members of the board began to push for expansion of Time into the entertainment business. A committee was formed to create a plan for the 1990s. The recommendation was to expand into entertainment and to consider buying a company to expand the business. Potential candidates, including Paramount (P) and Warner were considered and investigated. Warner was identified as the best prospect, because its businesses were compatible with Time (D) and it was stronger than the other candidates in the entertainment field. Negotiations began; Warner wanted a stock-for-stock swap; Time wanted to control management and the board. In early 1989 the parties reached a decision on the major issues; in March 1989 the boards approved the merger proposal, with a .465 premium in shares to Warner due to its compromise on the management issue and the fact that it was growing faster than Time. New York Stock Exchange rules required that Time's stockholders approve the deal; Delaware law required that Warner stockholders approve. Time also adopted several defensive measures (a no-shop rule; letters from banks that they would not finance any competing offer for Time, etc.). Time was concerned that by making the merger offer with Warner, other companies would think it (Time) was in "play." Time also appointed a committee of outside directors to oversee the merger process. June 23 was set as the stockholder vote date. On June 7, Paramount made an all-cash offer of $175 for each of Time's shares; several conditions were placed on the offer. Time's independent directors, the full board, and management met many times to consider the offer and were advised by financial advisers as to the cash value price for Time (they indicated that P's offer was inadequate). The market price for Time's stock began to rise, exceeding the $175 offer; Time sought to get the New York Stock Exchange to release its requirement of stockholder approval, which the Exchange refused to do. Time's board finally voted that P's offer was a threat to Time's long-range plans, its plan to preserve its culture, and that the combination with Warner was a better long-term value for shareholders. In addition, the board voted to recast its arrangement with Warner into an all-cash buyout of 51% of Warner in order to make its proposal more clearly comparable to Paramount's proposal (this in order to prevent shareholder confusion over the offers). Warner agreed to the new proposal. Paramount raised its offer several times to $200 per share. When these offers were rejected, P sued to enjoin the Time-Warner deal. The trial court denied P's request for a preliminary injunction on the basis that P was unlikely to prevail on the merits. On appeal the trial court was affirmed. P argued that (i) the original Time-Warner deal in March 1989 resulted in a change of control and Time was put up for sale (thus triggering the duties set forth in the *Revlon* case) and that D failed to maximize shareholder values by rejecting P's offer; and (ii) that P's offer triggered *Unocal* duties by D and that in adopting defensive measures, D's board violated its fiduciary duties to its shareholders. The following opinion is the appeal court's decision.

   b) **Issues.** First, did D's board have *Revlon* duties? If so, were they breached? Second, did *Unocal* duties apply? If so, were they breached?

c) **Held.** There were no *Revlon* duties here. There were *Unocal* duties, but they were ***not*** breached by D's actions.

(1) Directors have a duty to manage the corporation; this does not belong to the shareholders. This includes the right to set a corporate course of action. *The board is required to act in an informed manner*. But it is not under any per se duty to maximize shareholder value in the short term, even in the context of a takeover offer. The real issue here is whether entering into the proposed merger with Warner put Time up for sale, thus raising a *Revlon* duty to treat all buyout proposals equally. Here, Time's board in negotiating with Warner did not make the dissolution or breakup of Time inevitable (in comparison with *Revlon*, where the breakup was inevitable). There are two situations where *Revlon* duties apply: where the corporation initiates an active bidding process to sell the company; and where in response to a takeover bid, the corporation abandons its long-term strategy and seeks an alternative bidder. On the other hand, where the corporation receives an offer and then adopts defensive measures so as to continue its own corporate strategy, no *Revlon* duty exists. Here there is no *Revlon* duty: one does not arise simply because D was concerned that it was being put in play by the Warner offer; nor does the second Time-Warner deal show any intent of D to abandon its long-range strategy or show any inevitability that Time was up for sale.

(2) With respect to P's *Unocal* claim, there is ample evidence that D's decision to expand its business by merger with Warner was entitled to protection of the business judgment rule (that is, all that directors must show is they acted with good business judgment).

As to the second Time-Warner deal, the trial court found it was done as a defensive measure to protect against the success of the P's offer. In this case, *Unocal* does apply. Thus, the business judgment rule does ***not*** apply until the requirements of *Unocal* are fulfilled. Thus, the board has the burden of proving that it had (i) reasonable grounds for believing that a danger to corporate policy and effectiveness existed; and (ii) that the defense measures applied were reasonable in light of the threats posed.

Directors prove the first part by demonstrating good faith and a reasonable investigation. We have held in the past that a refusal to entertain a buyout offer may comport with a valid exercise of a board's business judgment, even where the offer is an all-cash, all-shares offer falling within a range of values that a shareholder might reasonably prefer. *Unocal* stands for the broad proposition that the board may consider a broad range of matters as a threat to the corporation posed by a takeover offer; inadequate price is not the single determining factor. So the board is not limited to comparing the value alone in competing offers. Nor is the court to substitute its judgment for the board's judgment by simply calculating the values of competing offers. Here the Time board not only considered the relative values of P's and Warner's offers, but the board reasonably concluded that P's offer posed other fundamental threats to D (P's offer was conditional; it threatened D's culture, etc.). Thus, the evidence supports the trial court's finding that D's conclusion that P's offer posed a threat to corporate policy was in good faith and not dominated by motives to either entrench management or other self-interest. It is also clear that D diligently sought information concerning its corporate policy, considered all possible alternatives (including a possible arrangement with P) in pursuit of its policy. Rejection of P's offer was not uninformed.

Finally, the response to the threat posed must be reasonable. The corporation that receives a buyout offer is not obligated to drop its corporate plans and pursue the offer, unless there is no reasonable basis to pursue its corporate strategy further. Here the board has a strategy and reacted to P's offer as a threat, but its response did not force its strategy on the shareholders. First, P could have tendered for all the shares of Time-Warner after their merger. Or P could have removed the conditions to its offer, putting more pressure on D's board to consider its offer.

2) **The defensive use of ESOPs and lockups--NCR Corp. v. AT&T Co.,** 761 F. Supp. 475 (D.C. Ohio 1991).

a) **Facts.** AT&T made a hostile cash tender offer for all of NCR's common stock at $90 per share. NCR had a three-year staggered board; however, by calling a special meeting of shareholders, the entire board could be replaced by a vote of 80% of all outstanding NCR shares; 70% of NCR's shares had been tendered to AT&T; it called for a special meeting for March 28, 1991. NCR had considered ESOP on prior occasions, primarily as a way of putting more stock in friendly employee hands, but it had never been able to resolve various complications involved with adopting such a plan and so the idea had been dropped. In December 1990, in the face of AT&T's offer, NCR's board began considering an ESOP again; the same problems existed, but NCR management chose to ignore them and go forward. The employee benefits people in NCR were not consulted; skimpy information was given to directors; in addition, such plans were less attractive from a tax standpoint than earlier, yet the plan was adopted. Thus, on February 20, 1991, nine days before the record date for determining votes at the special meeting, NCR issued 5.5 million shares of convertible preferred stock to an ESOP trustee at $90.75 per share. Each share was convertible into eight-tenths of a common share at $113 per share (25% above the market price); but each share got one full vote per share. Further, each of NCR's 24,000 salaried employees got one free share, whether or not they elected to participate in the ESOP. Also, the remaining unallocated shares would be voted by the trustee, in the same way employees voted the shares they owned. So about 8% of NCR's voting power was placed in employee hands. The plan was financed by the trustee issuing NCR a non-recourse promissory note; NCR was to provide the trustee with the necessary funds annually to pay for the note (if employee purchases of stock was insufficient to do so). No legal opinion was secured that the stock was validly issued (and there is doubt that it was). Further, holders of the preferred stock were benefited by a "reset" provision, so that if the NCR stock dropped (as it would if AT&T's offer were defeated), the conversion price for preferred stockholders will be reset at a lower price; this could cause a substantial dilution to the common shareholders. Also, preferred stockholders have the option at any time of redeeming for the conversion price of the common stock, *or* getting back their original price for the preferred, so they cannot lose either way. Everything is loaded against AT&T, so the incentive is for employees owning the stock to vote against AT&T's offer; i.e., if AT&T wins, the preferred stock owned is converted to cash and put in a retirement plan—the preferred stockholder loses the profit potential of participation in the ESOP plan. Further, if AT&T goes away, the price of the common stock of NCR will drop and the reset provision will apply, dropping the conversion price for preferred stockholders. So it is clear that the 8% of NCR's voting power in the ESOP will vote against AT&T's offer; with stock controlled by management, it appears that AT&T will not get the 80% it needs to replace NCR's board.

NCR sought a declaratory judgment that the ESOP was valid; AT&T counter-claimed, requesting that the ESOP shares be enjoined from voting at the special meeting.

b) **Issue.** Is the primary purpose of the ESOP to serve a valid corporate purpose or is it to be a defense against a hostile takeover attempt, allowing management to entrench itself?

c) **Held.** The primary purpose is to serve as a defense to a hostile takeover attempt.

   (1) Where a good corporate purpose is furthered, and this is the principal motivation for an action by the board, the fact that the consummation of a transaction may also have some effect on securing control of the corporation is immaterial. The issue is simply, is the transaction fair to the corporation?

   (2) If the transaction is legal, and there is a legitimate purpose, then the courts will use a balancing test to determine if the purpose other than securing control was the primary purpose.

   (3) Here there was a control purpose; there also appears to be a purpose to give an ownership incentive to employees.

   (4) Use of the balancing test leads to the conclusion that the primary purpose here was to entrench management: the timing of the adoption of the plan, the size of the shares put into the plan; giving stock to salaried employees and then allowing all shares in the plan to be voted by these employees; the fact that all discussions of the plan were in a context of trying to ward off the tender offer; the personnel department had no input into adoption of the plan; the preferred stock was structured so that holders would vote against AT&T.

   (5) NCR offers the defense that AT&T's offer was seriously undervalued and it acted to protect NCR shareholders; but it offered no evidence of this fact.

   (6) Delaware law allows directors to act in their best "business judgment" in adopting defensive plans, but only after showing (i) that there are reasonable grounds for believing that a danger to corporate policy and effectiveness exists, and (ii) that the defensive measures chosen were adopted by the board because of their reasonable relation to the threat posed. NCR

did not prove either of these preconditions for invoking use of the business judgment rule.

(7) Finally, the plan is unfair to NCR itself; the corporation foots the bill for the plan; it did not even get outside financing for the plan so that money could have flowed into NCR for use in expanding its business; also, the preferred stockholders participating in the plan gained an unfair advantage over common stockholders. Thus, AT&T has met its burden of proof on the counterclaim. The ESOP is invalid and unenforceable.

7. **State Anti-Takeover Legislation.** Many states now have statutes regulating takover bids.

a. **First-generation statutes.** The so-called first-generation statutes imposed very stringent requirements on takeover bids. In *Edgar v. MITE Corp.,* 457 U.S. 624 (1982), the Supreme Court held one such statute, the Illinois Takeover Act, unconstitutional. The Court considered the following theories:

1) **Supremacy Clause.** Three of the six judges who passed on the merits of the case held that the Illinois statute was unconstitutional under the Supremacy Clause, on the ground that a major objective of the Williams Act was maintaining a neutral balance between management and the bidder, and the Illinois Act violated this balance.

2) **Commerce Clause.** All six judges who addressed the merits held that the Illinois Act violated the Commerce Clause, by:

a) Directly regulating commerce taking place across state lines, because it applied to prevent an offeror from making an offer even to non-Illinois shareholders; and

b) Imposing an excessive burden on interstate commerce, by permitting the secretary of state to block a nationwide tender offer.

b. **Second-generation statutes.** After the decision in *Edgar v. MITE Corp.,* a number of states adopted "second-generation" takeover statutes. These statutes fall into two major categories: "fair-price" statutes and "control share acquisition" statutes.

1) **Fair price statutes.** Under the fair price statutes, an acquiror must pay all shareholders the "best price" paid to any one shareholder.

2) **Control share acquisition statutes.** Under control share acquisition statutes, if a designated stock-ownership threshold is crossed by an acquiring shareholder, he cannot vote the acquired shares without the approval of a majority of the disinterested shareholders.

3) **Applications--CTS Corp. v. Dynamics Corp. of America**, 481 U.S. 69 (1987).

a) **Facts.** Indiana passed a Control Shares Acquisitions Act (CSAA) that applied to any business incorporated in Indiana that has: (i) 150 or more shareholders; (ii) its principal place of business, its principal office, or substantial assets within Indiana; and (iii) either: (a) more than 10% of its shareholders resident in Indiana, (b) more than 10% of its shares owned by Indiana residents, or (c) 10,000 shareholders resident in Indiana. An entity acquires "control shares" in such a corporation whenever it acquires voting power to or above 20%, 33.3%, or 50%. Voting power of these acquired shares is only granted on petition and approval of a majority vote of all disinterested shareholders of each class of stock. The acquirer can request a meeting for such vote within 50 days; if voting power is not granted, the corporation *may* buy back the stock, or if no petition calling for a vote is asked for, the corporation can buy back the stock.

Dynamics owned 9.6% of CTS Corporation, an Indiana corporation. CTS elected to be governed by the new Act. Dynamics tendered for 1 million shares of CTS, which would bring its interest to 27.5%. Dynamics sued, alleging that the Act violated the Commerce Clause and was preempted by the Williams Act. The district court agreed with Dynamics; the circuit court affirmed. Dynamics appealed.

b) **Issues.**

(1) Does the Federal Williams Act preempt Indiana's state law?

(2) Does the state law violate the Commerce Clause?

c) **Held.** No to both issues. Reversed.

(1) The state law is not preempted by the Williams Act.

    (a) The state law is consistent with the intent of the Williams Act —it protects the shareholders against both management *and* the tender offeror. Neither contending party gets an advantage; it does not impose an indefinite delay on tender offers; it does not impose a government official's view of fairness on the buyer and selling shareholders. The shareholders can evaluate the fairness of the proposed terms.

    (b) If the tender offeror fears an adverse shareholder vote, it can make a conditional offer, accepting shares on condition that the shares receive the voting rights within a certain time period.

    (c) The Williams Act does not preempt all state regulation of tender offers, or state laws that limit or delay the free exercise of power after a tender offer (*example*: staggering the terms of the members of the board of directors).

(2) The state law does not violate the Commerce Clause.

(a) The state law does not discriminate against interstate commerce by imposing a greater burden on out-of-state offerors than Indiana offerors.

(b) The law does not adversely affect interstate commerce by subjecting activities to inconsistent regulations of more than one state. It applies only to corporations incorporated in Indiana.

(c) It is an accepted practice for states to regulate the corporation it creates. Thus, it is appropriate for the state to regulate the rights that are acquired by purchasing the shares of the corporation in order to promote stable relationships among the parties involved in the state's corporations.

(d) It is not for this Court to decide, or the intent of the Commerce Clause to promote, any specific economic theory—i.e., whether tender offers are good or bad.

(e) There is no conflict with the provisions or purposes of the Williams Act.

d) **Concurrence** (Scalia, J.). If the law does not discriminate against interstate commerce or risk inconsistent regulation, then it does not offend the Commerce Clause. It is irrelevant whether it protects the shareholders of Indiana corporations.

e) **Dissent** (White, Blackmun, Stevens, JJ.). The law undermines the policy of the Williams Act by preventing minority shareholders in some cases from acting in their best interests by selling their stock. Thus, the law directly inhibits interstate commerce (i.e., the interstate market in securities).

c. **Other statutes.** Some new ("third-generation") statutes do not fall into either the control-share acquisition or the fair-price patterns. For example, the New York statute provides for a five-year delay between the time a tender offer occurs and the time the target can be merged or otherwise combined with the bidder, unless the transaction was approved by the target's board of directors prior to the date control was acquired. [N.Y. Bus. Corp. Law §912] The Delaware statute imposes a prohibition on combinations between the bidder and the target, subject to certain exceptions, for three years. [Del. Gen. Corp. Law §103]

1) **Application--Amanda Acquisition Corp. v. Universal Foods Corp.**, 877 F.2d 496 (7th Cir. 1989).

a) **Facts.** Wisconsin passed an anti-takeover statute which provided that no firm incorporated in Wisconsin *and* having its headquarters, substantial operations, or 10% of its shares or shareholders there, could engage in a business combination with a shareholder holding 10% or more of the voting stock for three years after the interested stockholder's acquisition date, *unless* the board approved such a

Amanda
Acquisition
Corp. v.
Universal
Foods Corp.

subsequent combination before the stock acquisition date. Thus, if A bought 10% of XYZ Corp. and then wanted to merge XYZ, this could not be done unless A got board approval for his purchase or the merger before the tender offer. Even after the time is up, the bidder has to get a majority of the remaining shares to approve the business combination. Ninety percent of all tender offers are contingent on a follow-up merger between bidder and target. Plaintiff (Amanda) tendered for more than 10% of Universal; it sues to have the state statute declared unconstitutional as a violation of the Commerce Clause and as preempted by the Williams Act.

b) **Issue.** Is the Wisconsin law preempted? Is it a violation of the Commerce Clause?

c) **Held.** No to both issues.

(1) Section 28(a) of the 1934 Act provides that states may enact laws that do not conflict with the 1934 Act or rules under the Act. The 1934 Act has no provisions dealing with mergers with controlling shareholders after a tender offer.

(2) Courts are reluctant to infer preemption of state laws in areas traditionally regulated by the states; mergers and sales of assets are areas regulated by the states.

(3) The basic idea of preemption is larger than the idea that Congress in drafting the Williams Act wanted to create a neutral battleground between bidder and target. States may still favor one or the other on certain conditions.

(4) What must be observed is the federal process of making tender offers. The Wisconsin law does this. It also further regulates internal corporate affairs by preventing business combinations after the tender offer for a period of years. This makes tender offers in Wisconsin less attractive; but so does a state law allowing staggered boards of directors, and such a law is within the power of the states to enact.

(5) Federal law does not grant investors the right to receive tender offers. So there is no problem with Wisconsin enacting a law which discourages them, as long as the process of making them is left alone, as required by the Williams Act.

(6) There is no discrimination here by state law against interstate commerce; both intrastate and interstate commerce are treated the same.

(7) So the question is whether the law unreasonably injures interstate commerce. But the recent trend of the Supreme Court is to only look at the discrimination issue. It has avoided the issue of whether the benefits of the state law outweigh the consequences to interstate commerce from the regulation.

(8) Here the law regulates the internal affairs of Wisconsin corporations. No interstate transaction is regulated or forbidden. All investors, in-state and out-of-state, are treated alike; all bidders are treated alike.

(9) Wisconsin does not have to leave bidders with a meaningful opportunity for success in a tender offer.

(10) Finally, bidders have options: since all have the same constraints, they can lower the price offered to take account of the law, or they can operate an acquired company as a subsidiary for three years, etc.

d) **Comment.** The language of the case is overbroad. The Supreme Court will undoubtedly look at state regulations in terms of how much impact they have on interstate commerce, even if they are not discriminatory. And the courts may also want to look at the "neutral battlefield" concept as a basis for determining whether a state law is preempted by the Williams Act.

8. Going Private and a Corporation's Purchase of Its Own Stock.

a. **Introduction.** There are several possible situations here. First "going private" is a situation where a group of controlling shareholders take the corporation public and then wish later to buy out the minority, public shareholders so that the company can be private once again. Then there are "management buyouts," by which the management of a corporation, owning a small percentage of the stock, secures debt financing to use in buying out all other shareholders (any shareholders declining to sell face the possibility that there will be no market for their stock after the buy-out is done). Then there is the situation where a corporation may simply wish to buy back some of its shares to reduce the number outstanding.

1) **Application--Kaufmann v. Lawrence,** 386 F. Supp. 12 (S.D.N.Y. 1974).

Kaufmann v. Lawrence

a) **Facts.** Wells, Rich, Greene, Inc., a successful advertising firm started by Lawrence, sold shares to the public twice, for amounts aggregating $14 million. An expert valued the stock currently at $20 to $22 per share; but the market was depressed ($5), and Lawrence and the board of directors made an offer of $3 in cash plus an $8 note per share to buy out all shares except those owned by officers and directors. Plaintiff is a shareholder who sues in a class action to enjoin the going private offer, under sections 14(e) and Rule 10b-5. Plaintiff argues that there were failures to disclose in the offering documents, including a failure to disclose what the officers and directors had originally paid for their stock.

b) **Issue.** Is there anything inherently wrong or illegal with a company's offering to buy back all of its publicly held stock at a price much lower than the shareholders paid for the stock?

c) **Held.** No. The company can make the offer, buy back the stock, and if fewer than 300 shareholders remain afterward, it can avoid any reporting under the 1934 Act, so that it will be a private company. It makes no difference whether the transaction is "fair" or "unfair." Management may take advantage of an economic downturn and a low market value for the company stock.

b. **Reasons for a buyout.** There are several.

1) **Justifiable reasons.** Management may feel that the stock is undervalued and that earnings per share of the company can be increased by reducing the number of shares outstanding.

2) **Manipulative reasons.** There are also many manipulative reasons for such purchases (such as in the context of a tender offer fight—to prevent the tender offeror from being able to buy the securities).

c. **Applicable rules and regulations.** The following rules apply to a corporation's purchase of its own shares.

1) **No outright prohibitions.** There are no outright prohibitions in the securities laws on the issuer purchasing its shares when they have been tendered by another company.

a) **Tender offer provisions.** As a matter of fact, such an offer is *exempt* from the provisions of sections 13(d) and 14(d) of the 1934 Act. However, a tender offer by the issuer *is* subject to the fraud provisions applicable to tender offers generally (*see* discussion of section 14(e), *supra*).

b) **General liability provisions.** In addition, there are some general liability provisions in the 1934 Act that may apply to the issuer's purchase of its own shares. For example, section 9(a)(2) (applicable to purchases and sales of securities list on a national exchange), and Rule 10b-5 (applicable to all securities transactions) have been applied in situations where one company purchased shares on the market in order to defeat the tender offer attempt of another company. [Crane Co. v. Westinghouse Air Brake Co., *supra*]

2) **Manipulative market transactions.** Early cases in the federal courts took the view that—absent some market manipulation, or failure to disclose full information concerning the transaction to the shareholders affected—a company's tender offer for its own shares did *not* raise a federal question under the 1934 Act, at least where the sole ground for attacking the transaction was that it was "unfair" to minority shareholders. [Popkin v. Bishop, 464 F.2d 714 (2d Cir. 1972)] However, where a corporation purchased its own shares as part of a plan to manipulate the market price for its securities, several provisions of the 1934 Act *were* held to apply. [S.E.C. v. Georgia-Pacific Corp., Fed. Sec. L. Rep. (CCH) para. 91,692 (S.D.N.Y. 1966)]

a) **Example.** In 1976, in a situation where the parent corporation attempted to merge the remaining 10% of its 90% owned subsidiary (paying cash for the minority shareholders' stock), the Second Circuit held that a Rule 10b-5 issue *was* raised by allegations that the transaction was unfair to the minority shareholders who were cashed out in the transaction. However, the Supreme Court later rejected the theory that a company's purchase of the shares of minority shareholders in order to merge a subsidiary corporation into the parent—in full compliance with state law, but with no business purpose other than to eliminate minority shareholders—stated a claim under Rule 10b-5 in the absence of any misrepresentation or failure to disclose material facts. [Green v. Santa Fe Industries, 533 F.2d 1283 (2d Cir. 1976), *rev'd*, 430 U.S. 462 (1977)]

(1) Note. A crucial factor in the *Santa Fe* decision was the existence of an *adequate state remedy* (appraisal of the fair market value of the minority shareholders' stock by the court).

(2) Note. Thus, it appears that, under the federal securities laws, there are no outright prohibitions on the issuer purchasing its own shares, even when the sole purpose is to reduce the interest of minority shareholders, at least where the only allegation is "unfairness" of the purchase terms and the minority shareholders have an adequate state remedy.

3) Safe harbor rule. The S.E.C. has adopted Rule 10b-18 to provide a "safe harbor" from liability for manipulation in connection with purchases by an issuer, and certain related persons, of the issuer's common stock. The issuer or other person will not incur liability under the antimanipulative provisions of section 9(a)(2) or Rule 10b-5 if purchases are effected in compliance with the safe harbor rule. [*See* S.E.C. Release No. 34-19244 (1982)] In order to come within the safe harbor, an issuer must comply with the rule's so-called purchasing conditions:

a) Single broker-dealer limitation. All Rule 10b-18 purchases must be made from or through only one broker or dealer on any single day. However, the single broker-dealer limitation does not apply to Rule 10b-18 purchases which are not solicited by or on behalf of the issuer or an affiliated purchaser.

b) Timing conditions. Essentially, a Rule 10b-18 purchase cannot constitute the opening transaction and cannot be made during the one-half hour of trading, with regard to exchange-traded securities and other securities as to which last-sale information is reported to the consolidated trading report tape for the securities markets. As to NASDAQ securities, if a Rule 10b-18 purchase is made in any other manner than on a national securities exchange, such purchase will be allowed if a current independent bid quotation for the security is reported in Level 2 of the NASDAQ reporting system.

c) Price conditions.

(1) Reported securities. The price limit for Rule 10b-18 purchases of reported securities would be the higher of the last sale price reported in the consolidated system or the highest independent published bid, as defined in Rule 11Acl-1(a)(9), regardless of the market reporting that figure.

(2) Exchange-traded securities. The price limit applicable to purchases of exchange-traded securities in transactions on exchange is the higher of the highest current independent quotation or the last sale price on such exchange.

(3) NASDAQ securities. Rule 10b-18 purchases of NASDAQ securities otherwise than on an exchange may be made at a net price no higher than the lowest current independent offer quotation reported in Level 2 of NASDAQ.

(4) Over-the-counter securities. Rule 10b-18 purchases of securities (that are neither NASDAQ securities nor reported securities) otherwise than on an exchange may be made at the lowest current independent offer quotation ascertained on the basis of reasonable inquiry.

d) Volume limitations. Under Rule 10b-18, an issuer may purchase up to 25% of the average daily trading volume in the stock during the preceding four calendar weeks. Block purchases (as defined in the rule) and privately negotiated purchases are *not* required to be included in computing the 25% limitation. The Commission concluded that a 25% purchasing condition was appropriate in that S.E.C. cases concerning manipulation in the context of issuer repurchases have historically involved conduct outside the conditions of Rule 10b-18, including a volume limitation of 25%.

(1) Note. Paragraph (c) of Rule 10b-18 provides that no presumption shall arise that purchases not in conformity with the limitations of the safe harbor rule violate the antimanipulative provisions of the securities laws. Thus, Rule 10b-18 safe harbor operates to impose no per se volume prohibition on issuer repurchases, and the Commission noted that there may be circumstances in which an issuer would be justified in exceeding the volume conditions.

e) Disclosure requirements. Rule 10b-18 does not contain any express disclosure provisions. The obligation to disclose information concerning repurchases of an issuer's stock depends on whether the information is material under the circumstances. The S.E.C. has also pointed out that other relevant provisions of the federal securities laws, and existing policies and procedures of the various self-regulatory organizations, impose disclosure responsibilities that appear to be sufficient to ensure that investors and the marketplace in general receive adequate information concerning issuer repurchases.

(1) But note. Rule 10b-18 is *not* a safe harbor for violations of Rule 10b-5 which may occur in the course of an issuer repurchase program but which do not entail manipulation. For example, Rule 10b-18 confers no immunity from possible Rule 10b-5 liability where the issuer engages in repurchases while in possession of favorable, material nonpublic information concerning its securities.

f) Amendment to Rule 10b-6. Rule 10b-6 prohibits an issuer from purchasing its own securities of a specific class when such securities are the subject of a distribution. This had been interpreted to mean, for example, that if securities convertible into common stock were outstanding, then the issuer could not purchase any of its common stock (since the convertible securities might be convertible—in effect, the underlying common stock was still being distributed). Paragraph (f) of Rule 10b-6 has been amended to eliminate the need for an issuer or any person whose purchases would be attributable to the issuer to seek specific exemptive or interpretive relief from Rule 10b-6 to permit purchases of any class of the issuer's stock solely because the issuer is involved in a technical distribution.

4) **Other S.E.C. rules under the 1934 Act.** Section 13(e) of the 1934 Act provides that the S.E.C. may make rules and regulations governing an issuer's purchase of its own registered securities. The S.E.C. has adopted several rules pursuant to this authority:

a) **Rule 13e-1.** This rule precludes an issuer from purchasing its own shares during a tender offer by another party after that party has filed its schedule 13D statement and given the issuer notice, but *only until the issuer has filed certain information* with the S.E.C. and distributed this information to its equity security holders (e.g., the amount of securities to be purchased, the purpose of the purchases, etc.). An "issuer" for purposes of Rule 13e-1 includes any person controlling the issuer; hence, most officers, directors and issuer pension funds would be covered.

b) **Rule 13e-3.** This rule covers certain "going private" transactions where the securities involved are registered under section 12 of the 1934 Act or are issued by a company required to file periodic reports pursuant to section 15(d) of the 1934 Act. It requires extensive disclosures, prohibits fraud or untrue statements, and requires compliance with specific administrative procedures.

c) **Rule 13e-4.** This rule has been adopted by the S.E.C. to regulate tender and exchange offers made by an issuer for its own securities. This rule applies to any issuer who has a class of equity securities registered pursuant to section 12 of the 1934 Act or is required to filed periodic reports pursuant to section 15(d) of the 1934 Act. The rule prohibits fraud or untrue statements in covered transactions and requires that extensive disclosures be made in advance to the issuer's shareholders. Schedule 13e-4 sets forth the information that must be filed with the S.E.C. on commencement of the tender offer. The rule also regulates the manner in which the offer may be made (similar to section 14(d) of the 1934 Act)— i.e., tendered shareholders have withdrawal rights, etc. [*See* SEA Release No. 16112 (1979)]

d) **Rule 10b-6.** This rule prohibits an issuer from purchasing its own securities of a specific class when such securities are the subject of a distribution. This had been interpreted to mean, for example, that if securities convertible into common stock were outstanding, then the issuer could not purchase any of its common stock (since the convertible securities might be convertible—in effect, the underlying common stock was still being distributed). Now that rule 13e-4 has been adopted (*see* above), the S.E.C. has adopted an amendment to Rule 10b-6 that exempts tender offers from 10b-6 if the tender offer would be subject to Rule 10b-6 solely because the issuer has outstanding a class of securities which is immediately convertible into or exchangeable for the security that is the subject of the tender offer. [SEA Release No. 16645 (1980)]

IV. CIVIL LIABILITIES UNDER THE FEDERAL SECURITIES LAWS

A. IMPLIED CIVIL LIABILITIES

1. **Introduction.** The express civil liabilities in the securities acts have not historically been as important (with the possible exception of section 11 of the 1933 Act) as the implied liabilities. The reason for this is that plaintiffs have preferred an action under Rule 10b-5 of the 1934 Act or some other implied civil liability provision. Courts generally held that these implied civil liabilities were subject to fewer restrictions than the actions under one of the express liability sections. However, the express liability provisions have become more important recently because the Supreme Court has begun to restrict the availability of causes of action under Rule 10b-5 and has held that no implied civil liability will arise merely as the result of a violation of some section of the securities statutes or an S.E.C. rule.

2. **Regulation of Proxy Solicitations.**

    a. **Power of attorney.** A proxy is a power of attorney to vote shares owned by someone else. At common law, proxies were illegal, but today state statutes permit proxies.

    b. **Regulation by the states.** The regulation of shareholder proxies is a central part of state corporate law. Thus, the states regulate other important aspects of proxy solicitation, including the extent to which the expenses of a proxy contest can be paid by the corporation and how the shareholders' meeting is conducted (including matters relating to the counting of proxies, etc.).

        1) **State remedies.** Thus, remedies for fraud in solicitation of proxies may be available under state law.

        2) **Federal remedies.** But the federal courts have exclusive jurisdiction over the application for the federal proxy rules.

    c. **Overview of the federal proxy rules.**

        1) **Proxy solicitation as a means of corporate control.** The solicitation of proxies by corporate management (or by a faction competing against management) has become the most effective means of establishing or maintaining control over the corporation—i.e., control may be maintained, not by purchasing a majority of the outstanding voting stock, but rather by soliciting proxies from many individual shareholders whose aggregate votes constitute the needed majority.

        2) **The basic provision of the 1934 Act.** To prevent abuses in the proxy solicitation process, authority to regulate proxies of registered securities is given to the S.E.C. in section 14(a) of the 1934 Act.

3) Purposes of the rules adopted by the S.E.C. Under the authority given by section 14(a) of the 1934 Act, the S.E.C. has adopted rules for the regulation of proxy solicitation. These rules are designed to accomplish three objectives:

a) Full disclosure. Those soliciting proxies or attempting to prevent others from soliciting them must give full disclosure of all material information to the shareholders being solicited. [*See* SEA Rules 14a-3 to 14a-6]

b) Fraud. The use of fraud in the solicitation of proxies is made unlawful. [*See* SEA Rule 14a-9]

c) Shareholder solicitation. Also, shareholders (other than management) may also solicit proxies from other shareholders, and management must include in its proxy statement proper proposals made by these shareholders. [*See* SEA Rule 14a-8]

4) Securities to which applicable. The federal proxy rules are applicable to all companies with securities registered under section 12 of the 1934 Act (i.e., to all "registered" companies (*see supra*).

d. The disclosure requirements.

1) Where proxies are solicited—the proxy statement. The proxy rules require that anyone soliciting proxies must submit the material used in the solicitation to the S.E.C. in advance of the solicitation. The proxy rules set forth what must be disclosed to the shareholders (essentially all material facts regarding matters to be voted on by the shareholders; also, participants in the proxy solicitation must be identified, etc.). [*See* SEA Schedule 14A]

2) Where proxies are not solicited—the information statement. Where a matter requires shareholder vote (such as occurs at an annual meeting of shareholders), then even if proxies are *not* being solicited, the issuer must still file with the S.E.C. (and distribute to shareholders) the information which would be required to be transmitted in a proxy statement (if proxies were actually being solicited). [*See* SEA §14(c) and Schedule 14C] In effect, this requirement ensures that the corporation periodically reports to its shareholders.

3) Distribution of annual reports. In addition, where a proxy solicitation is made by management for a shareholders' meeting where directors are to be elected, then the proxy statement (or the information statement where proxies are not actually solicited) must be accompanied by an annual report by the issuer. Among other things, this report must contain certified financial statements for the previous two years.

e. What constitutes a proxy solicitation? A "solicitation" is any communication to the shareholders which is reasonably calculated to result in (i) the granting, (ii) the withholding, or (iii) the revocation of a proxy. [*See* SEA Rule 14a-1]

1) Thus, the proxy rules even apply to situations where the party sending the communication is not actually soliciting a voting proxy.

2) For example, the party may send a communication attempting to influence the shareholders *not* to give their proxies to management. This is covered by the proxy rules.

f. Shareholder lists.

1) Normally state law governs the matter of when a corporation must make a shareholders' list available to a shareholder.

2) The federal proxy rules do *not* require that management provide a shareholders' list in all cases, but where management is itself soliciting proxies, management must either provide a shareholder a complete shareholder list or mail a shareholder's solicitation material to the other shareholders.

g. Shareholder proposals.

1) **Introduction.** As an alternative to an independent proxy solicitation, a shareholder who would be entitled to vote at the shareholders' meeting to which a proxy statement sent by management relates (and who is a shareholder at the time the proposal is submitted) may serve notice on management of his intention to propose action at the shareholders' meeting.

   a) If the notice of proposed action conforms to the proxy rules, then management must set forth the proposal in its own proxy statement and make provisions in its proxy form for an indication of shareholder preference with respect to the proposal (at no expense to the proposing shareholder). [*See* SEA Rule 14a-8]

   b) The shareholder may also include a 200-word statement in support of the proposal.

2) **Bases for turning down shareholder proposals.** Where management opposes the shareholder proposal, it must file the proposal and the reasons opposing it with the S.E.C. The S.E.C. will review the proposal and give an indication whether it agrees or disagrees (in the form of an indication as to whether it would issue a no-action letter if management omits the proposal from the proxy solicitation). Management may properly turn down shareholder proposals in the following situations:

   (i) *Not a proper subject for action by shareholders.*

   (ii) *Proposals relating to "ordinary business operations" of the issuer.*

   (iii) *Proposals not relating to a corporate purpose* (such as promotion of a religious cause, etc).

   (iv) *Elections of directors.* The shareholder's proposal method may *not* be used as a means of opposing management's proposal for the election of directors, nor may it be used to counter proposals submitted by management. [*See* SEA Rules 14a-8(a) and (c)]

h. Proxy contests.

1) **Typical situations.** Typically, this type of fight arises where (i) the insurgent shareholders have acquired a substantial position in the company and want to control the company through the election of a majority of the directors (and so solicit shareholder proxies in order to elect their slate of directors), or (ii) the insurgent shareholders have proposed a merger or have tendered the shares of the company and company management seeks to avoid such a loss of control to the insurgents by merging with another company (a so-called defensive merger, which must be voted on by the company's shareholders; thus, management solicits proxies in favor of the defensive merger and the insurgents oppose such a favorable vote).

2) **The atmosphere of a proxy contest.** A proxy contest can involve many mailings and personal solicitations of the shareholders and the expenditure of a lot of money. It is a situation in which violations of the proxy rules frequently occur.

3) **Contests for the election of directors.** Sometimes the proxy contest takes the form of a contest for the election of directors. [*See* SEA Rule 14a-11(d)]

i. **Exemptions from the proxy rules.**

1) **Solicitation of ten or fewer persons.** Anyone (other than management) may solicit proxies from 10 or fewer persons without having to comply with the proxy rules. [*See* SEA Rule 14a-2(a)]

2) **The exemption for beneficial owners.** The beneficial owners of securities may solicit a proxy from the registered owner without having to comply with the proxy rules. [*See* SEA Rule 14a-2(c)]

j. **Enforcement provisions.**

1) **In general.** An action may be brought for any violation of the proxy rules, and the courts will fashion whatever relief is appropriate in the circumstances.

2) **Antifraud provisions.** Normally actions claiming violation of the proxy rules are brought under the antifraud provisions relating to the solicitation of proxies. [*See* SEA Rule 14a-9] The purpose of these antifraud provisions is to protect the shareholders and the integrity of the shareholder voting process (ensuring that there is a disclosure to shareholders of all material facts necessary to an intelligent decision on matters where shareholders' proxies are solicited).

3) **Implied private cause of action--J.I. Case Co. v. Borak,** 377 U.S. 426 (1964).

J.I. Case Co. v. Borak

a) **Facts.** Borak (P), a shareholder in J.I. Case Company (D), alleges that D provided false and misleading proxy information in violation of section 14(a) of the Securities Exchange Act of 1934. Specifically, he argues that a merger already consummated with another corporation would not have been approved by the shareholders but for the misleading proxy statements. P seeks to have the merger declared void. He also seeks damages for himself and other shareholders and any further relief as equity should require. The United States district court denied jurisdiction to grant the private relief pleaded, on the basis that the 1934 Act did not provide a private cause of action. The court of appeals reversed. The United States Supreme Court granted certiorari.

b) **Issue.** Where there is false and misleading information in the proxy statement in violation of section 14(a) of the Securities Act of 1934, and where the transaction (merger) is now complete and the proxies were necessary to the shareholder vote approving the transaction, do the shareholders possess personal direct, derivative, or other cause of action under section 14(a) of the Act?

c) **Held.** Yes. The decision of the court of appeals is affirmed.

(1) Though the proxy statute makes no specific references to a private right of action, one of its chief purposes is "the protection of investors," which certainly implies the availability of judicial relief to private parties when necessary to achieve that result.

(2) Derivative actions by shareholders *also* fall within the sweep of the Act, for to deny such would be tantamount to a denial of private relief.

(3) In granting relief, the court may provide such remedies as required to make effective the purposes of the Act, including the unwinding of a merger. Remedies are not limited to prospective relief.

(4) The action is remanded for a trial on the merits.

d) **Elements of a cause of action.** The elements of a cause of action for fraud are discussed in the following sections of the outline.

3. **Actions for Misstatements or Insufficient Disclosure in a Tender Offer—Section 14(e).** As stated earlier, it is unlawful for any person not to file a section 13(d) report when such person acquires the beneficial ownership of 5% or more of the outstanding shares of an equity security registered under section 12 of the 1934 Act. And, similarly, it is unlawful to engage in (or oppose) a tender offer without meeting the disclosure requirements of section 14(d)(1) (*see* discussion, *supra*). Finally, it is unlawful under section 14(e) for any person to make untrue statements or to omit to state material facts, or to engage in any scheme of deception or fraud in connection with any tender offer request or in opposition thereto. To establish a cause of action for damages under section 14(e), a plaintiff must be able to prove each of the following elements:

a. **Standing to sue.** The matter of who has standing to sue in tender offer cases was left in a state of substantial confusion by the Supreme Court decision in *Piper v. Chris-Craft Industries*, 430 U.S. 1 (1977).

1) **Former law.** Before the *Chris-Craft* decision, section 14(e) had been held to protect both selling and nonselling shareholders of the tendered company, the tendered corporation itself, and the tender offeror (e.g., against the tendered company which resists the tender offer). Even though section 14(e) was originally intended to protect only the selling shareholders, all of the above were held to have standing to complain of violations of the tender offer rules. [Electronics Speciality Co. v. International Controls Corp., 409 F.2d 937 (2d Cir. 1969)] Thus, until *Chris-Craft*, standing under section 14(e) was usually granted liberally to all persons who had reasonably been caused damage by the acts or omissions of other parties involved in a tender offer. This position seemed in accord with the language of section 14(e).

2) **Test for implied private actions--Piper v. Chris-Craft Industries,** 430 U.S. 1 (1977).

Piper v.
Chris-Craft
Industries

   a) **Facts.** Chris-Craft Industries (CCI) bought 13% of Piper's shares for cash on the market. It then approached Piper management about a merger and was refused (January 22, 1969). It then tendered Piper shares for cash at $65/share (market price was $53/share) and by February 3 had acquired 304,606 shares. Piper decided to fight the takeover attempt and sent a letter to its shareholders arguing against the CCI takeover (the circuit court found that the letter contained misrepresentations about the CCI offer). Then Piper entered into an agreement with Grumman Aircraft for Grumman to buy 300,000 shares at the same price CCI had paid for its tendered shares, giving Grumman an option to cancel the purchase; it disclosed the Grumman agreement to the public and to its shareholders but did not disclose the option to cancel. Then CCI began an exchange offer (registered under the 1933 Act with the S.E.C.)—its stock for Piper stock. The offer did not become effective until May 15. In the meantime, Piper made a deal with Bangor Punta Corporation for Bangor to buy the stock owned by Piper management for securities of Bangor and to tender enough other shares to get control. As soon as the deal was announced, Bangor put out a press release disclosing that it was going to offer securities to Piper shareholders worth $80 per Piper share (this was on May 8, just before CCI's exchange offer was made). This violated Rule 135 of the 1933 Act. As a result, CCI had to amend its offer to increase the price offered per share to be competitive with the Bangor offer. Both obtained about 120,000 shares with their offers. Bangor included in its registration statement a material omission (i.e., it listed on its books a railroad as worth $18 million, when it was trying to sell the railroad and had a best offer of only $5 million). Prior to the effective date of the exchange offer, Bangor had also gone to three mutual funds and negotiated a cash purchase of 120,000 shares, in violation of Rule 10b-6 of the 1934 Act (making purchases of the same stock that is part of the offering when there is an offering of the stock in registration). After the exchange offers concluded, both Bangor and CCI had about the same amount of stock; Bangor then continued to buy more shares for cash on the market until it got 51%. CCI ended up with 42%. CCI sued Piper for violations of section 14(e), Bangor for violations of 14(e) and Rule 10b-6, and the underwriter of Bangor's exchange offer. The circuit court, after protracted litigation, held that all defendants had violated the securities laws, that Bangor would not have gotten control but for these violations, but that CCI had not shown that it would have gotten control but for the violations. It nevertheless gave CCI damages in the amount of the difference between CCI's cost basis for the shares it had purchased and what they could be sold for after Bangor got control, plus interest to the date of the judgment. In addition, an injunction was issued which denied Bangor's right to vote 231,000 of the shares it had purchased for a five-year period (in effect, leaving the control of Piper in the joint control of CCI and Bangor for five years). Ds appeal.

b)   Issue. Does CCI have standing under either section 14(e) or Rule 10b-6 to sue?

c)   Held. No. Judgment for Ds.

(1)   A tender offeror, suing in its capacity as a takeover bidder, does not have standing to sue for damages under section 14(e); hence, the court of appeals erred in holding that Chris-Craft, as a defeated tender offeror, had an implied cause of action for damages under that provision.

    (a)   The legislative history shows that the sole purpose of section 14(e) was the protection of investors who are confronted with a tender offer. Congress was intent on regulating takeover bidders, who had previously operated covertly, in order to protect shareholders of target companies; tender offerors, the class regulated by the statute, were not the intended beneficiaries of the legislation.

    (b)   The creation of an implied cause of action for damages by judicial interpretation, such as is urged by Chris-Craft, is not necessary to effectuate Congress's objectives in enacting section 14(e). This conclusion is confirmed by the four factors identified in *Cort v. Ash*, 422 U.S. 66 (1975), as "relevant" in determining whether a private remedy is implicit in a statute not expressly providing one: (i) Chris-Craft, a member of the class whose activities Congress intended to regulate for the benefit of target shareholders, was *not* "one of the class for whose *especial* benefit [section 14(e)] was enacted . . ."; (ii) although nothing in the legislative history manifests an intent to deny a damages remedy to tender offerors, there is no material showing an intention to create such a remedy, and the pervasive legislative history negates any claim that the statute was intended to provide tender offerors with additional weapons in contests for control; (iii) it is not consistent with the underlying legislative purpose to imply a damages remedy for the tender offeror in a statute especially designed to protect shareholders of target corporations, particularly where the damages award (here $36 million to Chris-Craft) favors the tender offeror, not the "injured" shareholders of the target; and (iv) the cause of action by a tender offeror is one appropriately "relegated to state law," to the extent that the offeror seeks damages for loss of an opportunity to control a corporation.

(2)   In the context of this case, Chris-Craft has no standing to sue for damages on account of the asserted Rule 10b-6 violations by the successful competitor, since Chris-Craft's complaint is not that the price paid for the target company's shares was influenced by the Rule 10b-6 violations, but that the opportunity to gain control of the target company was lost by virtue of those violations. Thus, Chris-Craft's complaint does not implicate the concerns of Rule 10b-6, which is aimed at maintaining an orderly market for the distribution of securities free from manipulative influences.

(3) The courts of appeals erred under the circumstances presented here in awarding Chris-Craft injunctive relief. The case was tried in the district court exclusively as a suit for damages after Chris-Craft expressly waived any claim to injunctive relief. Under these circumstances, this Court's holding that Chris-Craft has no cause of action for damages under either section 14(e) or Rule 10b-6 renders the injunction granted by the district court inappropriate, premised as it was upon the impermissible award of damages.

d) **Concurrence.** CCI had standing to sue under an implied cause of action for damages under section 14(e). However, CCI did not show that the securities law violations of Ds caused its losses. Causation in a suit by a tender offeror to recover damages for violations by its competitors is a more complex issue than it is for a shareholder of the tendered company bringing suit to recover. The tender offeror must prove that the violations caused the shareholders of the tendered company to act in a certain way; in addition, the offeror must show that the shareholders' reactions caused the injury to the offeror. Thus, the presumption in the *Mills* case that there is causation from a showing of an omission of a material fact holds for the first part (showing that the shareholders were caused to act as they did), but this does not prove that CCI lost the battle for control as a result. CCI has failed to prove causation.

e) **Dissent.** In competing tender offers, Bangor violated section 14(e); CCI had 556,206 shares and was after control with its offer. CCI alleged that Bangor's violation prevented it from getting control and raised the cost it paid for the shares it bought (and lessened the value of the shares it did purchase).

(1) CCI was one of the shareholders of the tendered-for company by Bangor; it claims to have suffered harm in this respect, and this type of harm was meant to be covered by section 14(e). Bangor's getting control was the cause of this lost.

(2) Even in its interest as a tender offeror, CCI should have standing.

(a) A private remedy is implied from section 14(e), and enforcement of the purposes of the Act should be given to those best able to enforce it. The contestants to a tender offer are the parties most interested and in the best position to enforce the Act. The tender offeror is in the best position to see that the shareholders' interests are protected against management.

(b) The S.E.C. and the lower courts have consistently found that the tender offeror has standing. If this is not the case, it is hard to see what section 14(e) adds to Rule 10b-5.

(c) *Cort v. Ash* does not come to a contrary result. In *Borak* the primary beneficiaries of a cause of action were some individual shareholders, rather than the corporation. The Supreme Court allowed a cause of action since there was a "statutory basis" for inferring a cause of action. The same is true in this case. Also, it is error to argue that congressional desire to protect shareholders is in some way inconsistent with providing a tender offeror with a right to damages.

(d) Congressional intent seems to be to give the tender offeror a fair or equal opportunity with management to present its case. Disallowing standing gives incentive to management to misrepresent and violate the Act.

(e) A damage action is necessary to protect the shareholders of Piper who took CCI stock. The Piper shareholders who took Bangor stock can be protected by other remedies.

(3) Even if the damage remedy is set aside, this does not mean that the equitable remedy should have been set aside. CCI did not really make a binding election of remedies.

b. **Comments to the *Piper* case.**

1) The Court indicated in dictum that nontendering shareholders of the tendered company would have standing to sue under section 14(e) (e.g., where they did not tender their shares due to misrepresentations about the tender offer made by the management of the tendered company); but the Court did not clarify the issue of whether management (on behalf of the tendered company) would have standing to sue the tender offeror.

2) Note that subsequent to the *Piper* case, a court held that tender offerors did not have standing to sue under either sections 9(e), 10(b), or Rule 10b-5 of the 1934 Act for injuries allegedly incurred in a tender offer contest. [Crane Co. v. American Standard, Inc., 603 F.2d 244 (2d Cir. 1979)]

Touche Ross & Co. v. Redington

4. **Standards for Implying a Private Right of Action--Touche Ross & Co. v. Redington,** 442 U.S. 560 (1979).

a. **Facts.** Weis Securities, a registered broker-dealer, in 1969 retained Touche Ross (D) to serve as its auditor and to prepare filings with the S.E.C. (including an annual report of financial condition as required by section 17(a) of the 1934 Act) and the New York Stock Exchange. In 1973, Weis was adjudged a bankrupt and Redington (P) was appointed trustee. Despite advances made by the Securities Investor Protection Corporation to pay Weis customers who had deposits with Weis, there still existed several million dollars of unsatisfied claims. P and the Securities Investor Protection Corporation sued D on its own behalf and on behalf of unsatisfied customers for damages in district court, alleging that Weis falsified financial reports required under section 17(a), and that D failed to follow proper auditing procedures to discover such fraud. The district court dismissed the complaint and the appellate court reversed. The Supreme Court granted certiorari.

b. **Issue.** Do customers of securities brokerage firms which are required by section 17(a) of the 1934 Act to file certain financial reports with regulatory authorities have an implied cause of action for damages under section 17(a) against accountants who audit such reports based on misstatements contained in the reports?

c. **Held.** No. Judgment of the appellate court reversed.

1) Whether the violation of a federal statute which does not expressly grant a cause of action will be held to imply a cause of action is a matter of statutory interpretation of the intent of Congress.

2) Section 17(a) requires broker-dealers to keep information and file certain reports with the S.E.C. It confers no rights on any private party, nor does it proscribe any conduct as unlawful.

3) Section 17(a) gives the S.E.C. the necessary financial information to monitor the financial health of registered broker-dealers. It does not purport to give investors a remedy if a broker-dealer becomes insolvent.

4) There is no indication of congressional intent as to whether a private right of action should be available.

5) Where Congress intended a private remedy to exist in the 1934 Act, it so stated, as in, e.g., sections 9(e) and 16(b).

6) Section 18(a) creates a private cause of action against persons (including accountants) who make false statements in reports filed with S.E.C. However, the cause of action is limited to persons who purchase or sell securities in reliance on the reports. Without congressional intent to the contrary, we are reluctant to imply a remedy broader than what Congress provided in this section.

7) The other tests of whether a private remedy will be implied (as set forth in *Cort v. Ash, supra*—i.e., whether such a remedy is necessary to effectuate the purposes of the Act, etc.) are irrelevant if it does not appear that there was legislative intent to create such a remedy.

8) The Court has followed a stricter standard since we implied a remedy for violation of section 14(a) in the *Borak* case.

9) If injustice results from this decision, Congress must remedy it.

d. **Concurring** (Brennan, J.). When the plaintiff is not one of the class for whose special benefit the statute was enacted and there is no indication of explicit or implicit legislative intent to create a remedy, no cause of action will be implied.

e. **Dissent** (Marshall, J.). All four factors cited in *Cort v. Ash* are fulfilled here—the plaintiff is one of the class for whose benefit the statute was enacted; there is an implicit or explicit indication of legislative intent to create a remedy; it is consistent with the underlying purposes of the legislative scheme; and the cause of action is not one appropriate to relegate to state law.

f. **Comment.** *Redington* represents the current trend of the courts in being reluctant to imply a private right of action. The trend is based on the Supreme Court's reliance on the statutory language and legislative history of the securities laws, the supposed intent of Congress to avoid the overlap of the federal securities laws, and the concern that in the past it has been too easy to recover under the securities laws, resulting in the filing of unwarranted suits in order to recover their settlement value. Underlying this trend, however, is the Court's apparent belief that the marketplace should be freed from undue regulation and that more of the regulatory burden should be placed on the states.

Merrill
Lynch,
Pierce,
Fenner &
Smith, Inc.
v. Curran

5. **The Commodity Exchange Act--Merrill Lynch, Pierce, Fenner & Smith, Inc. v. Curran,** 456 U.S. 353 (1982).

a. **Facts.** The Commodity Exchange Act (CEA) oversees the futures trading of commodities. A futures contract is an agreement to take delivery of a certain amount of a commodity in the future (for example, a person might agree to sell a quantity of grain at today's price for delivery in 90 days). The CEA includes general antifraud provisions. The CEA (with its amendments) provides for a Trading Commission and an administrative system for hearing claims, but it says nothing about private judicial remedies for injured persons.

Four cases are consolidated. P1 sues a commission merchant registered with the Trading Commission for violations of the CEA (making misrepresentations, making trades solely to generate commissions, etc.); P2 sues the New York Mercantile Exchange and its officials for futures trading to enforce its rules when it knew that a scheme to manipulate futures prices in the potato market was going on; P3 and P4 sue firms of futures commission brokers, alleging that they knew of the illegal scheme to manipulate the market and nevertheless aided those involved in violating trading limits.

b. **Issue.** Are private judicial remedies to be implied under the CEA?

c. **Held.** Yes. Decisions of lower courts for Ps affirmed.

1) Whether a private cause of action will be implied depends on the intent of Congress.

2) Prior to the amendments to the CEA in 1974 (and prior to the *Cort v. Ash* decision), federal courts regularly implied private rights of action. The fact that Congress scrutinized the CEA in 1974 and said nothing implies that it intended to leave the private remedy. A review of legislative history also leads to this conclusion (since rather than abolish implied private remedies, which were being brought against exchanges for violation of section 5a(8)—failure to enforce exchange rules—and creating a disincentive for exchanges to enact more rules to protect trading, Congress created a Commodities Futures Trading Commission with authority to enact more rules governing the exchanges).

3) New informal enforcement procedures were enacted, but the congressional testimony indicates that these were a supplement to and not a displacement of judicial actions.

4) The 1974 Amendments also provided exclusive jurisdiction over commodity trading to the Commodities Futures Trading Commission, but the Senate added section 2(a)(1), which provided that nothing limited or changed existing jurisdiction already in the courts.

5) Purchasers and sellers of futures contracts have standing to assert the types of claims brought here by Ps.

a) Section 4b seems to clearly support an action by an investor against a broker. But in the three manipulation causes of action, the sections violated are general and do not confer special rights on any class of persons. Thus, if the *Cort v. Ash* test were being applied, these courses of action would fail. But we have held that Congress meant to continue the pre-1974 remedies.

b) Before 1974, private actions were being implied against exchanges. Congress meant to continue this.

d. Dissent.

1) The majority relies on the holdings of pre-1974 lower court cases. These cases were very few, and they were wrong.

2) There is no affirmative evidence in the 1974 hearings that Congress meant to uphold implied private remedies. Indeed, in the section where remedies are listed under the CEA, nothing is mentioned of implied remedies.

6. Implied Civil Liability Under Rule 10b-5 of the Securities Exchange Act of 1934.

a. Prohibition against fraud. Rule 10b-5 makes it unlawful, in connection with the purchase or sale of any security, for any person, directly or indirectly by the use of any means or instrumentality of interstate commerce, or of the mails, or of any facility of any national securities exchange:

1) To employ any device, scheme, or artifice to defraud;

2) To make any untrue statement of a material fact or to omit to state a material fact necessary in order to make the statements made, in light of the circumstances under which they were made, not misleading; or

3) To engage in any act, practice, or course of business which operates or would operate as a fraud or deceit upon any person. Note that 10b-5 covers "fraud" generally (i.e., devices, schemes, acts, practices, etc.) and not merely misrepresentations or omissions to state material facts.

b. Securities and securities transactions covered by the rule. Rule 10b-5 is very broad in its application to securities transactions.

1) **Securities to which applicable.** For Rule 10b-5 to apply, a "security" must be involved. The term is defined about the same as under the 1933 Act.

2) **Applicable to all security transactions.** The courts have indicated that securities transactions on exchanges, over-the-counter transactions, and all private transactions are under the coverage of the rule. [*See* Fratt v. Robinson, 203 F.2d 627 (9th Cir. 1953)]

3) **Purchases and sales.** Rule 10b-5 applies to both purchases and sales in all contexts.

4) **Interstate commerce requirement.** In order for the rule to apply, the means of interstate commerce, the mails, or a national securities exchange must be used "in connection with" the purchase or sale of securities.

    a) The courts have held that the misrepresentation itself need not be transmitted by the jurisdictional means; it is sufficient if *any part* of the securities transaction involves the use of the means of interstate commerce (such as the delivery of the securities). [*See* Fratt v. Robinson, *supra*]

c. **Remedies and limitations.**

1) **An implied private right of action.** Rule 10b-5 does *not* give a specific private right of action, but the courts have implied such an action.

2) **S.E.C. actions.** The S.E.C. may also bring criminal actions under the rule or actions for injunctions.

3) **Statute of limitations.** There is no specific statute of limitations applicable to Rule 10b-5. Normally, a relevant state statute is applied (i.e., the state's fraud statute).

4) **Actions where the 1933 Act provisions also apply.**

    a) **Buyers' actions against sellers.** The court began to apply Rule 10b-5 to situations involving defrauded buyers, which raised the issue of possible conflict with sections 11, 12(1) and particularly 12(2) and 17(a) of the 1933 Act (since the 1933 Act also applies generally to defrauded purchasers).

    b) **Where other sections of the 1934 Act apply.** It is clear that Rule 10b-5 may be applied to many situations where other provisions of the 1934 Act may also apply. [*See, e.g.,* Ross v. A.H. Robins Co., 607 F.2d 545 (2d Cir. 1979)] *Ross* held that Rule 10b-5 applied in a situation where section 18 (with its more stringent requirements) also applied. But note that the Supreme Court has been looking more carefully at these possible conflicts and has had the tendency not to cumulate the use of liability sections.

Herman & MacLean v. Huddleston

    c) **No conflict with section 11 of the 1933 Act--Herman & MacLean v. Huddleston,** 459 U.S. 375 (1983).

        (1) **Facts.** On October 30, 1969, Texas International Speedway (TIS) sold over $4 million in common stock to the public, which was used to build an automobile speedway. The company went bankrupt on November 30, 1970. In 1972 Huddleston and Bradley (Ps) instituted a class action pursuant to Rule 10b-5 against the participants of the TIS offering, including the accounting firm of Herman & MacLean (Ds). Ps claimed that Ds had engaged in a fraudulent scheme to conceal the real financial condition of TIS. The trial court instructed the jury that plain-

tiffs only had to prove their case by a preponderance of the evidence. The jury found for the plaintiffs and Ds appealed. The circuit court found that a 10b-5 cause of action could be maintained even though section 11 of the 1933 Act also applied to the transaction. However, the circuit court also held that a 10b-5 cause of action had to be proved by clear and convincing evidence. The Supreme Court granted certiorari.

(2) Issues.

    (a)   May a cause of action be brought under Rule 10b-5 when section 11 of the 1933 Act also would apply?

    (b)   Is preponderance of the evidence the correct standard of proof in a Rule 10b-5 cause of action?

(3) Held. (a) Yes. (b) Yes. Affirmed in part, reversed in part.

    (a)   Rule 10b-5 and section 11 were intended to address different types of wrongdoing. Section 11 applies to misrepresentations in a registration statement; it imposes a stringent standard of liability and applies to specifically named persons. Rule 10b-5 is a general antifraud provision, but plaintiff must carry a heavier burden to prove the cause of action. There is no good reason to carve an exception out of 10b-5 for conduct that is actionable under section 11, since the basic purpose of the 1933 Act is to provide greater protection to purchasers of registered securities. And having both remedies furthers the broad remedial purposes of the securities laws.

    (b)   In a typical suit for money damages, plaintiff must prove the cause of action by a preponderance of the evidence. The S.E.C. has held that a section 17(a) action under the 1933 Act is proved by a preponderance. The basis for a clear and convincing standard is that it was used in civil fraud cases at common law. But one of the purposes of the federal securities laws was to rectify deficiencies in the common law remedies. Since Congress has not indicated exactly what the standard should be, it is up to the courts. Clear and convincing evidence should only be required where it is important to allocate the risk of error in a certain way. The balance of interests in this case warrants the use of the preponderance standard. Defendants risk the shame from a finding of fraudulent conduct; but defrauded investors are the persons that Congress sought to protect.

d) Where there is a conflict with section 12(2) of the 1933 Act. There are cases which have held that Rule 10b-5 may be used where otherwise the plaintiff would have a cause of action under section 12(2) of the 1933 Act. [*See* Ellis v. Carter, 291 F.2d 270 (9th Cir. 1961)] Thus, the question is, under which section is a cause of action the easiest to prove?

    (1)   Section 12(2) is subject to the defendant's due care defense, has more stringent venue provisions, and generally has a shorter statute of limitations.

    (2)   But Rule 10b-5 requires that plaintiff must prove an intentional misstatement by defendant.

e) **Where both section 17(a) of the 1933 Act and Rule 10b-5 may apply.** (*See* the discussion concerning implied causes of action pursuant to section 17(a), *infra.*)

d. **Jurisdiction and service of process.** One of the reasons that Rule 10b-5 has been used so frequently is its broad procedural provisions.

1) **Jurisdiction.** The federal courts have exclusive jurisdiction over all civil actions arising under the rule, regardless of the amount in controversy.

2) **Venue.** Suit may be brought in any district court in which any act or transaction constituting the violation occurred, or in any district where the defendant is found, is an inhabitant, or transacts business.

3) **Service of process.** Process may be served anywhere in the world.

7. **Section 17 of the 1933 Act—Criminal Liability and Implied Civil Liability.**

a. **Criminal liability and injunctions.** It is unlawful under section 17(a) of the 1933 Act for any person in the offer or sale of securities by use of any means or instruments of transportation or communication in interstate commerce or by the use of the mails, directly or indirectly:

1) To employ any device, scheme, or artifice to defraud; or

2) To obtain money or property by means of any untrue statement of a material fact or any omission to state a material fact; or

3) To engage in any transaction, practice, or course of business which operates or would operate as a fraud or deceit upon the purchaser. All criminal actions and all injunctions brought by the S.E.C. under the 1933 Act are based on section 17.

b. **Implied civil liability.** There is judicial authority for the fact that this section also includes an "implied" civil liability, permitting private persons to bring an action thereunder (thereby avoiding the more stringent provisions of sections 11 and 12, such as the privity requirement). [*See* Osborne v. Mallory, 86 F. Supp. 869 (S.D.N.Y. 1949)] As the next case indicates, however, there is judicial authority to the contrary (i.e., that there is no implied private right of action for damages under section 17).

Landry v. All American Assurance Co.

c. **No implied right of action under section 17(a)--Landry v. All American Assurance Co.,** 688 F.2d 381 (5th Cir. 1982).

1) **Facts.** Shareholders (Ps) bought stock in a bank for $60 per share; shortly thereafter, serious financial problems were revealed and the stock dropped to $4 per share. Ps sued the Bank and several of its officers (Ds) under Rule 10b-5 and section 17(a) of the 1933 Act. The trial court found, on Ds' motion for a summary judgment, that no private rights of action would be implied under section 17(a) and that, while Ds had recklessly made misrepresentations, Ps had not exercised due diligence in purchasing the stock and so were precluded from recovery. Ps appealed.

2) Issue. Will a private cause of action be implied under section 17(a)?

3) Held. No. District court affirmed.

a) Historically plaintiffs have sued under both Rule 10b-5 and section 17(a), and courts usually decided the cases under 10b-5. But everyone assumed that there was a private cause of action under section 17(a).

b) Recently, however, the Supreme Court has limited 10b-5 (to intentional acts) and held that the culpability required to prove a cause of action in an S.E.C. enforcement action under section 17(a) varies with the subsection involved. [*See,* e.g., Aaron v. S.E.C.—plaintiff only needs to prove negligence under 17(a)(2) and (3)]

c) Thus, the issue of whether a private cause of action will be implied under 17(a) is an important one. Initially the Supreme Court would have decided the issue using the *Cort v. Ash* test: (i) is the plaintiff one of the class for whose special benefit the statute was enacted; (ii) is there any indication of legislative intent to create such a remedy; (iii) is it consistent with the underlying purposes of the legislative scheme to imply such a remedy; and (iv) is the cause of action one typically relegated to state law?

d) But the Supreme Court in *Touche Ross & Co. v. Redington* (*supra*) and in *Transamerica Mortgage Advisors, Inc. v. Lewis*, 444 U.S. 11 (1979), has emphasized an examination of the language, legislative history and purpose of the provisions being considered (i.e., the first three elements of the *Cort* test). The ultimate question is whether Congress intended to create a private cause of action.

e) Applying these tests, it is clear that there should be no private right of action implied here:

(1) The statutory language does not suggest such an action.

(2) The legislative history suggests that no civil liability would attach under section 17(a).

(3) It is inconsistent with the purposes of the 1933 Act to imply a remedy since sections 11 and 12 are express remedies and have more stringent requirements of proof than 17(a).

(4) The matters regulated by states usually are not ones that federal courts will imply a remedy for; the legislative history is clear that the 1933 Act was passed to deal with matters which the states were not dealing with adequately.

f) The outcome of the first three factors of the test, along with awareness of the Supreme Court's conservative interpretation of the *Cort* test, indicates that no remedy should be implied.

B. FAULT REQUIRED

1. Liabilities Under the 1933 Act.

a. Introduction. The first major objective of the 1933 Act is to provide full disclosure of material information to potential investors of newly issued securities. The second objective is generally to prevent fraud and/or misrepresentation in the interstate sale of securities. The liability provisions of the 1933 Act are organized around these two basic objectives.

1) Liability for improper disclosure. For example, in a registration statement, the issuer may misrepresent a material fact to the purchaser, or fail to state a material fact. Liability is provided for under section 11 of the Act. Or, in the prefiling period, the issuer or the underwriter may make an improper offer to the potential purchaser in violation of section 5 of the Act. Liability is provided for in section 12(1) of the Act. · Section 12(2) is a liability provision that covers fraud or misrepresentation in a prospectus or oral communication in connection with an initial offering of securities.

2) Liability for fraud or misrepresentation in general. In addition, the Act includes liability provisions that cover fraud or misrepresentation in the interstate sale of securities in general (i.e., whether or not registration with the S.E.C. is involved). [*See* the discussion of section 17, *supra*]

3) Comparison with the common law. In general, the liability provisions of the 1933 Act afford remedies to defrauded purchasers that are more liberal than those available at common law. At common law, a defrauded purchaser of securities had to prove the same elements to recover as any other defrauded purchaser of goods. These elements included:

(i) **Material facts.** Plaintiff had to show that the defendant seller of the securities had misstated a *material fact*, or failed to state a material fact that the seller was under a duty to disclose.

(ii) **Reliance.** Plaintiff also had to show that she had relied on the misrepresentation.

(iii) **Privity.** Plaintiff also had to show that there was privity of contract between herself and the defendant (i.e., that plaintiff had purchased the security from the specific defendant-seller who was being sued).

(iv) **Cause of loss.** Plaintiff had to show that defendant's misrepresentation was the actual cause and the proximate cause of plaintiff's loss.

(v) **Scienter.** Finally, the defendant must have had actual knowledge of the misrepresentation or omission. That is, defendant's misrepresentation must have been intentional.

All of the remedies under the 1933 Act were designed to make recovery easier for defrauded *purchasers* of securities by lightening the burden of proof they had to carry with respect to the above elements of a cause of action.

b. **Liability for false or misleading statements or omissions in the registration statement or prospectus—section 11 of the Act.** Section 11 of the 1933 Act imposes liability on designated persons for material misstatements or omissions in an effective *registration statement* or *prospectus*.

1) **Persons subject to liability.** The following persons can be held liable under section 11 for material misstatements in the registration statement or prospectus:

a) **Every person who signs the registration statement.** The following persons *must* sign the registration statement:

(i) The issuer;

(ii) The principal executive officers of the issuer;

(iii) The chief financial officer of the issuer;

(iv) The principal accounting officer of the issuer; and

(v) A majority of the members of the board of directors of the issuer.

[SA §6(a)]

b) **Every person who was a director of the issuer.** Every person who was a director of the issuer at the time the registration statement became effective can also be liable, even if such person did not sign the registration statement.

c) **Every person who is named (with his consent) as about to become a director.** Every person who is named (with his consent) in the registration statement as about to become a director of the issuer may also be held liable.

d) **Every "expert" who gives a certificate that part of the registration statement was prepared by him.** All "experts" who certify that they prepared part of the registration statement may be held liable under section 11. For example, accountants are "experts" as to the certified financial statements included in the registration statement.

e) **Every underwriter involved in the distribution.** Underwriters may be held liable under section 11.

f)   Control persons. And finally, persons who "control" any person who is liable under section 11 may also be held liable. [*See* SA §15]

2)   Elements of the plaintiff's cause of action.

a)   Material misstatements or omissions. Plaintiff must prove that there has been a misstatement or omission of a fact and that the fact was material.

b)   Elements required in a common law action not required in section 11 actions. Section 11 has essentially eliminated some of the requirements that were included in common law fraud actions against sellers of securities.

(1)   Privity of contract. For example, any person acquiring a security which was the subject of a defective registration statement may sue under section 11.

(a)   Thus, the purchaser need not have privity with the issuer. For example, A may recover if she purchases securities from B that are part of the registered offering (B having purchased them from the issuer) even though A is not in privity of contract with the issuer. And the purchaser may sue other liable parties (such as directors, underwriters, etc.) other than the issuer.

(b)   However, there is a *tracing requirement*. That is, the plaintiff must be able to trace the securities she purchased back to the defective registration statement.

(2)   Reliance. In general, plaintiff need not prove that she purchased in reliance on the misstatement in order to recover. However, if the issuer sends out an earnings statement covering the period of one year after the effective date of the registration statement, then a person *thereafter acquiring* some of the registered securities must prove reliance on the misrepresentation or omission in order to recover. [*See* SA §11(a)] But the plaintiff need not have read the registration statement to prove reliance. She could have relied on secondary sources that repeated the misstatement.

3)   Defenses available to defendants to avoid liability.

a)   Defenses available to the issuer. The issuer has the following defenses to a section 11 action (all of which may also be claimed by any other defendant):

(i)   The issuer can show that the alleged statements were actually true.

(ii)   The issuer can also show that the misstatements or omissions were not of material facts.

(iii)   Finally, the issuer can show that the plaintiff-purchaser knew of the misleading statements or omissions and invested in the securities anyway.

(1)   Statute of limitations. Under section 11, the period of limitations is one year after discovery of the false statement, with an overall limitation of three years after the security is first validly offered to the public.

b)   Statements made by nonexperts. Section 11 makes a distinction for liability purposes between "experts" (those who certify part of the registration statement as being true, such as certified public accountants who certify that the financial statements were prepared according to generally accepted accounting principles) and "nonexperts" (i.e., all others who may be held liable pursuant to section 11), *and* between the standard of care required of nonexperts reviewing material prepared by other nonexperts and that required of nonexperts reviewing statements of experts.

(1)   Nonexperts as to their statements made in the registration statement. A lawyer who is a member of the issuer's board of directors and who drafts the registration statement (and collects facts from the issuer in order to do so) is an example of a "nonexpert" who makes statements that appear in the registration statement.

   (a)   Standard of diligence required. In order to avoid liability under section 11, nonexperts must meet the following tests of "due diligence" regarding statements they make in the registration statement: (i) the nonexpert must *actually believe* that the statements made were true, and (ii) the *belief must be reasonable*.

   (b)   Reasonable investigation. In order to have a reasonable belief, the nonexpert must have made a *reasonable investigation* of the facts. Section 11 indicates that the test for defining the scope of a "reasonable investigation" is what a "prudent person would do in the management of his own affairs."

   (c)   No single standard. As a practical matter, however, there is no single standard. The courts look at each individual defendant, and based on his position with the issuer, his responsibilities relative to the issuer and the registration statement, his background, skills, training, and access to information, they determine what he should have done to fulfill the obligation to make a "reasonable investigation."

(2)   Nonexperts reviewing statements in the registration statements made by other nonexperts. A nonexpert not involved in actually drafting the registration statement (such as a member of the issuer's board of directors) may also have potential liability under the Act. To avoid liability the nonexpert will have to show that the due diligence appropriate to his position has been exercised. Part of this responsibility must be exercised with regard to statements made in the registration statement by other nonexperts (i.e., the director must review the registration statement written by the nonexpert lawyer).

   (a)   Standard of diligence required. The standard of diligence required is the same as for nonexperts concerning statements they made in the registration statement (*see* above).

(b) **Examples of nonexperts.** The underwriters, executive officers of the issuer, and members of the board of directors are examples of nonexperts.

c) **Statements made by experts.** Statements are also made in the registration statement by experts (for example, accountants must prepare and certify the issuer's financial statements).

(1) **Standard of diligence required of experts.** Statements made by experts must meet the following tests:

(a) The experts must *actually believe* that the statements they made are true; and

(b) The belief *must be reasonable*. In order for belief to be reasonable, the experts must have made a *reasonable investigation* into the facts supporting the statements made. Normally, this means that the expert must perform up to at least the standards of the profession (for example, accountants must make an investigation of the facts that would conform to the standards of financial results according to the generally accepted accounting principles of the S.E.C.).

(2) **Nonexperts reviewing statements made by experts.** Nonexperts (such as an outside director) are held to a lower standard of care with respect to reviewing statements made by experts than with respect to reviewing statements made by other nonexperts (for example, an outside director, a nonexpert, relying on the certified financial statements of the accountants, who are experts).

(a) The nonexpert must only show that he did not believe the statements made by the expert were untrue and that he had no reasonable ground to believe they were untrue. No investigation need be made by the nonexpert in the case.

(b) In most cases, nonexpert defendants will be able to meet this burden of proof (for example, most of the nonexperts in *Escott*, discussed below, were not held liable for the misrepresentations of the issuer made by the expert accountants).

Escott v.
BarChris
Construction
Corp.

4) **Application of due diligence standard--Escott v. BarChris Construction Corp.,** 283 F. Supp. 643 (S.D.N.Y. 1968).

a) **Facts.** Purchasers (Ps) of BarChris's convertible debentures offered pursuant to a registration statement brought an action under section 11, claiming that the registration statement contained material misstatements and omissions. BarChris was building bowling alleys for a small down payment and an installment contract from the purchaser, which contract was either discounted (to give BarChris cash) or the alley was sold to a finance company and leased back (with BarChris guaranteeing the loan). BarChris was in a cash bind and the industry was overbuilt. At the time of registration it overstated sales and earnings by significant margins (such as the backlog of orders, overstated by 75%, etc.). The action is against those who signed the registration statement and those who participated in the sale of the debentures (Ds); BarChris was bankrupt.

b) **Issue.** Did Ds meet the required standard of due diligence to avoid liability under section 11?

c) **Held.** No.

(1) Nonexperts, with respect to parts of the registration statement not prepared by experts, must, after a reasonable investigation, have reasonable grounds to believe and actually believe that the statements made were true and that there were no omissions of a material fact. A reasonable investigation is one that a prudent person in the management of his own property would conduct. With respect to statements made by experts, nonexperts must show that they had no reasonable ground to believe and did not believe that the statements made were untrue or that there was a material omission.

(2) The only expert was the accounting firm as to their audited financial statements. Neither the lawyer for the company nor the lawyer for the underwriting firm (although participating in writing the registration statement) are experts.

(3) The only expert part of the registration statement is the certified financial statements, not statements in the body of the registration statement that purport to be based on the financial statements.

(4) Kircher (treasurer, chief financial officer, and director) did not meet the standard of due diligence with respect to either the expert section or the nonexpert section of the statement. He knew all of the relevant facts; he was in a position to know of all of the misrepresentations and omissions; he worked on the registration statement; and he lied to those checking on its accuracy. It is not a defense that he was never specifically asked for the information. He must show the necessary actual belief and reasonable belief in the accuracy of the statement, which he could not do.

(5) Birnbaum (secretary, house counsel, and director) met the burden with respect to the experts but not with respect to the nonexpert portion. His position gave him access to contracts, minutes, etc., and while it appears that he did not actually know of the misstatements, he made no investigation into the facts but simply relied on statements of the corporate officers.

(6) Auslander (outside director) joined the board a month before the offering; he read a draft of the statement but made no investigation of any of the facts. He could rely on the expert portion, but he breached his duty with respect to the nonexpert portion.

(7) With regard to Grant (director and outside lawyer, drafter of the registration statement), more was required of him due to his unique position in drafting the registration statement. He did not know the statement was false, but he did not make a reasonable investigation. He need not have done an audit, but he could not accept the word of management; he must check matters that are easily verifiable, such as contracts and agreements, the backlog figures, minutes of meetings, conflicts of interest by manage-

ment, etc. Here he could rely on the expert portion, but he did not meet his burden with respect to the nonexpert portion of the statement.

(8) Coleman (a director and representative of one of the underwriters) met with BarChris management and asked several important questions, but once the offering was decided upon, he did not follow up and investigate any of these matters, but left the investigation to his underlings. A reasonable investigation would have discovered some of the misrepresentations. He is liable with respect to the nonexpert portion of the registration statement, but not with respect to the expert portion.

(9) The underwriters were represented by counsel, who made a cursory review of the important questions that had been asked initially, but essentially took management's word or answers to the questions, rather than conducting an independent analysis or investigation (such as of the backlog figures, etc.). The underwriter is not the same as an outside director (who can rely to some extent on management); the underwriter has an interest adverse to the company and is responsible to the public. It must make an independent investigation, which the underwriter here did not do. Thus, the underwriter here did not meet the due diligence test with respect to the nonexpert portions of the statements.

(10) The accountants are experts with respect to the financial statements. They must conduct an investigation that meets the standards of their profession. Here they had a young, relatively inexperienced accountant doing the audit for 1960 (and the subsequent investigation before the registration statement was filed). He should have discovered several important misrepresentations (such as the fact that BarChris had not sold one bowling alley that was included in income, but was still leasing and operating the alley). In the investigation after the audit (and prior to the filing of the registration statement), the accountants accepted the word of management with respect to several important matters that should have been investigated (such as reading corporate minutes, reading the prospectus and checking its facts, etc.). The burden of proof was on the accountants, and they did not meet it.

5) Damages.

a) **Formula for damages.** The plaintiff may recover the difference between the price paid for the stock (but not exceeding the price at which the security was offered to the public) and the price at which is was sold prior to suit. Alternately, if the purchaser has not sold the securities when the suit is filed, the purchaser may recover either (i) the difference between the price paid (not exceeding the offering price) and the value of the security at the time of suit, or (ii) the price at which it was sold after suit was instituted (but before judgment) if the damages in this case are less than the value at the time of suit. For example, if X bought stock in a registered offering for $10, and it was selling at $5 at the time of suit and X sold it for $6 prior to filing suit, X can recover only $4 per share.

b)   Causation of damages.

(1)   Plaintiff need not prove that the decline in value of the securities was caused by the misrepresentation (note that this was an element of plaintiff's cause of action at common law).

(2)   However, *defendant* may prove that all or some portion of the damages represents other than the depreciation in value resulting from the misrepresentation or omission of material fact in the registration statement.

c)   Limitation on recovery amount. In no case shall the amount recovered exceed the price at which the security was offered to the public. [*See* SA §11(g)]

d)   Underwriter liability. Also, an underwriter cannot be held for more liability in total than the offering price of the securities that the underwriter sold to the public. [*See* SA §11(a)]

c.   Liability for offers or sales in violation of section 5—section 12(1) of the Act. Section 12(1) provides that any person who offers or sells a security in violation of any of the provisions of section 5 of the 1933 Act shall be liable to the purchaser (i) for the *consideration paid* (with interest), less the amount of any income received on the securities, or (ii) for *damages* if the purchaser no longer owns the security.

1)   Liability for any violation of section 5. Liability under section 12(1) attaches for *any violation* by any person *of section 5* (e.g., a sale of unregistered securities, failure to deliver the required prospectus, making an illegal offer in the prefiling period, etc. (*see* discussion, *supra*)).

2)   Rescission or damages. The remedy of rescission of the transaction is available, or, if the purchaser no longer owns the security, an action for damages may be brought.

3)   Defenses to a section 12(1) cause of action.

a)   No violation of section 5. The defendant may prove that no violation of section 5 ever occurred (i.e., the offering was exempt from the registration provisions of section 5).

b)   No privity. Section 12(1) imposes a condition of direct privity of contract between the plaintiff-purchaser and the seller-defendant. A common defense to a section 12(1) action, therefore, is that no privity exists.

c)   Statute of limitations. The period of limitations is one year after the violation, but in no event more than three years after the security was validly offered to the public. This seems to mean that if a portion of the securities issue is sold after three years from the first offer, section 12(1) is not available (even if there is a violation of section 5 of the Act).

d) **Laches.** It has been held that laches is not a defense in a section 12(1) action where the period of limitations has not yet run. [Straley v. Universal Uranium & Milling Corp., 289 F.2d 370 (9th Cir. 1961)]

4) **Liability of controlling persons.** Every person who controls any person who is liable under sections 11 and 12 of the Act is jointly and severally liable with the liable persons, *unless* such controlling person or persons had no knowledge of, nor reasonable grounds to believe in the existence of, the facts on which the liability of the controlled person is alleged to rest.

d. **General civil liability under the Act—section 12(2).** This section provides that *any person* who offers or sells a security (whether or not the sale is exempted from registration by the provisions of the Act) by the use of any means of interstate commerce and makes an untrue statement of material fact (or omits to state a material fact) in connection therewith (the purchaser not knowing of such untruth or omission), and who cannot sustain the burden of proof that he did not know and in the exercise of reasonable care could not have known of such untruth, is liable to the purchaser of such security. [*See* SA §12(2)]

1) **Scope of section 12(2) actions.** Section 12(2) applies whether or not the securities were registered pursuant to section 5 of the Act, whether they were offered under an exemption to the Act or not, and whether the securities were offered in writing or orally.

2) **Plaintiff's case.** Plaintiff must show the following:

a) **Use of jurisdictional means.** The cases have held that the language of section 12(2) requires that liability be limited to persons "who offer or sell by use of any means or instruments of transportation or communication in interstate commerce or the mails." [United States v. Robertson, 181 F. Supp. 158 (S.D.N.Y. 1959)]

(1) Most decisions have indicated that this requirement is satisfied where *any* part of the sale (including delivery after the sale) involves such means.

(2) Also, as long as *any means of doing interstate commerce* is used, this is sufficient (even though the transaction itself does not involve or cross more states than one). [Lennerth v. Mendenhall, 234 F. Supp. 59 (N.D. Ohio 1964)]

b) **Sale by means of a prospectus or an oral communication.** Section 12(2) also requires that the offer or sale of securities occur by means of a "prospectus or oral communication" that includes the misrepresentation or fails to disclose the material fact.

c) **An untrue statement or omission of material fact.**

d) **Defendant's knowledge of the untrue statement.** The plaintiff must also *plead* that the defendant knew, or in the exercise of reasonable care should have known, of the untrue statement. Defendant then carries the burden of proof on this issue (i.e., to show that he did not know, and in the exercise of reasonable care should not have known, of the untrue statement).

3) **Defenses.** The following are defenses to a section 12(2) action:

a) **Lack of knowledge.** Defendant may show that he did not know, and in the exercise of reasonable care could not have known, of the untrue statement.

b) **Exercise of reasonable care--Sanders v. John Nuveen & Co.,** 619 F.2d 1222 (7th Cir. 1980), *cert. denied*, 450 U.S. 1005 (1981).

Sanders v.
John Nuveen
& Co.

(1) **Facts.** A class (Ps) of 42 purchasers of unsecured short term promissory notes (aggregating $1,612,500 issued by Winter & Hirsch, Inc. (WH), a consumer finance company) sued Nuveen (D), the exclusive underwriter of the WH notes (which were sold through its branch offices), and corporations controlling D. D prepared and circulated to prospective customers commercial paper reports on the WH paper. Several Ps received the report; others had oral statements made to them about the quality of the WH paper by D's salesmen. WH's financial statements, which were reproduced in D's reports, were false; in fact, WH was bankrupt at the time of the sale of the notes by D. D did not know this, but relied on the financial statements of WH, which had been prepared by public accountants. D had sent an analyst to interview WH and had checked with several bank creditors of WH before agreeing to underwrite the commercial paper. Shortly after the underwriting, WH defaulted. In an earlier decision the court had held that D had violated Rule 10b-5 for failing to make an adequate investigation of WH (the sale of the commercial paper was exempt from registration under the 1933 Act), but that decision had been overruled when the Supreme Court decided in *Ernst & Ernst v. Hochfelder (infra)* that scienter was an element of a Rule 10b-5 cause of action; the case was then remanded to the district court for a determination of Ps' claims under section 12(2) of the 1933 Act. The district court found for Ps and the case was appealed to this court.

(2) **Issues.**

(a) Does section 12(2) require an underwriter to make a reasonable investigation of the facts concerning the issuer before underwriting its securities?

(b) If so, did D make such a reasonable investigation?

(3) **Held.** (a) Yes. (b) No. Affirmed.

(a) Section 12(2) prohibits the offer or sale of a security by "means of a prospectus or oral communication" which includes an untrue statement or omission of a material fact.

1] There were material misrepresentations and omissions in D's commercial paper reports. This fulfills the prospectus requirement.

2]   Section 12(2) does not have a reliance requirement, so the individual Ps need not have read this report.

3]   The market price for the commercial paper was affected by the dissemination of the false commercial paper report of D, since this paper misrepresented the financial condition of WH.

(b)   D can defend a section 12(2) claim by showing that "in the exercise of reasonable care it could not have known" of the misrepresentation.

    1]   The district court found that an underwriter had a duty to make an investigation of the issuer in order to show that it had exercised "reasonable care." Also, this investigation had to look at more than published data.

    2]   There is no significance to the difference in language in section 11 of the 1933 Act (which requires a "reasonable investigation") and "reasonable care" under section 12(2).

    3]   What is reasonable care depends on the circumstances; it will not always be the same under section 12(2) as it is for a registered offering under section 11.

    4]   There is evidence to support the district court's decision that the investigation by D here was not sufficient to display reasonable care.

(4) Petition for certiorari denied. (This is the *dissenting opinion* of Justice Powell in the denial of the petition for certiorari.)

There is a difference between section 11 and section 12(2). "Investigation," as required by section 11, demands a greater undertaking than "care" (as required by section 12(2)). The S.E.C. itself has recognized the difference, indicting that exemptions to registration would be impaired if section 12(2) imposed the same standard on disclosures that section 11 does on registered offerings of securities.

Also, section 11 gives a lower standard of care (does not require an investigation) when a person is reviewing the statements of experts, such as the financial statements of accountants. The circuit court opinion thus seems to require a greater degree of care under section 12(2) than even section 11 would have required had the offering been a registered offering.

Certiorari should have been granted.

c)   **Waiver and estoppel.** Defendant may claim the defenses of waiver and estoppel where it can be shown that plaintiff has shown sufficient approval or acceptance of defendant's misconduct.

d)   **Plaintiff's knowledge.** Defendant can also show that the plaintiff knew of the untrue statement.

e)   **No privity.** There must also be privity of contract between any person who offers or sells to the "person purchasing such security from him" (section 12(2)).

The issue is (as it is in section 12(1)): who is the "seller"? The courts have given a broad interpretation to this term in section 12(2) actions, extending the concept of "seller" to include persons who "participate" in the sale of the stock to plaintiff-buyer.

(1) **Brokers, dealers, and agents.** Brokers and agents (selling on behalf of their principals) have been held to be "sellers" (e.g., where a broker solicits a buy order for a seller). [Wilko v. Swan, 127 F. Supp. 55 (S.D.N.Y. 1955)]

(2) **Other persons participating in the sale.** The test is whether the injury to plaintiff-buyer flows directly and proximately from the actions of the particular defendant; i.e., but for the presence of the defendant in the negotiations surrounding the sale, would the sale to buyer have been consummated?

f) **Statute of limitations.** The period of limitations is one year after discovery of the false statement but not more than three years after the sale. [*See* SA §13] It is uncertain whether laches applies to section 12(2) actions.

4) **Remedies.** The buyer may sue for rescission, receiving the consideration paid for the securities, plus interest, less any income received; or the buyer may sue for damages if the securities have already been sold.

5) **Does not apply to offers or sales in the secondary market.** Note that at one time it was thought that section 12(2) prohibited fraud generally in the interstate offer or sale of securities, whether the offer or sale be in connection with an initial offering of securities or an offer or sale of already issued securities in the secondary markets. Recently a court has held that section 12(2) applies *only* to offers or sales in initial offerings of securities. [*See* Ballay v. Legg Mason Wood Walker, Inc., 925 F.2d 682 (3d Cir. 1991)] The court reasoned that otherwise Rule 10b-5 would require scienter and 12(2) could apply to the after-trading markets and have a negligence standard apply. Thus, section 12(2) was limited to initial offerings only.

2. **Fault Standards Under the 1934 Act.**

a. **Fault required under Rule 10b-5.** A major issue in actions brought under Rule 10b-5 of the 1934 Act (discussed in greater detail *infra*) concerns the standard of care a defendant will be held to in a securities transaction.

1) **Resolution by the Supreme Court.** After a long period of controversy, the issue of the standard to be applied in private damage actions has now been resolved (to some degree) by the Supreme Court, which held in *Ernst* (below) that in order for liability to exist under Rule 10b-5, it must be shown that defendant had "scienter" (i.e., actual intent to deceive, manipulate, or defraud).

2) **Rule 10b-5 intentional act requirement--Ernst & Ernst v. Hochfelder,** 425 U.S. 185 (1976).

    a) **Facts.** Ernst & Ernst (D), an accounting firm, audited the books of a small securities firm and prepared its statements to the S.E.C. and the Midwestern Stock Exchange. Customers of the firm (Ps) gave the firm's president money in the form of personal checks to be invested in "escrow accounts." In fact, the president embezzled the money. To prevent detection of the fraud, the president had a firm rule that no mail addressed to him or to the firm in his care could be opened by any other person. Ps charge that if the auditing firm had not been negligent in its audit, it would have discovered this rule and an investigation would have led to the fraud. No reports of the escrow accounts ever showed up in the financial statements prepared by D. The district court granted D's motion for summary judgment. The circuit court reversed. The Supreme Court granted certiorari.

    b) **Issue.** Does Rule 10b-5 apply where D has been negligently nonfeasant in performing its duties, thus aiding and abetting the perpetration of a fraud?

    c) **Held.** No. Judgment reversed.

        (1) D is *not* liable unless Ps can show *intentionally* fraudulent conduct by D. Congress did not intend for negligent conduct to be proscribed by the statute.

    d) **Dissent** (Blackmun, Brennan, JJ.). The investor/victim should be allowed to recover. Congress intended the laws to be broad enough to protect P.

    e) **Comment.** The Court reserved for future decision the question whether recklessness was sufficient to show liability. However, most of the lower courts have held that a cause of action under Rule 10b-5 may be based on reckless conduct.

b. **Scienter for S.E.C. injunctive actions--Aaron v. S.E.C.,** 446 U.S. 680 (1980).

    1) **Facts.** Aaron (D) was a managerial employee of a broker-dealer, charged with supervising the sales agents of the firm and maintaining the "due diligence" files for the securities for which the firm was acting as a market maker. One such security was Lawn-A-Mat, Inc. For a period of a year, two of the firm's salespeople were repeatedly making false and misleading statements in connection with efforts to solicit orders for the purchase of Lawn-A-Mat shares. Investors complained, for the company's lawyer complained, and D had reason to know that the statements were false since he kept the official information in the due diligence file on the company. Nevertheless, D took no steps to supervise or halt the activities of the salesperson (other than telling them that there had been complaints). The S.E.C. brought an action for an injunction against D (and several others) for violations of section 17(a) of the 1933 Act and section 10(b) and Rule 10b-5 of the 1934 Act. The district court granted the injunction; the circuit court affirmed, and the Supreme Court granted certiorari.

2) **Issue.** Is the S.E.C. required to establish scienter as an element of a civil enforcement action for an injunction against violations of section 17(a) of the 1933 Act and section 10(b) and Rule 10b-5 of the 1934 Act?

3) **Held.** Yes. Judgment reversed.

    a) Injunctions may be brought for violations of the 1933 Act under section 20(b) of that Act, and for violations of the 1934 Act under section 21(d).

    b) As far as section 10(b) is concerned, *Ernst & Ernst v. Hochfelder* held that scienter had to be proved in order to bring an implied private right of action for damages. This was based on a reading of legislative intent, the plain meaning of the language of the section, and the fact that Congress in other places had expressly indicated other standards if it wanted such standards.

        (1) The rationale of *Hochfelder* means that scienter is an element of a section 10(b) violation regardless of the identity of the plaintiff or the nature of the relief sought.

        (2) The case of *S.E.C. v. Capital Gains Research Bureau*, 375 U.S. 180 (1963), is distinguished since it dealt with section 206(2) of the Investment Advisers Act, which has different wording and deals with a different situation (investment advisers, who have a fiduciary relationship with their clients).

    c) As far as section 17(a) is concerned, the language of the provision controls.

        (1) Section 17(a)(1) makes it unlawful to employ any device, scheme, or artifice to defraud. This proscribes only knowing or intentional conduct.

        (2) Section 17(a)(2) prohibits any person from obtaining money or property by means of an untrue statement of a material fact or an omission of a material fact. This is devoid of a scienter requirement. Thus, the S.E.C. may bring an action based on negligence.

        (3) Section 17(a)(3) makes it unlawful for any person to engage in any transaction, practice, or course of business which *operates* as a fraud or deceit. This is similar to the language used in section 206(2) of the Investment Advisers Act, focusing on the effect of conduct by a person rather than on the intent behind the conduct. Therefore, intentional conduct need not be shown.

    d) The language of sections 20(b) of the 1933 Act and 21(d) of the 1934 Act does not add anything to the analysis. They simply say that injunctions can be brought for violations of the sections of the Acts.

4) **Concurring** (Burger, C.J.).

    a) No matter what the standard of conduct is, it is clear that the district court was correct in granting an injunction, since there was intentional conduct here.

b) I agree that sections 10(b) and 17(a)(1) require scienter and that 17(a)(2) and (3) do not. This drives a wedge between sellers and buyers (since the 1933 Act and section 17(a) apply only to sellers, while 10(b) applies to both buyers and sellers), but this is the way Congress wanted it.

c) In practical terms this decision may not make any difference, since it is traditional in granting an injunction that it must be shown that there is a reasonable likelihood that the wrong will be repeated, which is shown by the fact that past wrongs were intentional (not just negligent).

5) Concurring in part, dissenting in part (Blackmun, Brennan, Marshall, JJ.).

a) Sections 17(a) and 10(b) are the primary antifraud provisions of the federal securities laws. The court's holding undercuts the S.E.C.'s authority to police the marketplace.

b) It is unclear that the words of the statutes themselves call for so restrictive a definition; usually meaning is imparted to words by the mischief that is to be remedied.

c) The Court previously recognized in *S.E.C. v. Capital Gains Research Bureau*, 375 U.S. 180 (1963), that scienter (required in actions for fraud at law) is often dispensed with in actions in equity for injunctions.

d) The Court has misconstrued the structural interrelationship among the equitable remedy provisions of the 1933 and 1934 Acts.

(1) In *Hochfelder* the Court noted that Congress had placed limitations on private causes of action for negligence under the Acts, and that to allow actions for negligence in private actions under 10(b) would destroy the effect of these other provisions. But there is no such danger here, since injunctions are initiated by the S.E.C.

(2) The consistent pattern of the Acts is to grant the S.E.C. broad authority to seek enforcement without scienter, unless criminal punishments are involved. When Congress meant scienter, it used such words as "willful," "knowing," etc., which it did not use in 17(a) or 10(b).

(3) The Court has destroyed the harmony between 10(b) and 17(a) by making distinctions (on the basis of alleged differences in the wording) between them. Rule 10(b) was passed for the very reason of supplementing section 17(a).

Adams v. Standard Knitting Mills

c. Fault standard for proxy rules--Adams v. Standard Knitting Mills, 623 F.2d 422 (6th Cir. 1980), *cert. denied,* 449 U.S. 1067 (1981).

1) Facts. Chadbourn, a public company, agreed to merge with Standard, an over-the-counter company that rarely traded, for common and preferred stock having the same market value as the Standard stock. Dividends were to be paid on the preferred stock and it was to be redeemed for cash (a portion of the shares each year). Chadbourn had loan agreements which restricted its ability to pay dividends on all of its stock and to redeem stock. In the body of the proxy statement these restrictions were described, but the heading of the paragraph was "common stock." In a footnote in the financial statements, the restrictions were described as restrictions only on common stock. A year after the merger, Chadbourn suffered a major loss, wiping out its retained earnings. It could no longer pay dividends or redeem the preferred stock. The former Standard share-holders sued Chadbourn, Standard (and its management), and others, including Peat Marwick (the accounting firm which prepared the financial statements of Chadbourn that went into the proxy statement soliciting the approval of Standard shareholders to the merger). Control of Chadbourn has been given to these shareholders and all parties have settled, except Peat Marwick. The district court found for plaintiffs against Peat Marwick in an action based on Rule 10b-5 and Rule 14a-0 for including false statements in the proxy statement. Peat Marwick appeals the decision of the district court.

2) **Issue.** Will the outside accountant who has negligently included false statements in the proxy statement be held liable for damages under Rule 10b-5 or Rule 14a-9?

3) **Held.** No. District court is reversed.

a) The statements included in the proxy materials were misleading or ambiguous at best.

b) Peat Marwick's attention was called to the mistake just after the proxy materials were sent out and before the shareholder vote. The partner in charge made a note of it but never got it corrected. Nevertheless, the mistake was only negligent; it was an oversight.

c) Liability under Rule 10b-5 must be based on intentional or reckless conduct.

d) The issue under Rule 14a-9 is not liability of the issuer of the proxy statement, but of the outside accounting firm.

(1) There must be a showing in this case of scienter or reckless conduct.

(2) The same standard should apply as applies in Rule 10b-5.

(3) Potential liability for relatively minor mistakes by accountants would be enormous under a negligence standard.

(4) The legislative history talks about intentional mistakes.

(5) Rule 14(e) as applied to tender offers requires scienter.

C. CONDUCT CREATING LIABILITY

1. The Type of Information that Must be Disclosed.

Feit v. Leasco
Data Process-
ing Equip-
ment Corp.

a. Misrepresentation of "facts" under section 11 of the 1933 Act--Feit v. Leasco Data Processing Equipment Corp., 332 F. Supp. 544 (E.D.N.Y. 1971).

1) **Facts.** Leasco (D) discovered that Reliance Insurance Co. had in excess of $100 million in surplus that could be distributed; it approached Reliance management for a merger. Reliance resisted. D tendered the shares of Reliance directly (Reliance brought a lawsuit and informed shareholders that it was not a good deal). Then D met with Reliance and gave Reliance management a long-term contract, with the president receiving D options, an increase in salary, etc. As a result of this contract, Reliance management terminated its resistance and D made another tender offer (this time of a preferred stock plus a warrant to purchase D common stock) on August 16, 1968. D did not disclose, in the registration statement of its stock used in the offering, the estimated amount of the surplus. At the date of the offering, the Reliance stock was selling for $67 per share (prior to the tender offer it had been selling for around $30) and the package of D securities for $72. Later the D package dropped in price. A Reliance shareholder (P), sues under sections 11 and 12(2) of the 1933 Act, section 14(e) of the 1934 Act and Rule 10b-5 of the 1934 Act.

2) **Issue.** Was there a material misrepresentation by D?

3) **Held.** Yes. Judgment for P.

   a) An estimate of "surplus" (the portion of cash that could be transferred from Reliance to D) should have been made in the registration statement. It was a material fact.

   b) A material fact is one where it is more probable than not that a significant number of traders (anything in the order of 10%) in the stock would have wanted to know the fact before deciding to deal in the security.

   c) D could have made the estimate. There were existing estimates by security analysts; D itself had made an estimate; the relationship with Reliance after the management contract was not so hostile that an estimate from Reliance could not have been gotten; and within several months D itself made an estimate in a subsequent registration statement.

   d) Section 11 damages are adequate to give P a remedy, so other sections of the securities acts need not be considered.

   e) Hodes, the lawyer-director for D, was so involved in the offering and knew so much about the deal that he will be treated the same as director-managers. All of these persons are liable since they did not make a reasonable investigation of the facts and they did not have a reasonable or actual belief that the registration statement was accurate. These persons are virtual guarantors of the accuracy of the registration statement.

f) The underwriters are not liable. They were represented by counsel; the issue was raised, but they had evidence of the hostility of Reliance and no one at D indicated that this hostility had abated. They were entitled to rely on the D management in this case.

g) Damages are based on the price paid (which is determined by taking the market value of the Reliance shares on the day before the offer was made) less the price at the time of sale. However, D can show that the drop in value of the securities was based on other causes (and here an allowance will be made for the decline in the general level of the stock market by using the percentage decline in the Standard and Poor's index).

b. **Merger negotiations, asset appraisals, and earnings projections--Starkman v. Marathon Oil Co.,** 772 F.2d 231 (6th Cir. 1985).

Starkman v. Marathon Oil Co.

1) **Facts.** Marathon (D) stock was at $68 per share; anticipating a hostile tender offer, it prepared an appraisal of its assets (which included a statement of unproven oil reserves that required complex estimates of future oil prices; this information could not be included on the regular company balance sheet); it had the First Boston brokerage firm do the same. D also prepared a five-year forecast of earnings and cash flow. Mobil then made a bid at $85 per share. D's board issued a press release stating that the offer was grossly inadequate and that it was recommending that shareholders reject it, and that the company would consider several other alternatives, including merger with a different company or staying independent. A letter saying the same went to shareholders and a report was filed with the S.E.C. At this time, D was negotiating a friendly takeover with U.S. Steel; U.S. Steel got the report on assets, the First Boston report, and the projections, all of which had been prepared to argue for the best price possible in the event of a takeover. None of this information was publicly disclosed. On November 17, U.S. Steel and D reached agreement. The merger was signed on November 18, providing for a two-stage deal with a value to D's shareholders of $125 per share. On that same day, Starkman (P) sold his stock on the open market for $78 per share. P sues on the basis that, under Rule 10b-5, D should have disclosed (i) the U.S. Steel negotiations, (ii) the asset reports, and (iii) the projections. The district court granted summary judgment for D. P appeals.

2) **Issue.** Were the negotiations and the reports material facts that should have been disclosed?

3) **Held.** No. Affirmed.

a) The general rule is that there must first be a duty to disclose, and if that exists, then "material facts" must be disclosed, but only if nondisclosure would make other information already given misleading.

b) With regard to the asset appraisals and earnings projections, Rule 14e-2 of the 1934 Act requires a target company to make a statement to its shareholders on its position relative to a tender offer, and under Rule 14d-9, a report following Schedule 14d-9 must be filed with the S.E.C. (which requires a statement of the reasons the target has taken the position it has). But there is no rule specifically requiring internal or other asset appraisals or earnings projections.

(1) The S.E.C.'s policy on the disclosure of such "soft" information has moved to allowing its disclosure in some situations.

(2) Until after U.S. Steel's offer, Regulation S-K actually prohibited disclosure in any document filed with the S.E.C. of any estimates of possible oil and gas reserves.

(3) Also, earnings forecasts were not required by the S.E.C. in any context; asset appraisals were only required in freeze-out mergers.

(4) The cases in this circuit have held that soft information must be disclosed only if the values involved are as certain as hard facts. Under this standard D had no duty to make a disclosure here.

c) With respect to the U.S. Steel negotiations, the S.E.C. and the courts have held that as long as merger discussions are preliminary, general disclosure that such alternatives are being considered is adequate; a duty to disclose terms and parties arises only after an agreement in principle has been reached.

Basic, Inc. v. Levinson

c. **Preliminary merger negotiations--Basic, Inc. v. Levinson,** 485 U.S. 224 (1988).

1) **Facts.** Officers and directors of Basic, Inc., including Ds, opened merger discussions with Combustion Engineering in September 1976. During 1977 and 1978, Basic publicly denied three times that it was conducting merger negotiations. On December 18, 1978, it halted trading on the New York Stock Exchange, saying it had been approached. On December 19, 1978, it announced that the board had approved Combustion's $46 per share tender offer. Levinson and others (Ps) are a class of shareholders who sold their stock after Basic's 1977 statement of denial and before the trading halt on December 18, 1978. They sue under Rule 10b-5. The district court, on the basis of a "fraud on the market theory," adopted a rebuttable presumption of reliance on the misrepresentation by members of the class. On a motion for summary judgment, the district court ruled for Ds, holding that at the time of the first announcement in 1977, no negotiations were actually going on, and that the negotiations conducted at the time of the second and third announcements were not destined with reasonable certainty to become a merger agreement. The court of appeals affirmed the holding about reliance, but reversed the summary judgment. It held that preliminary merger discussions could be material. Further, it held that once a statement is made denying the existence of discussions,

then even discussions that might otherwise have been immaterial can become material. The Supreme Court granted certiorari.

2) Issues.

a) Is the standard used to determine whether preliminary merger negotiations must be disclosed a materiality standard under Rule 10b-5?

b) Is it appropriate to use a rebuttable presumption of reliance for all members of a class on the basis that there has been a fraud on the market?

3) Held. (a) Yes. (b) Yes.

a) The *TSC Industries* test is the test of materiality for Rule 10b-5 cases; that is, a fact is material if there is a substantial likelihood that a reasonable shareholder would consider it important.

b) With contingent events like mergers (that may or may not happen), the probability that the merger will occur and the magnitude of the possible event are looked at. All relevant facts bearing on these two issues should be considered.

c) An absolute rule (such as the one requiring that a preliminary agreement be arrived at before negotiations are material), while convenient, is *not* in accord with the *TSC Industries* test. Likewise, the circuit court was wrong also. If a fact is immaterial, it makes no difference that Ds made misrepresentations about it.

d) Thus, the case must be remanded to consider whether the lower court's grant of summary judgment for Ds was appropriate.

e) Reliance is an element of a Rule 10b-5 cause of action. It provides a causal connection between a defendant's misrepresentation and a plaintiff's injury. But this causal connection can be proved in a number of ways. In the case of face-to-face negotiations, the issue is whether the buyer subjectively considered the seller's representations. In the case of a securities market, the dissemination or withholding of information by the issuer affects the price of the stock in the market, and investors rely on the market price as a reflection of the stock's value.

f) The presumption of reliance in this situation assists courts to manage a situation where direct proof of reliance would be unwieldy. The presumption serves to allocate the burden of proof to defendants in situations where the plaintiffs have relied on the integrity of the markets, which Rule 10b-5 was enacted to protect. The presumption is supported by common sense. Most investors rely on market integrity in buying and selling securities.

g) Ds can rebut the presumption. First, Ds could show that misrepresentation or omission did not distort the market price (for example, Ds could show that market makers knew the real facts and set prices based on these facts, despite any misrepresentations that might have been made). Or Ds could show that an individual plaintiff sold his shares for other reasons than the market price, knowing that Ds had probably misrepresented the status of merger negotiations.

4) **Dissent** (as to the fraud-on-the-market theory).

    a)   The fraud-on-the-market theory should not be applied in this case.

    b)   The fraud-on-the-market theory is an economic doctrine, not a doctrine based on traditional legal fraud principles. If Rule 10b-5 is to be changed, Congress should do it.

    c)   It is not clear that investors rely on the "integrity" of the markets (i.e., on the price of a stock reflecting its value).

    d)   In rejecting the original version of section 18 of the Securities Exchange Act, Congress rejected a liability provision that allowed an investor recovery based solely on the fact that the price of the security bought or sold was affected by a misrepresentation. Congress altered section 18 to include a specific reliance requirement.

    e)   The fraud-on-the-market theory is in opposition to the fundamental policy of disclosure, which is based on the idea of investors looking out for themselves by reading and relying on publicly disclosed information.

    f)   This is a bad case in which to apply the fraud-on-the-market theory. Ps' sales occurred over a 14-month period. At the time the period began, Basic's stock sold for $20 per share; when it ended, the stock sold for $30 per share, so all Ps made money. Also, Basic did not withhold information to defraud anyone. And no one connected with Basic was trading in its securities. Finally, some Ps bought stock after Ds' first false statement in 1977, disbelieving the statement. They then made a profit, and can still recover under the fraud-on-the-market theory. These Ps are speculators. Their judgment comes from other, innocent shareholders who held the stock.

United States
v. Matthews

d. **Uncharged criminal violations as omitted facts in proxy statements--United States v. Matthews, 787 F.2d 38 (2d Cir. 1986).**

    1) **Facts.** In 1972 Southland Corporation was sued by the New York State Department of Taxation for sales taxes on its franchised stores. DeFalco, a Southland employee, contacted Kelly, who set up a meeting with Mastropieri, a New York lawyer and city councilman. DeFalco testified that Mastropieri wanted a bribe to help, paid in the form of an airplane lease; Matthews (D), general counsel for Southland, rejected the idea. Then DeFalco sent a $96,500 bill from Mastropieri to Dole, Southland's vice president for franchises. The bill was paid, and Mastropieri wrote a check in the same amount to DeFalco and Kelly, who set up bank accounts and eventually embezzled the money.

    In the course of a business ethics review conducted by Matthews, questions were raised about the payment to Mastropieri, who was finally interviewed. He stated that he knew about the issue, that his fee was justified, that he had received the entire amount, and that none of the money was paid to anyone else and that no bribes were ever paid. No mention of the issue was included in the report given by D to the board of directors. The Government charged D and others for conspiracy to bribe members of the

New York State Tax Commission; he was also charged with having been elected a director of Southland by a false proxy statement which failed to disclose his part in the conspiracy.

The district court found D guilty of violating section 14(a) and Rule 14a-9 of the 1934 Act. D appeals.

2) **Issue.** Did D violate the proxy rules relating to being elected a director by not disclosing that he was part of a conspiracy to bribe state tax officials?

3) **Held.** No. District court reversed.

a) D was told about possible prosecutions in 1981 when he ran for the board; he did not disclose anything about them although he knew that he might be the "subject" of one or more of these investigations.

b) Later Mastropieri was convicted of participation in a conspiracy to bribe New York tax officials and Southland of misdescribing a bribe as a legal fee.

c) Finally Dole and D were indicted on the conspiracy to bribe and D on the proxy violation charge (the indictments now before us).

d) There was no bribe, and the Government has not proved what "facts" D should have told the Southland board. It does not appear that D could have told the board about anyone involved in a possible conspiracy without risk (e.g., of libel).

e) It is also unrealistic to have expected D to reveal that he was guilty (if he was) of the crime of conspiracy when he was not yet charged.

f) So the issue is whether D should have disclosed unadjudicated and uncharged allegations (that made him the subject of possible grand jury indictments at the time of the 1981 proxy statement) since it bears on D's morality and managerial fitness.

g) Attempts have been made to use Rule 14(a)-9 to get access to federal courts in order to redress state law claims of alleged mismanagement, breach of fiduciary duties, etc. As a result, the federal courts have held that the Rule only applies to items specifically mentioned or at least implicit in the S.E.C.'s rules.

2. **Who Must Disclose.**

a. **Trading by insiders and the duty to disclose under Rule 10b-5.** A simple definition is that an "insider" is someone with possession of material information about securities that is not possessed by others who are trading in the issuer's securities.

1) **Application of Rule 10b-5.** Rule 10b-5 does *not* mention "insiders" specifically, nor does it specifically require that one person having information not possessed by another disclose this information in a securities transaction. Nevertheless, the S.E.C. and the courts have used Rule 10b-5 to cover such transactions.

2) **Fiduciary relationship required.** The origin of the concept of an "insider" is the idea that where one person occupies a "fiduciary relationship" with another, this fiduciary must disclose relevant, material information to the person for whom he has the responsibility. Thus, if A is a corporate officer of XYZ, Inc. and possesses inside information, he should not trade on this information with B, an XYZ shareholder, without disclosing the information since A has a fiduciary relationship with B.

3) **Insiders defined.**

   a) **The test.** There are two elements which must be shown in order to designate someone an "insider":

      (1) The person must have a relationship giving *access*, directly or indirectly, *to information* about the securities which is intended to be available only for a business purpose and not for the personal benefit of anyone.

      (2) There must be an *inherent unfairness where the insider takes advantage of such information*, knowing it is unavailable to those with whom he is dealing.

   b) **Examples of insiders.**

      (1) Controlling shareholders, directors, and officers of a corporation are "insiders" with respect to information concerning the securities of that corporation. [*See* S.E.C. v. Texas Gulf Sulfur, 401 F.2d 833 (2d Cir. 1968), *cert. denied*, 394 U.S. 976 (1969)]

      (2) Tippers inside the corporation who pass along information to relatives, friends, and business associates (i.e., tippees) outside the corporation are insiders. In *Texas Gulf Sulfur*, these tippers were held liable for the profits made by the tippees.

      (3) Cases have also held the tippees from such insider tippers liable. [*See* In the Matter of Investors Management Co., SEA Release No. 9267 (1971)]

      (4) A broker who receives inside information from the corporation and uses it to assist his customers in making sales before public disclosure of a material fact is liable. [In the Matter of Cady, Roberts & Co., 40 S.E.C. 907 (1961)]

      (5) And in *Shapiro v. Merrill Lynch, Pierce, Fenner & Smith*, 495 F.2d 228 (2d Cir. 1974), a nontrading tipper (the underwriter of the issuer's securities) was held liable and so were the nontrading tipper's tippees (i.e., the clients of the tipper who sold the stock as soon as they received the inside information).

4) Elements of a Rule 10b-5 cause of action against insider trading. The elements are essentially the same as in other Rule 10b-5 actions, with the following differences:

   a) **Reliance.** Reliance may be an element in other 10b-5 settings, but in the situation where corporate insiders fail to disclose material facts and stock is traded over an exchange, the courts seem to treat the issue of materiality-reliance as one issue; i.e., did the defendant insider fail to disclose a material fact? If so, then the reliance element is also proved.

   b) **Affirmative duty to disclose.** Rule 10b-5 imposes an affirmative duty on insiders to disclose their material inside information to those who might reasonably be affected thereby *before* engaging in securities transactions in which the information would be material.

   c) **Due diligence required.** Defendants in corporate management can avoid liability by showing that they used due care in disclosing or in refusing to disclose.

      (1) This is a negligence standard, but note that the case that established it was *Texas Gulf Sulfur*, which was an S.E.C. action for an *injunction*. Subsequently the Supreme Court has held that intentional conduct must be shown in an S.E.C. injunctive action or in an action for damages.

      (2) In private damage actions, the Supreme Court has required that defendants must have knowingly misrepresented or omitted to state material facts before liability can be found. [*See* Ernst & Ernst v. Hochfelder, *supra*]

b. **Applications of Rule 10b-5 to insider trading.**

   1) **Outsiders may not have a general duty to disclose inside information-- Chiarella v. United States,** 445 U.S. 222 (1980).

      a) **Facts.** Chiarella (D) was a printer for a financial printing firm. He handled announcements of corporate takeover bids from which the names of the companies had been deleted. He surmised the companies and bought stock in the selling companies, then sold the stock after the takeover attempt, at a profit of $30,000. Pursuant to a consent decree with the S.E.C., D returned the profits he had made. Now, the United States (P) brings a criminal action for willful violation of section 10(b) of the 1934 Act. The district court convicted D, the circuit court affirmed, and the United States Supreme Court granted certiorari.

      b) **Issue.** Does a person who is not an insider of the issuer but who learns, from confidential documents, that the corporation is planning to attempt to gain control of a second corporation violate Rule 10b-5 if he buys stock and fails to disclose the impending takeover to potential sellers of the target company's securities?

      c) **Held.** No. Judgment reversed.

Chiarella v. United States

(1) Silence (nondisclosure) of material information in connection with the purchase or sale of securities may be a fraud under Rule 10b-5 *if there is a duty to disclose arising from a relationship of trust and confidence* (i.e., a fiduciary relationship between the parties to the transaction (for example, corporate managers and other insiders have such a duty to disclose a takeover attempt to their shareholders before trading in the company's stock).

(2) Here, D was not an insider and he received no confidential information from the target company. The trial court indicated that D had a duty to everyone (to all sellers, to the market as a whole, etc.) to disclose material nonpublic information before trading. The circuit court held that anyone (insider or not) who *regularly* receives material nonpublic information may not use it to trade before disclosure, since otherwise an unfair advantage is created in those with such information. But not every instance of financial unfairness is fraud under section 10(b). *And no duty to disclose arises unless there is some relationship of a fiduciary or trust nature between the parties*, which there was not.

(3) No general duty to disclose is evident from the language or legislative history of section 10(b). It is clear, for example, that the securities laws permit situations where one party has the advantage of nondisclosed information over other parties. For example, a party wishing to make a tender offer on a corporation can acquire up to 5% of that company's securities without disclosing its intentions.

(4) *We cannot address the question whether D breached a duty to the acquiring company* as the employee of a printer employed by the corporation, since this issue was not raised at trial and submitted to the trial court jury.

d) **Concurrence** (Stevens, J.). We have not decided that what D did is approved of, or that similar actions in the future will be held to be lawful. We only hold that D could not breach a duty he did not owe.

e) **Concurrence** (Brennan, J.). The correct rule is that a person violates section 10(b) when he improperly obtains for his own benefit nonpublic information which is then used in the purchase and sale of securities.

f) **Dissent** (Burger, C.J.). Rule 10b-5 requires that when a person misappropriates nonpublic information, he has an absolute duty to disclose that information or refrain from trading. The majority reverses because it believes that the district court instructed the jury that mere failure to disclose nonpublic information, however acquired, is a violation of Rule 10b-5 (an error since it leaves out the element of misappropriation of the information). This is an unduly restrictive reading of the district court's instructions, which can fairly be said to have stated the requirement of misappropriation.

g) **Dissent** (Blackmun, Marshall, JJ.). Even had D had the blessing of his employer, it would still be a violation of section 10(b). What is wrong here is the use of inside information as a result of access to such information which the ordinary investor does not have and which was not meant to benefit D. The majority has unduly restricted Rule 10b-5 adding the element of a special relationship akin to a fiduciary duty; it is emasculating Rule 10b-5.

h) **Comments.** This case can be read as saying that unless defendant is a corporate insider, there is no fiduciary duty to shareholders of the corporation to abstain from trading on inside information. However, there are several opinions here, so it is not clear what the case stands for.

(1) Possibly a person can obtain inside information (if *not* a corporate insider) by diligent search or even by accident and be able to trade on this information.

(2) Clearly, although the issue was not before the Court, some of the judges thought that if the issue had been clearly put that defendant "misappropriated" the inside information from his employer, this would be enough to make him a bad guy and create a duty to existing shareholders to disclose the information before trading.

(3) Clearly, some judges think that no matter how you get inside information, and no matter who you are, you should not be able to trade on it.

i) **Follow-up cases:**

(1) In *SEC v. Materia,* 745 F.2d 197 (2d Cir. 1984), *cert. denied*, 471 U.S. 1053 (1985), Materia (like Chiarella) was employed by a financial printer and used confidential information obtained in that capacity to trade in the stock of target corporations. The court held that Materia had criminally violated Rule 10b-5 under the misappropriation theory. *Chiarella* was distinguished on the ground that the instruction to the jury in that case had been much broader than the misappropriation theory (i.e., it covered all persons, however innocently they got the information).

(2) In *United States v. Newman*, 664 F.2d 12 (2d Cir. 1981), *cert. denied,* 464 U.S. 863 (1983), Courtois was employed in the mergers and acquisitions department of Morgan Stanley, an investment banking firm. Warner-Lambert Corporation retained Morgan Stanley to assess the desirability of making a tender offer for Deseret Pharmaceutical Corporation. Courtois learned of Warner's plan, and, acting with and through others, purchased Deseret stock at $28 per share. When Warner publicly announced the tender offer, the Deseret stock jumped to $38. The Second Circuit held that Courtois had criminally violated Rule 10b-5, based on the misappropriation theory.

j) **Private actions vs. criminal actions.** In a private rather than criminal action based on the same facts as *Newman, supra*, the Second Circuit held that although Newman and his associates had criminally violated Rule 10b-5 by trading on the basis of information they used in violation of Newman's fiduciary duty to his employer, they were not liable under private actions by those persons with whom they actually traded. An employee's duty to "abstain or disclose" with respect to his employer does not stretch to encompass a duty to disclose to the general public. [*See* Moss v. Morgan Stanley, Inc., 719 F.2d 5 (2d Cir. 1983), *cert. denied,* 465 U.S. 1025 (1984)]

Dirks v.
S.E.C.

**2) A further definition of an "insider" and market analysts as "outsiders"--
Dirks v. S.E.C., 463 U.S. 646 (1983).**

a) **Facts.** Dirks was an employee of a broker-dealer firm that specialized in providing investment analysis of insurance companies for institutional investors. He received information from Ronald Secrist, a former officer of Equity Funding (a New York Stock Exchange company) that its assets were vastly overstated since the company was creating false insurance policies. Dirks investigated by interviewing company officers and employees. Some of the employees verified the charge. Dirks discussed this information with some of his clients, who sold the stock, driving the market price down. Finally, the S.E.C. halted trading in the stock. Then the California Insurance Commissioner investigated and discovered the fraud. Equity Funding entered receivership. The S.E.C. sued Dirks under section 17(a) of the 1933 Act for aiding and abetting his clients who sold their stock based on the inside information. The circuit court affirmed the S.E.C.'s decision against Dirks. The Supreme Court granted certiorari.

b) **Issue.** Where the insider (Secrist) is not motivated by personal gain, is Dirks (a tipper), who got the inside information from an insider, and who gave it to tippees that traded on the information, in violation of section 17(a)?

c) **Held.** No. Circuit court is reversed.

(1) To be an "insider," a person must have a fiduciary relationship with the shareholders of the company whose stock is traded.

(2) The S.E.C.'s position is that a tippee from such an insider inherits the fiduciary duty of the insider if he knows the information is material and nonpublic and if he knows that the insider has a fiduciary duty not to disclose it.

(3) But a rule such as that suggested by the S.E.C. might inhibit market analysts from doing their work, which is to question corporate insiders and discuss this information with their clients.

(4) Hence, the motivation of the insider is critical. The test is whether the insider will personally benefit, directly or indirectly, for his disclosure. Absent some such personal gain, there is no breach, and the tippee who takes such information and gives it to those who might trade on it has not breached any duty, since his duty is derivative from the insider's duty. Gain might be monetary, reputational, etc.

d) **Dissent.** Secrist could not trade on his information. He could not get someone to do the trading for him. But this is what he did; he used Dirks to disseminate information to Dirks's clients, who traded with unknowing purchasers. It makes no difference to these unknowing shareholders whether Secrist had a good or bad purpose in disclosing the inside information. The breach is to take action disadvantageous to one to whom a duty is owed.

e) **Comment.** So not all corporate personnel that disclose inside information are "insiders"; it depends on their motivation.

f) Tipper and tippee liability.

(1) Broad rule rejected. The Court in *Dirks* rejected the broad rule that a person would be liable, as a tippee, solely because she knowingly received material nonpublic information from an insider and traded on it. Such a broad rule would conflict with the conclusion in *Chiarella* that only some persons, under some circumstances, will be barred by Rule 10b-5 from trading while in the possession of material nonpublic information. The Court was also concerned that a broad rule would inhibit the role of market analysts, who often, as part of their research into particular stocks, interview corporate executives and acquire information that may not have theretofore been public. However, the Court identified several kinds of cases in which *tippees would be liable.*

(2) Tippee liability based on fiduciary obligations of tipper. A person who receives information from an insider and trades on it is liable *if*—but only if—she receives the information improperly because the insider breached a fiduciary duty in communicating the information, *and the tippee knows or should know of the breach*. The primary test in *Dirks* for determining whether the communication of information by an insider constitutes a breach of fiduciary duty is whether the insider communicated the information to realize a gain or advantage. Not only are insiders forbidden by their fiduciary relationship from personally using undisclosed corporate information for the purpose of reaping personal gain or advantage, but also they may not give such information to others for that purpose. An insider who tips for that purpose breaches his fiduciary duty to the corporation. A tippee who knows or should know that the tipper, in disclosing inside information to the tippee, has breached his fiduciary duty to the corporation by using corporate information for his own gain or advantage, *will be liable as a knowing participant* in a breach of fiduciary duty. On the surface, this test seems narrow. However, the Court defined gain or advantage, in this connection, so broadly as to include most tipping activity.

(a) Tips to friends or relatives. There is a gain or advantage to the insider when he makes a gift of confidential information to a trading relative or friend. The tip to the relative or friend, followed by a trade by the tippee, is like a trade by the insider followed by a gift of his profits from the trade.

(b) Quid pro quo for past or future benefits. Even if the tippee is not a friend or a relative, the insider breaches his fiduciary duty, and the tippee is therefore liable, if there is a relationship between the insider and the tippee that suggests that the tip is a quid pro quo for a past or future benefit from the tippee.

(c) Tippers. Under *Dirks*, if a tippee will be liable, so will the tipper (*e.g.,* Dirks).

(d) Outsiders in special confidential relationship. Certain outsiders who receive information from the corporation as a result of a special confidential relationship could be liable, under a separate principle (*see* below).

g) "Temporary insiders." Where corporate information is legitimately revealed to an underwriter, accountant, lawyer, or other professional or consultant working for the corporation, that person may become a fiduciary of the corporation's shareholders regarding that information. [Dirks v. SEC, *supra*] The theory is that the person has entered into a special confidential relationship with the corporation and is given access to the information solely for corporate purposes. If such a person trades on the information, he will be just as liable as an ordinary insider (and he will be liable as a tipper if he improperly tips the information). Persons who acquire information in this way are sometimes referred to as "temporary insiders." Compare the status of these outsiders with the printer in *Chiarella*.

3) Private rights of action—Insider Trading and Securities Fraud Enforcement Act. The Insider Trading and Securities Fraud Enforcement Act of 1988 is intended in part to overrule the result in *Moss v. Morgan Stanley, supra*. Under one section of the Act, any person who violates Rule 10b-5 by purchasing or selling a security while in the possession of material nonpublic information is expressly made liable to ***any person in a private action*** who, contemporaneously with the purchase or sale, purchased or sold (as the case may be) securities of the same class. Liability under this provision is limited to the profit the defendant gained or the loss he avoided.

a) Note that Congress in 1984 also passed the Insider Trading Sanctions Act, providing for a penalty to be assessed on a suit by the S.E.C. against persons violating the insider trading prohibitions of the 1934 Act, of up to three times the amount of the "profit gained or loss avoided as a result" of such insider trading.

b) This Act is aimed at the trading of persons with advanced knowledge of takeover attempts of "market information," such as the *Chiarella* case.

c) To prove a cause of action, the S.E.C. has to prove a violation of the 1934 Act or its rules.

d) Then the court may, but is not required to, award three times profit or loss avoided from the use of inside information. This penalty is in addition to any other, as a result of a private action, S.E.C. disgorgement proceeding, etc. The penalty is paid to the U.S. Treasury.

e) Only violations that occur through the facilities of a national exchange or through a broker or dealer are covered.

4) Mail and wire fraud theories. A federal criminal statute concerning mail and wire fraud [18 U.S.C. §§1341, 1343] may render the misappropriation theory less important. In *United States v. Carpenter*, 791 F.2d 1024, *aff'd,* 484 U.S. 19 (1987), a *Wall Street Journal* reporter who wrote a widely read and influential column, participated, in violation of the *Journal's* confidentiality rules, in a scheme in which he provided two stockbrokers with securities-related information that was scheduled to appear in his column. Based on this advance information, the two brokers would buy or sell the securities before the column appeared, and sell or buy immediately thereafter. The reporter was found guilty of criminally violating Rule 10b-5, based on the misappropriation theory, and was also found guilty of federal mail and wire fraud, since the *Wall Street*

Journal was distributed by mail. The Rule 10b-5 violation was affirmed by an equally divided United States Supreme Court, without an opinion. Therefore, the Supreme Court's view of the misappropriation theory is still not clear. The mail and wire fraud conviction, however, was unanimously affirmed. The Court held that the interest of the *Journal's* owner in the confidentiality of the *Journal's* contents was a property right, and that by using the information for his own purposes, the reporter had obtained "money or property" (as required by the federal statute) from the *Journal* by fraud. Thus, as a practical matter, the status of the misappropriation theory under Rule 10b-5 has been rendered somewhat less important by the Court's adoption of a comparable theory in the interpretation of the mail and wire fraud statute. Most persons who misappropriate and then trade on information will now be guilty of the crime of mail and wire fraud, whether or not they are guilty of criminally violating Rule 10b-5. The mail and wire fraud statute, however, unlike Rule 10b-5, may not give rise to private actions.

5) **The requirements of "inside" information--United States v. Chestman,** 903 F.2d 75 (2d Cir. 1990).

a) **Facts.** Chestman was a stockbroker for Gruntal & Co. He became Loeb's broker, in the course of which he learned that Loeb was married to the daughter (Susan) of the sister of the 51% owner of Waldbaum's (i.e., Ira Waldbaum). Over the years, D made several trades in Waldbaum stock for Loeb. In November 1986 Waldbaum's entered into negotiations to sell to A & P stores for $50 per share (twice the market value). Ira told his sister (Shirley), who told Susan (and that it was confidential), who told her husband ("It is important not to tell anybody since it might ruin the sale"). The morning of November 26, Loeb called D and said, "I have some definite, accurate information," and asked what he should do; D did not say. D then bought 8,000 shares for his discretionary accounts, including Loeb. There is a dispute as to whether Loeb called back later that afternoon and ordered 1,000 shares for his account. The tender offer closed that afternoon, and the stock doubled the next day. The S.E.C. investigated; Loeb cooperated and disgorged his profits on the 1,000 shares. The S.E.C. went after D; he was convicted in the trial court of (i) violating Rule 10b-5; (ii) violating Rule 14e-3 of the 1934 Act; (iii) mail fraud; and (iv) perjury. He appeals.

b) **Issues.**

(1) On the Rule 10b-5 claim, did the government prove a misappropriation of nonpublic information, or a relationship of trust and confidence sufficient to establish an insider duty by D?

(2) Did the person upon whom the supposed mail fraud was committed have a recognizable "property" interest?

(3) Was there sufficient evidence to support the perjury conviction?

(4) What standard for conviction applies to Rule 14e-3, and did the S.E.C. have the requisite authority to pass a rule with this standard of fraud?

c) **Judge Miner's Opinion.**

(1) For D to be convicted of aiding and abetting Loeb in violating Rule 10b-5, it must be shown that Loeb breached a special relationship of trust and misappropriated valuable nonpublic information acquired in confidence; also, that D knew all of this and assisted. There is no evidence that D knew Loeb was breaching a confidential relationship by telling him the information. He did not know that there had been pledges of secrecy from Ira to Loeb; and there is no evidence in any event that there was an acceptance of such a duty by Loeb. For D to be liable as a "tippee," there must be evidence that Loeb furnished the information to D as a "tipper." There is the same failure relative to this information. Thus, there is no Rule 10b-5, insider liability.

(2) Mail fraud under 18 U.S.C. section 1341 requires a fraudulent obtaining of money or other property; "property" includes such intangible property as confidential, non-public business information. D is charged with being part of a fraudulent scheme engaged in by Loeb to obtain inside information from the Waldbaum family. But there is no basis for a determination that D was aware of the confidentiality of the information.

(3) In 1970 the S.E.C. adopted Rule 14e-3, which defines it as a fraudulent act to purchase or sell a security if one is in possession of material information relating to a tender offer, and the person knows the information is non-public and has been acquired directly or indirectly from the issuer, an offeror, or any person acting on behalf of the issuer. D challenges the rule as being outside the S.E.C.'s authority on the basis that it does not require a fiduciary duty or a duty to disclose; and on the basis that a quasi-negligence standard rather than scienter is required. However, I would affirm the Rule 14e-3 conviction; more than mere possession of inside information is required (i.e., knowing it is inside information and where it came from), and no reliance should be required.

d) **Judge Mahoney.** I agree that the convictions on securities fraud, mail fraud, and for perjury should be reversed, as Judge Miner said. But I also contend that the conviction for Rule 14-e3 should be reversed.

The S.E.C. exceeded its statutory authority in enacting the rule; it has no requirement that there be a breach of fiduciary duty (mere possession and use of inside information is enough). This is a broader definition of fraud than the S.E.C. has the power to enact.

e) **Judge Carman.** I also agree that the Rule 14e-3 should be reversed. The trial court did not instruct the jury as to the elements of fraud in connection with the rule. Section 14(e) of the 1934 Act is a fraud statute. The S.E.C. cannot enact a rule that brings about liability on lesser standards than the underlying enabling statute. The defendant under the rule could be liable but not be guilty of fraud. This is improper. The fault is not the S.E.C.'s. We should give the S.E.C. the presumption that it enacted a legitimate rule. But the trial court did not read the requirements of fraud into the rule and instruct the jury in this manner. So there should be a reversal. Specifically missing was a scienter instruction (a "willfulness" standard was used instead).

3. Misrepresentation, Fraud, or Deception.

a. Misrepresentation under Rule 10b-5. Rule 10b-5 requires that there be some misrepresentation, omission, or other deception in connection with the purchase or sale of securities. An issue has arisen in several contexts as to whether there has actually been such a "deception."

1) Situations where no one may have been deceived. The first context in which the issue has arisen occurs when no one may have been deceived by the "fraud."

a) Where all corporate directors are involved in the deception. The cases have held that even where all the directors of a corporation are involved in perpetrating the deception, there may still be a "fraud" on the corporation and its shareholders. [*See* Hooper v. Mountain States Securities Corp., 282 F.2d 195 (5th Cir. 1960), *cert. denied,* 365 U.S. 814 (1961)]

b) Fraud by all of the promoters, directors, and all present shareholders. There is also authority for the proposition that even where all the directors and all of the shareholders of the corporation are involved in the fraud, the corporation may still recover for the fraud. These situations occur where a corporation is initially being formed and all parties relating to the corporation are part of the fraudulent scheme. [*See* Bailes v. Colonial Press, 444 F.2d 1241 (5th Cir. 1971)]

2) Deception in connection with the purchase or sale of securities. The language of Rule 10b-5 requires that the fraud be "in connection with" the purchase and sale of securities.

a) Application--Superintendent of Insurance v. Bankers Life and Casualty Co., 404 U.S. 6 (1971).

> Superintendent of Insurance v. Bankers Life and Casualty Co.

(1) Facts. The stock of Manhattan Insurance Co. was sold by Bankers (D) to Begole for $5 million, who, in conspiracy with others, sold the bond portfolio of Manhattan for $5 million, and used the $5 million, through a complicated series of transactions, to pay off the bank loan used to pay D for the company. Thus, Manhattan sold its bonds but never received any of the proceeds and it ended up bankrupt. The Insurance Department of the State of New York (P) sued D and the bank (Irving Trust) under Rule 10b-5.

(2) Issue. Has there been a "deception" or "fraud" "in connection with" the sale of securities?

(3) Held. Yes. Remanded for trial on D's defenses. There has, however, been a deception in connection with the sale of securities.

(a) Manhattan is a "seller" of securities (its bond portfolio).

(b) The fraud or deception is the sale of Manhattan's bonds without its receipt of the proceeds.

(c) The fraud is "in connection with" the sale of the bonds (securities).

(d) Rule 10b-5 is not limited to situations concerned with preserving the integrity of the securities markets. However, it also was not meant to regulate transactions which comprise no more than internal corporate mismanagement.

(4) Comment. The Court notes that Rule 10b-5 was not meant to cover all of the situations of corporate mismanagement normally covered by state law, but it fails to state which ones are included and which excluded. Note also that Ds are being sued as aiders and abettors of Begole.

b) Sufficient connection. The language of Rule 10b-5 requires that defendant's fraud, misrepresentation, or omission must be "in connection with" the purchase or sale of a security by the plaintiff. The issue is whether the fraud or deception is so remote from plaintiff's purchase or sale transaction as to snap the necessary "connection."

(1) Fraud as part of the securities sales transaction. The fraud may occur as part of the securities sales transaction itself. For example, A sells to B, having inside material information which he does not disclose to B. It is clear in these cases that a sufficient connection exists.

(2) Fraud separate from the actual sales transaction. The more difficult cases are those where defendant's fraud is not directly related to the securities transaction itself. Thus, the issue is whether there is a sufficient connection.

3) Breach of fiduciary duties as "fraud." Federal courts have split on the question of whether a breach of fiduciary duty under state corporate law (e.g., breach of the directors' duty of loyalty or of due care) is a sufficient "fraud" for 10b-5 purposes. But the trend of opinions is now against finding a Rule 10b-5 cause of action.

a) Cause of action permitted. Some decisions can be read as permitting a 10b-5 cause of action even though a state cause of action for breach of fiduciary duty is also available. For example, a 10b-5 cause of action has been allowed in situations where a corporation (and its directors) issued stock for inadequate consideration—a breach of fiduciary duty under state law. [*See* Hooper v. Mountain States Securities Corp., *supra*]

b) Cause of action denied. Other decisions have held that no cause of action is available under Rule 10b-5 where state law provides an adequate remedy.

(1) Example. Rule 10b-5 has been held not to cover a cause of action for diversion and misuse of corporate assets by management, traditionally within the province of state law. [Mutual Shares Corp. v. Genesco, Inc., 384 F.2d 540 (2d Cir. 1967)]

4) Where the defendant follows procedures permitted by state law--Santa Fe Industries v. Green, 430 U.S. 462 (1977).

a) **Facts.** Santa Fe (D) owned more than 90% of the outstanding stock of a subsidiary corporation, and, desiring to eliminate the minority shareholders, used a Delaware short-form merger statute which allowed a corporation holding more than 90% of the stock of a subsidiary to merge the subsidiary corporation, paying cash to the subsidiary's minority shareholders, giving notice to them within 10 days of the merger and restricting the minority shareholders to an appraisal action in the state courts if they were dissatisfied with the price they received. D adopted the merger plan, disclosed all material information relative to the value of the subsidiary's stock, offered the shareholders $150 per share (when it had been appraised by a brokerage firm at $125/share), and notified the minority shareholders of their option to seek an appraisal in the state courts. A number of minority shareholders (Ps) sued in federal court to enjoin the merger or for damages from a violation of Rule 10b-5. They alleged that Rule 10b-5 was breached in that (i) there was no business purpose for the merger except to freeze out the minority, and (ii) a grossly inadequate price was offered. The district court dismissed. On appeal the dismissal was reversed and now D appeals.

b) **Issue.** Does Rule 10b-5 provide a remedy for breach of a fiduciary duty by officers and directors and majority shareholders (i.e., is there a fraud) in connection with a sale of the corporation's securities by its minority shareholders even if there is full disclosure of all the facts, no misrepresentations are made, and the transaction is permitted by state law?

c) **Held.** No. Judgment for Ps reversed.

(1) The states should be free to regulate the conduct of corporate officials except for the specific areas regulated by federal statute. Expansion of Rule 10b-5 to cover this form of activity would be an unnecessary intrusion on the powers of the states.

(2) Section 10(b) was designed to protect investors by requiring full and truthful disclosure so that investors could make informed choices as to their course of action.

(3) Here the investors were fully informed of their rights and options *and had an adequate state remedy (appraisal) for the wrong alleged* in the complaint.

d) **Comment.** The rationale of conservative opinions like *Green* is that 10b-5 is meant to control only the securities markets and fraud in the purchase and sale of securities, primarily in situations where there has been an affirmative misrepresentation or omission to state material facts. It was not meant to regulate all forms of corporate mismanagement—an area traditionally covered by state law. However, *Green* should be read narrowly since an adequate remedy was available to the minority shareholders (state law provided for court appraisal of the fair market value of their shares). In other situations, where the court considers the available state law remedies inadequate, Rule 10b-5 might still apply. It also seems clear that based on *Green* (at a minimum in the future) all the plaintiffs who wish to state a

10b-5 cause of action will attempt to show that there has been a material misrepresentation or omission of fact, whatever other fraud or deception might be present.

Goldberg v. Meridor

5) **Compare with prior case--Goldberg v. Meridor,** 567 F.2d 209 (2d Cir. 1977), *cert. denied*, 434 U.S. 1069 (1978).

a) **Facts.** UGO is a Panamanian company with its principal place of business in New York City. A controlling interest in UGO is owned by Maritimecor, a Panama corporation (Maritimecor in turn is controlled by Maritime Fruit, an Israeli corporation); the minority interest in UGO is publicly owned. A minority shareholder of UGO (P) brings a derivative action under Rule 10b-5 against Maritimecor (MTC), its parent, and others associated with it, alleging that MTC fraudulently caused it to go public to get a large amount of cash, then to make loans of $7 million to MTC, and then to issue over 4 million of its common shares to MTC for all of MTC's assets (except its 2.8 million UGO shares) and an assumption of all of MTC's liabilities (MTC having liabilities exceeding its assets). The district court required P to post security for expenses as required by a state statute or drop all state law claims (which P did). P claimed that there was no disclosure to him as to the unfair transfer made by UGO, nor of the conflict of interest of MTC and the UGO board members who approved the transaction. The district court dismissed on the basis that P had a chance to amend the complaint once and had not amended it to include proper allegations of nondisclosure of material facts, as required by Rule 10b-5. P appeals.

b) **Issue.** Should P be allowed to amend his complaint, and can P state a cause of action under Rule 10b-5?

c) **Held.** Yes. P should be allowed to amend the complaint, and the amended complaint will state a 10b-5 cause of action.

(1) P was only given the choice by the district court of complying with the state law about posting security for expenses or dropping state law claims. He was not given the choice of amending the complaint in order to state a claim under Rule 10b-5. He should be given that chance.

(2) Given that chance, P can state a claim under Rule 10b-5.

(a) Two press releases by MTC concerning the UGO merger painted a bright picture, when in fact MTC was experiencing financial difficulties. Hence P is not merely relying on the unfairness of the merger terms, but is claiming that there was a material nondisclosure and materially misleading disclosure.

(b) Shareholder approval of the merger by UGO was not required by Panama law. Where shareholder approval is not required, then a 10b-5 cause of action may arise based on fraudulent conduct, even without a violation based on nondisclosure or misrepresentations in disclosure.

(c) Rule 10b-5 protects corporations as well as shareholders. Here there is a fraud even though all of the UGO directors knew of the fraud. The minority shareholders of UGO have been deceived.

(d) The nondisclosures were material. First, had reasonable directors known the facts, they would not have voted for the transaction. Second, had the minority shareholders been informed, they could have sought and won an injunction against the transaction under state law (since there was no appraisal remedy given, an injunction would lie).

(e) The case is materially different on its facts from *Santa Fe Industries v. Green (supra)*.

d) Dissent. The deception (if there was one) was not material. No shareholder action was necessary to complete the merger. Even had the disclosure been made, there is nothing that P could have done to stop the transaction; hence, there is no way the disclosure or lack of it could be material. Also, here there is only a breach of fiduciary duty, a state law action, which is made to look like a nondisclosure case. Rule 10b-5 does not cover fiduciary breach cases when they are covered by state law.

b. Misrepresentation or nondisclosure necessary element of violation of the Williams Act--Schreiber v. Burlington Northern, Inc., 472 U.S. 1 (1985).

Schreiber v. Burlington Northern, Inc.

1) Facts. In December, Burlington Northern, Inc. (D) made a hostile tender offer to purchase 25.1 million shares of El Paso Gas Co. at $24 per share. D reserved the right to terminate the offer if any of several specified events occurred. The El Paso shareholders (Ps) fully subscribed to the offer by the December 30 deadline.

In January, after negotiations with El Paso, D announced the terms of a new and friendly takeover agreement, which included a new tender offer for only 21 million shares at $24 per share and recognition of "golden parachute" contracts between El Paso and four of its senior officers. The rescission of the December tender offer caused a diminished payment to Ps who had tendered during that offer. The January offer was oversubscribed and Ps who are tendered were subject to substantial proration.

Ps filed suit alleging that D, El Paso, and El Paso's board of directors violated section 14(e) of the Securities Exchange Act, which prohibits "fraudulent, deceptive or manipulative acts or practices . . . in connection with any tender offer." Ps argued that withdrawal of the December offer coupled with the substitution of the January offer was a "manipulative" distortion of the market. Ps also alleged that D violated section 14(e) by failing to disclose the "golden parachute" contracts offered to El Paso's officers. The district court dismissed Ps' suit, holding that the alleged manipulation did not violate section 14(e) because there was no misrepresentation. The court of appeals affirmed, holding that an "arguable breach of contract" was not a manipulative act under section 14(e). The Supreme Court granted certiorari.

2) **Issue.** Is misrepresentation or nondisclosure a necessary element of a violation of section 14(e) of the Securities Exchange Act of 1934?

3) **Held.** Yes. Judgment affirmed.

   a) The term "manipulative" as used in section 14(e) requires misrepresentation or nondisclosure. The term connotes conduct designed to deceive or defraud investors by controlling or artificially affecting the price of securities. Without misrepresentation or nondisclosure, section 14(e) has not been violated.

   b) Section 14(e) was added to the Securities Exchange Act as part of the Williams Act. The purpose of the Act is to ensure that public shareholders who are confronted by a cash tender offer will not have to respond without adequate information. Section 14(e) is directed at providing shareholders with complete and accurate information.

   c) Nothing in the legislative history suggests that section 14(e) serves any other purpose other than disclosure. Ps' interpretation of section 14(e) as including acts which, although fully disclosed, artificially affect the price of a target corporation's stock goes beyond the purpose of the statute. The term "manipulative" cannot be interpreted as an invitation to the courts to oversee the substantive fairness of every tender offer. This would inject uncertainty into the tender offer process.

   d) Ps' complaint seeks redress only for injuries related to the cancellation of the December tender offer. Since the alleged failure to disclose the "golden parachute" provisions related to the January offer, that claim bears no causal relationship to Ps' alleged injuries.

D. PERSONS ENTITLED TO SUE

1. **Section 11 of the 1933 Act—Liability for Misstatements or Omissions in a Registration Statement or Prospectus.**

   a. **Introduction.** Section 11 imposes liability on *designated* persons for material false or misleading statements or omissions in an effective registration statement or prospectus. [*See* SA §11(a)]

   b. **Privity of contract.** *Any person* acquiring a security which was the subject of a defective registration statement may sue under section 11. The purchaser need not be in privity with the issuer. But the purchaser must be able to trace the securities purchased back to the registration statement.

Barnes v.   c. **Recovery limited to traceable shares--Barnes v. Osofsky,** 373 F.2d
Osofsky   269 (2d Cir. 1967).

1) **Facts.** Aileen, Inc. had 1,019,574 shares outstanding, 205,966 of which had been issued pursuant to a 1961 registration statement and were traded on the American Stock Exchange. On September 10, 1963, it offered through an underwriter in a registered offering another 200,000 shares, which were listed and to be traded over the Exchange. The stock declined rapidly in price after the offering, and suits were brought alleging false statements in the prospectus. A statement was agreed upon, but three plaintiffs object in this action based on the fact that only people who can trace their shares purchased back to the registered shares are able to recover. Ps bought their shares shortly after the offering became public (in the trading market), but they cannot trace them back specifically to the registered shares.

2) **Issue.** Does a section 11 recovery cover only shares traceable to those offered pursuant to the registration statement?

3) **Held.** Yes.

    a) An incorrect prospectus can affect the price at which shares issued previously will trade. Section 11 is not limited to original purchases, and it is sometimes impossible to tell whether shares are traceable to newly issued shares.

    b) But section 11 seems to cover only those shares which are traceable. Specifically, its damage provisions all limit recovery to amounts related to the specific shares offered (i.e., section 11(g) indicates that the amount recoverable cannot exceed the price at which the security was offered to the public).

2. **Rule 10b-5 of the 1934 Act—Persons Protected.** Rule 10b-5 covers only deceptive transactions in connection with the "purchase" or "sale" of a security by the plaintiff.

    a. **Definition of purchase or sale.** "Purchase" and "sale" are defined to include "any contract to purchase or sell." [*See* SA §§3(13) and (14)]

        1) This suggests that something beyond a mere offer to purchase or an offer to sell must be involved before Rule 10b-5 applies.

        2) At the same time, an actual completed purchase or sale need not be involved, since the Act indicates that "any contract" to purchase or sell is sufficient.

    b. **Purchase or sale by the plaintiff.** The plaintiff must either be an *actual* "purchaser" or an *actual* "seller" of securities in order to have standing to maintain a 10b-5 cause of action. Contexts in which the issue has arisen:

        (i) The issue has arisen *where the plaintiff has not sold his stock but argues that the stock has depreciated in value due to the misrepresentations* made by the defendant. [*See* Greenstein v. Paul, 400 F.2d 580 (2d Cir. 1968)—held that no standing existed since no actual purchase or sale by plaintiff had occurred]

(ii) The issue has also arisen where plaintiff claims *he would have purchased stock* but for the negative statements made by the defendant (*see* the next case).

Blue Chip
Stamps v.
Manor Drug
Stores

1) **Where plaintiff is neither actual purchaser nor seller--Blue Chip Stamps v. Manor Drug Stores,** 421 U.S. 723 (1975).

a) **Facts.** Blue Chip (D) was subject to an antitrust consent decree requiring it to offer a substantial number of its shares to retailers who had used its stamp service. It registered the offering under the 1933 Act and about 50% of the stores purchased shares. Two years later, one of the nonpurchasing offerees (P) sued under Rule 10b-5 on the basis that the prospectus was overly negative so that P did not purchase, allowing D to later offer the shares to the public at a higher price. The circuit court found for P; the Supreme Court granted certiorari.

b) **Issue.** Does P, neither an actual purchaser nor seller, have standing to sue under Rule 10b-5?

c) **Held.** No. Judgment for D.

(1) The legislative history indicates that only actual purchasers or sellers are covered.

(a) The language of Rule 10b-5 indicates this.

(b) All lower courts considering the question have so held.

(c) Congress has not amended the section to broaden the language, although urged by the S.E.C. to do so.

(d) Where Congress wanted to cover more, it has specifically done so (for example, section 17 of the 1933 Act applies to "offerees").

(e) The 1934 Act has a provision (section 28(a)) limiting damages to "actual" damages. If only actual purchasers or sellers have a cause of action, then at least recovery is based on a demonstrable number of shares traded.

(f) Most of the sections of the securities acts passed at the same time as Rule 10b-5 relate to actual purchasers or sellers (i.e., sections 11 and 12 of the 1933 Act and section 18 of the 1934 Act).

(g) However, since Congress did not specifically consider the issue here, policy reasons should dictate the result in this case.

(2) Policy reasons:

(a) Rule 10b-5 lawsuits are particularly vexatious. The rule should therefore be limited. Such lawsuits frustrate normal business activity; they have a high settlement value; there are liberal discovery rules by which valuable business information can be obtained.

(b)   It is too easy to establish claims based on merely oral evidence put in by a plaintiff, with no verification (i.e., "I would have purchased"). Securities transactions take place across exchanges with no privity between seller and the would-be buyer; no verification of plaintiff's intention is generally available unless he actually decides to purchase.

2)   Injunction actions. An exception to the purchase or sale requirement has been held to exist where plaintiff seeks an injunction against the continuance by defendant of market manipulation violative of Rule 10b-5; here, status as a shareholder (without an actual purchase or sale in connection with the defendant's activity) is sufficient for bringing the injunctive action. [*See* Mutual Shares Corp. v. Genesco, Inc., 384 F.2d 540 (2d Cir. 1967); *but see* Cowin v. Bresler, *infra*]

c.   The privity requirement.

1)   The early view. The early view was that the plaintiff had to be in direct privity with the defendant in order to maintain a Rule 10b-5 action.

2)   Transactions over the securities markets. However, 10b-5 actions began to be brought in securities transactions consummated over the securities exchanges and in the over-the-counter market. Here the buyer normally does not know who the seller is—for example, A puts a buy order with his broker for 100 shares of XYZ Corporation. The order is executed over a securities exchange and A never sees the seller.

a)   At first it was held that, due to lack of privity, a 10b-5 action could ***not*** be sustained. [*See* Joseph v. Farnsworth Radio & Television Corp., 99 F. Supp. 701 (S.D.N.Y. 1951)]

b)   But the ***dissent*** in *Joseph* argued that as long as there was fraud or misrepresentation and plaintiffs relied on it, there could be recovery without a showing of privity.

3)   Recent decisions. The more recent decisions have moved away from requiring privity.

a)   **Situations involving affirmative misrepresentations.** Rule 10b-5 has been applied to situations where there are affirmative misrepresentations made even though there is no privity of contract between buyer and seller.

(1)   For example, in *Heit v. Weitzen*, 402 F.2d 909 (2d Cir. 1968), the court in effect overruled *Joseph*. Here the defendant corporation and some of its officers released false financial information, which plaintiffs relied on in buying the company's securities over an exchange. Rule 10b-5 was held to apply even

though there was *no contemporaneous selling of the company's securities by any of the corporate officers* (i.e., technically they were not the sellers in the securities transaction; hence, plaintiff had no privity with the officers making the affirmative misrepresentations).

b) **Situations of nondisclosure.** There was some speculation by commentators that where material facts are never disclosed at all (nondisclosure cases), there may be a requirement of some semblance of privity between the plaintiff and the defendant. But thus far the courts have not imposed such a requirement. [*See* Shapiro v. Merrill Lynch, Pierce, Fenner & Smith, Inc., 495 F.2d 228 (2d Cir. 1974), discussed *supra*]

3. **Section 14(a) of the 1934 Act—Proxy Regulation.**

a. **Introduction.** An action may be brought for any violation of the proxy rules. [*See* SEA Rule 14a-9]

Cowin v. Bresler

b. **Standing to sue--Cowin v. Bresler,** 741 F.2d 410 (D.C. Cir. 1984).

1) **Facts.** Bresler & Reiner, Inc. is a publicly owned company engaged in real estate. Cowin (P) is a minority shareholder. The company was controlled by Bresler and Reiner (Ds) (owning 70%); P claims that they manipulated the business for their personal profit (dealing with limited partnerships they controlled, repurchasing stock to limit the trading market, etc.). P seeks a common law remedy of (i) damages to the value of his stock, (ii) an injunction to prevent further violations, and (iii) a receiver to liquidate the company. P also sues under Rule 10b-5 for fraud in issuing false information which affected the value of the stock and under section 14(a) for issuing false proxy statements to elect directors.

Ds moved to dismiss the complaint. The district court held for Ds that (i) facts had not been alleged justifying the extreme remedy of a receiver, (ii) the common law claims should have been brought as a derivative suit, and (iii) the 10b-5 claims are really state actions for corporate mismanagement. The district court also dismissed the section 14(a) action by summary judgment, in that P did not have standing to sue because he had not personally relied on the alleged misrepresentations. P appealed.

2) **Issues.**

a) Does P have standing to bring a section 14(a) action?

b) In asking for an injunction under Rule 10b-5, must the fraud alleged have been in connection with the purchase and sale of a security?

3) Held. Yes to both issues.

    a)   P's common law claims are really ones that benefit all shareholders and belong to the corporation; thus, these claims should have been brought as a derivative suit and not individually.

    b)   P did allege sufficient facts to put the issue of a receivership before the court.

    c)   P did not allege that the violations of Rule 10b-5 occurred in connection with the purchase and sale of securities. But he asks for an exception to *Blue Chip Stamps* (*supra*) because this was a request for an injunction. But the statutory language requires that there be a purchase or sale, the same policy considerations mentioned in *Blue Chip* apply, and the Supreme Court was indicating in *Blue Chip* a broad policy statement and a wish to avoid consideration of individual facts of particular cases.

    d)   P does have standing to sue under section 14(a) despite the fact that he did not allege reliance on the alleged misrepresentations in the proxy statement.

        (1)   The Supreme Court has never severely limited the implied private right of action under section 14(a) as it has under Rule 10b-5.

        (2)   Unlike Rule 10b-5, neither section 14(a) nor Rule 14a-9 prohibits unlawful conduct in connection with particular activities (such as purchase or sale of securities); they contain a blanket proscription of fraud in connection with the solicitation of proxies.

        (3)   There is nothing in the statutory language that seems to require that P show that he was personally deceived (i.e., a reliance requirement).

        (4)   Finally, the injury P alleges (the election of Ds as directors) was not caused by his individual reliance on deceptive proxy solicitations; other shareholders elected Ds because they were deceived.

        (5)   Congress wanted to protect against this type of injury; individual reliance is irrelevant.

    e)   The district court had an alternative ground for dismissing the section 14(a) claim. P's injury was not causally related to the alleged proxy violations.

        (1)   P claims that the misleading proxy statement depressed the stock price, injuring him. But this did not happen as a result of some corporate action approved through the fraudulent solicitation of proxies.

        (2)   P also claims that the misleading proxies led to the election of the current directors, which led to fraudulent acts by these directors, thus

finally injuring him. Again, the injury to P is not a direct result of the corporate action authorized by the proxies solicited (election of directors); it is the subsequent breaches of fiduciary duties by the directors that caused the damage.

Ballay v. Legg Mason Wood Walker, Inc.

4. Application of Section 12(2) of the 1933 Act to Initial Distributions Only-- Ballay v. Legg Mason Wood Walker, Inc., 925 F.2d 682 (3d Cir. 1991).

    a. Facts. Ps brought a suit against D, a brokerage firm, for misrepresentations in connection with a sale of securities in the secondary trading market. Ps sued under both Rule 10b-5 of the 1934 Act *and* section 12(2) of the 1933 Act. They jury found for Ps on section 12(2) and Ds appeal.

    b. Issues.

        1) Does section 12(2) apply to trades in securities in the secondary trading market, or is it limited to the initial offering of securities?

        2) Was it error for the district court to refuse to charge the jury that the investors' reliance on their broker, as their agent, could establish a section 10(b) claim?

    c. Held. Section 12(2) applies only to initial distributions of securities, and there was only a harmless error. District court judgment for Ps is reversed.

        1) As to section 12(2), in order to apply, the communication must be by "prospectus or oral communication." These are related terms; prospectus means a communication in connection with a public offering of securities; thus, oral communication as used here is an oral communication in connection with an initial offering of securities. Congress did not intend a more expensive definition than this. If it covered secondary trading, then it would overlap with Rule 10b-5, allowing a party to use section 12(2) on a negligence standard and have to use Rule 10b-5 on an intentional conduct standard. Basically, the 1933 Act deals with initial offering; the 1934 Act and Rule 10b-5 deals with the secondary markets. Section 17(a) of the 1933 Act is an exception; parts of it apply also to secondary trading, but there Congress explicitly indicated it was to apply to secondary markets, and Congress used broader language than section 12(2) (i.e., general fraud-type language).

        2) There was no reversible error in the district court's refusal to give Ps' requested instruction to the jury on their broker's agency concerning the Rule 10b-5 claim.

5. Standing of a Shareholder of the Tendered Company to Sue in a Tender Offer.

    a. Introduction. It is unlawful to engage in or oppose a tender offer without meeting the disclosure requirements of section 14(d), or for any person to engage in fraud in connection with a tender offer. [*See* SA §14(e)]

b. **Standing to sue.** Although originally standing to sue was liberally granted to all persons who had reasonably been caused damage by fraudulent actions in connection with a tender offer, since *Piper v. Chris-Craft, supra,* the trend of the courts has been to limit standing.

c. **Tender offeror has no standing to sue--Kalmanovitz v. G. Heileman Brewing Co.,** 769 F.2d 152 (3d Cir. 1985).

Kalmanovitz v. G. Heileman Brewing Co.

1) **Facts.** In October 1962, Kalmanovitz (P) and the Jacobs group formed a partnership to make a tender offer for Pabst Brewing Co.; Jacobs already owned 1.14 million shares; P was to put up $26 million; the offer was at $24/share for 3 million shares. Pabst began talks with Heileman, which made an offer for 5.5 million shares at $27.50/share. P agreed with Jacobs to put up $44 million so they could go to $30/share (and was to receive 50% of any price Jacobs might receive above $24/share if Jacobs decided to sell its 1.14 million shares rather than go through with the tender offer). On November 23, 1982, P and Jacobs raised their offer to $35/share; Heileman announced that it would counter. Jacobs then called Heileman and settled for selling its shares in a new offer by Heileman at $29/share, plus $7.5 million to cover its expenses. P refused to accept Jacobs's offer of $5 million and went on to offer $40/share by himself, but Heileman's offer succeeded in gaining control.

P then sued Pabst, Jacobs, and Heileman on numerous claims, including claims for violations of SA sections 13(e), 14(d) and 14(e). The district court found that P had no standing and granted D's motion for a summary judgment.

2) **Issue.** Does P, based on his interest as a Pabst shareholder, have standing to sue under these statutes?

3) **Held.** No. District court judgment is affirmed.

a) The *Piper* case held that a tender offeror did not have standing under section 14(e).

b) We do not decide whether shareholders of the tendered company have an implied private right of action.

c) But assuming they do, we hold that P's real interest was as a tender offeror (he only owned 20 shares of Pabst) and not as a shareholder. hence, P should not be allowed to represent all the shareholders.

d. **Summary of the standing rules.** Section 14(e) prohibits material misstatements, misleading omissions, and fraudulent or manipulative acts, in connection with a tender offer or any solicitation in favor of or in opposition to a tender offer. Section 14(e) is closely comparable to Rule 10b-5, except that it does not contain the limiting language, "in connection with the purchase or sale" of securities, found in Rule 10b-5. It is not yet completely clear who may bring an action under section 14(e). A major Supreme Court decision, *Piper v. Chris-Craft Industries, Inc.*, 430 U.S. 1 (1977), lays down some important rules, but leaves a number of gaps.

1) **Suit by the offeror.**

   a) **Damages.** Under *Piper v. Chris-Craft Industries, Inc.*, the bidder does not have standing to sue for damages under section 14(e), particularly a suit against the target corporation's management for false statements made in opposition to the tender offer. The Williams Act was designed to protect shareholders of the target. It is not consistent with the underlying legislative purpose to imply a damages remedy for the bidder, particularly since the target's shareholders might end up bearing the burden of an award based on misrepresentations by the target's management.

   b) **Injunctive relief.** In *Piper v. Chris-Craft Industries, Inc.*, the Court left open the question of suits by the bidder under section 14(e) for *injunctive* relief against the target or its management. Lower courts have held that such a suit will lie. The bidder can also bring a suit for injunctive relief against competing bidders. Unlike damages, an injunction does not impose any burden upon the target's shareholders. Furthermore, an injunction prior to the time when the target's shareholders must decide whether to accept the tender offer allows them to make their decision in an environment purged of false and misleading information.

2) **Suit by target corporation.**

   a) **Damages.** Since *Chris-Craft* was based on the conclusion that the Williams Act was designed to protect the target's *shareholders*, the target corporation itself would not have standing to sue the bidder for damages under Rule 14e.

   b) **Injunction.** The target corporation *can* sue for an injunction against the bidder for violation of section 14(e), since such an injunction will protect the interests of the target's shareholders. [Gearhart Industries, Inc. v. Smith International, Inc., 714 F.2d 706 (5th Cir. 1984)]

3) **Suit by target's shareholders.**

   a) **Suit by tendering shareholders.** Based on the Court's interpretation of the Williams Act in *Piper v. Chris-Craft Industries, Inc.*, shareholders of the target have standing to sue for both damages and injunctive relief if they tender their shares on the basis of false and misleading information.

   b) **Suit by nontendering shareholders.** The Court did not express a view on this issue in *Piper v. Chris-Craft Industries, Inc.*, but since the statute does not contain the purchaser-seller limitation associated with Rule 10b-5, nontendering shareholders can probably sue under section 14(e), provided they can show damage resulting from a violation of that section.

E. PERSONS LIABLE

1. **Liability for Aiding and Abetting Under Rule 10b-5.** The courts have held that where there is a violation of Rule 10b-5, aiders, abettors, and co-conspirators may also be held liable.

   a. **Test for liability.** The following elements must be shown to hold an aider or abettor liable under Rule 10b-5:

      1) There must be a defendant who is held directly responsible for the violation of Rule 10b-5.

      2) The collateral participant must have had actual knowledge of the fact that his role was part of an activity that was improper.

      3) The collateral participant must have knowingly and substantially assisted the violation.

   b. **Application of three-prong test--Metge v. Baehler,** 762 F.2d 621 (8th Cir. 1985).

Metge v. Baehler

      1) **Facts.** IEI was in the real estate business. To acquire funds it formed a subsidiary (IMF), which sold unregistered one-year renewable securities (sometimes backed by mortgages on various properties). IMF ended up loaning the money raised to IEI on an unsecured basis. Eventually, due to poor projects, IEI went bankrupt; owners of the securities (Ps) received none of their principal and only 12.5% of the interest due them. As a class, they brought suit against BTC (a bank), which was lending IEI money, under Rule 10b-5 as an aider and abettor in the nondisclosure of material facts in connection with the sale of the unregistered securities. The district court granted D's motion for summary judgment. Ps appeal.

      2) **Issue.** Have Ps met the test for proving that there are facts sufficient to show the three elements to prove aiding and abetting, in order to avoid summary judgment?

      3) **Held.** Yes. Reversed and remanded.

         a) The three-prong test is:

            (1) A violation of Rule 10b-5 by a primary party. This is clearly proved.

            (2) Knowledge of the violation by the alleged aider and abettor.

            (3) Substantial assistance rendered by the aider and abettor. If defendant has a duty to act to disclose information to potentially injured parties, then inaction can be a basis for fulfilling this requirement. Or if no such duty exists, but it appears that defendant consciously intended to assist in perpetration of the

wrongful act, then inaction or lesser proof of substantial assistance is sufficient. In other words, these two elements are considered in relationship to one another; i.e., if there is a minimal showing of substantial assistance, then a greater showing of scienter is required.

b) There is sufficient proof of substantial assistance, based on the showing of intent here, to have sent the issue to a jury. Thus, the district court's finding of a summary judgment for BTC should be reversed.

(1) There is evidence that BTC knew that an increasing percentage of IEI's cash was coming from the sale of the certificates, that IEI was in serious financial condition, and that BTC kept IEI alive in order to collect as much of its loans to IEI as possible, to the detriment of the certificate holders.

(2) BTC sold a troubled real estate company, which it got in foreclosure of a bad loan, to IEI for cash, a $575,000 note, and 18% of IEI's stock, which BTC voted by proxy only when the loan was in default, which it frequently was. BTC had the right to sell the stock back to IEI at a profit. BTC also got frequent financial reports.

(3) From the beginning of the relationship, IEI was frequently threatened with bankruptcy and had annually increasing loans. Over a three-year period, BTC refinanced IEI several times, giving more money for more security and having IEI use the money to pay off unpaid principal and interest payments.

(4) Despite financial statements showing a minimum of $500,000 net worth, BTC knew that IEI was in serious shape; it knew that if IEI could not earn a profit, the net worth would rapidly disappear through foreclosure of various liens that secured most of the assets.

(5) There is also evidence that BTC knew of the sale of the thrift certificates and their importance financially to IEI. For example, one payment to BTC was made by an endorsed check from IMF to IEI. And BTC acted as the escrow agent for a trade by debtholders of IEI for certificates.

(6) Although it appears that BTC also lost $650,000 in principal and interest, it still may have benefited from the delay in IEI's bankruptcy by collection of over $300,000 that it was owed by IEI.

2. **Participant Liability Under Section 12 of the 1933 Act.** Sections 12(1) and 12(2) of the 1933 Act both require *privity of contract* between the buyer and the seller for liability to exist. Nevertheless, some courts have indicated that the

purchaser of securities may sue not only the actual seller of the securities but also others involved in the sale.

a. **Who is a "seller" under section 12(1)--Pinter v. Dahl,** 486 U.S. 622 (1988).   Pinter v. Dahl

1) **Facts.** Pinter is an oil and gas producer in Texas and a registered securities dealer. Dahl is a California real estate broker and investor in oil and gas projects, who met Pinter, investigated some oil leases owned by Pinter, and invested over $310,000 in the properties. Dahl told others about the venture; they never met Pinter or toured the properties; in effect, they took Dahl's word for it, and invested on average about $7,500 each. Pinter prepared the subscription agreement; these agreements stated that there was no registration and that Rule 146 and the private offering exemption was being relied on. Dahl received no commission. The venture failed; all money was lost. Dahl and the other investors sued under section 12(1) of the 1933 Act for rescission of the sale, alleging it was unlawful since it was not registered. Pinter counterclaimed on the basis that Dahl had promised to bring him sophisticated, qualified investors and to provide them the necessary information; thus, Dahl's suit must be barred by the equitable defenses of estoppel and in pari delicto. Further, Dahl may himself have been a "seller" within the meaning of section 12(1) and thus be liable for a contribution for the other plaintiffs' claims against Pinter. The district court granted judgment for plaintiffs and against Pinter's counterclaim. The court of appeals affirmed. The case is now in front of the Supreme Court.

2) **Issues.** First, is the common law defense of in pari delicto available in a private action brought under section 12(1) of the 1933 Act? Second, must one intend to confer a benefit on himself or on a third party in order to qualify as a "seller" within the meaning of section 12(1)?

3) **Held.** Yes, to both issues.

   a) The in pari delicto defense:

      (1) The in pari delicto defense is allowed in actions involving strict liability, since the need to deter illegality is present in situations involving these types of causes of action just as it is in other types of causes of action.

      (2) Under the *Bateman Eichler* case, the defense is available in private causes of action brought under the federal securities laws.

      (3) Under the first prong of the *Bateman* case, the defendant cannot escape liability unless as a direct result of the plaintiff's actions, the plaintiff bears at least substantially equal responsibility for the underlying illegality. In a section 12(1) case, plaintiff must be at least equally responsible for the actions that render the sale of the unregistered securities illegal. Knowledge that the securities are unregistered is not, by itself, enough.

      (4) Under the second prong of the test, a plaintiff's recovery may be barred only if preclusion of suit does not offend the underly-

ing statutory policies. Section 12(1) imposes strict liability for failure to register securities. Private enforcement is a primary tool in enforcing the 1933 Act. Where plaintiff is primarily an investor (even where he actively is involved in the distribution of the unregistered securities), barring suit by in pari delicto, would offend the underlying policy of the 1933 Act. Whether plaintiff is primarily an investor depends on all the facts (did he get compensation for helping, etc.).

(5) The record in this case is not adequate to make a determination of whether the two prongs of the *Bateman* test are satisfied.

b) The section 12(1) claim that Dahl was a "seller" and as such may be held liable for the sale of unregistered securities to the other investor-respondents:

(1) Section 12(1) provides that "Any person who . . . offers or sells a security" in violation of the registration requirement of the Securities Act "shall be liable to the person purchasing such security from him."

(2) Clearly, any person who passes title to a buyer may be liable.

(3) The Securities Act defines "sale" and "offer to sell" in such a way that solicitations of offers to buy are covered. Thus, liability extends beyond persons who actually have title to the securities. *Agents* of sellers would be covered.

(4) But section 12(1) also provides that only a defendant from whom the purchaser "purchased" the securities would be liable.

   (a) This means that for liability to exist, an actual sale must take place.

   (b) As long as a sale has taken place, others besides the person passing title, who are part of the selling process, may be liable persons. "Sell" and "offer" are terms related to "purchase"; hence, persons who solicit the purchase may be liable.

(5) Courts have long held that section 12(1) applies to brokers and dealers who solicit a sale. This furthers the purpose of the Securities Act because the solicitation stage is the most critical part of the selling process; this is the time when potential purchasers need the disclosure called for by the Act.

(6) Section 12(1), however, does *not* cover persons who urge a purchase but whose motivation is solely to benefit the buyer. It is uncommon to say that the buyer "purchased" from a person who gives gratuitous advice. This is not a "solicitation."

(7) Section 12(1) covers only those persons who successfully solicit the purchase, motivated at least in part by a desire to serve their own financial interests or those of the securities owner.

(8) The test used by some courts, i.e., "sellers are those whose participation in the buy-sell transaction is a substantial factor in causing the transaction to take place," is too broad. It goes beyond the language of the statute, which requires sellers to be limited to those that pass title and *persons who "offer" or who "solicit offers."* The substantial factor test would, for

example, extend liability to persons only remotely related to the relevant aspects of the sales transaction, such as accountants, lawyers, etc.

(9) It is impossible from the trial court record to determine whether Dahl had the kind of interest in the sales that would make him a liable person.

c) The trial court judgment is vacated and the case remanded for further proceedings.

3. **Liability of Controlling Persons.** Both the 1933 Act and the 1934 Act contain provisions making "controlling persons" liable for the securites law violations of persons they control.

a. **Liability under the 1933 Act.** The 1933 Act provides that any person who controls another person found liable under sections 11 or 12 is jointly and severally liable along with the liable party—*unless* the controlling person had no knowledge of, nor reasonable grounds to believe in, the existence of the facts that form the basis of the controlled person's liability. [SA §15]

b. **Liability under the 1934 Act.** The 1934 Act provides that controlling persons are liable for the securities violations of persons they control, unless they acted in "good faith" and did not directly or indirectly induce the acts that are the basis of the controlled person's liability. [SEA §20(a)]

c. **Compare.** Ignorance (i.e., no knowledge) is a clear defense to an action brought under section 15 of the 1933 Act, whereas a showing of "good faith" must be made under section 20(a) of the 1934 Act to avoid liability. At this point, however, it is still unclear just what "good faith" means.

d. **Application of agency principles.** A major issue in determining the liability of controlling persons is whether principles of agency apply in addition to liability under section 15 of the 1933 Act or section 29(a) of the 1934 Act. For example, may an employer of a person who violates the securities laws while acting within the scope of his employment be held liable on the basis of respondeat superior, even though the employer might not be liable under sections 15 or 20(a)? The courts are split over this issue.

e. **Common law agency principles applied--*In re* Atlantic Financial Management, Inc. Securities Litigation,** 784 F.2d 29 (1st Cir. 1986).

In re Atlantic Financial Management, Inc. Securities Litigation

1) **Facts.** Ps claim, in a Rule 10b-5 action, that Strong, chairman of AZL Resources, Inc., misrepresented certain facts, as a result of which Ps bought AZL stock and lost money. Ps sue for damages not only against Strong but also against AZL on a common law agency theory, contending that Strong's "apparent authority" permits holding AZL vicariously liable.

2) **Issue.** Is section 20(a) the exclusive remedy against controlling persons of those found liable pursuant to Rule 10b-5 of the 1934 Act?

3) **Held.** No. Common law agency principles may also apply.

    a) Whether common law agency principles apply depends on congressional intent in enacting the 1934 Act.

    b) The courts have tended to read congressional statutes (such as Rule 10b-5) that impose tortlike liability as embracing some of the common law agency principles where this will further statutory purposes.

    c) The issue is whether common law vicarious liability should be applied where a corporate officer had "apparent authority." The answer is "yes."

    d) We hold that section 20(a) is not an exclusive remedy.

        (1) The legislative history of the section seems to indicate that section 20(a) was intended to expand liability beyond common law agency, not to contract it (i.e., to reach even the parties that controlled corporate employers, such as shareholders or directors).

        (2) To find otherwise would make major changes in existing liability assumptions; for example, state misrepresentation law would follow agency principles and federal law would not.

        (3) Most courts have held that the section 20(a) remedy is not exclusive.

4. **Outside Directors.**

    a. **Introduction.** A director might participate directly in a violation of the securities laws that is charged to the corporation. Or the director may fail to fulfill his duty of "due diligence" pursuant to section 11 of the 1933 Act in relationship to a registered offering. Or an outside director may aid or abet the violation of the securities laws by a corporate officer. Alternatively, it might be found that such a director was a "controlling person" and as such he may be held liable under section 15 of the 1933 Act or section 20(a) of the 1934 Act. Finally, there is the question of whether an outside director might be liable where he did not actively aid or abet the violation and where he is not a controlling person. What this amounts to is the issue of whether the outside director has some duty to investigate or supervise what is said in securities transactions entered into by company officers.

Lanza v. Drexel & Co.

    b. **Liability of outside directors--Lanza v. Drexel & Co.**, 479 F.2d 1277 (2d Cir. 1973).

        1) **Facts.** The Lanzas (Ps) sold their company's stock to BarChris for BarChris stock. (For background, *see BarChris, supra.*) Coleman (D), a partner in the firm which eventually underwrote BarChris's securities offering, became a director of BarChris in April 1961. Negotiations to purchase Ps' stock began in March 1961 and were carried on by officers of BarChris without D's participation

or knowledge. Various material that was distributed to Ps by the officers contained material misrepresentations and omissions about BarChris. In August 1961, BarChris restated its earnings downward, and D began asking questions about the financial status of BarChris. From that time until the acquisition of the Lanzas' company was approved at a BarChris board meeting in November, the coverup of BarChris affairs gradually came to light (before the closing of the Lanza deal, D knew of BarChris's stringent cash position, of customer defaults, and of dissension among the BarChris officers, but apparently did not know that its published financial figures were also false). D did not know of the material misrepresentations and omissions made to Ps and he made no inquiry to determine what was being said to Ps. Shortly after the closing of the Lanza sale, BarChris entered bankruptcy; Ps had to pay $100,000 to buy their stock back from the trustee. They sued D and his firm (Drexel & Co.) under Rule 10b-5. The district court found for D; Ps appeal.

2) **Issue.** Does an outside director have a duty to convey all material adverse information to prospective purchasers of the corporation's stock where the director does not know that these prospective purchasers are not receiving all such information?

3) **Held.** No. Judgment for D. District court affirmed.

   a) There was no such duty at common law. Directors were to protect the interests of their shareholders. They could only be held liable for aiding or abetting a violation by company officers.

   b) The 1933 Act specifically provides for a director's duty; Rule 10b-5 says nothing about such a duty.

   c) Knowing participation by a director in a fraud perpetrated by the corporation or its officers will make an outside director liable. But there is no affirmative duty to investigate the representations made by company officers, nor to disclose all material adverse information known by the director where the director has no knowledge that the officers have not disclosed such information.

   d) It is sound policy to have outside directors on the board. It is impractical to have these directors check on all representations made in the course of a sale of the company's securities. To hold them liable for doing so will result in no outside directors being willing to serve.

4) **Note.** *Ernst & Ernst v. Hochfelder, supra*, held that a collateral defendant (there, an outside accounting firm) must have acted knowingly in order for Rule 10b-5 liability to result. This would seem to indicate that there is no duty to investigate the company's representations, but if the director knows or is reckless in not knowing of such misrepresentations, and does nothing, then the outside director could be held liable as an aider and abettor.

5. **Accountants.**

a.   **Liability under the 1933 Act.** A registration statement under the 1933 Act must contain certified financial statements. The accountants who certify the statements are subject to liability under section 11 of the Act as "experts." In this capacity, to avoid liability, the accountants must have had, after reasonable investigation, reasonable grounds to believe, and actually believe, at the time the registration statement became effective, that the statements made by them were true and that there was no omission to state a material fact. This holds the accountants to a standard of negligence in two respects: (i) in the conduct of the audit; and (ii) in the presentation of the information in the financial statements.

b.   **The 1934 Act.** Compare liability under the 1934 Act.

1)   **The standard of conduct required.** There might be a distinction made between (i) the manner in which the accountants conduct the audit (where the only relevant standard is negligence, since it is almost inconceivable that an accountant would deliberately omit some required auditing procedure), *and* (ii) the manner in which the accountants present the information about the issuer in the financial statements (here it is more likely that accountants might deliberately omit or misrepresent information about the issuer).

a)   **Auditing procedures.** *Ernst & Ernst v. Hochfelder, supra,* held that 10b-5 liability for accountants could only be based on intentional wrongdoing. This was a case where plaintiff alleged that the defendant accounting firm had negligently omitted proper auditing procedures, which would have discovered the issuer's fraud.

b)   **Statement of financial results.** Accountants have long had the responsibility of auditing a company and expressing an opinion about the financial statements. Traditionally, this opinion has been limited to whether the financial statements were compiled according to "generally accepted accounting principles." Liability arising out of giving these opinions has more or less rested on whether the accountants conformed to such principles. However, there is some evidence that the duties of accountants are being expanded.

(1)   For example, in *United States v. Carl J. Simon,* 425 F.2d 796 (2d Cir. 1969), an action for criminal liability under section 32 of the Securities Exchange Act of 1934 against the accountants of a major accounting firm, the court held that culpability did not depend on whether the accountants had followed generally accepted accounting principles (which they had) but on whether the financial statements certified by the accountant "fairly presented the financial position of the company" and whether, if they did not, the defendant-accountants had acted in "good faith."

(2)   The lack of "good faith" is probably equivalent to showing actual knowledge under *Ernst & Ernst v. Hochfelder.*

2)   **The ambit of responsibility.** The financial statements prepared by the accountants may be used in a registration statement, in connection with an underwriting where there is no registration statement, or in a private sale

of securities. One important question concerns the scope of liability; i.e., to whom will accountants be responsible?

a) Those who read the financial statements are owed a duty by the accountant based on actual reliance.

b) Those who do not read the statements, but who accountants could reasonably expect would rely on the statements, have been found by some courts to be owed a duty.

c. **Increased disclosure of relationship between accountant and clients.** The S.E.C. has also moved to require increased disclosure of the relationships existing between companies and their public accountants. [*See* SA Release No. 5550, SEA Release No. 11147, and Accounting Series Release 165 (1974)]

1) In monthly reports required of the company by the 1934 Act (8K), changes in accounting firms, resignation of firms, major disputes over accounting issues, etc., must all be disclosed.

2) In financial statements, accountants must disclose material disagreements with management, events that form a part of current financials that were the subject of the disagreement, matters accounted for differently from a previous accounting firm's methods, how the results would come out under methods preferred by previous accountants, etc.

3) Changes were also made in proxy regulations to require disclosure of accounting firms to be used by the company, the name of the previous accountant (if different), disclosure of the existence and composition of an audit committee of the Board of Directors, etc.

d. **Negligence standard applied in an enforcement proceeding--S.E.C. v. Arthur Young & Co.,** 590 F.2d 785 (9th Cir. 1979).

S.E.C. v. Arthur Young & Co.

1) **Facts.** Burke promoted several oil and gas ventures; Arthur Young (D) audited and prepared financial statements for some of these ventures. The S.E.C. brought actions under section 17(a), Rule 10b-5, and other provisions against Burke and brought an action against D for aiding and abetting, seeking an injunction prohibiting future violations. The trial court found for D. The S.E.C. appealed.

2) **Issue.** Is compliance with generally accepted accounting standards the appropriate standard of conduct under the securities law for accountants reviewing client work?

3) **Held.** Yes. Trial court judgment affirmed.

a) The granting or denying of injunctive relief is within the discretion of the trial court, and will not be disturbed unless there has been clear abuse. Thus, the S.E.C. must show that there was no reasonable basis for the trial judge's decision.

b) In a *statutory enforcement decision*, we assume that *Ernst & Ernst v. Hochfelder* does not require a finding of scienter—that liability can be based on negligence.

c) The S.E.C. argues that D had to perform in a manner that would have revealed to an ordinary prudent investor (who examined the accountant's reports) a reasonably accurate picture of the financial risks of investment in the venture.

d) This is more stringent than is required; it would make the accountant a guarantor of the client's honesty.

e) The accountant only needs to comply in good faith with generally accepted auditing standards of the profession, unless he discovers or deliberately refuses to become informed about material facts that should be disclosed.

6. **Liability of Lawyers.** The role of lawyers in the securities area is undergoing substantial change as a result of recent developments. Traditionally, lawyers have been advocates for their clients; however, the S.E.C. and the securities laws have recently moved them in the direction of becoming auditors, required to protect the interests of the public, as well as of their clients. The impulse behind this change in direction is consumerism—the idea that lawyers are in a key position with regard to securities transactions to protect the public interest.

a. **Liability to clients for malpractice.** Lawyers have always had the responsibility of performing competently for their clients; consequently, they may be liable to their clients for a knowing or negligent failure to do so. Third parties affected by the lawyer's malpractice may also have a cause of action against the lawyer.

b. **Liability as principals.** A lawyer may also be liable for a violation of the securities laws as a principal in a business transaction. For example, a lawyer may own securities and make a material misrepresentation in connection with their sale, or become a partner with someone else who violates the securities laws.

c. **Liability to those affected by securities transactions.** In addition, a lawyer may in some situations be liable to parties affected by a securities transaction in which she has acted purely as a lawyer on behalf of her client.

1) **Liability under the 1933 Act.** For example, in the situation where the lawyer drafts a 1933 Act registration statement for a client and the lawyer is also a director of the company, the lawyer may be liable to purchasers of the issuer's securities under section 11. [*See* Escott v. BarChris Construction Corp., *supra*]

a) **Liability as expert.** It is also clear that lawyers may be held as experts where they render their opinion as an expert in connection with a registration statement (e.g., giving an opinion concerning title to real property). (*See* discussion of the liability of expert, *supra*.) The issue in registration situations is whether the lawyer can be held liable as a lawyer for drafting the registration statement—even though, according to section 11, she does not have to sign it.

b) **Liability for preparing registration statement.** The S.E.C. has taken the position that lawyers can be held liable under section 11 to those purchasing securities from the issuer for mere preparation of the registration statement—even though the lawyer is not an expert and does not sign the registration statement (as a director, etc.).

    (1) **Duty to make independent investigation.** The rationale for the S.E.C. position is that lawyers should be held to a duty of *reasonable care* in investigating the facts and in disclosing any material facts discovered. Thus, a lawyer cannot take the word of her client for how things are; she must make an *independent investigation* of the facts. And if the lawyer discovers that a client has made misrepresentations or material omissions and insists on going forward with the registration statement anyway, she must disclose her discovery, possibly even to the S.E.C., or face possible liability as an aider or abettor.

    (2) **Actual knowledge may be required.** Although there are no judicial decisions on this specific point as yet, the case of *Ernst & Ernst v. Hochfelder, supra,* may have an effect on this area. If the basis of the action against the lawyer were Rule 10b-5, then a lawyer would not be held liable for damages unless she had actual knowledge of a securities law violation by her client and knowingly aided in the transaction. *Note:* To apply the *Hochfelder* case in this manner would deny the position of the S.E.C., which is that the lawyer must make a reasonable investigation of the facts.

2) **Liability as participant, aider, or abettor.** Lawyers may become so involved in a securities transaction that they depart from their role as lawyers and become involved as "participants" in the transaction. Where this happens and there is a violation of the securities laws, the lawyer may be liable under one of the general liability sections of the securities acts.

    a) **Lawyer as an aider and abettor in a private cause of action--Abell v. Potomac Insurance Co.,** 858 F.2d 1104 (5th Cir. 1988).

Abell v. Potomac Insurance Co.

        (1) **Facts.** Fryar masterminded the development of a home for severely mentally and emotionally disturbed patients in Cheneyville, La. He bought property for $100,000; named the place "Westside"; and got Booz, Allen to do a feasibility study (which was unfavorable), then got a favorable study. He got the town to underwrite a $13.5 million bond offering, to be paid back from revenues from Westside. Fryar formed All-American; the property was sold to All-American, then All-American sold it to Westside (to be paid from the offering) for $600,000 in cash and $1.9 million in bonds. None of this was disclosed in the offering document. Two weeks before the offering, the underwriter's law firm quit. Skye represented Westside; Wright, Lindsey & Jennings (WLJ) represented the underwriter. After the bond issue was sold, Westside went into bankruptcy. Bondholders (Ps) sued everybody, including the underwriter and its counsel, WLJ. The case was heard at several levels. This is the circuit court opinion relating to WLJ's liability under Rule 10b-5. The trial court had found against WLJ.

(2) Issues. (a) Is WLJ liable under section 12 of the 1933 Act? (b) Is WLJ liable as an aider and abettor under Rule 10b-5?

(3) Held. No to both issues.

(a) *Section 12.* Under the *Pinter* case decided by the Supreme Court, only narrowly defined persons are considered "sellers" under sections 12(1) or 12(2). Who passed title to the bonds? Who solicited the sales? From whom did Ps purchase? They did not buy from the law firms involved, nor did these firms offer the securities.

(b) Ps argue that WLJ, as counsel for the underwriter, which was held liable, has a duty to the investing public to ferret out and disclose fraud of its client. This is a form of vicarious liability. However, the duty WLJ had to investigate the facts is owed to its client. Only where some opinion is prepared explicitly for the plaintiff, for plaintiff's benefit, is the lawyer liable to a third party, not his client. Here, there was no opinion letter drafted for Ps. Here WLJ worked for the underwriting firm, had a duty to ensure its client's compliance, did not sign the offering document, and is listed only as passing on matters *for the underwriter.*

(c) *Rule 10b-5.* To be liable as an aider and abettor, there must be a primary violation. There was, by the underwriter. Further, to be a Rule 10b-5 aider and abettor, (i) the aider must have a general awareness of the violation; and (ii) the aider must have rendered substantial assistance. Here, WLJ rendered substantial assistance. "General awareness" means knowledge or actual awareness of the violation. How "knowing" it has to be may depend on how substantial the assistance that was rendered. Or, did WLJ know and intend to aid in the fraud? For a lawyer, to be liable under "knowledge" requires that the lawyer had clear intent to violate the securities laws, not just to assist in transactions in the ordinary course of legal business.

The evidence must be reviewed, on appeal, in the light most favorable to Ps. WLJ knew the underwriter was under S.E.C. investigations and other investigations for securities law violations. WLJ knew that the underwriter's counsel resigned; the original bond counsel resigned. WLJ did little to investigate what its client had done, or why counsel had resigned. It made changes in the offering asked for by Fryar, without questioning them. It did not properly investigate the offering document's factual statements. But WLJ provided only ordinary legal services; it may have recklessly disregarded its duties and ignored warnings, but it did not constitute actual knowledge or awareness or fraud.

The cause of action against WLJ is dismissed.

S.E.C. v. National Student Marketing Corp.

b) Lawyer liable as aider and abettor under Rule 10b-5--S.E.C. v. National Student Marketing Corp., 457 F. Supp. 682 (D.C. Cir. 1978).

(1) Facts. National Student Marketing (NSM) agreed with Interstate to an acquisition of Interstate based on an exchange of NSM shares for Interstate

230 - Securities Regulation

shares. As part of the negotiations, NSM gave Interstate favorable earnings projections for the coming year. White & Case (WC) represented NSM; Lord, Bissell, Brook (LBB) represented Interstate. Peat, Marwick (an accounting firm) was to provide Interstate with a letter prior to the closing that as of May 31 NSM's unaudited financial statements had been prepared in accordance with generally accepted accounting principles and were accurate, and that there had been no material adverse changes in the financial position of NSM as of five days before the closing of the transaction. In addition, WC was to give Interstate a letter that NSM had lawfully taken all steps necessary to close the transaction; LBB was to give NSM a similar letter that Interstate had taken all such steps. Through proxy solicitations, shareholders of both companies approved the merger. Prior to closing, Peat, Marwick knew that required adjustments would change the interim financial report of NSM (changing it to a loss), and that the year-end report would probably be only break-even (rather than the profit that NSM had represented to Interstate). NSM knew this information also. At the closing, which occurred on October 31, Peat, Marwick's letter stating that there was a loss on the interim financials came by telephone; it indicated that it had discovered changes in the interim financials of $880,000. Nothing was said about expected year-end results. But NSM's management indicated to Interstate that despite the adjustments, the year-end results would be as predicted. The WC partner (Epley) assured Interstate that the Peat, Marwick letter could be considered the necessary letter and that a signed copy would soon follow. After discussion by Interstate officers and its board, and advising with the lawyers, the closing proceeded. Soon after the closing the Peat, Marwick letter arrived, suggesting that there was a loss and that the closing should be postponed and shareholders of Interstate resolicited. Nevertheless, WC and LBB both issued their required letters and the Interstate shareholders were not informed of the Peat, Marwick letter. Further, some of the Interstate officers and directors who had received NSM stock in the merger, knowing about the Peat, Marwick letter (and without disclosing it), based on an opinion from LBB that a sale did not violate the securities laws, sold some of their NSM stock. The stock of NSM rose rapidly at first; then, with disclosures of its true financial position, the stock dropped drastically. The S.E.C. then brought this action, charging the two Interstate attorneys (and, vicariously, their firms) with aiding and abetting several securities law violations.

(2) **Issue.** Did the D attorneys for Interstate aid and abet violations of the federal securities laws?

(3) **Held.** Yes. But injunction denied.

(a) There must first be a violation of the securities laws to find aiding and abetting. Brown (director and officer of Interstate) and Meyer (LBB attorney) violated Rule 10b-5 and section 17(a) of the 1933 Act through participation in the closing of the merger and their subsequent sales of NSM stock.

(b) To prove aiding and abetting, the person must have a general awareness of his role as part of an overall activity that is illegal, and he must substantially and knowingly assist the violation.

(c) With respect to failing to take action to interfere with the closing of the merger, Ds knew all the facts and were present when the relevant events took place which were a fraud on the Interstate shareholders (failure to disclose the material facts about the financial condition of NSM). Their silence when they had a duty to their corporate client means they rendered substantial assistance to the fraud. Normally courts will give great leeway to an attorney's decision about materiality and the need to disclose, but here materiality was obvious, and Ds made no effort even to speak up about the issue. Thus, Ds cannot rely on the fact that mere "business judgments" were being made. They owed a fiduciary duty to client shareholders.

(d) Ds did not render substantial assistance to the merger violation through the issuance of their opinion. The letter was one of many conditions prerequisite to NSM completing the merger; it was for the benefit of NSM, and it largely dealt with formalities not incident to the fraud alleged.

(e) Ds' actions following the merger do not constitute aiding and abetting a securities fraud (i.e., the fact that they did not go to the S.E.C., demand rescission of the merger, etc.). Such actions do not have the needed relationship to a securities law violation (the merger had already been completed).

(f) The opinion of Ds relative to NSM stock sales subsequent to the merger did not substantially assist the sale of such stock. The opinions were not for the investing public, but were given to counsel for NSM and dealt only with factual issues concerning the application of Rule 133 of the 1933 Act (the exemption used for the sales).

(g) Injunctive relief is not appropriate here since there is no reasonable likelihood that Ds will repeat their violations of the securities laws. They have not historically engaged in such acts and their actions were not blatant and completely outrageous.

(4) Comments.

(a) The situation where lawyers frequently become involved in assisting clients in fraudulent conduct is where lawyers draft opinion letters which assist clients to complete a securities transaction. [*See* S.E.C. v. Spectrum Ltd., 489 F.2d 535 (2d Cir. 1973)—S.E.C. action for an injunction against a lawyer who wrote an opinion letter for a client that the client's stock could be sold without violating the private offering rules of the 1933 Act]

(b) There is an important issue in all aiding and abetting causes of action concerning the standard of culpability to be applied. Courts differ on whether to apply the same standard as is applied in causes of action against primary offenders [*see* S.E.C. v. Coven, 581 F.2d 1020 (2d Cir. 1978)] or a higher standard [*see* Woodward v. Metro Bank of Dallas, *supra*—scienter to be applied in all aider and abettor causes of action, no matter what the standard in primary cause of action].

(c) Note that prior to *Pinter v. Dahl* (*supra*), a lawyer or accountant assisting in a securities transaction might have been held pursuant to sections 12(1) or 12(2) of the 1933 Act as a "participant"; however, *Pinter* abolished the "participation" test and limited liability to persons who actually sell the securities or who offer or solicit offers for them.

(d) Note also that most of the successful actions against lawyers have been S.E.C. enforcement actions, *not* private damage actions.

d. S.E.C. injunctions against lawyers. The S.E.C. has traditionally used injunctions as a form of punishment (i.e., public advertisement that a lawyer has engaged in wrongdoing), as well as a means of preventing future violations of the securities laws. [S.E.C. v. Spectrum Ltd., 489 F.2d 535 (2d Cir. 1973)— S.E.C. injunction issued against attorney for *negligent* opinion letter to a client which supported a violation of the 1933 Act]

1) Although injunctions have traditionally issued on a showing of a negligent violation, after *Aaron v. S.E.C., supra,* the S.E.C. now has to show in 10b-5 actions that the lawyer knowingly violated the securities laws. This might mean, at the minimum, reckless conduct. [*See* McLean v. Alexander, 599 F.2d 1190 (3d Cir. 1979)] On the other hand, negligence is a sufficient basis for an injunction in an S.E.C. action under sections 17(a)(2) or (3) of the 1933 Act (although scienter must be shown under section 17(a)(1)). [Aaron v. S.E.C., *supra*]

e. The lawyer's professional conduct rules. The American Bar Association has set out general guidelines for the lawyer's relationship with clients. In some aspects, these rules are in sharp contrast with positions taken by the S.E.C. The rules do agree with the basic provisions of the securities laws that the lawyer cannot knowingly aid or abet a client in a violation of the securities laws. [*See* Rule 1.2(d)] The main controversy with the S.E.C. arises over the lawyer's duty under the Model Rules to protect the confidences and secrets of the client.

1) **Attorney-client relationship.** In general, the attorney has a relationship of confidentiality with the client; her duty is to protect this relationship and the interests of the clients. [Rule 1.6] Therefore, she should not act as an investigator for the S.E.C. However, the lawyer cannot go beyond certain bounds in protecting the client's interests; she does have certain duties to the public. [Rule 1.2(d)]

2) **Disclosure of confidential information.** The lawyer is not required to, but may, reveal the client's confidences or secrets only:

a) With the permission of the client; or

b) Where necessary to establish a claim or defense on behalf of the lawyer in a controversy between the lawyer and the client or to respond to allegations in any proceeding concerning the lawyer's representation of the client; or

c) When the lawyer knows that the client clearly intends to commit a crime that the lawyer believes is likely to result in imminent death or substantial bodily harm.

(1) Thus, on the one hand, it is clear that if a lawyer knows that the client is going to violate the securities laws and she continues to aid the client in doing so, she may be liable as an aider and abettor. [Rule 1.2(d)]

(2) However, the lawyer is not required to report this possible future action to anyone. The Rules clearly indicate that the lawyer may do so only where the violation is likely to result in imminent death or serious bodily harm. Note that the S.E.C. has argued that the lawyer should reveal to the S.E.C. *all* of the client's intended violations of the securities laws. [*See* S.E.C. v. National Student Marketing, *supra*]

d) Note that where the attorney knows that in the course of her representation the client has committed a crime or fraud on anyone, she should ask the client to rectify the act, but if the client does not, the attorney may not reveal the crime or fraud to affected persons. [*See* Rule 1.6]

3) **Where attorney believes client's conduct is illegal.** The attorney should resolve all doubts in favor of the client and, as long as it appears that the client will not knowingly engage in illegal conduct, the attorney may continue representation. However, if the lawyer knows that the conduct is illegal even after resolving all doubts in the client's favor, she may not continue to represent the client. [Rule 1.16(a)(1)]

4) **The entity is the client.** The Rules also provide that in the case of a corporation, the lawyer's client is the entity and not management. [Rule 1.13] This means that if management intends to violate the securities laws, or has in the past violated the securities laws, the lawyer may have a duty to report this to the corporation's board of directors and, in some cases, to the shareholders. In addition, given that the lawyer represents the entity and not individuals in management (such as the president), the lawyer must be careful to avoid conflicts of interest between clients (the entity *and* one or more of its officers or employees) by dual representation. [*See* Rule 1.7]

In the Matter of William R. Carter and Charles J. Johnson, Jr.

5) **Lawyer's duty to corporate entity--In the Matter of William R. Carter and Charles J. Johnson, Jr.,** SEA Release No. 17,597 [1981 Transfer Binder] Fed. Sec. L. Rep. (CCH) 82,847 (Feb. 28, 1981).

a) **Facts.** National Telephone Company ("National") was in the business of installing and leasing telephone systems which interfaced with AT&T telephone lines. Carter and Johnson were partners in the law firm of Brown, Wood, Ivey, Mitchell & Petty ("Brown-Wood"), and commenced representing National on an ad hoc basis in the spring of 1974. (In July 1974 Johnson was elected secretary of the company and in this capacity attended several of its board meetings, until resigning in May 1975.) National also employed in-house counsel and apparently prepared most of their reports for filing with the S.E.C. internally.

National employed Brown-Wood for specific matters, commencing with the preparation of an S-1 registration statement relating to a 1973 debenture offering. In this Rule 2(e) proceeding, Carter and Johnson were charged with willfully violating and willfully aiding and abetting violations of sections 10(b) and 13(a) of the 1934 Act and Rules 10b-5, 12b-20, and 13a-11 thereunder, as well as with having engaged in unethical and improper professional conduct.

Although Brown-Wood was primarily concerned with matters arising under the securities laws, National also relied on the firm in connection with the negotiation of a bank loan. National's business was growing rapidly, but each new phone system it leased involved heavy front-end installation and equipment expenditures, well in advance of the receipt of any rental income; hence, the more it grew, the greater its negative cash flow. In the spring of 1974 National had arranged with a consortium of banks for a $15 million term loan to be secured by an assignment of its lease receivables. Before the term loan could be finalized, however, National commenced taking down short-term advances and had used up substantially all of this line of credit by September 1974. National had a so-called wind-down plan which was to be resorted to if it exhausted its available credit and could not expand further. The plan involved terminating all sales personnel and leasing sufficient additional systems to use up its equipment inventory, and then becoming strictly a lease maintenance company, servicing the systems it had already installed, but "selling" no additional leases. By the time bank loan finally closed in December 1974, the company was facing a financial crisis. The banks, on advice of a consultant who recommended against the wind-down plan except as last resort, increased the amount of the term loan from $15 million to $21 million. Eighteen million dollars was taken down at the closing, of which $16.5 million was used to pay off the previous short term loans from the bank and $1.5 million was applied to other indebtedness. National still had $2 million in short term indebtedness after these transactions. Under the terms of the $21 million loan, National had the right to borrow only $1 million more (anytime prior to May 1). The remaining $2 million available under the loan agreement could be used only to implement the wind-down program, which was now referred to as the "lease maintenance program" (LMP). National would be required to implement the LMP under the terms of the loan agreement if it borrowed in excess of $19 million from the banks, or if its cash position deteriorated below certain specified ratios.

National's officers, many of its directors, and Johnson and Carter were all aware that the bank loan agreement would not provide adequate capital to sustain the growth that it had projected for fiscal 1975 in its June 1974 annual report to shareholders.

In January 1975 National was within $11,000 of exceeding the specified cash ratios for triggering the exercise of the LMP. In March it clearly became obligated to implement the LMP, although it failed to do so. In fact, no disclosure to the public was made of its obligation to implement the LMP until May 28, 1975, the day after the directors removed Hart, the president of National. Although not emphasized by the Administrative Law Judge (ALJ), it appears that through much of the crisis National and Hart were negotiating with an investment banking firm to undertake additional equity or other financing for National and had some expectation that such financing might take place. Such financing, however, never did materialize because of generally unfavorable market conditions. It also appears that right up to his removal Hart had been negotiating with the banks to waive National's obligation to implement the LMP. The banks, however, never agreed to such a waiver and through their attorneys were pressing from March 1 on for disclosure by National to the investing public of its obligation to implement the LMP and its implications. During all of this time Hart and National were releasing, in the form of letters and press releases and reports to shareholders, optimistic statements about the company's earnings and growth prospects, without qualifications concerning the difficult cash position of the company. The Brown-Wood firm was on the mailing list for all of these mailings, and in negotiations for the credit agreement (and in other meetings) had become fully informed of National's difficult financial circumstances.

Knowing that National had been giving very optimistic reports to the public (despite a poor cash position and the inability to locate additional financing), Johnson on

October 20, 1974, drafted a letter which inferentially referred to the wind-down plan by stating that the company regarded curtailment as advisable in view of the company's negative cash flow and adverse market situation for financing, and gave it to National's house counsel with the suggestion that such a letter be sent to all shareholders. It was not sent. In late March 1975 Carter and Johnson (having been informed by a consultant to the banks that National was obligated under the loan agreement to implement the LMP) advised Hart that immediate disclosure concerning the implementation of LMP was required and so advised him again on April 23. On May 1, Johnson drafted a disclosure letter relating to the implementation of LMP, which Hart did not send. Brown-Wood also advised house counsel to make disclosure of the LMP in the monthly Form 8-K report filed with the S.E.C. for April, but it was not made. Brown-Wood did nothing further until the directors on May 24 called a meeting on their own and for the first time Brown-Wood informed the directors of Hart's prior failure to follow their advice as to the necessity for disclosure. Johnson shortly thereafter drafted a press release describing National's condition. The company went into Chapter XI bankruptcy on July 2, 1975.

The specific actions that were the basis of the S.E.C.'s charges all occurred in December 1974 and January 1975.

Knowing (i) that National was experiencing a severe cash crisis which could affect the continued viability of the company, (ii) that the credit agreement would not solve the problem, (iii) that National's growth projections could not be achieved if the wind-down plan were implemented, and (iv) that National's management was unreceptive to making the disclosure which they were urged to make, after execution of the loan agreement, Carter and Johnson prepared a press release on December 20, 1974, describing the bank loan agreement, and early in January they prepared a Form 8-K for the month of December, which also described the loan agreement. The press release and the Form 8-K both referred to the increase of the line of credit from $15 million to $21 million, and reflected the fact that $16.5 million had been used to repay short-term debt. The press release stated that $1.5 million was to be applied for "operating expenses," a statement found by the ALJ to be incorrect since it was actually used to pay off indebtedness existing at the time the loan was made. The press release then alluded to the lease maintenance program, not by fully explaining it and its implications (i.e., that it was a wind-down plan which the company was probably going to have to implement), but by referring to the $2 million which was available for "the purpose of funding a lease maintenance program in the event additional financing is not otherwise available." The third document was a letter to shareholders sent out by the company (without Brown-Wood's approval) on December 23, 1974. It also explained lease maintenance in a back-handed fashion, without referring to it, by stating that "we shall continue to limit installations substantially below our capability until the end of our fiscal year. . . ." The same letter assures this "will not be to the detriment of continuing earnings growth," and that National was "stronger now than ever before in its history." Carter and Johnson had earlier advised National not to issue any such statement unless it was cleared by them. They became aware of the contents of the shareholder letter on December 27, when an assistant at National, realizing that the company had ignored their advice, telephoned the text of the letter to them. Carter and Johnson agreed with the S.E.C. that the description of the amended loan agreement was not an adequate disclosure. But they also stated that if read in conjunction with the December 20 press release, the shareholder letter was not misleading. Johnson testified that, although he and Carter were not wholly comfortable with the letter, they were not uncomfortable with it. (Note that there was no determination that the shareholders would have been aware of the contents of the press release). From January 1975 until Hart's termination in

May, the company continued to issue optimistic public reports. Furthermore, on March 11, Hart falsely certified to the lending banks that the LMP had been implemented.

The Administrative Law Judge (ALJ) found that the press release and the Form 8-K were misleading for failure to disclose the likelihood that the LMP would have to be instituted, how it would function, and its implications from the standpoint of the company's growth. They were also misleading because of the failure to disclose that in view of the limited financing available to the company, its prior growth projections (which depended upon additional financing) were not realistic. Not only were counsel held accountable with respect to the inadequate disclosure, but also counsel were found to have assisted Hart in avoiding the inclusion of the LMP as part of the December 1974 Form 8-K by treating it as an instrument delivered to the banks and alluded to in the bank loan agreement, but not as an exhibit to the loan agreement, which would have had to be filed an as an exhibit to the 8-K. Hart's purported reason for not wanting the LMP filed with the S.E.C. was because of his concern over its impact on employee morale. The ALJ was moved to remark that if it would have been material to employees, it would have been material to investors.

The ALJ also found that the Brown-Wood attorneys failed to take appropriate steps to assure that adequate disclosures were made in the form of press releases and letters to shareholders and others at a time when optimistic information was communicated by the company to shareholders and the marketplace; for example, that the company's letter to shareholders (sent December 23, 1974) was materially misleading and that Carter and Johnson did nothing to correct it or to see that adequate disclosures were made. The ALJ also concluded that the attorneys thereafter continued to assist management in concealing material facts, and failed to inform the Board of Directors of management's unwillingness to implement the LMP and to make proper disclosure concerning it.

As a result of its findings the ALJ suspended Carter from practice before the Commission for a period of one year, and suspended Johnson for nine months. Carter and Johnson appealed the decision to the full S.E.C.

b) **Issues.**

(1) Must the lawyer report management's failure to comply with the duty of disclosure under the securities laws to the company's board of directors?

(2) Is specific intent the standard of culpability for an aiding and abetting violation under Rule 2(e)?

(3) Did the lawyers here aid and abet the company's violations of the securities laws in the press release and the Form 8-K filing with the S.E.C.?

c) **Held.** (1) Yes. (2) Yes. (3) No. Case dismissed against the lawyers.

(1) The Commission essentially made the same findings as to the material omissions or misstatements as the ALJ had. The Commission found that the December press release and the Form 8-K were misleading because of the failure to disclosure (i) the nature of the LMP, (ii) that cessation of all leasing activity would result from its implementation, and (iii) that the implementation of the LMP on the company's growth would be negative.

The Commission also agreed that National violated the federal securities laws through its continued failure to make adequate disclosures in public statements and in S.E.C. filings regarding its deteriorating cash position, its inability to meet earlier growth projections, the possible events and actual triggering of the LMP, and the impact that implementation of the LMP would have on National's growth.

(2) The initial Carter opinion did not make a precise distinction between its stated conclusions relative to primary violations of the securities laws and aiding and abetting liability. The S.E.C. did, holding that the lawyer's involvement in the affairs of the company was not sufficient to justify a finding that they were primary violators of the securities laws. With respect to the question of whether the lawyers had affirmatively and "willfully" aided and abetted their client's violations of the securities laws, the Commission held that in an aiding and an abetting charge pursuant to Rule 2(e) (where the S.E.C. must find a "willful" violation), *specific intent* to defraud (or at least recklessness) had to be proved.

(a) In analyzing whether the lawyers had violated this standard, the Commission began its analysis with a common statement of the aider and abettor concept. The aider and abettor is one who, when there has been a primary violation of the laws:

(i) Knows that the primary violator is engaged in activity that will deceive another or is illegal;

(ii) Renders substantial assistance to the primary violator; and

(iii) Is aware or knows that his role was part of the improper or illegal activity.

(b) As to the issue of whether the lawyers in Carter rendered "substantial assistance," the S.E.C. adopted an expansive definition, indicating basically that this element of an aiding and abetting charge in intrinsically easy to prove against any securities lawyer who "is inevitably deeply involved in his client's disclosure activities and often participates in the drafting of documents." The Commission also suggested that, in making a decision about this element of the aiding and abetting test, no distinctions should be made between oral or written advice, or between advice rendered in a separate document and work done on the actual disclosure documents, or between the lawyer who participates in the drafting of the disclosure documents and one who renders advice but who studiously avoids participation in the actual drafting process.

(3) The S.E.C. then focused on the critical issue of whether the lawyers had the necessary intent for culpability. The S.E.C. stated:

(a) "It is axiomatic that a lawyer will not be liable as an aider and abettor merely because his advice, followed by the client, is ultimately determined to be wrong. What is missing in that instance is a wrongful intent on the part of the lawyer. It is that element of intent which provides the basis for distinguishing between those professionals who may be appropriately considered as subjects of professional discipline and those who, acting in good faith, have merely made errors of judgment or have been careless. . . ."

(b) "Significant public benefits flow from the effective performance of the securities lawyer's role. The exercise of independent, careful, and informed legal judgment on difficult issues is critical to the flow of material information to the securities markets. Moreover, we are aware of the difficulties and limitations attendant upon that role. In the course of rendering securities law advice, the lawyer is called upon to make difficult judgments, often under great pressure and in areas where the legal signposts are far apart and only faintly discernible."

(c) "If a securities lawyer is to bring his best independent judgment to bear on a disclosure problem, he must have the freedom to make innocent—or even, in certain cases, careless—mistakes without fear of legal liability or loss of the ability to practice before the Commission. Concern about his own liability may alter the balance of his judgment in one direction as surely as an unseemly obeisance to the wishes of his client can do so in the other. While one imbalance results in disclosure rather than concealment, neither is, in the end, truly in the public interest. Lawyers who are seen by their clients as being motivated by fears for their personal liability will not be consulted on difficult issues."

(d) In reaching a decision on the charge of willful aiding and abetting the violation of the securities laws, the Commission stated that, with respect to the press release and the 8-K filing, it was a close judgment but that the "available evidence is insufficient to establish that either respondent acted with sufficient knowledge and awareness or recklessness to satisfy the test for willful aiding and abetting liability." The lawyers may have known about National's financial condition and the failure to disclose the details of the LMP and its effect if implemented, but they may not have known that failure to disclose such information was material since, among other things, they relied on Hart's assurances that other financing sources were available and he was pursuing them.

(4) With respect to National's continued failure to make material disclosures after January 1975, the Commission stated that the lawyers' *failure to act* did not manifest the required intent to foster or aid a violation of the securities laws by inaction or silence; rather, they made numerous attempts to get the client to make disclosures, were continually rebuffed, and were at a loss "for how to deal with a difficult client."

(5) In the second Carter opinion, the S.E.C. also addressed itself to the issue of whether Carter and Johnson had engaged in unethical or improper professional conduct. The Commission found that although their conduct was improper, they should not be sanctioned because "elemental notions of fairness dictate that the Commission should not establish new rules of conduct and impose them upon professionals who acted at the time without reason to believe that their conduct was unethical or improper." The S.E.C. noted that there are many generally accepted norms of professional conduct which it feels free to apply without prior

formal announcement. However, the responsibility of a lawyer in the situation of a client violating its disclosure obligations under the securities laws, in the Commission's view, had not been "firmly and unambiguously established."

(6) The S.E.C. suggested that considerable consensus did exist about certain ethical standards that applied to this case. For example, the corporation and not management is the securities lawyer's client. Also, the lawyer must not knowingly provide substantial assistance to a client engaged in illegal conduct. And the lawyer must make all reasonable efforts to prevent a client that proposes illegal conduct from engaging in the same. However, the S.E.C. stated that applying these general principles when members of the corporation's management refuse to take the lawyer's advice to make material disclosures is not "a simple task." For example, the fact that the company's management took the position from the beginning that it would disclose only what it absolutely had to was not a basis for resignation or of extraordinary action by the lawyers. But, as time went by, and it became clear that the company's management was not looking to its lawyers for disclosure advice but instead was resisting such advice and seeking to avoid the required disclosure altogether, then the normal lawyer-client relationship could be said to have terminated and the lawyer had a duty to "do more than stubbornly continue to suggest disclosure when he knows his suggestions are falling on deaf ears."

(7) The S.E.C. then stated its rule of law to cover this situation:

> When a lawyer with significant responsibilities in the effectuation of a company's compliance with the disclosure requirements of the federal securities laws becomes aware that his client is engaged in a substantial and continuing failure to satisfy those disclosure requirements, his continued participation violates professional standards unless he takes prompt steps to end the client's noncompliance.

(8) What steps does this rule require if corporate management refuses to make the required disclosures? The S.E.C. suggested that this is for the lawyer to determine:

> Resignation is one option, although we recognize that other considerations, including the protection of the client against foreseeable prejudice, must be taken into account in the case of withdrawal. A direct approach to the board of directors or one or more individual directors or officers may be appropriate, or he may choose to try to enlist the aid of other members of the firm's management. What is required, in short, is some prompt action that leads to the conclusion that the lawyer is engaged in efforts to correct the underlying problem, rather than having capitulated to the desires of a strong-willed, but misguided client.

(9) The S.E.C. went on to state that the lawyer need not actually succeed in persuading the client to follow his advice or resign in order to avoid S.E.C. discipline. "So long as a lawyer is acting in good faith and exerting reasonable efforts to prevent violations of law by his client, his professional obligations have been met."

F. MATERIALITY, RELIANCE, AND CAUSATION

1. **Materiality.** The misrepresented or undisclosed fact must be a "material" one. A number of tests of "materiality" have been suggested by the courts.

   a. **The reasonable person standard.** In *List v. Fashion Park, Inc.*, 340 F.2d 457 (2d Cir. 1965), *cert. denied*, 382 U.S. 811 (1965), the court stated that the "basic test of materiality . . . is whether a reasonable [person] would attach importance [to the fact] in determining his choice of action in the [securities] transaction in question."

   b. **Significant propensity to affect the voting process.** In *Gerstle v. Gamble-Skogmo, Inc.*, 478 F.2d 1281 (2d Cir. 1973), the court held, in a Rule 14a-9 case for misrepresentations in the proxy statement, that the test of materiality was whether the defect would have had a "significant propensity" to affect the voting process.

   c. **Substantial likelihood that fact would be considered significant.** And in the context of a proxy statement, the Supreme Court has given what appears to be the definitive test for materiality: Whether there is a substantial likelihood that a reasonable shareholder would consider the fact of significance in determining how to vote. [*See* TSC Industries v. Northway, Inc., below]

   d. **Materiality defined--TSC Industries v. Northway, Inc.**, 426 U.S. 438 (1976).

TSC Industries v. Northway, Inc.

   1) **Facts.** National Industries bought 34% of the common stock of TSC Industries and put five persons on the TSC board (one becoming chairman of the board, another chairman of the executive committee). Then a proposal was made by National to buy the remainder of TSC in a stock-for-stock exchange. The board of TSC approved (the five National directors abstaining). A shareholder of TSC, Northway, Inc. (P), brings this action pursuant to Rules 14a-3 and 14a-9, claiming that the joint proxy statement issued by TSC and National to solicit the approval of the TSC shareholders to the transaction contained false and misleading statements. The following were claimed as violations:

      a) A failure to disclose that the president of National was the chairman of the board of TSC and that the vice president was the chairman of the executive committee. Also that, because it owned 34% of the common stock of TSC, National may have been in "control" of TSC.

      b) The fact that the opinion issued by a brokerage firm that the terms of the transaction were fair to TSC shareholders was modified by a later statement indicating that the price on part of the stock issued by National would probably decline after the merger.

c) Also, the fact that about 9% of the stock purchases of National were by a mutual fund with connections to National or by National itself (which may have manipulated the stock price of National).

2) **Issue.** Were the statements or omissions "material"?

3) **Held.** No. The statements or omissions were not "material" as a matter of law; thus, summary judgment by P is denied.

a) A statement is "material" if there is a "substantial" likelihood that a reasonable shareholder would consider it important in deciding how to vote. This does not require proof of substantial likelihood that disclosure of the fact would have caused the reasonable investor to change his vote. It does contemplate a showing of substantial likelihood that, under all the circumstances, the omitted fact would have assumed actual significance in the deliberation of the reasonable shareholder.

b) Summary judgment issues only where the statements are such that reasonable minds cannot differ on the question of materiality. This is not the case here, so summary judgment should be denied and the issues tried.

c) The proxy statement did reveal that National controlled TSC (i.e., the stock ownership was revealed, the fact that National had five people on the board was revealed, etc.).

d) The brokerage firm indicated that a premium over market price was being paid for the TSC shares; even with the second letter revealing that this firm thought that the price of the National shares would decline after the merger, the fact that a premium is being paid is not disputed. Also, there is nothing to prove that the stock purchases by National and the mutual fund were for the purpose of manipulating the market price of National; nor is there anything to prove that such purchases were coordinated with the merger of TSC.

Virginia Bankshares, Inc. v. Sandberg

e. **Qualitative terms and proxy solicitation of unneeded minority votes--Virginia Bankshares, Inc. v. Sandberg,** 115 L. Ed. 2d 929 (U.S. 1991).

1) **Facts.** In 1986 First American Bankshares, Inc. (FABI), a bank holding company, began a freeze-out merger under Virginia state law in which First American Bank of Virginia (85% owned by FABI and 15% owned by 2,000 minority shareholders) was merged into Virginia Bankshares, Inc., a wholly owned subsidiary of FABI. FABI got an investment banker to give a report that $42 per share was a fair price. Virginia law required that the merger be submitted to vote at a shareholders' meeting, preceded by a statement of information given to shareholders. FABI instead solicited proxies for voting at the annual shareholders' meeting. In the proxy solicitation materials FABI urged approval of the merger because (i) it was an opportunity for minority shareholders to achieve a "high" value, and (ii) the price offered was "fair." Most minority shareholders approved, but P did not; she sued for damages in district court, on the basis that section 14(a) and Rule 14a-9 were violated by material misrepresentations in the proxy materials; she also sued under state law for breach of fiduciary

duties by the directors of FABI. P alleged that the directors had not believed the price was fair or high. The jury found for P and awarded her an additional $18 per share. The circuit court affirmed. The Supreme Court granted certiorari.

2) **Issues.** (a) Were the qualitative statements in proxy statements about a "high" price, etc. material and misleading? (b) Is there a federal claim under the proxy rules where P is a minority shareholder whose vote is not required to approve the transaction and where by solicitation of proxies no state law remedies otherwise available to P have not been lost?

3) **Held.** (a) The statements were material and misleading. (b) There is no cause of action under the proxy rules in this situation.

a) If a director makes a statement in proxy material of his reasons for doing something (or of his beliefs or opinions) and it is shown that the director did not really have these reasons or hold these beliefs, these statements can be material. These matters can usually be documented from corporate records. And here, the word "high" is not too vague; it has a basis in provable facts from established criteria in valuing companies. For example, P showed that the book value used to calculate $42 per share was not based on the appreciated value of the bank's real estate; also that market value as used was not reliable since the market for the stock was thin; also, that undisclosed valuations by the bank showed a value of $60 per share.

b) But in addition to showing an opinion or belief that was not in fact held, P *must also show* that the statement also said or implied something false or misleading about the subject matter. Here, not only did the directors give an opinion that the value was high (and this was a reason for the merger), but also there is an implied misstatement of actual fact that this was the reason and that the price was in fact high, which P showed proof of otherwise.

c) Here, one director of Virginia Bankshares was also a director of FABI, which was not disclosed. Virginia state law provided that such a freeze-out merger could be attacked afterward by minority shareholders if they could show conflicts of interest that may have injured them. This provision could be avoided if (i) minority shareholders approved the transaction after disclosure of the material facts concerning the transaction; (ii) the directors ratified the transaction after disclosure; or (iii) the transaction could be proved to be fair. P argues that because the proxy solicitation allowed Ds to avoid these state law provisions (otherwise available to the minority shareholders) because the minority approved the transaction in the proxies, then there is causation (the proxy solicitation provided an essential link in the chain of approving the transaction, and a section 14(a) cause of action should exist).

d) However, in this case there is no such causal sequence. This procedure is too hypothetical. It allows actions where the shareholders' vote is not necessary to the transaction.

(1) Implied private rights of action under federal securities laws are based on congressional intent. They should not be expanded beyond that intent.

(2) Congress was not clear in how far an implied private right should go in the case of section 14(a); however, where it did want private rights, it specified them in specific sections of the securities laws.

(3) So policy concerns must be looked at to determine the scope of the private right in this case.

    (a) It is too speculative to allow a dissatisfied minority shareholder to allege that without the proxy solicitation a timid management would not have been able to pass the corporate action, which approval was secured by misrepresentation.

    (b) And, on the other hand, directors in the future would simply make a few statements about plans to proceed without minority endorsement (if they did not get it in the proxy solicitation).

(4) There have been cases where proxy solicitation has been a link in the process of preventing a class of shareholders from resorting to a state remedy otherwise available; e.g., a minority shareholder induced by a misleading proxy statement to forfeit a state-law right to an appraisal remedy. [Swanson v. American Consumers Industries, Inc., 475 F.2d 516 (7th Cir. 1973)] But this case does not require the court to decide whether section 14(a) provides a cause of action for lost state remedies since there is *no* indication that will occur here. Virginia law indicates that minority shareholder ratification of a merger overcomes any problem of a conflict of interest. But state courts would not accept the giving proxies based on a material misrepresentation as a minority shareholder approval.

Judgment is reversed.

4) **Concurrence** (Scalia, J.). There is a standard misrepresentation of fact here; i.e., that (of the directors' opinion *and*) of the accuracy of facts on which the opinion was assertedly based. No new rule is needed to decide the case.

5) **Dissent** (Kennedy, Marshall, Blackmun, Stevens, JJ.). The majority has misrepresented the status of non-voting causation in proxy cases. Courts have applied this theory to cases for 25 years. The Court simply wanted to restrict a well-established implied right of action.

2. **Reliance.** "Reliance" is a showing by the plaintiff that he *actually relied* on the material fact that was misrepresented. That is, reliance is a showing that the misrepresentation was *the cause of plaintiff's entering the transaction*.

a. **Standard for causation.** In determining transaction causation, the courts generally apply the *substantial factor test*. Plaintiff has to show that the belief in the misrepresentation was a "substantial factor" in his having entered the transaction. [*See* List v. Fashion Park, Inc., 340 F.2d 457 (2d Cir. 1965)]

b. **Relationship to materiality.** When a fact is material, there is a strong indication that the plaintiff would rely on it and it would be a substantial factor in causing the plaintiff to enter the transaction. On this basis, reliance would seem to flow as a logical assumption from a showing of materiality; however, one does not *necessarily* follow the other. For example, a material fact could be misrepresented and plaintiff could know about it and enter the securities transaction anyway (i.e., no reliance is shown). Or conceivably, plaintiff might not know about it and it might be shown that even had he known, plaintiff would still have entered the transaction (i.e., plaintiff likes to invest in insurance companies, and buys them at their market price without any other information).

c. **Early cases.** The early cases (involving plaintiff and defendant in a personal, *face-to-face* relationship) required that plaintiff show that he actually relied on defendant's material misrepresentation. This type of case still seems to require actual reliance.

d. **Modern trend.** The modern trend of the cases is, however, toward limiting the necessity of showing reliance, since most transactions occur over exchanges and it is difficult for individual plaintiffs to show reliance on misrepresentations that may in fact have affected the price at which they purchased or sold securities.

1) **Situations involving affirmative representations and open-market transactions.** In cases involving affirmative misrepresentations where plaintiffs purchase or sell securities on the *open* market, two types of cases arise:

    a) **Actual reliance.** It is possible that plaintiff actually read and relied on statements made by the defendant. If there is a reliance requirement, this would fulfill it.

    b) **Effect on the market.** The other alternative is simply for plaintiff to allege that defendant's statements affected the market price at which plaintiff sold his stock (i.e., a material fact was misrepresented and it is the cause of plaintiff's loss, since the market price of the stock was affected). Note that this does not show that the plaintiff relied on the misrepresented fact. As a matter of fact, plaintiff in this situation would not argue that he personally read or relied on defendant's statements at all.

        (1) Class actions in this type of situation have been allowed where no actual proof has apparently been required from each plaintiff in the class of his actual personal reliance. [*See* Green v. Wolf Corp,, 406 F.2d 291 (2d Cir. 1968); *but see* Rifken v. Crow, 574 F.2d 256 (5th Cir. 1974)]

        (2) And in *Mitchell v. Texas Gulf Sulfur Co.*, 446 F.2d 90 (10th Cir. 1971), the court indicated that while there was a reliance requirement, it was satisfied if the misrepresentation was a "substantial factor" in determining the plaintiff's course of conduct (a similar requirement to "materiality").

(3)   So while in this context there may be no case which specifically dispenses with the reliance requirement, there are cases that seem to indicate that a plaintiff whose loss can be shown to have been caused by market factors affected by defendant's statements can recover without a showing of specific individual reliance on these misrepresentations.

(4)   Note that if defendant did undertake to show that plaintiff had *not* relied and was successful (e.g., by showing that plaintiff actually knew about the misrepresentation and invested anyway), it is probable that plaintiff could *not* recover. Thus, in some sense a reliance requirement must continue to exist. In other words, *there may be a rebuttable presumption of reliance* from a showing of misrepresentation of a material fact. Lack of reliance can always be shown.

(5)   *See also* the *Basic, Inc. v. Levinson* case, discussed *supra*, for more on the "fraud on the market" theory—i.e., where securities are sold in a well-developed market, a plaintiff may be able to prove reliance on a misrepresentation by alleging that she relied on the integrity of the market.

(a)   In an open and well-developed securities market, material misrepresentations (or the withholding of material information) generally affects the price of the stock. Since purchasers rely on the price of the stock as a reflection of its value, they may be defrauded even if they do not directly rely on the misstatements. [Basic, Inc. v. Levinson, *supra*]

(b)   The effect of the fraud on the market theory is to create a *presumption* of reliance. The defendant can rebut the presumption by showing, for example, that a misrepresentation in fact did not lead to a distortion of price, or that an individual plaintiff traded or would have traded despite knowing the statement was false, or that before the plaintiff traded, the correct information credibly entered the market.

2)   Situations involving disclosure of material facts. Another type of situation occurs where the reliance issue is raised—i.e., where the defendant fails to disclose material facts (nondisclosure cases).

a)   The issue. The reliance issue here is whether the plaintiff *would have* acted differently if he had known of the material fact (i.e., *would* plaintiff have relied on the material fact *if* it had been disclosed?).

b)   Using materiality to make an inference. This is asking a hypothetical question. In trying to answer it, the courts have resorted to making an inference from the fact of materiality. That is, if it is shown that a *reasonable investor* would have considered the fact important in making a decision (materiality), then no reliance need be shown. [*See* Shapiro v. Merrill Lynch, Pierce, Fenner & Smith, Inc., 495 F.2d 228 (2d Cir. 1974), discussed *supra*]

c)   Analysis. Of course, what may be going on here is the simple recognition by the courts that in a nondisclosure case it is extremely unlikely that actual reliance can be shown or that the defendant could show plaintiff's nonreliance. Thus, the language of these opinions would seem to dispense with the reliance requirement. However, if by some remarkable set of circumstances defendant could prove that plaintiff would not have relied on the omission, then it is probable that plaintiff could *not* recover (and in this sense there is still a reliance requirement).

3. **Causation and Causation-in-Fact.** Courts have consistently stated that the defendant's action must have "caused" the plaintiff's injury.

    a. **Standard for causation.** In order to show causation, the plaintiff must be able to show that the defendant's deception was a *substantial factor* in causing the loss.

    b. **Types of situations in which the issue arises.** There are many different situations in which the issue of causation arises (such as in fraud cases, mismanagement of assets, etc., or in affirmative misrepresentations made about the issuer—i.e., that conditions are better than they are, or worse than they are, etc.). Each of these situations (and others) must be looked at on the basis of the particular facts, although the courts have not been careful to do this. For example, where the corporation sells stock for inadequate consideration, it is clear that the sale of stock is the source of loss to the corporation (and its shareholders). But where management of the corporation breaches some fiduciary duty (such as by engaging in a transaction in which they have a conflict of interest), this may or may not be the cause of a drop in the price of stock bought by plaintiff (the drop in the stock could have been caused by other market factors).

    c. **Relationship to materiality.** It seems almost inevitable that a court would find that once materiality has been shown (i.e., that a reasonable investor would have wanted to know the fact), causation has also been shown. Some courts have so stated (at least in the nondisclosure area). But it is also conceivable that a fact could be material but not the cause of loss. For example, it may be material to know that management engages in transactions in which their interest and the corporation's interest conflict, but it might not be the cause of plaintiff's loss (i.e., the price of the stock which plaintiff bought might have gone down due to general market factors).

    d. **Relationship to reliance.** Reliance is a showing that the fact was material to the plaintiff—that it was a substantial factor in causing him to enter the transaction in which he experienced a loss.

        1) It sometimes appears that a finding of reliance is enough for a court to hold that there is the necessary causation—i.e., that transaction causation is equated with loss causation.

        2) For example, where XYZ's earnings have gone down and this information is disclosed to some parties (A) and not others (B), and B buys XYZ stock without the material information, then B may recover from XYZ and perhaps from A. [*See* Shapiro v. Merrill Lynch, Pierce, Fenner & Smith, Inc., *supra*]

a)   It is clear that in this situation the fact is material. It is also clear that a reasonable investor and the plaintiff here (B) would have relied on the fact had he known about it. Thus, there is a finding that there is transaction causation. But is it the nondisclosure that caused the loss? Or is it the drop in earnings? Courts seldom make this distinction, so in many cases a showing of materiality and/or reliance amounts to a showing of causation.

Schlick v.
Penn-Dixie
Cement Corp.

e.   **Application--Schlick v. Penn-Dixie Cement Corp.**, 507 F.2d 374 (2d Cir. 1976).

1)   **Facts.** Penn-Dixie (D) owned 53% of Continental and had six of the nine directors. D merged Continental into a wholly owned subsidiary. One of the minority shareholders (P) of Continental brings an action under Rule 10b-5 and section 14(a) on the basis that D manipulated and depressed the market value of Continental stock (traded on the New York Stock Exchange) by utilizing Continental's assets for its own benefit (bank accounts were used as compensating balances for D's own borrowings; Continental funds were used for a D real estate venture; excessive costs were charged to Continental; an accounting change was made that reduced the earnings of Continental, etc.). P also alleges that D tried to raise the price of its own stock by having the Continental pension fund buy D's shares off the market, and that D brought about the merger at an unfair exchange ratio to Continental's minority shareholders. P charges that the proxy statement used to solicit Continental shareholder proxies to approve the merger was materially defective since it failed to disclose the manner in which D had inflated the value of its shares at the expense of Continental. The district court dismissed the complaint for failure to state a cause of action. P appeals.

2)   **Issue.** Has a claim under Rule 10b-5 or section 14(a) been stated?

3)   **Held.** Yes. Lower court judgment reversed on both the 10b-5 and 14(a) claims.

a)   With regard to the Rule 10b-5 claim, D's activities to lessen the value of Continental shares are a "fraud." There is a connection between the security transaction and the misconduct. P must show both causation ("loss causation") and reliance ("transaction causation").

(1)   Transaction causation is showing that the violations *caused plaintiff* to engage in the securities transaction. In a misrepresentation case, this means plaintiff must show that he relied on the misrepresentation. In a nondisclosure case, plaintiff must show that the omissions were "material." They were here.

(2)   Loss causation is a showing that the economic harm to plaintiff resulted from the misrepresentations, omissions, or fraud. It is clear that the fraud here resulted in the unfavorable merger exchange ratio.

b)   With regard to the section 14a-9 claim, P has alleged both loss causation (i.e., an unfair exchange ratio based on D's manipulation of Continental) and transaction causation.

(1) It is clear that there is a loss causation. The issue is transaction causation, since the majority could have effectuated the transaction without the vote of minority shareholders (thus, the omission of fact was not central to getting proxies to vote in favor of the transaction).

(2) Transaction causation is broader than this, however. Here it may be held that the minority shareholders were deceived by the action of those making the corporate decision to merge (and then voting for it). The decision on cause should uphold the purpose of the proxy rules, and to require disclosure of material facts to shareholders (even when the majority has enough votes to approve the transaction) upholds the intended purposes (since the majority will be loath to reveal unsavory material facts, and the market will benefit from such disclosure).

G. PROCEDURE, DEFENSES, AND REMEDIES

1. **Jurisdictional Means.** The regulatory sections under the 1933 Act (e.g., section 12(2), etc.) all require that the prohibited conduct must occur by use of means or transportation, or communication in interstate commerce. There is a similar requirement for Rule 10b-5. But there are differences in the specific requirements as well, as indicated by the language of the various statutes.

2. **Location of Jurisdiction.** According to section 22(a) of the 1933 Act, jurisdiction of federal courts in federal district courts is concurrent with jurisdiction in state courts. However, jurisdiction of the 1934 Act causes of action is exclusively in the federal courts.

3. **Venue.** Under the 1933 Act, venue may be in any district in which the offer or sale of securities took place, if the defendant participated therein, and under the 1934 Act in any district where any act or transaction constituting the violation occurred. In addition, under both acts, venue may also be in any district in which the defendant is an inhabitant or transacts business or is found.

4. **Arbitration Under the 1933 Act--Rodriguez de Quijas v. Shearson/ American Express, Inc.,** 490 U.S. 477 (1989).

   a. **Facts.** Ps are individuals who invested $400,000 in securities with defendant broker. Ps signed customer agreement with provision providing for binding arbitration unless unenforceable under state or federal law. Ps sued on the basis that their money was lost in fraudulent transactions, under section 12(2) of the 1933 Act, several provisions of 1934 Act, and state law. The district court ordered that all claims be submitted to arbitration, except the 1933 Act claim, which was governed by *Wilko v. Swan,* 346 U.S. 427 (1953). The court of appeals reversed, holding that the 1933 Act claim was also to be submitted to arbitration since *Wilko* was obsolete. The Supreme Court granted certiorari.

Rodriguez de Quijas v. Shearson/ American Express, Inc.

b. **Issue.** Is a predispute agreement to arbitrate claims under the 1933 Act unenforceable, requiring resolution of the claims only in a judicial forum?

c. **Held.** No.

1) The *Wilko* court did not accept that arbitration was merely a form of trial to be used in lieu of a court trial. It also concluded that the 1933 Act was intended to protect buyers of securities, who often do not deal at arm's length and on equal terms with sellers, by offering them a wider choice of courts and venue than is enjoyed by participants in other business transactions, making the right to select the judicial forum a particularly valuable feature of the 1933 Act. These reasons do not justify the interpretation that section 14 of the 1933 Act prohibits agreements to arbitrate future disputes related to the purchase of securities.

2) *Wilko* reflected the old judicial hostility to arbitration. This has changed.

3) The right to select the judicial forum is not such an essential feature of the 1933 Act that section 14 may be construed to bar any waiver of this right.

4) The 1933 Act enacted substantive provisions which gave advantage to buyers of securities (i.e., placing burden on seller to prove lack of scienter when a buyer alleges fraud) and procedural provisions (i.e., broad venue provisions, etc.). But there is no basis for holding that the prohibition in section 14 against waiving compliance with any provision of the 1933 Act as applying to these procedural provisions.

5) Similar procedural measures were present in other statutes where this Court has allowed enforcement of predispute arbitration provisions. [*See, e.g.,* Shearson/American Express, Inc. v. McMahon (1934 Act)] Indeed, the language of section 29(a) of the 1934 Act is exactly like section 14 of the 1933 Act.

6) The strong language of the Arbitration Act indicates that arbitration agreements shall be valid except on such grounds as exist in law or equity for revocation of a contract. Under this statute, the party opposing arbitration carries the burden of showing that Congress intended in a separate statute to preclude a waiver of judicial remedies, or that such a waiver of judicial remedies inherently conflicts with the underlying purposes of the other statute.

7) Petitioners have not carried their burden of showing that arbitration agreements are not enforceable under the Securities Act.

8) Arbitration could also be denied where the party opposing it can prove that the agreement to arbitrate resulted from fraud or overwhelming economic power that would allow for revocation of the contract. There is no factual support to prove such a situation here.

9) The *Wilko* case is overruled. The *McMahon* case and *Wilko* are inconsistent, and *McMahon* led plaintiffs to manipulate their claims by adding a 1933 Act claim so as to escape *McMahon*.

10) Our ruling is applied to this case. Only where there are special circumstances is a new ruling applied only prospectively. This result does not produce substantial inequitable results; Ps did not agree to the arbitration provision in reliance on *Wilko*'s giving them a way out.

d. **Dissent** (Stevens, Brennan, Marshall, Blackmun). *Wilko* has been followed for so long as precedent that only Congress should overturn it.

5. **Evidentiary Privileges.** Issues involving the attorney-client privilege to keep client communications confidential can often arise in securities law practice. The situation is unique in that often the client is disclosing information that is then meant to be disclosed to others in various registration documents.

a. **Waiver through client disclosure--*In re* Subpoenas Duces Tecum to Fulbright & Jaworski and Vinson & Elkins,** 738 F.2d 1367 (D.C. Cir. 1984).

In re Subpoenas Duces Tecum to Fulbright & Jaworski and Vinson & Elkins

1) **Facts.** Ps asked for enforcement of four subpoenas requesting that Ds produce documents that would assist them in a suit against Tesoro Petroleum Corporation and its officers and directors. Ps allege that Tesoro manipulated its stock price in order to buy back its stock and go private, thus avoiding S.E.C. disclosures, including the need to disclose illegal payments to foreign governments.

Tesoro had hired Fulbright to conduct an investigation for it concerning such illegal payments. Fulbright's report, notes, and various corporate documents were voluntarily turned over to the S.E.C. in connection with its voluntary disclosure program (promising wrong-doers lenient treatment for cooperation). After reviewing the records, the S.E.C. filed suit against Tesoro, then resolved the issues in a consent decree. The S.E.C. then turned some of the documents over to the Department of Justice (for a grand jury proceeding); the grand jury subpoenaed the remaining records of Ps from the S.E.C. The district court granted Ps' request for enforcement of the subpoenas.

2) **Issue.** Did Ds' voluntary release of information to the S.E.C. act as a complete waiver of the attorney-client and work product privileges with respect to that information relative to other parties?

3) **Held.** Yes. Affirmed.

a) **The attorney-client privilege.** Any voluntary disclosure by the holder of the privilege is inconsistent with the confidential relationship of attorney-client and thus waives the privilege. Ds argue that the waiver was limited to the S.E.C., but a client cannot waive the privilege in circumstances where it is beneficial and maintain it in other circumstances.

b) **The work product privilege.** This is broader and is meant to promote a lawyer's preparation as opposed to society's interest in revealing all material facts relating to a dispute. Thus, disclosures made in pursuit of trial preparation and not inconsistent with maintaining secrecy against opponents should be allowed without waiving the privilege. Here, however, the privilege is waived:

(1) Ds seek to gain an advantage greater than the law need allow to foster a healthy adversary system. The S.E.C. was an adversary party; the voluntary disclosure to the S.E.C. simply meant lesser punishment. It is not fair to waive the rule against one adversary party while retaining it against others. Ds knew that there would be litigation with others when they disclosed to the S.E.C.

(2) There were no expectations by Ds that they would get confidentiality from the S.E.C. The S.E.C. regulations granting such confidentiality relate only to formal administrative proceedings and not to the voluntary disclosure program. Also, Ds claim that the S.E.C. promised confidentiality in private letters, but this does not seem to be the case; also, the letters were sent after the S.E.C. already had the information. It also makes no difference that the S.E.C. has proposed legislation that would preserve confidentiality of information submitted to the S.E.C.

(3) Finally, there are no policy factors that call for a special exception for the S.E.C.'s voluntary disclosure program. Ds could have done the work and then refused to cooperate with the S.E.C., or only disclosed the information if the S.E.C. had promised to keep the information confidential.

In re International Systems and Controls Corporation Securities Litigation

b. Exceptions to the work product rule--*In re* International Systems and Controls Corporation Securities Litigation, 693 F.2d 1235 (5th Cir. 1982).

1) Facts. International Systems (D) did business throughout the world. Ps allege that D regularly bribed foreign nationals to get contracts. D in 1976 appointed a special audit committee of two directors, assisted by an outside law firm and an accounting firm. In 1978 the S.E.C. issued a subpoena for the records of the investigation, then filed a complaint; ultimately, a consent decree was entered.

One of the plaintiffs brought a derivative suit against the board members; another filed a class action against the directors, officers, and the accounting firm. Both sought the records of the investigation.

The district court found that all of the information was protected by the work product rule but ordered some of it disclosed. D appeals.

2) Issues.

a) Can a corporation assert the work product rule against its own shareholders?

b) If the corporation continues to engage in a crime or fraud while the work product is developed, does this create an exception to the nondiscovery work product rule?

3) Held. a) Yes. b) Yes. Remanded.

a)   In *Garner v. Wolfinbarger*, 430 F.2d 1093 (5th Cir. 1970), *cert. denied*, 401 U.S. 974 (1971), it was held that the attorney-client privilege could be asserted by the corporation against its shareholders, except where the suit by shareholders was against officers and directors for acting against the corporation's interests. In that case the shareholders should have an opportunity to show that the privilege should not apply.

b)   Work product is attorney work prepared in anticipation of litigation. In this situation there is no community of interest between shareholders and their corporation. So the *Garner* rule on attorney-client privilege should not apply. Also, the *Garner* rule uses a different standard for requiring disclosure from that for disclosing work product. [*See* Fed. R. Civ. P. 26(b)(3)]

c)   Work product can only be disclosed if (i) there is a substantial need for the materials, and (ii) the plaintiff cannot get the materials without substantial hardship.

Here plaintiffs have only taken one deposition; this is not sufficient proof that undue hardship would be involved in getting the information Ps require another way. There has been no proof that undue expense will be required, and Ps have not shown that they cannot get the information they seek in other ways.

d)   There is an exception to the protection of work product when it can be shown that (i) the client was engaged in ongoing fraudulent activity when the work product was sought or produced, and (ii) the work product was reasonably related to the fraudulent activity.

6.   The Defense of Lack of Due Diligence. Where defendant lacks mutual knowledge of the fraud, yet has acted in a reckless manner, many courts will find him liable under a 10b-5 theory. However, the Supreme Court in *Hochfelder*, *supra*, reserved for future decision the question of whether reckless conduct was sufficient to find liability in private damage actions.

a.   **Definition.** Reckless conduct has been defined as a "highly unreasonable omission, involving not merely simple or even inexcusable negligence, but an extreme departure from the standards of ordinary care, and which presents a danger of misleading buyers or sellers that is either known to the defendant or is so obvious that the actor must have been aware of it."

1)   As stated above, nearly every reported decision of the lower courts since *Hochfelder* has held that reckless conduct is a sufficient basis for civil liability under Rule 10b-5.

2)   One result of the availability of recklessness as a basis for the imposition of Rule 10b-5 liability is an expansion of the possibility of a 10b-5 recovery by plaintiffs beyond what it appeared to be when *Hochfelder* was first decided.

b.   **Defense of "due diligence."** The breadth of situations permitting 10b-5 recovery has been further widened by courts restricting the availability of the defense of "due diligence." In many cases since *Hochfelder*, the courts have narrowed the extent to which a defendant can resist a 10b-5 action on the basis that plaintiff's reliance on defendant's omissions or misrepresentations was not justified, and would have been prevented had plaintiff exercised "due diligence."

1) Prior to *Hochfelder*, the approach of the federal courts had varied somewhat; essentially, however, the courts had adopted a standard of negligence in determining whether a plaintiff had exercised due care in pursuing her interests.

2) Following *Hochfelder*, the courts seem to have reexamined the due diligence defense and have held that mere negligence on plaintiff's part may not be enough to preclude a 10b-5 action. If the contributory fault of the plaintiff is to cancel defendant's wanton or intentional fraud, plaintiff's action may have to reach the level of gross conduct as compared to the action of defendant.

Dupuy v.
Dupuy

c. **Standard applied--Dupuy v. Dupuy,** 551 F.2d 1006 (5th Cir. 1977).

1) **Facts.** The Dupuys were brothers involved in the real estate development business as partners. They formed Lori Corporation and acquired a long-term lease on property suitable for a hotel in the French Quarter of New Orleans. Each owned 47% of the corporation and each put in $1,880 in capital. Milton (P) ran the business on a day-to-day basis; he had little education but a great deal of experience; Clarence (D) was a lawyer. P initially got a monthly salary. In March of 1972 D cut off the monthly salary; since P could not borrow on his other holdings, he asked D to buy his interest and was forced to take other employment, which he did for a time until ill health forced him to quit. Shortly after P was forced out of his job, where he had begun to negotiate for a deal to build the hotel, D began separate negotiations which culminated in a deal to finance and build the hotel; as part of this deal, D transferred Lori's lease (representing that he had the authority of the corporation to do so) and received 40% of the hotel deal himself (Lori also got 40%). D also told P that nothing was happening and the deal was dead. In ill health, P pressed D to buy his interest in Lori; he did not check with anyone else about the status of the hotel deal, but relied totally on his brother's representations. The value of Lori's interest in the hotel deal was valued at various amounts, from $500,000 to $3 million. There is a dispute about what D paid for P's interest (P saying $10,000; D saying $45,000). The trial jury found for P and assessed damages at $900,000. The trial judge granted D judgment notwithstanding the verdict. P appeals.

2) **Issue.** Does D have a good defense to P's cause of action under Rule 10b-5 that P did not exercise reasonable diligence in protecting his own interests?

3) **Held.** No. The trial court's ruling of judgment notwithstanding the verdict is reversed. A new trial is granted on the issue of the amount of damages.

a) There are two rationales for the due diligence defense:

(1)   Only those who have pursued their own interest with care and good faith should qualify for the implied private right of action pursuant to Rule 10b-5.

(2)   By requiring plaintiffs to invest carefully, the antifraud policies of the securities laws are advanced and the stability of the markets protected.

b)   The due diligence defense is separate and apart from any of the elements of a Rule 10b-5 cause of action. For example, it is not a matter of proving lack of a justifiable basis for reliance. Thus, even though some courts in nondisclosure cases have abandoned the reliance requirement, this is irrelevant to the due diligence issue. It still must be proved.

c)   The test used to be one of negligence, based on whether a reasonable investor with the attributes and in the situation of the plaintiff would have exercised greater diligence.

d)   The *Hochfelder* decision by the Supreme Court has caused courts to reexamine the negligence standard. Most have decided that now the defendant must prove that the plaintiff was at least reckless in not protecting himself.

(1)   The reason for this is that the policy of deterring intentional conduct (by the defendant) outweighs the policy of deterring negligent conduct. *Hochfelder* requires that plaintiff prove that defendant acted intentionally or recklessly. So defendant should have to prove that plaintiff at least acted recklessly.

(2)   The other reason for finding that plaintiff must be at least reckless is that there is no reason to shift the loss that occurs from one party to the other if they are equally at fault; but if the plaintiff has only been negligent and the defendant acted intentionally, there is a good reason to have the defendant shoulder the loss.

e)   The most important reason for requiring recklessness in the due diligence defense is that otherwise the scope of actions under Rule 10b-5 would become so narrow as to almost eliminate use of the Rule to patrol securities violations. Plaintiff already has to prove the defendant acted intentionally; to then let the defendant off if he could prove plaintiff acted negligently means that Rule 10b-5 would be limited to only the most extraordinary cases of fraud.

f)   The trial court's jury instructions were adequate to ask whether P had been reckless in not investigating the background facts of his sale of stock to his brother. There is sufficient evidence from which the jury could reasonably have found that P did not have sufficient knowledge of the risk of D's forming a deal, or that he had formed such a deal.

g)   In many cases the fact that plaintiff put pressure on the defendant to buy the stock would weigh heavily in determining that plaintiff had some obligation to make an investigation. But here the jury could have found justification for P's not doing so—his history of reliance on his brother, and the fact that he was very ill.

4) Comment. Note that this defense is really limited to face-to-face transactions, as was the case here.

7. **Common Law Defenses--Bateman Eichler, Hill Richards, Inc. v. Berner,** 472 U.S. 299 (1985).

a. **Facts.** Lazzaro, a registered broker working for Bateman Eichler (D), and Neadeau (D), president of T.O.N.M. Oil and Gas Exploration Corporation, conspired to provide investors (Ps) with false and misleading (apparently inside) information about gold property discoveries by T.O.N.M. in order to drive the price of T.O.N.M. stock up. After Ps bought stock, the price collapsed. Ps sued under Rule 10b-5; Ds argue that there should be no recovery because Ps are in pari delicto. The district court found for Ds; the court of appeals reversed. The Supreme Court granted certiorari.

b. **Issue.** Does the common law defense of in pari delicto bar a private damages action under the federal securities laws against corporate insiders and broker-dealers who fraudulently induce investors to purchase securities by misrepresenting that they are conveying material nonpublic information about the issuer?

c. **Held.** No, not necessarily. Affirmed.

1) A private action for damages under the securities laws may only be barred on the ground of plaintiff's own culpability where, as a result of his own actions, plaintiff bears at least substantially equal responsibility for the violations he seeks to redress.

a) There are often important distinctions between the relative culpabilities of tippers, securities professionals who pass along inside information, and tippees.

b) Tippee's use of inside information does not violate Rule 10b-5 unless the tippee owes a duty to disclose the information. [*See* Chiarella v. United States, *supra*]

c) A tippee's duty is merely derivative from the other insiders.

d) The insider breaches a duty to the issuing corporation as well as to the shareholder to whom he buys or sells. The tippee only breaches a duty to the shareholder.

e) The insider also breaches a duty to the tippee where the tipper-insider passes on false information.

f) Here Ds masterminded the scheme; Ps were unwitting dupes.

2) The common law defense of in pari delicto should also be rejected where the primary objective of protecting the investing public is furthered.

a) Barring private actions such as this one would result in a number of fraudulent schemes going undetected by the S.E.C., since there would be no incentive for Ps to bring a private action.

b) Insider trading is deterred by bringing enforcement pressures on the sources of the abuse of inside information—the corporate insiders and broker-dealers.

c) The tippees are still at risk—guilty tippees, by bringing an action, expose themselves to the possibility of substantial civil penalties by shareholders and to criminal penalties.

8. **Dismissal of Derivative Suits; Application of State Law in Federal Courts-- Joy v. North,** 692 F.2d 880 (2d Cir. 1982).

a. **Facts.** Joy brought a shareholder's derivative suit on behalf of Citytrust Bancorp against its wholly owned subsidiary and its officers and directors in federal district court, alleging common law breach of trust and of fiduciary duty as well as violation of the National Bank Act, which limits aggregate loans to a single entity to 10% of a bank's combined stockholder equity. The loans were made to a developer in connection with the construction of an office building; the loans turned out to be poor loans. Joy first demanded that the directors of Citytrust bring the action, which they refused to do. *Burks v. Lasker*, 441 U.S. 471 (1979), was then decided, which held that federal courts must apply state law in determining the authority of a committee of independent directors to discontinue derivative suits. The board of Citytrust then authorized a Special Litigation Committee, composed of two independent directors assisted by counsel. This Committee issued a report recommending that suit against 23 defendants (20 of whom were outside directors) be discontinued since there was no reasonable possibility that they would be found liable. It also recommended that settlement be considered against the insider defendants, and that if this failed, consideration again be given to discontinuing the lawsuit (although there was a possibility that they were negligent in making the loans). Joy refused to withdraw the action against the outsiders; defendants filed a motion to dismiss, which the district court granted, at the same time putting the Committee's report under seal. The district court indicated that since no Connecticut case or statute existed (the corporations were domiciled in Connecticut and the district court was there), the state law would be the weight of authority elsewhere. It held that Connecticut law permits the use of such a committee and that the business judgment rule limits judicial scrutiny of its recommendations to the good faith, independence, and thoroughness of the Committee. Joy appealed from this ruling.

b. **Issue.** Did the district court apply the proper scope of judicial review to a board of director's Committee decision that a shareholder's derivative suit should be discontinued?

c. **Held.** No. District court decision is reversed.

1) The issue is what the Connecticut Supreme Court would do.

2) Officers and directors of a corporation are not held for negligence in decision making except in limited circumstances. This is called the "business judgment rule," which is based on the fact that shareholders can voluntarily choose their investments and that after-the-fact litiga-

tion is an imperfect basis on which to evaluate corporate business decisions.

3) Derivative suits are brought on behalf of the corporation by a shareholder; there are dangers in such suits, such as the fact that sometimes the benefits to the corporation and its shareholders are offset by the costs, delay, etc., involved in the suit.

4) Whether to bring a lawsuit is a business decision. Where the allegations are not against the directors that make the decision whether to sue, their decision will be upheld unless plaintiff can prove bad faith. When the suit is against some of the directors, no demand need be made on the directors to bring the suit, but the directors can form a special litigation committee of independent directors to evaluate the merits of such a suit.

5) Since such committees are appointed by the defendant directors to the lawsuit, it is not cynical to expect that such committees will tend to view derivative suits against the other directors with skepticism. Further, courts are competent to review the decisions of such committees.

6) Judicial review of committee recommendations should be based on the following guidelines, which apply only to cases involving allegations of acts resulting in direct financial harm to the corporation and a diminution of the value of the shareholders' investment.

7) The burden is on the committee to show that the action is more likely than not to be against the interests of the corporation. The court's review is to determine the balance of probabilities as to likely future benefit to the corporation. Where the court determines that the likely recoverable damages discounted by the probability of finding liability are less than the costs to the corporation in continuing the action, it should dismiss the case. The costs that may be properly taken into account are attorneys' fees, other out-of-pocket expenses related to the litigation, time spent by corporate personnel, and indemnification expenses. Where the court finds a likely net return but one that is not substantial in relation to shareholder equity, it may then consider the impact of distraction of key personnel and potential lost profits that may result from the publicity of a trial. Other indirect costs should not be taken into account.

8) The Committee report should not be sealed; it is part of the court record and the basis of the adjudication. Absent compelling reasons, it cannot be sealed.

9) As to this case, there is a good possibility of liability in general. As to the outside persons, it appears that liability is possible, and as to the insiders it seems more than just possible. Thus, if liability exists back to the beginning of the time the loans were made, recovery could be several millions of dollars, which far exceeds the cost of litigation. Since the probability of a substantial net return is high, the recommendations of the litigation committee should be rejected.

d. **Dissent.** Only two state courts have addressed this issue. New York courts have held that the substantive merits of an independent director committee's decision to terminate derivative litigation against defendant corporate directors are beyond judicial scrutiny, and that a court's role in such cases is limited to determining whether the committee acted independently, thoroughly, and in good faith. The other position, similar to the majority here, is the position of the Delaware courts.

The New York position is superior. The majority's position opens up many unanswered questions, such as whether the court will look at evidence that was not presented to the committee, etc. Also, the formula for calculating net benefits is cumbersome, indefinite, and unworkable. Finally, courts are not equipped to make business decisions as to whether a corporation should pursue a lawsuit. Finally, the majority's decision is not made out of a concern for greater corporate accountability, but from an anti-business bias. Pervasive government regulation of business has largely been a failure, and states continuing it are likely to see businesses move to other states. For these reasons, the Connecticut Supreme Court should adopt the New York position.

9. **Statutes of Limitation; Rule 10b-5--Lampf, Pleva, Lipkind, Prupis & Petigrow v. Gilbertson,** 115 L. Ed 2d 321 (U.S. 1991).

a. **Facts.** D, a law firm, helped prepare the offering documents and tax opinions for seven partnerships to buy and lease computer equipment, which were sold to plaintiffs as tax shelters in 1979-81. The partnerships failed; in late 1982 the IRS began investigating the tax deductions, which were subsequently disallowed. In late 1986 and 1987, plaintiffs issued in federal district court for Oregon under Rule 10b-5. The court held that the complaints were not timely under Oregon's two-year statute of limitations, which was adopted by the court (summary judgment). The circuit court reversed the summary judgment, but held that the same statute of limitations applied. The United States Supreme Court granted certiorari to review the case.

b. **Issue.** Does a uniform federal statute of limitations apply to Rule 10b-5 causes of action in federal courts?

c. **Held.** Yes.

1) Usually when Congress has failed to provide a statute of limitations for federal causes of action, a federal court "borrows" the local time limitation most analogous.

2) However, when a state limitation period would frustrate the policies of the federal law, federal courts look to a federal law for a suitable period.

3) First, the court determines whether a uniform statute of limitations should be adopted. Then, if there should be a uniform standard, the question is whether it should be a state or federal source. Where forum shopping would take place, arguably a federal source should apply. But to overcome the presumption of state adoption, it must be shown that a federal source affords a closer fit with the cause of action than state law.

4) Here Congress did not create a Rule 10b-5 cause of action; it was implied by the federal courts. So Congress did not consider the limitation period. However, if it had, it would probably have adopted the same or similar period to that which it adopted when it adopted related remedies in the 1934 Act and indicated a limitations period for these sections of the Act. The 1934 Act contains a number of express causes of action; most of these carry a one- and three-year statutes of limitations.

5) Congress has recently passed section 20A of the 1934 Act, adding remedial provisions against insider trading, and including a five-year statute of limitations. But Congress only meant to alter remedies available to these cases.

6) Thus, the Rule 10b-5 case must be brought within one year of discovery of the fraud, and in any case, within three years of when the fraud was committed.

d. **Concurrence.** Absent a congressionally created limitations period, state law should govern, or if inconsistent with federal law, then there should be no limitations period. Here there is an implied cause of action; the best approach is that adopted by the majority.

10. Actions for Rescission and Damages.

a. **Action for rescission.** A seller suing under Rule 10b-5 can recover her securities and a buyer can recover the amount she paid for the securities. There are limitations in rescission, however, such as waiver, laches, estoppel and impracticality (as in unwinding the merger of two publicly traded companies). Or the remedy may just be available (e.g., where the defendant-purchaser has sold the securities purchased from the plaintiff).

b. **Damages.** There are several basic formulas for awarding damages in private actions: First, plaintiff may be awarded restitution, i.e., the difference between the value of what she gave up and the value of what she received in the transaction. Alternatively, plaintiff may recover damages based on the defendant's profits. As a third option, plaintiff may recover the benefits of the bargain she made.

1) **Restitution.** Most courts grant the plaintiff damages based upon restitution (what she has lost), but the restitution formula is applied differently by different courts.

a) **Value measured after "reasonable time."** Some courts have placed a time limitation on measuring plaintiff's damages. Thus, plaintiff would recover the difference between the value of what she gave up—as of a reasonable period of time after the discovery of the fraud—and the value of what she received. [Mitchell v. Texas Gulf Sulphur Co., 446 F.2d 90 (10th Cir. 1971), *cert. denied*, 404 U.S. 1004 (1971)]

b) **Value measured at time of trial.** Some courts are more lenient, giving plaintiff damages based on the difference between the value of the securities at the time of the trial and the value of consideration paid by or to the plaintiff. [Yzel v. Fields, 386 F.2d 718 (8th Cir. 1967), *cert. denied*, 390 U.S. 951 (1968)]

2) Defendant's profits. More and more courts now appear to prefer a "disgorgement of profits" rule to mere restitution. Thus, a defrauded seller would sue for the profit the buyer had made on the transaction. [Ohio Drill & Tool Co. v. Johnson, 498 F.2d 186 (6th Cir. 1974)]

3) Benefit of the bargain--Osofsky v. Zipf, 645 F.2d 107 (2d Cir. 1981).

Osofsky
v. Zipf

    a) Facts. McDermott & Co. (D) and United Technologies competed in tender offers for Babcock & Wilcox, D offering to buy a percentage of B & W and then promising to merge B & W at about "the same price it paid for the shares in the tender offer." After a series of offers and counteroffers, D acquired 49% of B & W at $62.50 per share, after United dropped out of the bidding war. Then D proposed a merger with B & W, offering a package of preferred and convertible preferred shares for the remaining B & W common stock. A brokerage firm indicated to B & W shareholders that the D preferred stock being offered was valued at about $62.50 per share. The B & W shareholders approved the merger. Shareholders (Ps) sue on the basis of sections 14(e) and 14(a) of the 1934 Act for material misleading statements. The district court granted D's motion for summary judgment on the basis that Ps could not get damages based on the "benefit of the bargain" and that they had suffered no "out-of-pocket" damages. Ps appeal.

    b) Issue. What is the proper measure of damages pursuant to section 28(a) of the 1934 Act, which provides that damages shall not exceed "actual damages"?

    c) Held. The proper measure of Ps' damages should be based on the "benefit of the bargain." The district court judgment is reversed.

        (1) The language of section 28(a) was designed to prevent double recovery by those who assert both federal and state causes of action based on the same conduct. It is also meant to prohibit recovery of punitive damages.

        (2) The purpose of this section is to give plaintiffs recovery for their economic losses for violations of the 1934 Act, whether this be out-of-pocket losses or loss of their bargain.

        (3) Situations where the buyers were buying highly speculative stock and courts denied the "benefit of their bargain" as damages are distinguished. Those cases (e.g., where the plaintiff-buyer invested in a speculative gold mine) are ones where benefit of the bargain damages are very uncertain and speculative. That is not the case here.

        (4) Here we have a seller, in a merger situation, where the seller was promised $62.50 per share of its common stock, and the package of preferred stock it received was worth approximately $59.88. This is a material difference.

(5) Granting loss of the bargain damages upholds the policy of the 1934 Act, since in many tender offers the shareholders of the tendered company will receive a premium price, so that the only damages they suffer for misrepresentation or fraud is the loss of their expected bargain. Nor is it draconian to require tender offerors to pay what they promised the shareholders of the tendered company they would pay.

4) Unlimited liability. An unresolved issue is whether a defendant can be held liable for the total amount of damages suffered by all plaintiffs in a Rule 10b-5 case—despite the fact that this amount would far exceed the profit made by the defendant. There is authority that apparently would permit such unlimited damages.

a) **Example—affirmative misrepresentation.** In an affirmative misrepresentation case, the defendant was a corporate officer who had bought his company's stock on the basis of inside information. He was held liable to the plaintiffs who sued, with no apparent allowance for the fact that he also might later be sued by other plaintiffs who had also sold their stock on the exchange during the same period. If such additional plaintiffs did sue, defendant's liability could exceed his trading profits many times over. [*See* Mitchell v. Texas Gulf Sulphur Co., *supra*]

b) **Example—nondisclosure.** In a nondisclosure case, the Second Circuit did not limit the possible extent of defendant's liability; however, in remanding the case to the district court, it noted that the lower court should inquire into factors that could possibly circumscribe unlimited damages. [Shapiro v. Merrill Lynch, Pierce, Fenner & Smith, Inc., *supra*]

c) **Attempts to limit liability.** Courts have attempted to find a rationale for limiting a defendant's liability in a Rule 10b-5 action. For example, one court indicated that in order for 10b-5 liability to exist, there must be "trading causation" between plaintiff's losses and defendant's trading on the basis of the undisclosed inside information. [*See* Fridrich v. Bradford, 542 F.2d 307 (6th Cir. 1976), *cert. denied*, 429 U.S. 1053 (1977)]

Elkind v. Liggett & Myers, Inc.

d) **Liability for nondisclosure--Elkind v. Liggett & Myers, Inc.,** 635 F.2d 156 (2d Cir. 1980).

(1) **Facts.** Liggett & Myers (D) assisted financial analysts in their projections of company earnings by reviewing reports they prepared. They did not, however, release their own projections or attempt to correct these reports where they differed with company projections. In 1972, reports had been circulating that the company was going to have a good year, with earnings expected to increase by at least 10%. By midyear, the company's projections indicated that its earnings would not be this good. D's officer met with an analyst on July 10 and disclosed that sales of two product lines were slowing and that a midyear earnings statement was due in a week; on July 17 it was disclosed that it was a "good possibility" that earnings would be down over the previous year. The analyst immediately traded 1,800 shares based on this information. The next day the adverse earnings report was released. A class of shareholders (Ps) bought Liggett shares

without the benefit of the inside information. D appeals a judgment for Ps.

(2) Issue. Where there has been a nondisclosure of material facts generally but the company discloses such information to a financial analyst who trades on the information, is the company liable to purchasers who bought without such information?

(3) Held. Yes. Judgment affirmed.

(a) Where the company gets intimately involved with those analysts who are preparing financial reports on the company, it may be appropriate to attribute those reports to the company. But this degree of involvement did not occur here, so the company is not obligated to correct the earnings projections made by financial analysts by disclosing its own earnings projections.

(b) D did not make false statements simply by asserting that 1972 would be "a good year"; D did not disclose its earnings projections, and it did not impliedly agree with what financial analysts were saying.

(c) The company does not have to disclose material inside information, but it is a violation to disclose such information to a favored few. If this occurs, it is a Rule 10b-5 violation.

(d) Those who trade during a period of tippee trading but who do not have access to the same inside information may recover either against the individual tippee or the company that disclosed the inside information.

(e) There is a difficult situation where the company gives information to financial analysts. Companies are encouraged to do this, but they must not give inside information without disclosing it generally to the public.

(f) The information in the July 10 disclosure was not material (not reasonably certain to have a substantial effect on the market price of the stock; not likely to have affected the decision of a potential buyer or seller), since it was fairly well known in the marketplace already.

(g) The July 17 information was material. And there is scienter, since D knew it was material and that the outsider was reasonably likely to take advantage of the information.

(h) In face-to-face, affirmative misrepresentation cases, the out-of-pocket measure of damages is appropriate.

(i) But in the nondisclosure case of open-market purchases, the trader does not have an absolute right to know inside information. In this situation, there are several possibilities for a measure of damages:

1] Out-of-pocket measure (difference between price paid and value when bought). This is inappropriate in this type of case. In addition, there are problems with calculations of this measure; e.g., how is "value" of the stock during the period of nondisclosure to be determined? Also, unlimited damages under this provision are unfair to the corporation's shareholders (i.e., all open-market purchasers may bring a cause of action against the tipper and tippee no matter how little profit they made nor how great the damages).

2] Alternatively, recovery could be limited to the erosion of the market price of the security that is traceable to the tippee's wrongful trading. There are problems with this causation-in-fact measure. It is very difficult to prove such causation.

3] The best alternative is to allow recovery of post-purchase decline in market value up to a reasonable time after the purchaser learns of the tipped information or after there is a public disclosure of it, but limit the amount of recovery to the amount gained by the tippee as a result of selling at the earlier date rather than delaying sale until the parties could trade on an equal basis. Thus, if A (with inside information) sells 100 shares at $10/share, and B buys 100 shares at $11, then the inside information about poor earnings is released two days later and the stock drops to $5/share, A's liability is limited to $500 (note that B's actual damages are $600). The problem here is that it violates the normal rule that ordinarily gain to the wrong-doer is not a prerequisite to liability for violation of Rule 10b-5. Also, in some cases, the market could drop very substantially due to factors other than the nondisclosed information, and the tippee may be liable for very heavy damages beyond his gain. Also, where total losses of all plaintiffs exceed the defendants' total gain, a pro rata recovery will be given.

(j) Here the inside information was given out on July 17. The same information was publicly disclosed at 2:15 p.m. on July 18 and printed in the *Wall Street Journal* on the morning of July 19. The only purchasers who were damaged were those buying from the afternoon of July 17 to the morning of July 19. The stock closed at $55¼ on July 17, and $52½ on July 18. Purchasers had a reasonable time to decide what to do until the close of the market on July 19, when the stock went to $46⅞. Thus, the total maximum liability of D is $9.35 per share x 1,800 shares.

5) **Punitive damages.** There are no punitive damages available under Rule 10b-5.

6) **S.E.C. actions.** The S.E.C. may also bring a criminal action under Rule 10b-5, an action for an injunction, or an action to recover trading profits made by the defendants.

S.E.C. v. MacDonald

a) **S.E.C. action for disgorgement of profits--S.E.C. v. MacDonald,** 699 F.2d 47 (1st Cir. 1983).

(1) **Facts.** MacDonald (D) was on the board of directors of Realty Income Trust (RIT). While the real estate trust was doing poorly and negative information was in the news and the stock was down, RIT successfully acquired a major office building and succeeded in leasing

its empty space. Prior to this news being publicly released, D purchased 9,600 shares of RIT. On the announcement, the stock went up $1 per share in two days. A year later D sold his stock at a $6 per share profit. The S.E.C. sued D under Rule 10b-5 to have him disgorge his profits. The district court held that D must disgorge all of his profits, even though the usual measure of damages in a private right of action is the price for which the stock is purchased subtracted from the price to which it rises within a fairly reasonable period of time after the public announcement. Price rises after that time are thought to be due to other developments. D appeals.

(2) **Issue.** Did the district court apply the proper measure of damages in an S.E.C. enforcement action under Rule 10b-5 for purchasing stock based on inside information?

(3) **Held.** No. District court reversed.

(a) In private actions involving the purchase of securities that are publicly traded, plaintiffs usually are able to recover the price for which D purchased the stock subtracted from the price to which it rises within a reasonable time after the material facts are disclosed.

(b) After a reasonable time, plaintiffs can buy the stock and participate in any further rise in value. D should not be penalized for this subsequent rise. To hold otherwise would permit the plaintiffs to profit from further appreciation but to protect against subsequent depreciation.

(4) **Dissent.** The majority's opinion is correct for a damage action between two private parties. Here, however, the S.E.C. represents the whole defrauded market, and public equity should permit a court to safeguard the integrity of the securities markets by imposing in a proper case the civil sanction of full disgorgement of the actual profits of an illegal bargain. Even this measure is not a good deterrent since not all those who use inside information are caught, and if they are caught they only have to give up what they have gained; there is not much deterrent effect to the remedy. Thus, the lower court should have the discretion to order disgorgement of any amount up to D's full profits, depending on the circumstances of the case.

11. **Injunctive Actions.** A plaintiff who is injured by violation of the liability provisions of the 1934 Act may, as an alternative to an action for damages, also sue for an injunction. Injunctions are usually sought in contested tender offer and proxy fight cases.

   a. **Relevant distinctions.** The cases that deal with injunctions under the tender offer rules must be carefully distinguished in two respects. First, as to their factual circumstances—i.e., whether they relate to the preliminary filing requirement of section 13(d), section 14(d) disclosure requirement for tender offers or the section 14(e) antifraud provision (this is relevant since there are standing questions with respect to each section). And second, the cases differ significantly when a preliminary injunction as opposed to a permanent injunction is sought.

b. **Permanent injunctions.** Before the court will permanently enjoin the making of a tender offer, plaintiff must show that it will suffer irreparable injury as a result of defendant's violation of the tender offer rules.

Rondeau v.
Mosinee
Paper Corp.

1) **Irreparable injury standard--Rondeau v. Mosinee Paper Corp.,** 422 U.S. 49 (1975).

    a) **Facts.** Rondeau (D) began to buy common stock of Mosinee (P), acquiring over 5% without filing a section 13(d) report. P notified D that a report was required; D hired a lawyer and, on determining the need to file the report, did so, indicating that when he began buying stock it was because he thought the stock a good buy, but he now had an intention to take over control of the company by making a cash tender offer. P then sued for an injunction to (i) prohibit D from voting his stock, (ii) prohibit him from acquiring any additional shares, and (iii) require that he divest himself of his interest in P. D moved for summary judgment, which the district court granted. This was reversed by the circuit court (and an injunction was granted preventing D from voting the stock for five years). The district court had found that the violation had not been willful, that D had not formed the intent to take over P until the time he disclosed it, and that P had suffered no irreparable harm from the violation.

    b) **Issue.** Did the circuit court use the proper standard in granting an injunction in a section 13(d) case?

    c) **Held.** No. Circuit court reversed; judgment for D.

        (1) The purpose of the Williams Act is to give shareholders confronted with a cash tender offer adequate information regarding the offering party and its intentions.

        (2) Incumbent management is only to be given an adequate opportunity to respond and explain its position to the shareholders.

        (3) None of the evils aimed at occurred here. No tender offer was made and there is no indication that violations will occur in the future if a tender offer is made.

        (4) Shareholders who sold before the report was filed can bring damage actions.

        (5) The purpose for issuing an injunction is that irreparable harm is threatened, not that punishment is needed for those who violate the technical provisions of the tender rules.

    d) **Dissent.** The Williams Act is a prophylactic measure to make sure that *shareholders and management* are notified at the earliest possible time of a potential shift in management control. A violation of rules is enough to show an actionable harm; no other harm need be shown to grant an injunction.

e) **Comment.** If the standard for a permanent injunction is a probability of *irreparable* harm, then this would also have to be shown to get a preliminary injunction after this case.

c. **Preliminary injunctions.** A plaintiff seeking a preliminary injunction against the defendant-tender offeror must meet the burden of showing either (i) probable success if the case were to go to trial on the merits and the possibility of irreparable injury, or (ii) the existence of serious questions concerning material misrepresentations or omissions by the offeror and a balance of hardships in plaintiff's favor. [General Host Corp. v. Triumph American, Inc., 359 F. Supp. 749 (E.D. Wis. 1973)]

H. LIABILITY FOR SHORT-SWING PROFITS FROM INSIDER TRANSACTIONS

Section 16 of the 1934 Act is designed to prevent "insiders" from using inside information to make profits in the purchase and sale of the issuer's securities.

1. **Basic Provisions of Section 16.**

   a. **Registered securities.** Section 16 applies to companies having equity securities which are registered under section 12 of the 1934 Act.

   b. **Insider reports.** The 1934 Act requires that "insiders" report their beneficial interest in registered equity securities and any purchases or sales thereof. [*See* SEA §16(a)]

   c. **Profits on the purchases and sales.** Any profit made by an insider in the purchase and sale of an equity security within six months belongs to the corporation. [SEA §16(b)] Thus, if A (an officer of XYZ Corporation, which has its common stock registered under section 12 of the 1934 Act) buys 100 shares for $5 per share and then sells these shares for $10 per share within six months, he is liable to XYZ for the profit of $5 per share.

   d. **Rationale of section 16.** The rationale of section 16(b) is that "insiders" are assumed to possess material information about the issuer and such information may be used as a basis for purchasing or selling the issuer's equity securities at an advantage over persons from whom the securities are purchased or to whom they are sold.

      1) However, there are loopholes. For example, suppose A (an insider) has owned XYZ shares for over six months. He becomes aware of unfavorable conditions in XYZ (which are not disclosed to the public). He may sell his shares based on this inside information and not incur liability under section 16(b).

2. **Procedural Aspects of Section 16 Actions.**

a. **Federal courts.** Federal courts have exclusive jurisdiction over section 16 actions.

b. **Service.** There is nationwide service of process.

c. **Statute of limitations.** Section 16(b) indicates that there is a two-year statute of limitations from the date when the profit is realized by the insider. The statute is tolled if the insider has not filed the required section 16(a) reports (until such time as the profits are discovered or with reasonable diligence should have been discovered).

d. **Corporation or derivative suit.** The corporation may sue for the profit made by its insider, or if the corporation declines to proceed, *any* security holder of the corporation may bring a derivative action on behalf of the corporation. The S.E.C. has no authority to seek injunctive or other relief for the violation of section 16(b).

e. **Attorney's fees.** Attorney's fees are recoverable as part of the plaintiff's judgment.

   1) They often provide the main motivation for bringing a 16(b) action (i.e., lawyers look for section 16 situations and then find a shareholder on whose behalf they can sue).

   2) These types of lawsuits are made even easier by the fact that under section 16(b) an action may be brought by *any* security holder (i.e., the plaintiff need not be the owner of equity securities, nor must he have owned the securities at the time the wrong occurred; thus, plaintiff can purchase securities subsequent to the date of the wrong and still bring an action).

3. **Strict Liability.**

a. **The general rule.** The general rule is that there are no defenses to a section 16(b) action if the elements of a cause of action are present (i.e., an "insider," a registered equity security, a matching purchase and sale within the required time period). Thus, historically it has made no difference that the insider cannot be shown to have had access to any inside information, or cannot be shown to have used inside information in effectuating the matching purchase and sale within six months at a profit, etc.

b. **Exceptions to the general rule.** However, to an increasing extent, courts are looking into the substance of transactions alleged to have violated section 16(b) to determine whether in fact there was a violation of the underlying rationale of the section (the abuse of inside information), and, where such an abuse is not shown, they are refusing to impose liability in certain cases (even though there is a matching purchase and sale by an insider within six months) (*see* discussion *infra*).

4. **Insiders Defined.** "Insiders" under section 16 are officers and directors of a company that has a class of equity securities registered under section 12 of the Act, and all persons owning (beneficially) more than 10% of any class of the company's equity securities registered under section 12 of the 1934 Act.

a. Deputization.

1) **Liability limited to specifically named defendants.** Section 16 specifically names the parties who are potentially liable under its provisions, and the courts have generally refused to expand the class of potential defendants (such as to persons possessing the same inside information as officers and directors).

2) **The deputization issue.** Situations arise, however, where an "insider" (such as a director of A) has other affiliations (such as being an officer of another corporation, B). While the insider himself (for himself) might not engage in any prohibited purchases or sales, the entity (B) with which he is affiliated may. In these situations the plaintiff has sought to hold the affiliated entity (B) liable for its profits on the basis that it "deputized" the individual insider to act on its behalf (thus making the second entity also an "insider"). Whether deputization has occurred is a question of fact.

   a) **Establishing deputization--Feder v. Martin Marietta Corp.,** 406 F.2d 260 (2d Cir. 1969).

   Feder v. Martin Marietta Corp.

   (1) **Facts.** A shareholder of Sperry Rand (P) sued Martin Marietta (D) under 16(b) for profits made by D in the purchase and sale of Sperry stock bought while the president of D was a director of Sperry and sold after his resignation. Bunker was D's president. D began buying a substantial number of shares in Sperry; Sperry asked Bunker to join the board, but he refused. Once D's investment reached $10 million, D's board approved Bunker's appointment to the Sperry board. D's stock purchases continued (101,300 shares being purchased while Bunker was on the board). Then Bunker resigned and a couple of weeks later D sold all of its Sperry stock (the 101,300 shares being sold within six months of their purchase). The trial court found that Bunker was not appointed as D's agent or deputy on the Sperry board, and so dismissed the suit. P appeals.

   (2) **Issue.** Was Bunker, a director of Sperry, deputized by D to act as its representative on the Sperry board, thus making D a "director" of Sperry?

   (3) **Held.** Yes. Dismissal reversed. Judgment for P. Case remanded to consider the damages issue.

      (a) The trial court based its decision on the fact that Sperry took the initiative in asking Bunker to join the board and that it was Bunker's reputation as an engineer that was the basis of the invitation.

      (b) But the trial court's finding was clearly erroneous. It failed to consider the reasonable inferences to be made from other facts.

         1] Bunker was responsible for the investment activity of D.

2] The position on Sperry's board allowed Bunker access to insider information on Sperry that could be used in investing in Sperry stock by D.

3] Bunker received reports on Sperry's future outlook and discussed Sperry with its officers.

4] Inside reports of D indicate that it used the information from Sperry in making investment decisions on Sperry stock.

5] All of this might not be enough to hold that Bunker was D's deputy. But Bunker's letter of resignation to Sperry indicates that he was invited to be a board member because of D's stock ownership in Sperry, that D's board allowed Bunker to take the position only after D owned $10 million in Sperry stock, and that D followed a pattern of putting its people on the boards of other companies that it invested in.

(c) It has previously been held that 16(b) imposes a liability for profit made from short-swing purchases and sales where a person was a director at the time of sale even though he was not a director at the time of purchase. Here Bunker was a director at the time of purchase but not at the time of sale. D is still liable for short-swing profits.

1] S.E.C. Rule X-16A-10 indicates that if a transaction has been exempted from 16(a), it will not be subject to 16(b). But courts may review S.E.C. rules. Since a purchase and sale within six months (where a director resigns before the sale) may be motivated by inside information, if Rule X-16A-10 exempts such a transaction from 16(b), the Rule is invalid.

2] 16(b) itself may impose liability only on those subject to 16(a), but since the S.E.C. itself in the form it uses for 16(a) reporting (Form 4) requires ex-directors to report sales or purchases in the month that their directorates terminate, it seems that 16(b) is meant to cover situations where sales are made after a director resigns. It is simply a logical extension of what the S.E.C. has already done to cover the situation where a former director sells stock that was purchased by him while a director.

(4) Dissent. An exception to the strict liability of 16(b) was given for conversion situations. The majority has turned that exception into a total destruction of the intent and meaning of 16(b), thus destroying the prophylactic effect of 16(b).

b. **Officers.** An officer is defined as "a president, vice president, treasurer, secretary, comptroller, *and any other person who performs* for an issuer functions corresponding to those performed by the foregoing officers (even though not having such a title)." [*See* SEA Rule 36-2] So title alone is not determinative of liability; functions performed count.

c.   **The ten percent holder.** Every person who directly or indirectly is the "beneficial owner" of more than 10% of any class of registered equity security is subject to the provisions of section 16.

1)   **Beneficial ownership.** In calculating 10% ownership, it is "beneficial ownership" that counts.

   a)   **Family ownership.** The S.E.C. has indicated that a person is regarded as being the beneficial owner of securities held in the names of his or her spouse and minor children, since ordinarily such a person has the benefits equivalent to ownership. [*See* SEA Release No. 7793 (1966)]

2)   **Purchases and sales of all equity securities included.** To be an "insider" by virtue of stock ownership, a person must beneficially own more than 10% of some class of registered equity security. But once qualified as an "insider" (by owning 10% of any *registered* equity security, or because of being an officer or director of a company with a class of registered equity security), the insider is liable for purchases and sales of *any* equity security of the issuer, whether or not it also is registered.

3)   **Convertible equity securities.**

   a)   **Introduction.** A convertible debenture is an equity security. Thus, the 10% holder of such a registered security would be an "insider" and subject to the reporting requirements of section 16(a).

   b)   **Calculating the ten percent for liability purposes.** However, in *Chemical Fund, Inc. v. Xerox Corp.*, 377 F.2d 107 (2d Cir. 1967), the court held that for the purposes of determining whether the holder of convertible securities is a 10% holder for section 16(b) purposes, the holder of convertible securities is deemed the owner of the underlying securities *only*, and all of such underlying securities owned by the holder will be deemed to be outstanding in making the 10% calculation. The rationale of the decision was that the Act was aimed at those insiders who exercise control of the corporation (which is done through voting), so that ownership of nonvoting securities is not relevant.

4)   **Timing of ownership.** While *officers* and *directors* need not hold *both* positions at the time of purchase *and* sale, the language of the statute indicates that the liability of 10% holders applies only where such ownership exists both at the time of purchase *and* at the time of sale. Note that transactions occurring within six months *prior* to the date that an officer or director became such are not counted in creating purchases and sales. But transactions after termination may be matched with purchases or sales while the person was an officer or director.

   a)   **Purchase by stages.** Section 16(b) does not cover any transaction where a more-than-10% beneficial owner was not such both at the time of the purchase and sale, or the sale and purchase, of the security involved. In *Foremost-McKesson, Inc. v. Provident Securities Co.*, 423 U.S. 232 (1976), the Supreme Court held that in the case of a purchase-sale sequence, a beneficial owner is not liable unless he was a more-than-10% owner *before* he made the purchase in question. To put this differently, the purchase that first lifts a beneficial owner above 10% cannot be matched with a subsequent sale under section 16(b).

(1) **Example.** D purchases 6% of the outstanding shares of C Corp. on January 2, an additional 6% on February 1, and another 6% on March 1. D sells all of these shares at a substantial profit on April 1. The profit on the January 2 and February 1 purchases is not subject to section 16(b), because D was not a more-than-10% beneficial owner at the time he made either purchase. The profits on the March 1 purchase are subject to section 16(b), because D held a 12% interest at that time.

(2) **Sale followed by purchase.** The *Foremost* case involved a purchase followed by a sale. However, a sale by a more-than-10% beneficial owner reducing his interest to less than 10%, followed by a purchase within six months, presents greater potential for abuse. In such a case, the defendant would presumptively have had access to inside information prior to the first leg of the swing, and such information might well carry over to the second leg. Thus, the opinion in *Foremost* left open the question whether a sale-purchase sequence by a person who was a more-than-10% beneficial owner at the time of the sale might result in liability under section 16(b).

b) **Application.** Where A owns 12%, then sells 3% within six months, and then immediately sells the remaining 9%, he can only be held for profits on the sale of the first 3% (since at this point he owned 10%; thereafter, at the sale of the 9%, he did not own 10%). [*See* Reliance Electric Co. v. Emerson Electric Co., 404 U.S. 935 (1972)]

5. **Transactions Covered by the Rule.** The following elements must be shown to sustain a section 16(b) cause of action:

a. **Transactions in equity securities.** The transactions must involve an "equity" security.

1) **Rights to acquisition.** Conversion privileges, warrants, and other acquisition rights to equity securities are sufficiently connected with an underlying equity security to be included in the definition of a security. [*See* SEA §3(a)(10)]

b. **The purchase and sale requirement.** There must be a matching purchase and sale, or sale and purchase. Either the defendant may purchase at a low price and then sell at a higher price or sell and then buy back at a lower price.

1) **Security conversions.** There are many types of conversion transactions (such as conversion of preferred stock into common, debentures into common, etc.). The authority as to whether a "purchase" and/or a "sale" is involved in these conversions is mixed.

   a) **Simplistic approach.** Earlier judicial decisions seemed to take a simplistic approach to the question.

      (1) For example, in *Park & Tilford, Inc. v. Shulte*, 160 F.2d 984 (2d Cir. 1947), *cert. denied*, 332 U.S. 761 (1947), a call (option to buy) was issued by the company (which was controlled by defendant insiders) for conversion of preferred stock into common; defendants converted. The court held that the conversion was a "purchase" of the common.

      (2) However, other cases have taken exactly opposite positions, such as *Ferraiolo v. Newman*, 259 F.2d 342 (6th Cir. 1958), *cert. denied*, 359 U.S. 927 (1959), which held that a conversion of preferred into common was not a purchase of the common.

      (3) Finally, the S.E.C. adopted Rule 16b-9, which indicates that a conversion of one security into another (under certain conditions), according to the provisions of a corporate charter or other governing instrument, is neither a purchase nor sale.

   b) **The policy approach.** In addition, courts have begun to look at the rationale of 16(b) in determining whether a conversion involves a "purchase" or "sale." For example, in *Blau v. Lamb*, 363 F.2d 507 (2d Cir. 1967), the court indicated that the test in conversion situations was whether the transaction is one which could possibly support the speculative, short-term profit-taking by insiders that section 16(b) was designed to prevent. The rationale is that while section 16(b) precludes an inquiry into whether defendants in fact have relied on inside information, it does not follow that this section should apply to transactions that could not possibly result in the wrong that section 16(b) is aimed at preventing.

2) **Recapitalizations.** It appears that most recapitalizations (i.e., where XYZ corporation exchanges one security for another outstanding security) do **not** involve any purchase or sale of new stock, since (i) all similarly situated shareholders are similarly treated, (ii) shareholder approval of the transaction is normally required, and (iii) each shareholder simply continues his investment in the corporation in a different form. [*See* Roberts v. Eaton, 212 F.2d 82 (2d Cir. 1954), *cert. denied*, 348 U.S. 827 (1954)]

3) **Reorganizations.** Generally when a corporation is merged or sold in exchange for stock there is a "sale" of securities surrendered and a "purchase" of the securities received.

   a) **Tender offers and defensive mergers.** The tender offer involves the direct purchase of the shares of the target company (A) by the tendering company (B). Typically, the tendering company (B) may begin by purchasing a minority interest in the target company (A) and then may attempt to negotiate a merger with another company (C). In this case, the tendering company (B) may own A's shares and find itself in a difficult situation with respect to section 16(b).

(1)   If B should fail in its tender offer and sell A's shares, there may be a violation of section 16(b) if its purchase and sale of A's shares have occurred within less than six months.

(2)   Or if C gains control and merges A into C, then if B exchanges its A shares for C shares, B may still have violated section 16(b).

(3)   Note that there is no problem for B unless it first acquires 10% or more of a class of registered equity security (so that B becomes an "insider").

Kern County Land Co. v. Occidental Petroleum Corp.

b)   **Ten percent shareholder not "insider"--Kern County Land Co. v. Occidental Petroleum Corp.**, 411 U.S. 582 (1973).

(1)   **Facts.** Occidental (D) made a tender offer on May 8 for Kern stock (which resulted in the purchase of 500,000 shares, or more than 10%); the offer was renewed on May 11 and terminated by acceptance of an additional 387,549 shares on June 8. Kern sought a defensive merger with Tenneco (P), and D (seeing that it was going to lose the battle), within six months of the date it had first acquired the 10% interest, entered into an option with P giving P the right to purchase D's Kern stock for $105 per share. The option was exercisable by P six months and one day after the date on which D's tender offer for Kern stock was to expire (i.e., on December 11). The option price paid to D was $10 per share, to be part of the purchase price if P exercised its option. Then the Tenneco-Kern merger plan was approved on July 17 and closed on August 30. At this time D got the right to exchange its Kern stock for P preferred stock. On December 11, P exercised its option to buy D's Tenneco preferred stock. D made more than $19 million on the transaction. P sued D for this profit under section 16(b), alleging that the execution of the option and/or the merger were "sales" by D, occurring within six months of the purchase date.

(2)   **Issue.** Has there been a matching "purchase" and "sale" for section 16(b) purposes?

(3)   **Held.** No. Judgment for D.

(a)   D purchased 10% of Kern stock by May 11. And there was a sale—the merger—by August 30. But D, in this factual context, did not have the position of an insider, either when it first made its tender offer, or after it bought 10%, or at the time of the sale. It could not have had access to any inside information. It was in a battle with Kern for control.

1]   It makes no difference that D had the intention to make a tender offer and then reap a profit when a defensive merger was made. There was still no abuse of inside information. If this type of transaction is to be controlled, it must be under some other section of the securities laws.

2] D did not vote for the merger. It was an involuntary party to the merger. It had tried to get injunctive actions to prevent the closing of the merger within the six-month period, but failed. Had D voluntarily sold the Kern stock within the six-month period, then there would be a 16(b) "sale."

(b) Also, the granting of an option to purchase stock is not normally regarded as a "sale" by the grantor of the option. Here there is not a sufficient possibility of the abuse of inside information to call the option a "sale."

1] It was done for the mutual advantage of D (to get out of a minority position) *and* P (to get rid of a large minority shareholder).

2] The transaction was between P and D (not with Kern).

3] D gave P an option to buy, which it would only exercise if its stock price remained steady. If the stock dropped more than $10 per share (the option price), P would not exercise the option, and D would be left to take its loss. It is hard to see how D could speculate on inside information under this arrangement.

4] The exercise date was over six months in the future (the period beyond which 16(b) was not to operate).

5] The option itself did not amount to a sale since the option price was fair and it was not inevitable that the option would be exercised. Further, D did not give up all of its rights attached to the stock as of the option date.

(4) Dissent. An exception to the strict liability of 16(b) was given for conversion situations. The majority has turned that exception into a total destruction of the intent and meaning of 16(b), thus destroying its prophylactic effect.

c) **Comment.** Note that *Kern County Land, Blau v. Lamb*, and other cases that look at the policy of section 16 are opening up a defense to potential defendants that previously appeared to be closed under the strict liability theory (*see supra*). At least in the context of corporate combinations, the courts seem to be following a "subjective" approach, which is leading to a case-by-case determination as to whether there should be liability. The test is whether, in the factual context of the case, there has been a violation of the policy of section 16(b), which is directed against the speculative use of inside information.

4) **Derivative securities.** The S.E.C. has now made it clear that transactions in derivative securities (options on XYZ common stock, calls on XYZ common stock, etc.) are matchable against transactions in the underlying equity security *and* against equivalent derivative securities. [*See* S.E.A. Release No. 28869 (1991)] Thus, section 16(b) would apply to all of the following:

a) A, an insider, buys 1,000 shares of IBM common stock on 1/1/93 for $100/share, and sells the stock on 3/30/93 for $110 per share.

b) A buys 10 IBM call options covering 1,000 shares on 1/1/93 for $9,875, exercisable at $100 on or before 6/30/93. On 3/30/93, A sells the call options for $13,625.

c) A buys 1,000 shares on 1/1/93 for $100,000 ($100/share). On 3/30/93, A buys 10 put option contracts (covering 1,000 shares) expiring 6/30/93 with a total exercise price of $115,000, for $7,500. This guarantees A a profit: exercise the put option and sell the 1,000 shares for $115,000 ($115,000 less $100,000, less $7,500 = $7,500).

c. **The time requirement.** The matching purchase and sale must occur within a period of *less than* six months.

    1) **Introduction.** Section 16(b) may be applied to any matched "purchase" and "sale" or "sale" and "purchase" from which a profit is realized, if the matched transactions occur within a period of *less than* six months.

        a) Thus, to determine whether 16(b) applies, you must look backward and forward for six months from *any* transaction that is either a purchase or sale.

        b) Suppose, for example, that A buys 100 shares of stock for $10 per share; in a month he sells the stock for $9 per share; then in a month buys for $8; and in another month sells for $7. In three months he has lost $300, but he is still liable under section 16(b) since the $9 sale can be matched with the $8 purchase.

    2) **The general rules as to "purchases" or "sales."** For years, the general rule was that for the purposes of section 16(b), a "purchase" occurred when the purchaser incurred an irrevocable liability to take and pay for the stock, and a "sale" occurred when the seller incurred an irrevocable liability to deliver and accept payment for the stock.

    3) **Applications of the general rule.** The general rule stated above was more difficult in application than it appeared to be on the surface.

        a) **Shares to be determined on contingent events.** For example, in some instances, shares are to be delivered as part of a purchase price based on future contingent events.

            (1) For example, Company A may buy Company B and promise to pay additional shares of stock to B in the event that the market price of A's stock declines over a certain period of time. If the stock price of A goes down, then A must pay more of its shares to B. When are these contingent shares of A "purchased"?

            (2) In *Booth v. Varian Associates*, 334 F.2d 1 (1st Cir. 1965), *cert. denied*, 379 U.S. 961 (1965), the court held that the contingent shares were purchased on the date of their delivery (not the contract date, although the parties were committed as of this date).

(3) Thus, it appears that courts will look first to the intention of the parties as expressed in their agreement; if no intention is expressed, then the transaction will be presumed effective on its actual consummation.

b) **Option agreements.** An option to purchase is ***not*** an irrevocable liability. Therefore, most courts held that receiving such an option was not a "purchase." [*See* B.T. Babbitt, Inc. v. Lachner, 332 F.2d 255 (2d Cir. 1964)] Note, however, that this may not be good reasoning, since having an option gives the purchaser a fixed purchase price and puts an insider in a good position to profit by inside information.

c) **New rule.** Consequently, the S.E.C. has now indicated that the acquisition of an option is the purchase of the underlying equity security, rather than the date of the exercise of the option. [S.E.A. Release No. 28869 (1991)]

6. Damages Under Section 16(b).

a. **The general rule.** The amount of damages is the "profit realized" in the matching transactions, which is the difference between the purchase price and the sale price. [Smolowe v. Delendo Corp., 136 F.2d 231 (2d Cir. 1943), *cert. denied*, 320 U.S. 751 (1943)]

1) **Maximum profit.** Whatever matching of purchases and sales that will produce the maximum profit is the one used (disregarding the matching of certificates, etc.). Therefore, if 100 shares are purchased at $1 per share and 100 at $2, and six months later 100 shares are sold at $10 per share, the recoverable profit is $9 per share.

2) **Loss transactions.** Any transactions producing losses are ignored.

b. **Interest.** Interest on the profit is given in the discretion of the court, based on considerations of "fairness."

c. **Dividends.** Whether dividends paid on securities held during the six-month period are part of the "profit" realized depends on the circumstances.

1) **Not included.** Dividends are not included in the following situations:

a) Where they are declared on stock prior to purchase by the insider.

b) Where they are declared prior to the person's becoming an insider.

c) Where they are declared on specific certificates which were not sold at a profit. There is contra authority on this point, however. [*See* Western Auto Supply Co. v. Gamble-Skogmo, Inc., 348 F.2d 736 (8th Cir. 1965), *cert. denied*, 382 U.S. 987 (1966)—holding that dividends paid on an equivalent number of shares to the number sold were part of the profit]

2) Included. Courts are unanimous that dividends declared while the owner is an insider on the actual shares sold are part of the "profit."

d. Control premium. Some courts have allowed a special item of damages in certain transactions where the purchase and sale involved the acquisition of control of a company.

1) For example, in *Newmark v. RKO General, Inc.*, 425 F.2d 348 (2d Cir. 1970), RKO acquired a controlling interest in Central Airlines for cash and the exchanged shares of Central Airlines for shares in Frontier (which RKO controlled) in a merger.

2) To the "profit" realized by RKO (the difference between its cash cost of the Central shares and the market value of the Frontier shares it received in the merger), the court added 15% as a "control premium," on the theory that these shares were more valuable to the defendant than to an ordinary investor, since these shares allowed the defendant to control Frontier.

V.   S.E.C. ENFORCEMENT ACTIONS

A.   S.E.C. INVESTIGATIONS

1.   **Introduction.** Section 21(a) of the 1934 Act provides the S.E.C. with the power to conduct investigations regarding violations of the statute and the rules and regulations thereunder.

2.   **Stages of the Investigation.** Investigations go through two stages:

   a.   **Informal inquiry.** Initially the S.E.C. begins an informal inquiry into a possible violation. Witnesses are interviewed but no one is required to talk with the S.E.C. if he does not wish to.

   b.   **Formal investigation.** The second stage is a formal investigation. The staff of the S.E.C. asks the Commission for an order based on a showing of likelihood of a violation of the securities laws. A formal order then permits the staff to issue subpoenas duces tecum and to examine witnesses under oath. There is no punishment for failure to respond; the S.E.C.'s only recourse is to initiate a proceeding in court to enforce compliance.

3.   **Confidentiality.** The S.E.C. warns witnesses to keep their testimony confidential; however, there is no statutory basis for this S.E.C. position.

4.   **Right to Counsel.** A person who is subpoenaed to testify in a formal investigation has the right to be represented by counsel during his own testimony. He has no right, however, to have counsel present during the taking of testimony from other witnesses. [S.E.C. v. Meek, Fed. Sec. L. Rep. (CCH) 97,323 (10th Cir. 1980)]

5.   **Submissions of Intended S.E.C. Targets.** The S.E.C. has an informal practice of permitting persons who have been targeted as potential defendants in an injunction action the opportunity to make a formal, written presentation to the S.E.C. itself. No formal rule permits this as of right.

6.   **Parallel Proceedings.** S.E.C. investigations are "parallel proceedings" from the time they are initiated, since the end result may be either a recommendation to file an injunctive action or a reference to the Justice Department with a recommendation that it initiate a criminal prosecution by bringing the matter before a federal grand jury.

   a.   *Miranda* **warnings.** Thus the S.E.C. staff always gives a form of "*Miranda* warning" to the witnesses it summons to testify, advising them that the investigation may lead to a criminal prosecution.

   b.   **Right to refuse to testify.** Thus, witnesses have the right to refuse to testify on the basis that their answers may tend to incriminate them.

   c.   **Parallel investigations.** It may also happen that the S.E.C. is conducting an investigation at the same time that the Justice Department is conducting a grand jury investigation into the same matter, either as a result of referral by the S.E.C. or otherwise.

7. **Section 21(a) Reports.** This section of the 1934 Act allows the S.E.C., in its discretion, to publish information concerning violations of the securities laws. Section 15(c)(4) also provides that the S.E.C. may publish its findings relating to violations of sections 12, 13, and 15(d). The S.E.C. has followed a policy of referring to these sections as a basis for issuing reports which document probable violations of the securities laws, without any formal administrative proceedings. Many of these reports concern persons (such as directors of corporations) over which the S.E.C. has no formal administrative authority to impose disciplinary actions (as the S.E.C. does over broker-dealers, etc.). In addition, the S.E.C. has negotiated with such persons the terms of written statements which amount to confessions of wrongdoing and which also frequently contain "undertakings" as to certain remedial action that the wrongdoer agrees to implement in return for the S.E.C. not instituting a formal investigation or an injunctive action. These actions by the S.E.C. have been criticized as the creation of an unauthorized form of administrative remedy having no statutory basis. [*See In re* Spartek, Inc., SEA Release No. 15567 (1979)]

B.   S.E.C. INJUNCTIVE ACTIONS

1. **Introduction.** After a formal investigation of possible wrongdoing, the S.E.C. may recommend an enforcement action. The most frequent action of the S.E.C. to enforce securities law violations, other than administrative actions to discipline persons registered with it, is for an injunction in federal district court, enjoining those who have allegedly violated or are about to violate the securities laws. [*See* SEA §21(d); *see also* SEA §27 (giving federal district courts jurisdiction) and SA §20(a)]

2. **Consents.** Usually defendants do not litigate; they agree to a "consent injunction," which is entered in court when the complaint is filed.

3. **Consequences.** An injunction can be a severe punishment. Many provisions of the securities laws disqualify persons from engaging in many aspects of the securities business if they have had an injunction entered against them. Also, as a result of the injunction, private civil actions may be filed against the defendants.

4. **Culpability Standard.** *See* the discussion of the *Aaron* case, *supra*.

5. **Bases for Injunctions.** An injunction is supposed to be granted in order to prevent future wrongs, not to punish for past ones. But the S.E.C. has often used the injunction for this latter purpose.

S.E.C. v.
Unifund, SAL

a. **Basis for a preliminary injunction--S.E.C. v. Unifund, SAL,** 910 F.2d 1028 (2d Cir. 1990).

1) **Facts.** In 1989 Rorer began confidential negotiations to merge with Rhone, a French corporation. In mid-January 1990, massive trading occurred in Rorer stock, just before the merger was announced. The S.E.C. investigated, and brought this action for a preliminary injunction against Unifund (based in

Lebanon) and Tamanaco (based in Panama). Both purchased large amounts of stocks and options, and sold on the merger announcement, for large profits. The federal district court issued the TRO, which forbade future violations of Rule 10b-5, required that both defendants retain any unsold securities in their accounts as well as the proceeds from securities already sold, and required that their trading accounts be frozen to preserve the assets there for payment of possible remedies. The district court indicated that the standard was "a strong prima facie case of violation of section 10b and a reasonable likelihood that the wrong will be repeated." The court relied on unusually heavy trading of Rorer stock and circumstantial evidence proving that the trades were based on inside information (there were connections with a Florida brokerage firm, and a broker there indicated he had received a tip that something was going on with Rorer stock). The district court found a likelihood of future violations due to the fact that Ds regularly traded in securities. Ds appeal.

2) **Issue.** What is the appropriate standard of proof the S.E.C. must meet for a federal court to issue a preliminary injunction?

3) **Held.**

a) By section 21(d) of the 1934 Act, the S.E.C. may seek injunctions from the federal courts. The S.E.C. does not have to show the risk of irreparable injury, or the unavailability of remedies at law.

b) Generally a preliminary injunction seeks to preserve the status quo while the S.E.C. investigates. In this circumstance, the S.E.C. must prove that there is a likelihood of success on the merits (i.e., it must show a prima facie case). However, if the relief sought by the S.E.C. goes beyond preserving the status quo, then tougher measures of proof should be required (possibly a "strong" prima facie case, etc.).

c) First, the S.E.C. seeks a prohibition against future securities law violations. This goes beyond preserving the status quo; it has grave possible consequences (subjecting Ds to contempt if they trade in violation of the law). Thus, the S.E.C. must show a substantial likelihood of success as to the existence of a current violation and the risk of repetition. The S.E.C. cannot show this here; it has not proven the identity of a tipper, nor that Ds knew that there was fiduciary duty not to trade on the information they had. All that has been shown is unusual trading activity and some circumstantial connection with possible abuse of inside information.

d) The S.E.C. also seeks to freeze the assets in Ds' accounts, in order to back up a possible disgorgement order if it wins on the merits. This ancillary relief is proper. Thus, it is proper to freeze amounts up to and including the three times insider profits allowed by section 21A of the 1934 Act. It is not proper to keep the Ds from trading in their accounts, but if the assets fall below a certain level, the S.E.C. may require that the accounts be replenished. Finally, the S.E.C.'s meager showing is not sufficient to freeze the accounts forever; 30 days is enough, unless the S.E.C. within that time indicates a date on which it is ready for trial.

b. **Action for a permanent injunction--S.E.C. v. Caterinicchia,** 613 F.2d 102 (5th Cir. 1980).

1) **Facts.** Trustee Loan made small consumer loans; it got its cash by the sale and renewal of eight-month subordinated commercial notes, which it offered through newspaper ads that touted a high rate of interest and safety. Trustee had an exemption for the sale of the notes from Alabama state law, and used the intrastate exemption for the sale of the notes under federal securities law. No financial information on Trustee was disclosed in the brochure given to investors. In fact, Trustee had lost money five out of the past six years, and at one point was insolvent. Caterinicchia took over as president by buying a majority interest in the stock of Trustee; he continued the program of selling the notes. The state securities commissioner issued a ruling that sale of the notes was no longer exempt and required that the renewal of notes not be automatic and that financial information be disclosed to investors. Trustee continued to renew the notes automatically unless investors requested redemption. The S.E.C. also questioned whether the intrastate exemption was available, since some of the noteholders had moved out of state after buying the notes. Trustee began to redeem these notes. The S.E.C. suggested that there were nondisclosure of material facts about the financial condition which violated the antifraud provisions of the federal securities laws and suggested that the company's financial condition be disclosed to all noteholders. Caterinicchia delayed, hoping to turn the company into a profitable operation before such revelations were made. Finally, Trustee filed a petition in bankruptcy under Chapter XI of the Bankruptcy Act. The S.E.C. brought this action for a permanent injunction based on violations of section 17(a) of the 1933 Act and Rule 10b-5 of the 1934 Act. The district court found violations, but refused to grant the permanent injunction on the basis that there was no likelihood of continuing violations. The S.E.C. appeals.

2) **Issue.** Should a permanent injunction issue under the facts of this case?

3) **Held.** No. There is sufficient evidence to support the district court's determination.

   a) Ds are not currently violating the law. In this circumstance, there must be a reasonable likelihood that there will be further violations for an injunction to issue.

   b) The S.E.C. must show something beyond past acts to prove this.

   c) The district court had the discretion to issue an injunction or not; its decision will not be disturbed except for clear abuse.

   d) An injunction sought by the S.E.C. is not "extraordinary" relief. It will be granted whenever there is about to be a violation of the securities laws.

   e) There is sufficient evidence to support the district court's finding. The basis that the S.E.C. claims the district court used was not the basis of the district court's decision:

(1) The basis was not that the bankruptcy court would supervise Ds. The district court was aware that this supervision would last only one year.

(2) The court was also aware that Ds continued to renew notes after the state and the S.E.C. ordered them to discontinue doing so.

(3) Nor was the basis of the decision that the manner used by Ds to raise money was public advertising which could easily be detected by the S.E.C.

f) The basis of the decision is that the S.E.C. did not prove that Ds were likely to violate the securities laws in the future. It concluded that the past violations resulted from a misguided attempt to protect the investors by saving the company from bankruptcy and liquidation.

6. **Ancillary Relief.** The S.E.C., when it settles with a defendant, often asks for and gets a variety of ancillary remedies designed both to remedy the consequences of past wrongs and to prevent future ones:

a. **Appointment of a receiver.** Where the defendant is a corporation and its affairs are in bad condition, a receiver may be appointed.

b. **Disgorging of profits.** The defendant may be required to disgorge profits made in connection with securities law violations (such as the use of inside information).

c. **Appointment of special counsel.** The defendant may be required to appoint "special counsel" to investigate and report on all past securities law violations.

d. **Appointment of independent directors.** The defendant may be required to appoint independent persons to the board of directors who have been approved by the S.E.C.

7. **Collateral Estoppel.** If the S.E.C. injunction action is litigated, then all of the factual issues that are litigated and decided by the court may not be litigated again in a separate action against the defendant. Thus, to avoid this possibility in subsequent civil actions by private parties based on the S.E.C.'s injunction action, defendants are highly motivated to settle actions with the S.E.C. without going to trial. Of course, in settlements where defendants admit facts and these admissions become part of a consent injunction, the collateral estoppel effect is still present.

C. S.E.C. ADMINISTRATIVE PROCEEDINGS

1. **Notice and Hearing.** In most instances where the S.E.C. may take action against a company or a person, it may be done only after notice and an opportunity for a hearing. Furthermore, the proceedings must be conducted pursuant to the requirements of the Administrative Procedure Act (much like a court trial).

2. Ex Parte Proceedings. In addition, the S.E.C. may suspend trading in nonexempt securities, without any notice or hearing to the company involved, for a period of 10 days. [*See* SEA §12(k)] Renewals of this period must be based on new circumstances arising after the original suspension notice. [S.E.C. v. Sloan, 436 U.S. 103 (1978)]

3. Burden of Proof. Most of the formal administrative proceedings conducted by the S.E.C. are disciplinary proceedings to punish alleged violations of the securities laws by persons required to be registered with the S.E.C. and expressly subjected by these laws to such administrative sanctions by the statutes (e.g., registered broker-dealers, investment advisers, etc.).

    a. Hearing. Hearings are conducted before an administrative law judge; his decision is then reviewed by the full Commission, and an appeal is available to the circuit court.

Steadman
v. S.E.C.

    b. Preponderance of evidence proof standard--Steadman v. S.E.C., 450 U.S. 91 (1981).

        1) Facts. The S.E.C. initiated a disciplinary action against Steadman (D) pursuant to section 9(b) of the Investment Company Act of 1940 and section 203(f) of the Investment Advisers Act of 1940 for numerous violations in his management of several mutual funds registered under the Investment Company Act. After an evidentiary hearing before an administrative law judge, where a preponderance of the evidence standard was applied, the Commission held against D and entered an order permanently barring D from associating with any investment adviser or affiliating with any registered investment company, and suspending him for one year from associating with any broker or dealer in securities. D sought review.

        2) Issue. In a disciplinary proceeding by the S.E.C., is a preponderance of the evidence the appropriate standard of proof to show fraud?

        3) Held. Yes. District court affirmed.

            a) Where Congress has not set the degree of proof for the party carrying the burden of proof, the court may set the standard.

            b) Here Congress has set the standard:

                (1) The securities laws themselves do not set a standard.

                (2) But the Administrative Procedures Act does, which governs all agency hearings. Section 7(c) indicates that sanctions shall not be imposed except when supported by and in accordance with "substantial evidence." This implies a quantity of evidence. The words "in accordance with" imply that the agency must weigh the evidence and decide based on the weight of the evidence.

                (3) Section 10(e) has the same language, but this section refers to the standard for judicial review of the agency's actions.

(4)   The legislative history of the House of Representatives clearly indicates that the standard meant to apply was "preponderance of the evidence."

c)   This result is confirmed by the fact that the S.E.C. has always used this standard in its disciplinary administrative hearings.

4)   Dissent. The Court has imposed very severe sanctions—permanently barring a professional from his profession and the sale of the mutual fund management company that D owns. In this situation, as well as where the prosecution is for fraud (as it is here), the standard should be "clear and convincing evidence." This was the common law standard. This is the backdrop against which Congress passed the securities laws. Congress itself gave no specific indication of its intent on this issue. Also, the Administrative Procedure Act was not passed until seven years after the two Acts under which D was disciplined.

5)   Comment. Note that the Fifth Circuit held that when the S.E.C. imposes a drastic sanction on a defendant, the S.E.C. has an obligation to carefully articulate exactly why a lesser sanction will not suffice. This holding was not disturbed by the Supreme Court.

4.   Administrative Proceedings Against Professionals Pursuant to Rule 2(e).

a.   Introduction. Any person compelled to appear before any administrative agency of the United States has the right to be represented by counsel. Furthermore, any member of the bar of the highest court of any state may represent others before any agency (except the Patent Office) on filing a written declaration that he is currently qualified and is authorized to represent the particular party. Additionally, the Securities and Exchange Commission has enacted the "S.E.C. Rules of Practice" to provide for efficient and expeditious conduct of its own administrative proceedings. Rule 2 sets out the requirements for persons who may appear and practice before the Commission, and subsection 2(e) gives the S.E.C. the power to suspend or disbar persons practicing before it. This power, as exercised by the S.E.C., is currently the subject of substantial controversy.

b.   Bases for disbarment or suspension. There are several bases under Rule 2(e) for the S.E.C. to deny a lawyer the privilege of practicing before the Commission. The most commonly referred to bases are stated in Rule 2(e)(1), which sets forth several bases for action against a lawyer if one of them is found by the S.E.C. to exist as a result of a hearing:

1)   The first such basis is that the lawyer lacks the "requisite qualifications" to represent others.

2)   The second basis is that the lawyer lacks the necessary "character or integrity."

3)   The third basis is that the lawyer has engaged in "unethical or improper professional conduct."

4) The fourth basis is that the lawyer has "willfully" violated or willfully aided and abetted the violation of the federal securities laws. No definition of the key word "willfully" is given in the rule.

c. **Prohibition of practice before the commission.** If there is a sufficient basis under Rule 2(e), pursuant to the terms of Rule 2(e)(1), the Commission may deny a professional, either temporarily or permanently, the privilege of appearing or practicing before it "it any way." Rule 2(g) defines "practicing before the Commission" as including: "(1) transacting any business before the Commission; and (2) the preparation of any statement, opinion or other paper by any attorney, accountant, engineer or other expert, filed with the Commission in any Registration Statement, notification, application, report or other document with the consent of the attorney, accountant, engineer or other expert." This provision clearly prohibits an attorney from representing a client in a formal or informal administrative proceeding before the S.E.C. It also specifically provides that participation in any way in preparing documents to be filed with the Commission is prohibited. And the S.E.C. staff has also taken the position that it even encompasses the giving of any advice relating to any of the federal securities laws.

d. **History of the use of Rule 2(e).** The ethical conduct of lawyers has always been supervised by the general disciplinary system maintained by the courts and the state bar associations. Additionally, since 1935 Rule 2(e) has been used by the S.E.C. to regulate the conduct of lawyers involved in securities transactions. The S.E.C. initially took the approach of policing and disciplining unethical lawyer conduct occurring in face-to-face contact with Commission members and employees, such as might occur in an administrative hearing. Alternatively, most of the early proceedings were ones where the lawyer could be said to have attempted to subvert the integrity of the S.E.C.'s regulatory processes by intentionally filing false information in required S.E.C. reports.

In 1970 Rule 2(e) was amended to proscribe conduct which was a willful violation or a willful aiding and abetting of a violation of the securities laws (if such was established after a hearing before the S.E.C.). Shortly thereafter, the S.E.C. began to assert its present position that, in effect, it may discipline any lawyer who fails to perform what the Commission deems to be a duty to the S.E.C., even if the lawyer's conduct occurs in a securities transaction to which the federal securities laws apply generally and the conduct occurs in the privacy of the lawyer's office. In effect, the S.E.C. launched the beginning of its attempt to conscript lawyers in private practice as an extended enforcement arm of the Commission. This is what has caused the controversy since this kind of role for the attorney conflicts with the traditional paradigm of the lawyer-client relationship.

e. **The statutory basis for Rule 2(e).** The S.E.C. has never claimed that it has express statutory authority to discipline lawyers who appear before it. Rather, the S.E.C. bases its authority on its general rulemaking powers under the separate federal securities acts, and on its inherent authority under the securities laws in general. There has not been a lot of judicial review of the S.E.C.'s position, but what there has been has been generally supportive of the Commission. For an important case illustrating application of Rule 2(e), *see In the Matter of Carter and Johnson*, S.E.A. Release No. 17597 (1981), *supra*.

5. **Sanctions for Failure to File Required Reports.** Pursuant to section 15(c)(4) of the 1934 Act, the S.E.C. has the right to impose administrative remedies for late or tardy filings under sections 12, 13, 14, or 15 of the 1934 Act. Such sanctions may also apply to any person who "was the cause" of such a violation.

6. **Self-Regulatory Enforcement of Stock Exchanges and Organizations of Broker-Dealers.** These organizations have adopted rules that go beyond the 1934 Act and S.E.C. rules (i.e., "just principles of trade"). Section 6(b) of the 1934 Act also provides that members of national exchanges may be disciplined by the exchanges for violations of the 1934 Act and its rules. Sections 19(d)-(h) deal with the procedural requirements for disciplinary actions by self-regulatory organizations and review by the S.E.C. Rule 19d-1 requires that the S.E.C. be notified of final actions. And, pursuant to 19(e), final actions may be appealed to the S.E.C. Under section 21(f), however, the S.E.C. cannot itself bring an injunction action to enforce the rules of a self-regulatory organization *unless* it finds (i) that the organization is unable or unwilling to take appropriate action, or (ii) such action is otherwise necessary in the public interest or for the protection of investors.

D. NEW SANCTIONS FOR THE S.E.C.

The Securities Enforcement Remedies and Penny Stock Reform Act of 1990 have provided the S.E.C. with new injunctive and administrative remedies that will probably encourage the S.E.C. to conduct more of its enforcement efforts in-house rather than through the federal courts.

1. **Injunctive Remedies.** The Remedies Act amended section 20 of the 1933 Act, section 21 of the 1934 Act, section 42 of the Investment Company Act, and section 209 of the Investment Advisers Act to allow the S.E.C. to seek a *monetary penalty* in any civil injunctive action it brings (in addition to asking for disgorgement of profits). The penalties run from $5,000 per violation for individuals and $50,000 for corporations, up to $100,000 for individuals and $500,000 for corporations for fraud and injury done to other persons. Furthermore, section 20(b) of the 1933 Act and section 21(d) of the 1934 Act have been amended to enable courts to bar individuals from serving as officers or directors of any publicly reporting company.

2. **New Administrative Penalties.** The Remedies Act also amended section 8 of the 1933 Act, section 9 of the Investment Company Act, and section 203 of the Investment Advisers Act, and added new section 21C to the 1934 Act to provide the S.E.C. with an administrative cease-and-desist authority. Thus, the S.E.C. may proceed against any party it suspects has violated or may violate the federal securities laws and order that party to cease the violation, disgorge profits, and take steps to comply with the law. The S.E.C. may also order temporary cease-and-desist orders, without notice to defendants, and without a hearing. The temporary orders remain in effect until an administrative proceeding for a permanent order is resolved, unless the defendant appeals the temporary order to the S.E.C. and then to a federal district court. These procedures are a substitute for proceeding in the old way in front of federal courts.

VI. CRIMINAL ENFORCEMENT AND THE RACKETEER INFLUENCED AND CORRUPT ORGANIZATIONS ACT

A. INTRODUCTION

Criminal prosecutions under the federal securities laws are increasingly common. Section 24 of the 1933 Act and section 32(a) of the 1934 Act are broadly worded, each making it a "felony" for any person to "willfully" violate any statutory provision of either statute or any rule or regulation thereunder. Sentences are up to five years under the 1933 Act and 10 years under the 1934 Act.

Often the criminal statutes may be used to punish technical violations of the laws as a way of convicting a defendant of an easier-to-prove crime, or as a lesser offense if the defendant cooperates.

As alternatives, federal prosecutors may use federal mail and wire fraud statutes, or the RICO statute, which has harsher sentences and an express private cause of action authorizing injured victims to sue for treble damages.

B. PROCEDURAL ISSUES

1. **Criminal Prosecutions.** United States Attorneys bring criminal prosecutions in the federal system. The S.E.C. informally or formally (after a Commission vote) refers matters it wants prosecuted.

2. **Dual Prosecutions.** The S.E.C. may refer a criminal matter and simultaneously pursue its other remedies—injunction, etc. It will not bargain *not* to refer the case to a United States Attorney.

3. **Discovery.** In *criminal cases* discovery occurs through a grand jury. A defendant may plead the Fifth Amendment. In *civil cases*, the Fifth Amendment is less of a shield.

   a. **Discovery in parallel prosecutions--S.E.C. v. Dresser Industries, Inc.,** 628 F.2d 1368 (D.C. Cir. 1980), *cert. denied*, 449 U.S. 993 (1981).

   S.E.C. v. Dresser Industries, Inc.

   1) **Facts.** Beginning in 1973, the problem of corporations making illegal payments to government officials of the United States and foreign countries, and failing to disclose these payments in appropriate corporate finance reports to the S.E.C., came to light. The S.E.C. developed a Voluntary Disclosure Program whereby companies could investigate such payments and make disclosures in their reports to the S.E.C. and thereby be less likely to be prosecuted by the S.E.C. than if the S.E.C. itself made such an investigation. Dresser made such an investigation and filed several 8-K monthly reports with the S.E.C. disclosing such illegal payments in general terms. The S.E.C. asked for the underlying details of the violations, in line with its guidelines for the Voluntary Disclosure Program. Dresser refused, indicating that the disclosures would endanger some of its employees working abroad. The Justice Department had also

begun investigating such payments; the S.E.C. gave the Justice Department its files of companies involved in the Voluntary Disclosure Program. The Justice Department presented the Dresser case to a grand jury, which subpoenaed the Dresser documents. The S.E.C. then issued a formal order of investigation with a subpoena. Dresser filed suit to enjoin action by both the S.E.C. and the Justice Department. The district court held for the Justice Department and the S.E.C.; a special panel of the circuit court held that the subpoenas should be enforced but that the information received by the S.E.C. should not be given to the Justice Department. Dresser appealed.

2) **Issue.** At this stage of the criminal proceeding, should the S.E.C. be prohibited from giving information it receives pursuant to its subpoena in a formal civil investigation to the Justice Department, which is conducting a parallel criminal investigation?

3) **Held.** No. Panel decision of the circuit court is reversed.

   a) The civil and criminal laws frequently overlap. The Constitution does not normally require a stay of civil proceedings until the criminal action is over. But courts may, in their discretion, stay civil proceedings, postpone civil discovery, or impose protective orders when the interests of justice require it.

   b) The strongest case for doing so occurs where a party under indictment for a serious criminal offense is required to defend a civil administrative action for the same matter and where the latter, if not deferred, might undermine the party's Fifth Amendment rights, expand the rights of criminal discovery, and expose the basis of the defense to the criminal action in advance of the criminal trial.

   c) This is not a strong case for protection. No indictment has been returned; Fifth Amendment rights are not yet threatened; the S.E.C. subpoena does not require Dresser to reveal the basis of its defense.

   d) Securities law expressly provides that the S.E.C. can investigate violations and transmit evidence to the Justice Department, which may institute criminal actions. [*See* SEA §21(b)] Effective enforcement of the securities law requires that the S.E.C. and the Justice Department be able to investigate possible violations simultaneously. Both civil and criminal investigations take time; parallel investigations must proceed if the statute of limitations is to be complied with and timely investigations of evidence made.

   e) The prejudice to Dresser is speculative at this point. The Panel's modification of the district court order should be overturned. No party requested such a modification. The statute imposes no such limitation. Congress meant that the S.E.C. be able to share with the Justice Department at this point in an investigation. There is no precedent of the courts to support this modification. No compelling purpose is served thereby.

   f) On the other hand, there are significant advantages at this preliminary stage of the proceedings in allowing cooperation. Dresser's right to a speedy trial is promoted. Effective enforcement of the securities laws is also advanced.

g)   Any injustice which occurs at a later stage of the proceedings can be prevented at that time.

C.   CRIMINAL PROSECUTIONS UNDER THE FEDERAL SECURITIES LAWS

1.   **Introduction.** According to section 24 of the 1933 Act and section 32(a) of the 1934 Act, any "willful" violation of the statutory provisions or the rules thereunder is a criminal violation. Section 32(a) has several different added provisions: a second clause provides that it is a criminal violation to willfully and *knowingly* make false or misleading statements in various filings. Then, the last clause provides that there is no violation *if* defendant proves he had *no knowledge* of an applicable rule or regulation.

United States
v. Dixon

2.   **Willful and Knowing Violation of the 1934 Act--United States v. Dixon,** 536 F.2d 1388 (2d Cir. 1976).

   a.   **Facts.** Dixon was president of AVM Corp., a reporting company under the 1934 Act. He was convicted under section 32(a) for failing in a proxy statement and in a Form 10K filing to disclose that the company had lent him $65,000 during 1970 (any loan above $10,000 had to be disclosed in the proxy statement; amounts above $20,000 in the 10K). Just before the close of the year, Dixon had switched some of the loan to his father and had taken out a bank loan to pay down the remainder to $19,100. Then in February, Dixon reborrowed the money. In March, the proxy and 10K were filed. There was testimony that AVM's financial officer had given Dixon the correct information on amounts that had to be disclosed; and there was some testimony that the outside accountant had told Dixon that on the 10K report he did not have to report anything if the amount *at year end* was under $20,000. The proxy statement and 10K were prepared in draft form by the company's general counsel, with blanks (including blanks for officer loans) that officers filled in when the draft was circulated. Dixon argued that he did not knowingly violate the law. Dixon appeals the decision of the trial court.

   b.   **Issues.** Did Dixon have the state of mind required for a conviction? Was the jury properly charged?

   c.   **Held.** Yes to both questions.

      1)   Violation of the rules requires only a showing of willfulness. Violations of filing requirements must be both willful and knowing.

      2)   Willful here means simply that defendant knew that he was doing a wrongful act. Knowing means that defendant's act involved a significant risk of actually accomplishing the violation that was intended.

      3)   Here Dixon knew that content of proxy statements and 10K reports were prescribed by rules. Dixon also indicated that he knew that officer loans were covered by rules.

4)	It seems the trial court believed that Dixon knew that the rules were not satisfied by having a sufficiently low balance at year end, however high the amount had been previously. But this need not be proved; all that need be proved here is that Dixon did an intentional act that was wrongful. He may have thought that he was avoiding a different rule than the one that existed, but this does not excuse him. He knew there was a rule; if he had wanted to be sure to follow it, he could have checked on its provisions.

d.	**Comment.** Note that if Dixon had been prosecuted under the willful and knowing clause for a false filing, would proof that Dixon knew he acted illegally have been required? And what does the last clause of section 32(a) mean—a defendant can escape if he had no knowledge of the rule? It would have to mean that defendant did not know that there was an applicable rule, not that he did not know some specific aspect of the rule.

3.	**The Attorney-Client Privilege--United States v. Bilzerian,** 926 F.2d 1285 (2d Cir. 1991).

a.	**Facts.** Bilzerian (D) was convicted on nine counts of an indictment charging violations of the securities laws and fraud on the I.R.S. The transactions occurred in the stock of four companies; he was convicted and sentenced to four years in prison and a $1.5 million fine. D raised money from investors, funnelled it through trusts, and represented in filings with the S.E.C. related to tender offers that the money was his personal money; he hired brokers to buy stock in target companies for him, but kept in broker name, to delay filing reports; he bought stock in privately negotiated deals and represented that they were bought in the market; and he had a broker-dealer buy stock from him to keep in the broker's account, without disclosure that the stock belonged to D and would later be purchased by D from the broker ("parking"). D defended on the basis that he did not intend to violate the law, and that he had no knowledge that he had committed any violations. He was prosecuted under Rule 10b-5 and Section 32(a). D asked that he be able to testify that he did not believe that he had violated the law and not be cross-examined regarding his communications (relating to his belief) with his lawyer. The trial judge ruled that if he testified regarding his good faith, this would open the door to cross-examination with respect to his basis for this belief, and cross-examination on his communications with his attorney regarding these matters would be allowed. D declined to testify. D appeals the trial court's ruling on this issue.

b.	**Issue.** Was the trial court correct in ruling that D's testimony as to his belief and knowledge that he was not violating the law provided a waiver of confidential communications between D and his attorney regarding D's belief?

c.	**Held.** Yes.

1)	D claims that his testimony would not have disclosed the existence of any attorney-client communication, so the attorney-client privilege should not have been waived. But the privilege may implicitly be waived when D asserts a claim that in fairness requires examination of protected communications. Here D wanted to testify that he thought his actions were legal; this would have put his knowledge of the law and the basis for his understanding in issue. His conversations with his lawyer regarding the legality of his schemes would then be relevant to his intent.

2) The trial court's ruling did not prevent D from denying criminal intent. D could have denied criminal intent without asserting good faith, or he could argue his good faith in defense counsel's opening and closing statements, or by examination of witnesses.

3) There was no abuse of the trial court's discretion in ruling that the attorney-client privilege would be waived if D testified as to his state of mind of good faith.

d. **Comment.** Note also that a showing that defendant relied on the advice of counsel in acting may be sufficient to show that defendant did not knowingly violate the law. [*See* United States v. Crosby, 294 F.2d 928 (2d Cir. 1961).

United States
v. Mulheren

4. **Market Manipulation--United States v. Mulheren,** 938 F.2d 364 (2d Cir. 1991).

a. **Facts.** Mulheren (D) was the chief trader and general partner of Jamie Securities Co. He was charged with a 42-count indictment in June 1989, and convicted on several charges. This case concerns an appeal of his conviction for market manipulation of Gulf & Western common stock. In 1985 Boesky and Icahn bought approximately 5% each of G & W stock, then tried to take over the company, which was resisted by Davis, G & W chairman. Finally, Boesky offered to sell his stock back to G & W for $45 per share, slightly above the market. D had done business with Boesky on several deals, and inquired about G & W (there were rumors in the press of the takeover). D then met with Davis, offering to monitor Boesky and suggesting cooperation in another takeover. Davis and Boesky agreed to the sale back at the last traded price of October 17. At 11 a.m. on the 17th, Boesky called D and indicated that G & W was a great stock at a price under $45, and that it "would be great if the price were to reach $45." Shortly thereafter D began buying G & W, eventually purchasing 75,000 shares, and raising the price to $45 per share. The S.E.C. charged D with buying the stock solely to manipulate the market price for Boesky, and not with an investment intent. D was charged with violating Rule 10b-5 and convicted. D appeals on the basis that there was no sufficient evidence to prove beyond a reasonable doubt that D's intent was market manipulation; and that even if he had had such an intent, there was nothing illegal in the way he purchased the stock.

b. **Issue.** Was the evidence of intent to manipulate the market sufficient for a jury to find that such was D's intent, beyond a reasonable doubt?

c. **Held.** No. Conviction overturned.

1) There must be substantial evidence in the record to show that there was evidence beyond a reasonable doubt that D intended to manipulate the market.

2)   Further, the government's theory is questionable; i.e., that it is illegally manipulative for an investor who is neither a fiduciary nor an insider to engage in securities transactions in the open market with the sole intent to affect the price of a security. We will assume this is true, however.

3)   First, it was not proved beyond a reasonable doubt that D even knew that Boesky had a stock position in G & W. Boesky never testified he told D; D testified that he had not read the speculation in the press; and in the meeting of D with Davis, D said he did not think Boesky had a position.

4)   Further, the government did not prove beyond a reasonable doubt that D purchased the 75,000 shares for the purpose of manipulating the price of G & W stock:

   a)   In the telephone conversation with Boesky, the meaning is unclear from what was said. It is not clear that Boesky asked D to push the price of G & W up. Why limit it to $45 per share? Also, for weeks D had been asking Boesky about G & W as an investment.

   b)   The stock price went down after Boesky sold his stock; D lost over $64,000 on the purchases.

   c)   D could have raised the price to $45 per share with a purchase of 5,000 shares; why 75,000?

   d)   Boesky's comments to D could be interpreted as a stock tip.

   e)   The broker who executed D's trades did them properly.

   f)   D's purchases were 70% of the market trades during the time they were executed; this does not prove anything without more. Trading was light.

   g)   D sold call options after the purchase of 75,000 shares; this was a hedge. They were sold after Boesky had already sold his stock.

   h)   The fact that D continued to do business with Boesky after he lost money on the G & W stock does not prove anything beyond a reasonable doubt.

D.   THE FEDERAL MAIL AND WIRE FRAUD STATUTES

The mail fraud [18 U.S.C. §1341] and wire fraud [18 U.S.C. §1343] statutes have enormous reach. The elements of the offenses:

(i)   A scheme to defraud, and

(ii) A mailing of a letter or use of the interstate phone as part of the scheme, but not necessarily by the defendant (by anyone, as long as use of the mail or phone was foreseeable).

(iii) No damages need be proved.

(iv) But there must be a showing of specific intent to defraud.

One of the main issues has been what type of fraud must be shown. In 1988 Congress passed 18 U.S.C., section 1346, which provides that "scheme or artifice to defraud" includes any scheme to deprive another of "the intangible right of honest services." In *Carpenter v. United States*, 484 U.S. 19 (1987), the Supreme Court held that depriving the *Wall Street Journal* of "confidential business information" by one of its writers in a stock scheme was fraud. Further, it seems clear that if a fiduciary trustee of funds accepts a kickback from a broker to trade through the broker's firm with trust funds, this might qualify as fraud, even though the fiduciary has no intent to cause his beneficiary any loss.

E. THE RACKETEER INFLUENCED AND CORRUPT ORGANIZATIONS ACT

1. **Introduction.** When it was first enacted, the Racketeer Influenced and Corrupt Organizations Act of 1970 ("RICO") appeared to be directed at the unlawful activities of organized crime. However, the statutory language is sufficiently broad to bring a variety of business frauds within the scope of its civil sanctions. Thus, the civil liability provisions of RICO threaten to revolutionize all of securities litigation, completely contrary to any discoverable intent of Congress.

2. **The Key Statutory Provisions.** The following are the key statutory provisions of RICO:

   a. **Civil damage provision.** The civil damage provision [18 U.S.C. §1964(c)] creates a *private* right of action with treble damage recovery (plus attorneys' fees) for "any person injured in his person or property by reason of a violation of section 1962."

   b. **Participation in an interstate business.** It is unlawful for any person employed by or associated with any enterprise in or affecting interstate commerce to conduct or participate, directly or indirectly, in the conduct of such enterprise's affairs through a pattern of racketeering activity. [18 U.S.C. §1962(c)]

   c. **Racketeering activity.** Section 1961(1) defines a "pattern of racketeering activity" as at least two occurrences within 10 years of any of several specifically listed offenses, one of which is "fraud in the sale of securities." (*Note*: The list of predicate offenses is long and includes most violent offenses under state law as well as federal labor, securities, bankruptcy, wire and mail fraud offenses.)

3. **The Elements of a RICO Cause of Action.** There are two elements of a RICO cause of action:

a. The defendant must violate section 1962, which has seven subparts: (i) the defendant, (ii) through commission of two or more acts, (iii) which constitute a "pattern" (iv) of "racketeering activity," (v) directly or indirectly invests in or maintains an interest in or participates in or operates (vi) an "enterprise," (vii) the activities of which affect interstate commerce.

b. The plaintiff must have been injured in his property or business by reason of a violation of section 1962.

4. Jurisdiction. The RICO statute confers jurisdiction on the federal district courts to entertain civil actions, but it does not say whether this jurisdiction is concurrent with the state courts or exclusive. There is very little case law on this issue yet; what little there is favors the view that jurisdiction is concurrent. [Cianci v. Superior Court, 40 Cal. 3d 903 (1985)]

5. The "Enterprise" Element.

a. **Definition of the element.** As with almost every other aspect of this cause of action, there is confusion with respect to the meaning of the term "enterprise." The common sense idea is that of an "activity."

b. **Statutory definition.** But the statute defines an enterprise as a collection of people; specifically, an enterprise includes (i) any individual, partnership, corporation, association, or other legal entity, and (ii) any union or group of individuals associated in fact although not a legal entity. [18 U.S.C. §1961(4)]

c. **Applications.**

1) **Illegal activity as an enterprise--United States v. Turkette,** 452 U.S. 576 (1981).

   United States v. Turkette

   a) **Facts.** A single individual (D) was the leader of a group of other individuals who engaged in various illegal activities, including narcotics, gambling, etc. The district court convicted D; on appeal, the circuit court held that an "enterprise" included only legitimate businesses. The case was appealed to the Supreme Court.

   b) **Issue.** Does an "enterprise" under section 1962(c) include both legitimate and illegitimate businesses?

   c) **Held.** Yes. Reversed.

      (1) The language of section 1962(c) does not distinguish between legitimate and illegal businesses.

      (2) In section 1961(4), two divisions of enterprises are set forth: (i) individual, partnership, corporation, or other legal entities; and (ii) any union or group of individuals although not a legal entity. The second category does not simply give an enumeration of specific examples of the first category. It is an entirely separate category, broad

enough to include groups conducting criminal as well as legal businesses.

(3) This interpretation does not create any inconsistencies in the sections of the statute. There must be an enterprise (it can be criminal activity) and there must be a pattern of "racketeering activity," or specific criminal acts (a list of which is given in the statute). The same criminal acts may be used to prove the existence of an "enterprise" and the "racketeering activity."

(4) Section 1962(c) also proscribes investment of income derived from racketeering activity in an enterprise or the acquisition of an interest in any enterprise through racketeering activity. These sections are aimed at preventing racketeers from investing in either criminal or legitimate businesses.

(5) Section 1964 provides various civil remedies, including divestiture, dissolution, etc. These remedies are not just applicable to legitimate businesses.

(6) The effect of the inclusion of illegal businesses in the definition of "enterprise" is to involve the federal government in prosecution of criminal activity that was formerly thought to belong only to the states.

2) **Single person as an enterprise.** It is clear that a single person and his activity can constitute an enterprise. *See* section 1961(4), which mentions "any *individual*, partnership," etc.

3) **Part of a business.** A part of a business may qualify as an "enterprise" so that it can be shown that the enterprise is being conducted through a pattern of racketeering activity.

6. **Racketeering Activity.**

a. **Introduction.** In order for a violation of section 1962 to occur, the defendant must conduct or be involved in an enterprise through a pattern of "racketeering activity."

b. **Injury apart from the individual offenses.** It is not necessary that plaintiff prove a separate injury occurring as a result of the pattern of racketeering activity. Injury occurring from the conduct prohibited by the statute (section 1961(1)) is sufficient. [American National Bank & Trust Co. v. Haroco, 473 U.S. 606 (1985)]

Sedima, S.P.R.L. v. Imrex Co.

c. **Prior racketeering conviction not required--Sedima, S.P.R.L. v. Imrex Co., 473 U.S. 479 (1985).**

1) **Facts.** Sedima (P), a Belgian corporation, entered into a joint venture with Imrex (D), a United States company, to supply electronic components to another Belgian company, splitting the profits. After

initiating $8 million in orders, P charged D with inflating expenses and not splitting profits and sued for treble damages under RICO.

The district court dismissed, holding that for there to be a section 1962 injury, there must be an injury different from a direct injury due to the racketeering activities named in section 1962. The court of appeals affirmed on the same basis as the district court *and* because defendants had not previously been criminally convicted of one of the named criminal acts mentioned in RICO, such as mail or wire fraud or under RICO itself (a requirement the court read into section 1964(c)). The Supreme Court granted certiorari.

2) Issues.

a) For RICO to apply, must there be a prior criminal conviction for racketeering activity?

b) Must the racketeering activity involved be somehow different from the specifically named criminal activities in section 1962?

3) Held. a) No. b) No. Reversed.

a) There is no place in any of the RICO sections where a prior conviction of defendant for racketeering activity is required in order for a plaintiff to pursue treble damages in a private action under section 1964(c). There is nothing in the legislative history to indicate this either.

(1) The court of appeals reached this result to try to limit RICO private damage actions in some way.

(2) It is not clear whether the acts creating liability under section 1962 (although they are criminal acts under the statutes involved) must be proved beyond a reasonable doubt in a section 1964(c) civil RICO action.

(3) This construction does not raise serious constitutional questions: the same acts can create criminal as well as civil liability, the treble damages are not clearly punitive, etc.

(4) The purpose of RICO was to allow private parties to supplement government criminal actions with civil actions; this purpose would be obviated if treble damage actions could only be brought against those already brought to justice.

b) A violation of section 1962(c) requires (i) conduct (ii) of an enterprise (iii) through a pattern (iv) of "racketeering activity." Other than this, there is no requirement that the "racketeering activity" be separate from the harm or damage done from the specific criminal acts mentioned in section 1962.

c) RICO is to be read liberally in order to effectuate its remedial purposes.

d) It is irrelevant that most RICO cases are being brought against ordinary businesses and not against apparent mobsters. If a change in the breadth of the statute is to occur, Congress must make it.

4) Dissent (Marshall, Brennan, Blackmun, Powell, JJ.).

a) The Court's interpretation of the civil RICO statute validates the federalization of broad areas of the state common law of fraud. Congress did not intend this to happen.

  (1) The only limitation on the inexorable expansion of the federal mail and wire fraud criminal statutes has been prosecutors' discretion.

  (2) But there is no restraining influence on prosecutors in civil RICO actions.

b) RICO is also displacing other areas of federal law; e.g., one offense under RICO is "fraud in the sale of securities." Plaintiffs would rather pursue a RICO claim (treble damages) than a claim under the 1935 Act or the 1934 Act.

c) Only 9% of all civil RICO cases have involved allegations of criminal activity normally associated with professional criminals, the central purpose Congress sought to promote.

5) Dissent (Powell, J.).

a) The language of RICO can be read more narrowly to confine its reach to the type of conduct Congress had in mind.

b) For example, section 1961(5) defines "pattern" of racketeering activity to require at least two acts of racketeering activity. Section 1961(1) states that such activity means any number of acts. Thus, the definition of "pattern" may be interpreted as meaning that the presence of the named acts is just the beginning in proving a "pattern." The pattern element is designed to limit its application to planned, ongoing continuing crime; this is unlike the criminal acts in this case.

6) Comment. Note that this case involves a corporate defendant, and that, by not requiring that there be a prior criminal conviction, RICO is being applied to possible first-time offenders (rather than proven, habitual criminals). Also, the conviction does not require a criminal standard of proof and treble damages are awarded—a very severe penalty for a corporate defendant.

H.J. Inc. v. Northwestern Bell Telephone Co.

d. A "pattern" of racketeering activity--H.J. Inc. v. Northwestern Bell Telephone Co. 492 U.S. 229 (1989).

1) Facts. Ps, customers of Northwestern (D), filed a class action in 1986 in federal district court, alleging violations of section 1962 of RICO. Ps sought an injunction and treble damages under RICO's civil liability sections, 1964(a) and (c). Also joined was the Minnesota Public Utility Commission, which was responsible for setting utility rates. Ps alleged that Northwestern bribed members of the MPUC with cash gifts and other benefits to influence the setting of rates in excess of fair and reasonable rates. This occurred between 1980 and 1986. Ps' first claim was a pendent state claim asserting that D violated the state bribery statute as well as common law bribery. The second claim alleged violation of section 1962(a) of RICO, in that D derived income from a pattern of racketeering activity involving acts of bribery and used the income therefrom to engage in its business as an interstate enterprise. Count three claimed a violation of section 1962(b) in that, through the same pattern of activity, D acquired an interest in the MPUC, also an interstate enterprise. Count four claimed a violation of section 1962(c) in that Ds participated in the affairs of the MPUC through this pattern of racketeering activity. Count five claimed that Ds conspired together to violate sections 1962(a), (b), (c), thus violating section 1962(d). The district court granted Ds' motion to dismiss the complaint on the basis that all fraudulent acts were part of a single scheme and so there was no "pattern' of illegal activity as required by RICO. The court of appeals affirmed. The Supreme Court granted certiorari.

2) **Issue.** Did the court apply the correct standard for determining whether a "pattern" of racketeering activity exists?

3) **Held.** No. Court of appeals is reversed.

   a) RICO imposes criminal and civil liability on those who engage in certain "prohibited activities." Each prohibited activity is defined in section 1962 to include, as a necessary element, proof either of "a pattern of racketeering activity" or "of collection of an unlawful debt." "Racketeering activity" is defined to mean "any act or threat involving" specified state law crimes, an "act" indictable under various specified federal statutes, and certain federal "offenses"; but the term "pattern" is defined only as requiring "at least two acts of racketeering activity" within a 10-year period. [*See* 18 U.S.C. §1961(5)]

   b) RICO has extremely broad application because the offenses that qualify are broad (securities fraud, etc.) and Congress and the courts have not come up with a meaningful concept of "pattern."

   c) In determining what is meant by "pattern" of racketeering activity, the wording of the statute and its legislative history are the guides. There is nothing in either to suggest that acts of racketeering form a pattern only when they are part of separate illegal schemes. We also do not agree with the courts that have held that a pattern is established when two predicate acts of racketeering are shown. It is also not necessary to prove that the perpetrator is involved in organized crime.

   d) Something more than merely two predicate acts must be shown, but the concept encompasses the possibility of multiple predicate acts within a single scheme where the acts are related and amount to or threaten the likelihood of continued criminal activity.

   e) The definition of pattern in section 1961(5) is not so much a definition as a statement of minimum necessary conditions: at least two acts, the last of which occurs within 10 years of the first. While two acts are necessary, they may not be sufficient. Section 1961(5) does not indicate what these additional requirements are.

   f) The words "pattern of racketeering activity" themselves have significance.

      (1) A "pattern" is an arrangement or order of things or activity.

(2)   So the racketeering acts must fall into some kind of pattern, i.e., bear some kind of relationship to each other.

(3)   Since no definition as to the kind of relationship that must exist is given, it must be that Congress intended to take a flexible approach. Many relationships between predicate acts might constitute a pattern.

g)   The legislative history of RICO adds the following:

(1)   A pattern is not formed by sporadic activity. Two widely separated and isolated acts do not constitute a pattern.

(2)   There must be some relationship between the acts and the threat of continuing activity. There must be a threat of continued criminal activity.

(3)   RICO was Title IX of the Organized Crime Control Act. Title X of this Act has a definition of the relationship of criminal acts in creating a "pattern." "Criminal conduct forms a pattern if it embraces criminal acts that have the same or similar purposes, results, participants, victims, or methods of commission, or otherwise are interrelated by distinguishing characteristics and are not isolated events."

h)   The "continuity" requirement led the lower courts to create a test requiring multiple criminal schemes to create a pattern. But Congress did not intend that continuity might be shown only by proof of multiple schemes. The continuity or its threat may be shown in a number of ways, making it difficult to formulate in the abstract any general test:

(1)   A closed period of repeated conduct, or past conduct that threatens repetition can qualify.

(2)   Usually the acts extend over a substantial period of time.

(3)   Whether the predicate acts establish a threat of continued racketeering activity depends on the specific facts of each case.

(4)   An example: the threat of continuity may be established by showing that the acts or offenses are part of an ongoing entity's regular way of doing business.

i)   Ps alleged multiple predicate acts over a six-year period of time. These acts were related by a common purpose, to influence the MPUC to set higher than reasonable rates. It is possible that Ps could prove at trial that these acts, spread over a six-year period, also satisfy the continuity test (i.e., they were a regular way of conducting Ds' business, etc.). Thus, the court of appeals erred in affirming the district court's dismissal of Ps' complaint for failure to plead a "pattern of racketeering activity." This issue should be allowed to go to trial.

4)   **Concurrence** (Scalia, J., Rhenquist, C.J., O'Connor, Kennedy, JJ.). The majority has done nothing but give the same hints about what "pattern" means that have been given before. Nothing helpful has been given. So the courts of appeals will not be any more unified in the future than they have in the past.

This is intolerable with respect to RICO, since RICO is resulting in the federalization of broad areas of state and common law. We concur in that nothing in the statute supports the proposition that predicate acts constituting part of a single scheme can never support a cause of action under RICO.

7. The Predicate Offenses.

a.   **Introduction.** For RICO liability, there must be a pattern of listed acts that results in or constitutes "racketeering activity." [*See* 18 U.S.C. §1961(1)]

b.   **Common offenses.** Two of the most common offenses forming the basis of RICO liability are:

   1)   **Fraud in the sale of securities.** Compare this requirement with the provisions of Rule 10b-5 (fraud *in connection with* the *purchase* or sale of a security).

   2)   **Mail or wire fraud.**

8. Conducting an Enterprise Through a Pattern of Racketeering Activity.

a.   **Introduction.** For RICO to apply, there must be (i) racketeering activity, (ii) a pattern of such activity, (iii) an enterprise, and (iv) the enterprise must be conducted through this pattern of racketeering activity.

b.   **Congressional intent.** The original intent of Congress was apparently to use this provision to focus RICO on organized crime; that is, RICO was originally aimed at organizations whose major purpose was engaging in crimes of conduct, not legitimate businesses that happen to engage in some illegal activity.

   1)   One way that this issue arises is with the question whether the "enterprise" is a whole company, part of a company, or just the illegal activity. For example, where one of the salespersons of XYZ Co., a large corporation, is engaged in illegal activity, if the entire company were the enterprise, then it would be hard to find that the whole company was conducted through a pattern of one salesperson's racketeering activity.

c.   **Enterprise and person committing violations must be separate--Haroco, Inc. v. American National Bank and Trust Co. of Chicago,** 747 F.2d 384 (7th Cir. 1984), *aff'd on other grounds*, 473 U.S. 606 (1985).

Haroco, Inc. v. American National Bank and Trust Co. of Chicago

   1)   **Facts.** American (D) made loans to several plaintiffs at a rate of interest 1% over the bank's prime rate; Ps now claim fraud in charging higher interest rates and sue D, one of its officers (who is also a director), and its parent company, Heller International. Ps claim that D used the mails in furtherance of the scheme. Count I alleges that D violated section 1962(c) by conducting D's and Heller's affairs through a pattern of racketeering activity; Count II alleges that Heller and Grayheck (the officer-director) violated section 1962(c) by

conducting D's affairs through a pattern of racketeering activity. The district court dismissed for failure of Ps to state a claim. Ps appeal.

2) **Issues.**

    a) Must the "person" liable and the "enterprise" involved be separate?

    b) Are there allegations sufficient to avoid a motion to dismiss that a separate person conducted the affairs of an enterprise through racketeering activity?

3) **Held.** 1) Yes. 2) Yes. Reversed.

    a) According to the language of section 1961, the person conducting the affairs of the enterprise and the person constituting the enterprise could be the same. But section 1962(c) requires that the liable person be "employed by or associated with" the enterprise. So D, the corporation, cannot be *both* the liable person *and* the enterprise.

    b) However, section 1962(a) has no such limitation in its language. Here a person (such as a corporation, which is an enterprise under section 1962(c)) acts unlawfully (and thus is subject to the damages provisions) if it receives income from a pattern of racketeering activity in which the person has participated as a principal if the person uses the income in the operation of an enterprise affecting commerce.

        (1) Thus, if you can find a violation of section 1962(c) because there is both a separate enterprise and a liable person, the enterprise might still be liable under section 1962(a).

        (2) But D cannot be held liable under Count I for violation of section 1962(c) for conducting its own affairs through a pattern of racketeering activity.

    c) However, Ps also alleged in Count I that D violated section 1962(c) by conducting, through a pattern of racketeering activity, the affairs of its parent corporation, Heller (since D and its parent, Heller, are separate entities). The parent's affairs include D, the subsidiary.

4) **Comment.** This case raises the issue of what the enterprise is, and whether its affairs were conducted through a pattern of racketeering activity. A parent, Heller, and its subsidiary, D, are the enterprise. D is the liable person. Part of the enterprise, the subsidiary D, had some alleged fraudulent activity. This seems enough for the court to hold that the "enterprise" was conducted through a pattern of racketeering activity.

9. Respondeat Superior.

a. **Introduction.** Section 1962(c) does not make an "enterprise" liable under RICO. Only the "person" who conducts the enterprise is liable. Suppose then that A, an employee of XYZ Corporation, is found liable. The question is whether plaintiff could sue XYZ under the doctrine of respondeat superior because XYZ is A's employer.

b. **Respondeat superior doctrine does not apply--Schofield v. First Commodity Corp. of Boston,** 793 F.2d 28 (1st Cir. 1986).

   1) **Facts.** Schofield (P) claims that First Commodity Corp. (D) fraudulently induced her to invest in trading commodity futures; she brings several claims, including a RICO claim. The district court dismissed the RICO claim; P appeals.

   2) **Issue.** Can a corporate employer, who is the enterprise, be sued under respondeat superior?

   3) **Held.** No. Affirmed.

   a) The "person" who engages in a pattern of racketeering activity must be a separate entity from the enterprise in an action based on section 1962(c).

   b) The persons are D's account executives; D is the enterprise. The brokers are liable under RICO. The question is whether D, the brokerage firm, can be directly liable if the violations were the results of its policies. The language of section 1962(c) is clear that the answer is "no." The major purpose of RICO was to prevent the infiltration of legitimate business by organized crime. But the language of section 1962(c) does allow liability against the enterprise even if it is illegitimate.

   c) On the other hand, there is the possibility of liability against the enterprise under section 1962(a), which makes it unlawful for a "person" to receive income from a pattern of racketeering activity in which the person has participated as a principal, and to use or invest the proceeds in the operation of an enterprise affecting interstate commerce. Thus, this section prohibits D, the enterprise for section 1962(c) purposes, from taking proceeds of the racketeering activity and as a section 1962(a) person using the proceeds in its section 1962(a) enterprise. In other words, there is no prohibition in section 1962(a) against the "person" and the "enterprise" being the same entity.

   d) The next question is whether normal respondeat superior principles apply to employers of persons liable under section 1962(c), thus making the brokerage firm employer (D) liable for the actions of its broker employees. The answer is that the respondeat superior doctrine does not apply. If it were otherwise, the intent of Congress in not permitting the enterprise to be liable under section 1962(c) would be thwarted.

4) **Comment.** Other courts are contra on the respondeat superior question. [*See, e.g.*, Bernstein v. IDT Corp., 582 F. Supp. 757 (N.D. Cal. 1983)]

10. **Damages.** A person *injured in his business or property* may recover for the damages he sustains, which may be trebled. [*See* 18 U.S.C. §1954(c)] But personal injuries to the plaintiff are *not* recoverable (e.g., A, the plaintiff, refuses to pay protection money to the mob and his business is burned down and he is beaten up; A can recover for injuries to his business, but not for the personal injuries).

VII. TRANSNATIONAL TRANSACTIONS

A. INTRODUCTION

The securities markets are becoming global. This is due to increased sophistication of communication equipment, investors' desire to diversify, and the need of borrowers to tap the cheapest capital markets. Globalization presents regulation risks; i.e., a foreign corporation, listed on the London Exchange, but with many United States investors, perpetrates a stock manipulation scheme. Can United States regulators reach this corporation? Can the United States police the world? Or what if XYZ, Inc., a foreign corporation, wants to issue its stock in several foreign countries, including the United States. What law governs?

The United States tends to give broader reach to its anti-fraud laws than to its purely regulatory rules (such as those of the 1933 Act governing new issues, etc.).

B. TRANSNATIONAL SECURITIES FRAUD

1. **Introduction.** Section 2(7) of the 1933 Act defines interstate commerce to include commerce between a foreign country and any United States state. Section 30(b) of the 1934 Act excludes 1934 Act rules if a person transacts a securities business "without the jurisdiction of the United States," unless the United States has adopted rules to the contrary.

   Most courts applying United States securities laws on fraud to transactions having international contacts have focused on the intent of Congress in the reach of these laws.

2. **Application of Rule 10b-5.** Most cases of extraterritorial application of United States fraud laws have involved Rule 10b-5.

   a. **Situations where American investors are suing nonresidents--Leasco Data Processing Equipment Corp. v. Maxwell,** 468 F.2d 1326 (2d Cir. 1972). Leasco Data Processing Equipment Corp. v. Maxwell

      1) **Facts.** Leasco (P), a New York company, was approached in the United States by Pergamon, a British corporation controlled by Maxwell (D), about doing business together. P refused. D invited P personnel to England, and over a period of several months there were many meetings in both places, many telephone calls, etc. At these meetings, P alleges that D and the other defendants (parties associated with D) made many misrepresentations about the financial condition of Pergamon. Allegedly false financial reports prepared by a London accounting firm (Chalmers, Impey & Co.) were given to P. Richard Fleming, chairman of Fleming Ltd., and Banks, the president of a Fleming American subsidiary, visited P in New York and vouched for the accuracy of the Chalmers financial report. Kerman, a director of Pergamon and a senior partner in a law firm which represented Pergamon, met with P's people while they were in London, and a junior partner in the same law firm drafted the agreement between P and Pergamon and met with P in New York. After a tender offer agreement for P to buy

Pergamon was signed, D told P's management that they should buy Pergamon stock on the London Stock Exchange before the tender offer was announced. P bought $22 million in Pergamon stock, through its Dutch subsidiary corporation. (Unknown to P, 600,000 of the shares which P bought were sold by defendants.) P then discovered the misrepresentations made by D and the other defendants and called off the tender offer. P now sues under Rule 10b-5 for damages in connection with the purchase of $22 million in Pergamon stock.

2) **Issues.**

   a) Is there subject matter jurisdiction under Rule 10b-5 over the transaction?

   b) Is there personal jurisdiction over all of the defendants?

3) **Held.** a) Yes. There is a sufficient allegation of subject matter jurisdiction so as not to dismiss the complaint. b) Personal jurisdiction is sustained with respect to some parties and dismissed with respect to others.

   a) Most defendants are British citizens, although some subsidiaries of Pergamon are domiciled in the United States. P is a United States corporation. The stock purchase was made in England, but significant acts of misrepresentation occurred here. Pergamon stock was not traded in the United States.

   b) This is not the *Schoenbaum* case, where the fraudulent acts were all committed outside the United States, a foreign security was involved, and the issuer was not doing business in the United States.

   c) The *Restatement of Foreign Relations Law*, section 17, provides that there is jurisdiction where there is conduct within the country which relates to something located in this country. Also, where Congress expresses its intention to exercise jurisdiction, the United States courts must comply unless the exercise of jurisdiction offends the Due Process Clause.

   d) It appears that Congress meant Rule 10b-5 to reach situations where United States investors buy foreign securities in a foreign country (which are not traded here), *where acts of fraud have been practiced in this country* in connection with the purchase.

   e) It makes no difference that the actual purchaser is a foreign subsidiary of the American company.

   f) With respect to personal jurisdiction, Fleming Ltd. is subject to the United States courts (its officers made appearances in the United States in connection with making misrepresentations); but Chalmers, Impey & Co. is not. It did no act in this country (one basis for jurisdiction), and *the effect* of the financial reports it prepared in England on Leasco was not reasonably foreseeable (traditionally the second basis for exercising personal jurisdiction). The facts with respect to Kerman are too conflicting at this point to make a make a ruling (he knew that D was trying to make a sale to P, but his role is too unclear to make a decision on the basis of the conflicting affidavits).

b.   Situations where residents are suing United States residents--Bersch v. Drexel Firestone, Inc., 519 F.2d 974 (2d Cir. 1975).

1)   **Facts.** IOS was a Canadian company, with headquarters in Switzerland, which went bankrupt. It had previously offered its stock publicly in three separate offerings: the first, in Europe and Asia, was underwritten by six firms, two of which were American (but underwritten from their European offices); the second was underwritten by Crang in Canada and sold to Canadians; the third, by IOB (an IOS subsidiary based in the Bahamas), was offered outside the United States to employees of IOS, clients of IOS companies, and persons with business relationships with IOS. All offerings were made at the same time and at the same price. The financial statements were prepared by Arthur Andersen (whose principal office was in the United States). None were registered under the United States securities laws. Shortly after the offerings, the IOS stock collapsed. A United States citizen residing in New York (P), who purchased shares under the IOB offering, brings a class action under the 1933 Act, the 1934 Act, and for common law fraud, on behalf of all purchasers of the offerings, alleging fraud and misrepresentation in the offering. The defendants are various United States firms, such as Drexel (which underwrote the IOS issue in Europe and Asia).

2)   **Issue.** Is there subject matter jurisdiction under the United States securities laws for fraud?

3)   **Held.** Yes. Jurisdiction is sustained with respect to American purchasers of the IOS securities.

   a)   There were acts within the United States (meetings, use of American law firms, etc.) which would permit the United States to govern whatever consequences flowed therefrom, wherever these consequences appear. [Restatement (Second) of Foreign Relations Law §17]

   b)   But the issue is determining the intent of Congress as reflected in the securities laws.

   c)   The S.E.C.'s rule not to apply 1933 Act registration requirements to offerings of United States firms to foreigners abroad does not settle the case. The antifraud provisions of the 1933 Act and 1934 Act may have broader application.

   d)   *The antifraud provisions may not be applied on behalf of foreign investors.* There were some acts in the United States, but all the misrepresentations occurred abroad. Anything that took place here was merely preparatory and of small consequence to what occurred abroad.

   e)   The collapse of IOS had some generalized economic and financial effects in the United States, but these are not sufficient to confer subject matter jurisdiction over a damage suit by a foreigner under the antifraud provisions of the securities laws. Section 17 of the 1933

Act and 10b of the 1934 Act relate to acts in connection with the purchase or sale of a security—the intent is to protect purchasers or sellers of securities in which the United States has an interest.

f)   There is some debate about how Americans in the United States ended up buying some of the IOS stock. There is an S.E.C. order that IOS stop selling its securities to United States citizens, except those living abroad who are connected with IOS. But we hold that:

(1)   With respect to United States citizens in the United States, since there is an "effect" in this country, IOS, Cornfeld (the president), and Andersen (the accounting firm) are subject to the securities laws. And so is Drexel Firestone if it is shown at trial that the offering it underwrote (the largest of the three) was essential to the success of the IOB offering (where P bought his stock). It makes no difference whether significant culpable acts were committed in this country with respect to this transaction.

(2)   As to Americans abroad, as long as all of the acts connected with the securities sale were committed abroad (whether by foreigners or Americans), there is no subject matter jurisdiction. *But where there are significant acts done in this country*, there is jurisdiction. There were such acts here by Drexel, IOS, and Andersen (if a causal relationship between the Drexel offering and IOB offering is shown). Whether Cornfeld committed sufficient acts in the United States must be left to be determined at trial.

3.   The Tests Applied by the Courts.

a.   **Dual tests.** Courts seems to apply dual tests: is there a significant effect from the international transaction on United States investors? Second, did significant fraudulent conduct occur in the United States?

b.   **The effects test.**

1)   In *Schoenbaum v. Firstbrook*, 405 F.2d 200 (2d Cir. 1968), *rev'd on rehearing en banc*, 405 F.2d 215 (2d Cir. 1968), *cert. denied*, 395 U.S. 906 (1969), Acquitaine purchased additional shares of its subsidiary Banff Oil at an unfair price based on inside information about an oil discovery. An American shareholder of Banff sued under Rule 10b-5. Banff and Acquitaine were Canadian corporations, and all the events took place in Canada, but Banff was listed and traded on the American Stock Exchange. The court found subject matter jurisdiction and applied United States law. The rationale was that United States law would be applied to transactions in stocks which were traded in the United States (although the business transactions occur outside the United States), where application of United States law is necessary to protect American investors. Section 30(b) of the 1934 Act was held to apply only to transactions by foreign securities professionals, and even then only where the transactions

were outside the jurisdiction of the United States under the above rationale.

2) Query: what if foreign investors trade on inside information in a United States company which is listed for trading in London, and all purchases are done on the London Exchange? How far can the effects test be pushed? It is unlikely that even where a United States company is involved, if plaintiffs and defendants are all foreign citizens, United States fraud laws will probably not be applied.

c. **The conduct test.** Alternatively, courts may see that fraudulent conduct occurs in the United States and apply United States fraud laws. In the *Bersch* and *Learco* cases, the court applied a two-step test:

(i) Would foreign relations law allow application of United States law?

(ii) What is the intent of Congress as to the reach of United States law?

Courts have varied in their approaches. When the securities involved are not actually traded in the United States, some courts have held that for United States law to apply, the conduct occurring here must be actual fraud, with all of the elements of Rule 10b-5. [*See* IIT v. Vencaps, Ltd., 519 F.2d 1001 (2d Cir. 1975)] The rationale is that the objective is to prevent the United States from becoming a haven for securities fraud. Other courts have allowed subject matter jurisdiction in United States courts when *some conduct* occurs in the United States but the major fraudulent acts occurred elsewhere. [*See* Grunenthal GmbH v. Hotz, 712 F.2d 421 (9th Cir. 1983)] Much will depend on whether United States citizens are suing *or* the plaintiffs are foreign citizens suing United States defendants.

4. **The Restatement (Third) of Foreign Relations Law of the United States.** In 1986 the American Law Institute adopted the *Restatement (Third) of the Foreign Relations Law of the United States*, which indicates when United States courts should apply subject matter jurisdiction to cases having foreign contacts.

a. **The basic section.** Section 402 indicates that a state should prescribe law with respect to:

(1)(a) Conduct that, wholly or in substantial part, takes place within the state's territory;

(b) The status of persons, or interests in things, present within its territory;

(c) Conduct outside its territory that has or is intended to have substantial effect inside the territory.

(2) The activities, interests, status, or relations of its nationals outside as well as inside its territory.

b. **Qualification.** If section 402 is found to apply, then section 403 may limit application of United States law. Even when section 402 applies, a state may not prescribe law to activities, relations, status, or interests of persons or things having connection with another state when the exercise of such jurisdiction is "unreasonable." All relevant facts are considered in making a determination of "unreasonableness." Where two or more states have a reasonable basis for applying their law, all states should defer to the state having the greatest interest.

c. **Specific application of United States securities laws.** Section 416 provides:

1) The United States generally has jurisdiction to prescribe its securities laws with respect to:

    a) (i) Any transaction in securities *in the United States* to which a national or resident of the United States is a party, and (ii) any such offer;

    b) Or any transaction in securities carried out or intended to be in an organized United States securities market, or carried out predominately in the United States although not on an organized market;

    c) Conduct, wherever it occurs, if significantly related to a (1)(b) transaction, if the conduct has or is intended to have substantial effect in the United States;

    d) Conduct occurring predominately in the United States that is related to a securities transaction, even if it occurs outside the United States;

    e) Investment advice, solicitation of proxies carried out predominately in the United States.

2) Otherwise, jurisdiction of the United States depends on whether it is reasonable to apply United States law in light of section 403 above, giving particular weight to:

    a) Whether the transaction or conduct has or reasonably can be expected to have a substantial effect on a United States securities market for securities of the same issuer or holdings by United States nationals or residents of the securities of the same issuer;

    b) Whether negotiations are conducted in the United States;

    c) Whether the party sought to be subjected to United States courts is a United States national or resident, or persons sought to be protected are United States nationals or residents.

5. **Personal Jurisdiction.**

a. **Introduction.** Section 22(a) of the 1933 Act and section 27 of the 1934 Act provide that service of process may be on a defendant wherever he may be found. Thus, service may be made, under the law, wherever due process of law allows.

b. **Test.** The test seems to be that defendant may be served when he has taken purposeful action directed toward the United States and its effects in the United States were foreseeable. [*See* Asahi Metal Industry Co. v. Superior Court, 480 U.S. 102 (1987)—Japanese manufacturer sold product to Taiwanese assembler with an awareness that the product would end up in California. California court could assert personal jurisdiction over Japanese firm]

C. INTERNATIONAL ENFORCEMENT

1. **Discovery in Insider Trading Case--S.E.C. v. Banca Della Svizzera Italiana,** 92 F.R.D. 111 (S.D.N.Y. 1981).

S.E.C. v. Banca Della Svizzera Italiana

   a. **Facts.** One day before a cash tender offer for the stock of St. Joe Minerals Corp. was announced, Banca Della Svizzera Italiana (BSI), possibly for itself or for undisclosed principals from a Swiss branch, purchased call options on the Philadelphia Exchange and common stock of St. Joe on the New York Exchange. The next day the tender offer was announced, and BSI had made a $2 million profit. The S.E.C. sued for a TRO to prevent the transfer agent from disbursing any funds in BSI's account and for discovery, suspecting insider trading. The S.E.C. brings the action based on section 21(d) of the 1934 Act, for violation of Rules 10b-5 and 14e-3. Jurisdiction is based on section 21(e) and 27 of the 1934 Act, and jurisdiction over BSI exists by virtue of BSI's doing business in the United States (a branch is located in Manhattan).

   b. **Issue.** Should the court compel a foreign party that transacted purchases on American securities exchanges to make discovery and answer interrogatories concerning its undisclosed principals where the acts of disclosure might subject that party to criminal liability in its home country for violation of secrecy laws?

   c. **Held.** Yes. Discovery should be compelled.

      1) The S.E.C. has tried to work cooperatively with BSI to obtain the information it seeks about the clients of BSI. This has not worked.

      2) The Supreme Court has held that if the party resisting discovery resists disclosure in good faith because sanctions exist under foreign law, then this may be a basis to avoid discovery. Here, however, BSI may have deliberately used Swiss law to avoid disclosure *and* the vital national interests in enforcement of United States law outweigh other considerations:

         a) Section 40 of the Restatement of Foreign Relations code indicates that vital national interests may compel discovery from a foreign entity. Here the United States has the interest in the integrity of its financial markets, which is continually being thwarted by the use of foreign bank accounts. And the Swiss government has not expressly opposed the disclosure, nor has it confiscated the bank's records. The secrecy belongs to the bank customers, not the bank; they may waive it. And the Swiss government may choose not to prosecute the bank because a foreign government forced disclosure.

b)   Section 40 also mentions as a factor the extent and nature of the hardship that inconsistent enforcement actions would impose on the party which is subject to both jurisdictions. It is not certain that the bank will face any sanctions; if it does, it appears that they created the situation that would result in such sanctions.

c)   Finally, section 40 also mentions other factors: where the enforcement will occur (in the United States where the bank's lawyers are), nationality of the resisting party, extent that enforcement will result in compliance, etc. Here the bank is Swiss, but it is international in scope, with offices all over the world, hence they must expect to comply with the laws of many countries.

d.   **Comment.** Section 40 has been superseded by section 437 (Discovery and Foreign Government Compulsion: Law of the United States) of the *Restatement (Third) of the Foreign Relations Law*, which provides:

(a)   Subject to Subsection [c], a court or agency in the United States, when authorized by statute or rule of court, may order a person subject to its jurisdiction to produce documents, objects, or other information relevant to an action or investigation, even if the information or the person in possession of the information is outside the United States.

(b)   Failure to comply with an order to produce information may subject the person to whom the order is directed to sanctions, including finding of contempt, dismissal of a claim or defense, or default judgment, or may lead to a determination that the facts to which the order was addressed are as asserted by the opposing party.

(c)   In issuing an order directing production of information located abroad, a court or agency in the United States should take into account the importance to the investigation or litigation of the documents or other information requested; the degree of specificity of the request; whether the information originated in the United States; the availability of alternative means of securing the information; and the extent to which non-compliance with the request would undermine important interest of the state where the information is located.

(2)   If disclosure of information located outside the United States States is prohibited by a law, regulation, or order of a court or other authority of the state in which the information or prospective witness is located, or of the state of which the prospective witness is a national.

(a) The person to whom the order is directed may be required by the court or agency to make a good faith effort to secure permission from the foreign authorities to make the information available.

(b) Sanctions of contempt, dismissal, or default would not ordinarily be imposed on the party that has failed to comply with the order for production, except in cases of deliberate concealment or removal of information or of failure to make a good faith effort in accordance with paragraph (a).

(c) The court or agency may, in appropriate cases, make findings of fact adverse to a party that has failed to comply with the order for production, even if that party has made a good faith effort to secure permission from the foreign authorities to make the information available and that effort has been unsuccessful.

2. **Test Used by the Supreme Court.** The Supreme Court appears to follow the approach used by section 437 of the *Restatement*. Its test balances the need for international comity against the legitimacy of the discovery request. The factors considered by the Court are drawn from the factors mentioned in section 437(1)(c).

3. **Other Approaches to International Enforcement.** The process of using United States courts is very time consuming, and expensive, and not always successful. For example, what if the bank in the case above had not had a branch in the United States? Thus, the S.E.C. has resorted to other methods as well as using the courts; it has gotten the United States and several foreign countries to pass treaties on information exchange. And it has negotiated Memorandums of Understanding with many nations for joint cooperation in sharing information in securities law violation cases.

D. TRANSNATIONAL SECURITIES REGULATION

1. **Introduction.** The S.E.C. has taken a more cautious approach when it comes to applying United States regulatory securities laws (i.e., 1933 Act applied to security distributions, etc.). There are two reasons: more potential for regulatory conflicts with foreign governments; and second, foreign offerers may simply not offer securities in the United States or to United States residents. The issues in this area are: how to cooperate with foreign governments so that effective regulation does not disappear; and how to simplify regulation of foreign issues but not deprive United States investors of the information they need.

2. **Reducing the Regulatory Burden on the Foreign Issuer.**

   a. **Problems for foreign issuers.** Foreign issuers of securities in the United States face several problems: costs and delay of a United

States offering; obligation to report under the 1934 Act; accounting and auditing standard differences; threat of civil liability under the anti-fraud laws; greater likelihood of litigation in the United States. The S.E.C. has made an effort to simplify regulation for foreign issuers.

b. **The 1933 Act.** Special registration and reporting forms have been adopted for foreign issuers. Financial statements do not have to be prepared in accord with United States accounting principles, but issuers may have to show a reconciliation of some or all items, depending on the situation.

c. **The 1934 Act.** Although it appears on the face of the 1934 Act that a foreign issuer must file periodic reports with the S.E.C. under section 12(b) if a class of its securities is listed on a national securities exchange, or under section 12(g) if its securities are held by at least 500 shareholders and it has assets of more than $1 million, the S.E.C. has developed several exemptions (e.g., the class of the foreign issuer's securities not held by at least 300 United States residents; not listed on a national exchange; not listed on NASDAQ). Pursuant to Rule 12g3-2(b), firms not traded on NASDAQ or a national exchange but otherwise traded in the United States may simply give the S.E.C. the same information they give to regulators in their home country. Further, "foreign issuers" are exempt from the proxy rules and Section 16 liability for short-term trading. A foreign issuer is defined as an issuer organized or incorporated outside the United States, *unless* (i) more than 50% of its outstanding voting stock is held of record by United States residents, and (ii) any of the following conditions apply: (a) the majority of its executive officers and directors are United States citizens or residents; (b) more than 50% of its assets are located in the United States; (c) its business is administered principally in the United States. Furthermore, foreign issuers listing on NASDAQ or a national exchange must file an Annual Report on Form 20-F. Less significant detail is required than for United States companies.

d. **ADRs of foreign issuers.** Foreign companies often enter the United States markets by having a United States bank sell an American Depositary Receipt (ADR) based on shares issued by the foreign company abroad. An ADR is a negotiable receipt, usually issued by a United States bank, that evidences ownership of a specified number of foreign securities on deposit with the United States depositary (or a foreign bank). ADRs must either have been registered under the 1933 Act (Form F-6) or have been acquired by the depositary in a secondary market transaction (usually the case). And, the foreign issuer must enter the S.E.C.'s continuous disclosure system under the 1934 Act (at least complying with Rule 13g3-2(b)).

3. **Multijurisdictional Disclosure.** The S.E.C. has suggested that there are two approaches to disclosure by foreign issuers: developing common prospectus requirements with foreign countries, and following a reciprocal prospectus approach (each country accepts the other's requirements). The United States has reached an agreement with Canada on a disclosure system. [*See* SAR No. 33-6841, 1989] And it has proposed various reciprocal registration processes for other foreign issuers that meet certain qualifications (e.g., length of time traded on a recognized foreign exchange, size of assets, etc.). Usually what is required is that the foreign issuer provide the same information required to be provided in the foreign country.

4. Cross-Border Tender Offers.

a. **No impact in the United States of tender for a foreign company--
    Plessey Co. plc v. General Electric plc,** 628 F. Supp. 477 (D.C. Del.
    1986).

   1) **Facts.** General Electric Co. plc (GEC), a British company, made a
       tender offer in England for the stock of Plessey PLC, another British
       company. Plessey had ADRs listed on the New York Stock Ex-
       change and held by 3,000 persons in the United States. GEC made
       the offer only to owners of Plessey stock, explicitly excluding United
       States ADR holders. The only thing communicated to United States
       ADR owners was through the United States financial press, which
       published information based on a press release on the tender offer
       made by GEC in England, and a letter on the tender offer sent at
       Plessey's instigation by City Bank in New York to ADR holders.
       Plessey seeks a TRO in United States district court to force GEC to
       comply with disclosure requirements for tender offers under section
       14 of the 1934 Act.

   2) **Issue.** Does the United States tender offer laws apply to this tender
       offer by a British company for another British company?

   3) **Held.** No. TRO request denied.

       a) The press release on the tender offer is not an offer to United
           States ADR holders.

       b) The mailing by City Bank, instigated by Plessey, does not
           constitute a use of the United States mails by the tender offeror,
           GEC.

       c) There is less tendency by United States courts to apply United
           States regulatory securities laws than to apply United States
           securities fraud laws. No fraud is alleged here. And there is no
           strong United States interest in regulating this situation; the
           United States activities are small in comparison to what hap-
           pened abroad. Here a foreign bidder has avoided American
           channels in pursuit of another foreign company. The only act
           are a secondhand news account not attributable to GEC, and a
           mailing instigated by GEC. Thus, the American contacts here
           are minimal.

**5. Regulation S and Rule 144A—Offerings of Securities Outside the United
    States.** *See* the discussion at II.F.8.c.4).

VIII. REGULATION OF SECURITIES TRANSACTIONS BY THE STATES

A. INTRODUCTION

Both the Securities Act of 1933 and the Securities Exchange Act of 1934 preserve the power of the states to regulate securities transactions. [SA §18; SEA §28(a)] Every state has adopted some form of securities regulation, and every securities transaction may therefore be subject to the law of one or more of the states having contact with the transaction, as well as to federal law.

B. THE UNIFORM SECURITIES ACT

1. **Provisions of Act.** The Commissioners on Uniform State Laws have adopted a Uniform Securities Act, divided into sections concerning (i) fraud in general, (ii) broker-dealer registration, (iii) registration of new securities offerings, and (iv) remedy provisions.

2. **Adoption by the States.** In drafting their own securities laws, most of the states have adopted some part of the Uniform Securities Act, have used some of the concepts found in the federal acts, and have added some provisions of their own choosing. Yet despite their wide diversity, nearly all the states regulate both the original distribution of securities and the subsequent trading thereof (including the registration of broker-dealers).

C. THE ORIGINAL DISTRIBUTION OF SECURITIES

Since most states have securities laws regarding the original distribution of securities within their borders, an issuer making an original distribution within a state must usually comply with *both* the Securities Act of 1933 and the relevant state law.

1. **Blue Sky Laws.** The state statutes that regulate the original distribution of securities are called "blue sky laws." There are basically four different types of regulatory systems that may be set up by these state statutes:

   a. **Prohibition of fraud.** Some states simply prohibit fraud or misrepresentation in the purchase and sale of securities, and provide civil and criminal sanctions for violations.

   b. **Registration by notification.** Other states require that issuers file with state authorities certain material information about themselves and the securities to be issued. After the passage of a stated period of time, the registered securities may then be issued. Civil and criminal sanctions for violations are provided in these statutes as well.

   c. **Registration by qualification.** Some blue sky laws require the filing of comprehensive information (similar to a registration statement under the 1933 Act) and review of the offered securities by state officials prior to issuance. A typical standard use in such a review is whether the securities are being offered on a "fair, just, and equitable" basis.

d. **Registration by coordination.** Other states permit securities registered under the federal laws to be issued without further processing by the state.

2. **Exemptions from State Regulation.** State laws normally provide for a number of exemptions from the registration or other qualification requirements. The exemption may be based either on the type of securities transaction involved or on the type of securities themselves.

    a. **Limited offering exemption.** Many states recognize an exemption from registration if the securities are offered in a transaction that is "limited" in one of several ways:

        1) **Isolated transaction.** Some states exempt securities that are offered in a single, isolated transaction, to a limited number of purchasers.

        2) **Limited persons and time.** States may also recognize an exemption for securities offered to a limited number of persons during a specific period of time.

        3) **Private offerings.** Some states have an exemption similar to the exemption in the 1933 Act for purely "private offerings."

        4) **Limited number of shareholders.** An exemption may also exist for a sale of securities if the shareholders of the corporation after the sale do not exceed a specified number.

    b. **Other transaction exemptions.** States may provide for other types of transaction exemptions as well; e.g., some states recognize an exemption for preincorporation subscription agreements in certain situations.

    c. **Security exemptions.** In addition, the blue sky laws typically provide for a number of exemptions based on the type of security offered. For example, many states exempt:

        1) Government securities;

        2) Short-term commercial paper; or

        3) Securities issued by certain types of corporations regulated by government entities, such as public utilities, insurance companies, and banks.

    d. **Exemption for secondary distributions.** Many states regulate "secondary," as well as original, distributions, i.e., transfers of securities by shareholders after the original distribution is completed. Where this is the case, exemptions are provided to allow "ordinary trading transactions" to occur without impediment. Typically, the following transactions are exempted:

        1) Isolated or limited offerings by nonissuers; and

        2) Securities listed on stock exchanges or in certain financial manuals.

3. **Regulatory Authority of State Agencies.** The grant of authority to agencies that regulate the distribution of securities differs in each state. Some simply administer a general "fraud" standard, while others regulate under a "fair, just, and equitable" standard. The latter standard gives state agencies greater latitude in approving or disapproving a securities issue.

4. **Civil Liability Under Blue Sky Laws.** State statutes usually provide specific remedies for violation of their blue sky laws. If no such provision is made, the courts may also apply appropriate common law remedies.

   a. **Violation of registration requirement.** Most states that require registration of new securities offerings also provide liability for any violation of the registration requirement (similar to section 11 of the 1933 Act).

   b. **General liability provisions.** In addition, many states that have adopted modified versions of the Uniform Securities Act have included liability provisions similar to section 12 of the 1933 Act.

   c. **Liability of officers and directors.** Some state laws expressly provide for the liability of directors and officers of a corporation that sells securities in violation of the state statute. Even where the statute does not so provide, state courts generally hold that any officer or director who "participates" or "aids" in such sale is jointly and severally liable with the corporation.

   d. **Common law.** Even where there is no blue sky law, state courts have developed a common law to cover securities transactions. In some cases, this common law has been a mirror of the federal securities acts. [Diamond v. Oreamuno, 24 N.Y.2d 494 (1969)—state court used common law to uphold shareholder action against corporate management for abuse of inside information in selling corporate stock (an analogy to Rule 10b-5]

5. **Constitutional Law Problems.** Because the states and the federal government both regulate the distribution of securities, and each has its separate legal system set up to do so, problems may arise where securities transactions have contacts with more than one of these jurisdictional units. The court in which a securities action is brought must determine whether it has jurisdiction over the securities transaction in question and, if it does, which law it should apply.

   a. **Two basic problems.** Basically, the situation of multiple jurisdictional units creates two problems:

      1) **Jurisdiction question.** What courts can entertain litigation when a problem has contacts with more than one state?

      2) **Conflict of laws question.** What law will be applied to settle the issues that are raised?

   b. **Jurisdiction.**

      1) **State jurisdiction statute.** In deciding whether a state court has jurisdiction over a securities action, the first question is whether the state's jurisdiction statute purports to cover the transaction. This is a matter of statutory interpretation.

a) **Domestic corporations.** In almost every instance, a state's law will give jurisdiction to its courts over security transactions by domestic corporations (i.e., those incorporated in the state). However, some statutes do not purport to cover resident corporations' sale of securities to out-of-state residents, on the basis that the buyer's state of residence will assume jurisdiction over such transactions. [*See, e.g.,* Cal. Admin. Code, title 10, rule 260.105.2]

b) **Foreign corporations.** The difficult questions therefore arise with respect to security transactions by foreign (i.e., out-of-state) corporations—e.g., where XYZ, incorporated in State A, attempts to sell securities to residents of State B. The securities laws of most states govern such transactions if an "offer" or "sale" is made "within the state." [Kreis v. Mates Investment Fund, Inc., 473 F.2d 1308 (8th Cir. 1973)]

2) **Constitutionality of statute.** After the applicability of the state statute is determined, the constitutionality of the state's jurisdiction must be decided as well. For example, suppose that a foreign issuer offers to sell securities to a resident of State X by use of the mails, telephone, or other means of interstate commerce that do not require the offeror to be present in the state. If the state's statute purports to cover this situation, is the state statute constitutional?

a) **"Significant contacts."** Most states statutes do cover these types of situations. If the transaction has "significant contacts" with the state, this is sufficient to sustain the constitutionality of such a statute.

b) **Service of process.** Most states require a foreign corporation that enters its borders to issue securities to file a "consent" to service of process within the state. Where a foreign corporation does not physically enter the state, but solicits purchasers by using the means of interstate commerce (e.g., the mails), the state may rely on substituted service of process. [McGee v. International Life Insurance Co., 355 U.S. 220 (1967)—such service is constitutional]

c. **Conflict of laws.**

1) **Constitutional question.** The first conflicts issue involves a constitutional question: When can a state court constitutionally apply its own law to a case having contacts with more than one state? The answer is basically the same as noted above with respect to jurisdiction—i.e., when the local forum has "substantial contacts" with the transaction.

2) **Policy question.** Assuming the forum state has substantial contacts with the securities transaction, the second issue is: When will the state court apply its own law and when will it apply the law of another state having substantial contacts?

a) **Note.** Resolution of cases involving substantial contacts with more than one state can be very difficult, since they involve many competing considerations. Ultimately, the question can only be resolved by making a decision as to which state's law should apply—a policy question with which the law of Conflicts is concerned.

        b)   **Example.** To achieve a desired result, a California court applied California law to require cumulative voting of a Delaware corporation which had its principal office and business in California. However, the decision leaves unexplored many important questions, e.g., the full faith and credit to be given the corporate laws of other states, and the burden on interstate commerce when one state in effect regulates the corporate charters of out-of-state corporations. [*See* Western Airlines v. Sobieski, 191 Cal. App. 2d 399 (1961)]

     3)   **Federal law vs. state law.** Significant issues also arise with respect to conflicts between federal and state law. Where the basic cause of action is based on federal securities laws, state legal rules that impact significantly on the effectuation of federal rights, or that are inconsistent with federal policy underlying the federal cause of action, will also be treated as raising federal questions.

D. SECONDARY DISTRIBUTION OF SECURITIES

Many states have statutory provisions that regulate the trading of securities subsequent to their original distribution, as does the Securities Exchange Act of 1934.

1.   **General Fraud Provisions.** Nearly every state has some general provision against fraud, and a few states have provisions similar to Rule 10b-5 of the 1934 Act.

2.   **Registration of Broker-Dealers.** Many states also have provisions requiring the qualification and registration of persons involved in the securities business as broker-dealers. [*See* Uniform Securities Act §204]

3.   **Tender Offer Statutes.** In addition, many states have adopted special provisions governing the regulation of tender offers made on companies domiciled within the state's borders. Where the state statute is in too great a conflict with the purposes and manner of regulation of the federal laws, state law may be held preempted by federal law. Alternatively, the state law may also be held to impose an undue burden on interstate commerce and thus be invalid on this basis.

    a.   **Undue burden on interstate commerce.** A state tender offer statute may be found to be invalid under the Commerce Clause of the Constitution where it imposes an undue burden on interstate commerce. [*See* Edgar v. MITE Corp., 457 U.S. 624 (1982)]

    b.   **Preemption of state law.** In *Edgar*, the Supreme Court held that the Illinois takeover law was unconstitutional under the Commerce Clause of the Constitution. However, a majority of the Court could not agree that the Illinois law was also preempted by the Williams Act. Thus, *Edgar* left open the question of how far states could go in regulating takeovers. However, the post-*Edgar* trend is clearly that the courts are finding that the Williams Act does indeed supersede and preempt state laws.

TABLE OF CASES

(Page numbers of briefed cases in bold)